Genocide and Resistance in Southeast Asia

Other books and monographs by Ben Kiernan

The Samlaut Rebellion and Its Aftermath, 1967-70

Peasants and Politics in Kampuchea, 1942-1981 (co-author)

Revolution and Its Aftermath in Kampuchea (co-editor)

How Pol Pot Came to Power:
Colonialism, Nationalism and Communism in Cambodia, 1930-1975

Cambodia: The Eastern Zone Massacres

Burchett: Reporting the Other Side of the World, 1939-1983 (editor)

Pol Pot Plans the Future:
Confidential Leadership Documents from Democratic Kampuchea,
1976-1977 (co-editor)

Genocide and Democracy in Cambodia:
The Khmer Rouge, the United Nations, and the International Community
(editor)

The Pol Pot Regime:
Race, Power and Genocide in Cambodia under the Khmer Rouge, 1975-1979

Le Génocide au Cambodge, 1975-1979: race, idéologie et pouvoir

Conflict and Change in Cambodia (editor)

The Specter of Genocide: Mass Murder in Historical Perspective (co-editor)

Blood and Soil:
A World History of Genocide and Extermination from Sparta to Darfur

Ben Kiernan

Genocide and Resistance in Southeast Asia

Documentation, Denial & Justice in Cambodia & East Timor

Transaction Publishers
New Brunswick (U.S.A.) and London (U.K.)

Library of Congress Catalog Number: 2007037306
ISBN: 978-1-4128-0668-8 (case); 978-1-4128-0669-5 (paper)
Printed in the United States of America

Library of Congress Cataloging-in-Publication Data

Kiernan, Ben.
    Genocide and resistance in Southeast Asia : documentation, denial, and
    justice in Cambodia and East Timor / Ben Kiernan.
        p. cm.
    Includes bibliographical references and index.
    ISBN 978-1-4128-0668-8 (hardcover : alk. paper) —
    ISBN 978-1-4128-0669-5 (pbk. : alk. paper)
        1. Cambodia—Politics and government—1975-1979. 2. Cambodia—
    Politics and government—1979-   3. East Timor—Politics and
    government—-20th century. 4. Genocide—Cambodia. 5. Genocide—
    East Timor. I. Title.

DS554.8.K5834   2007
959.604'2—dc22   2007037306

for Joan and Peter, and Hugh Kiernan

SOUTHEAST ASIA

China

India

Burma

Laos

Thailand

Vietnam

Cambodia

Philippines

Brunei

Malaysia

Singapore

Indonesia

East Timor

Darwin

Papua
New Guinea

Map drawn by Laurent Bonneau.

Contents

Acknowledgements

I wish to thank my wife, Glenda E. Gilmore, and our children, Mia-lia, Derry, and Miles, for their patience and support in the writing of this book. I am also grateful to the National Humanities Center for its Horace W. Goldsmith Fellowship, which enabled me to complete the book, and to Irving Louis Horowitz of Transaction Publishers for encouraging me to publish it. The preface by David J. Case appeared in the *Yale Alumni Magazine* in November 2003. Chapter 1 first appeared in *Revolution and Its Aftermath in Kampuchea: Eight Essays*, edited by D.P. Chandler and Ben Kiernan (Yale Council on Southeast Asia Studies, New Haven, 1983). The research was assisted by a grant from the Christopher Reynolds Foundation. Research for chapter 2 was conducted with the aid of the Federation of American Scientists and its Preseident, Dr. Jeremy J. Stone. An earlier version of chapter 3 appeared in Mark Selden and Alvin Y. So, eds., *War and State Terrorism: The United States, Japan, and the Asia-Pacific in the Long Twentieth Century* (Rowman and Littlefield, Lanham, MD, 2004). Chapter 4 is reprinted with the permission of the authors from *Chega! The Report of the Commission for Reception, Truth and Reconciliation in Timor-Leste* (CAVR), October 2005. (The full report is online at: www.cavr-timorleste.org.) The articles reprinted in chapter 5 first appeared in *Nation Review* (Melbourne) in 1978 and 1980, and in the *Bulletin of Concerned Asian Scholars* in 1979. Those in chapter 6 first appeared in the *Illawarra Advertiser* (Wollongong, Australia), September 23, 1987, and in the *Far Eastern Economic Review* (Hong Kong), March 1, 1990. Earlier versions of chapter 7 appeared in *Human Rights Review* (April-June 2000), and of chapters 8 and 9, in *Critical Asian Studies* in 2001 and 2003. The articles in chapter 10 appeared in *Nation Review* and the *Bulletin of Concerned Asian Scholars* in 1979. Those in chapter 11 appeared in the *Bulletin of Concerned Asian Scholars* (1980), *Inside Asia* (1985), in the Australian newspapers *Sydney Morning Herald* (Aug. 13, 1985 and Aug. 27, 1986) and *Sun-Herald* (Sept. 22, 1985), and in the Bangkok *Nation* (May 7 and 14, and October 13, 1989). I wish to thank Bernice Daye, Joel Elliott and Laurence Mintz for their valued assistance in preparing the manuscript for publication.

Preface

David J. Case

Several hours north of Australia by turbo-prop plane, on a narrow coastal crescent below rugged mountains, lies Dili, capital of the world's newest independent nation. In the center of Dili, not far from the harbor, is the chief executive office building of the young government of East Timor. Above its entrance hangs a UN-blue tarp bearing the Portuguese words "Palacio das Cinzas": Palace of Ashes.

From out front, on one of the many pleasant lanes that transect this quiet city, passersby can see the sun shining straight through the openings where the second-floor windows should be. The roof is gone. The intact floor of the second story is all that prevents monsoon downpours from flooding the president's office below. Inside, the cement walls are heat-curdled and stained black; twisted steel reinforcing rods jut at odd angles from the ceiling.

Formerly a department of motor vehicles, the edifice was one of many across East Timor that were burned during the summer of 1999. On August 30, in a UN-sponsored referendum, the populace voted overwhelmingly for independence. The Indonesian military's response was to unleash thousands of murderous militia troops, who were so thorough in their work that, when the aggression was finally suppressed and international relief teams showed up, the relief workers had nowhere to stay. They resorted to leasing a huge floating hotel and sailing it into Dili's harbor.

Four years later, the new nation is recovering not only from the 1999 hostility, but also from the preceding twenty-four years of military occupation by Indonesia, which left a quarter of the population dead. Peaceful and picturesque but dirt poor, East Timor has no resources to repair the burned-out buildings that line its streets. And so for now, its first president, Jose Alexandre "Xanana" Gusmao, makes do with this charred carcass of a building. His staff works in cubicles separated by flimsy plywood.

It's nine o'clock in the morning, and the president is late to work; an assistant says that his meeting the night before lasted well into the morning hours. At the door of the Palace of Ashes, guards lean against an old wooden desk and smoke clove cigarettes, filling the lobby with a pleasant, spicy scent. Inside, as the day heats up, guests sit waiting on tattered upholstered chairs. They glance indifferently from time to time at a cartoon playing on a television in the corner, its colorful animated figures barely visible behind a blizzard of static.

Among the guests is Ben Kiernan, a tall, slender man with a well-trimmed beard and thick hair, brown but graying. For his audience with the president of East Timor, he wears khaki pants, a black short-sleeved polo shirt, and gray high-tech running shoes, and has brought along his sixteen-year-old son, Derry. Kiernan is the A. Whitney Griswold Professor of History at Yale, recruited in 1990 for his expertise in Southeast Asia. Fifty years old and originally from Australia, he is popular among students, and it's easy to see why. An avowed egalitarian—he would never think of excluding his son from this visit with a head of state—he is generous with his time, and he has an uncanny ability to make people feel welcome, important even, in his presence. One night after Kiernan has delivered a lecture in Canberra, I watch him give his e-mail address to a nervous undergrad seeking guidance. "I'm traveling so it might take me some time to respond, but I will get back to you," he assures her.

Kiernan is a scholar of comparative genocide—a professional chronicler of atrocity. For a quarter century he has studied some of humanity's most vile events, starting with a dissertation on the Khmer Rouge regime in Phnom Penh, which was responsible for the deaths of 1.7 million Cambodians. In 1998, he put Yale at the vanguard of a new academic field by founding the university's Genocide Studies Program, the first in the country, according to *Business Week*. It has conducted work on Rwanda, Bosnia, Sudan, and the Holocaust, among others.

But Kiernan has never been content to limit his work to academics. He is also known as a spokesman for the often-forgotten victims of mass murder. By 1978, as a young PhD student, he had begun urging Western nations to stop supporting the Khmer Rouge and to prosecute its leaders. The fight would pit him against Washington, which backed the regime for more than a decade. In the mid-1990s, when his side finally prevailed, Kiernan won a U.S. State Department grant to document the regime's crimes. The grant, administered by the Yale Center for International and Area Studies, enabled him to uncover the cache of records that, for the first time, irrefutably demonstrated that the Khmer Rouge leaders had personally ordered the torture and murder of citizens. The records paved the way for a UN tribunal.

These days, when he's not busy running the Genocide Studies Program or writing his history of genocide in the past five hundred years, Kiernan focuses his energy on East Timor. In 1999, he says, he saw a video clip on television of "an Indonesian-trained militia soldier hacking to death a Timorese, with a machete," and ever since he has been trying to help East Timor recover. The chance is remote that the men who supervised the barbarities committed here will be held accountable. That would require an international tribunal, and while the UN has raised this possibility, East Timor's leaders, running a country that is poor, internationally unimportant, and dependent on good relations with its former tormentor, can hardly spare the diplomatic capital needed to ensure that it materializes. Meanwhile, Ben Kiernan is doing his best to make sure the matter doesn't slip into oblivion.

Kiernan will spend part of the summer of 2003 chasing down transcripts of Radio Fretilin—clandestine broadcasts by Timorese resistance fighters, who used two-way radios to communicate with sympathizers in Darwin, Australia. During the Indonesian occupation, Radio Fretilin was often the only way for information about the military's atrocities to reach the outside world. "Radio Fretilin brought to the public's attention facts that were difficult for the Australian government to see published, because of the close relationship between Canberra and Jakarta," Kiernan explains. "The transcripts are a unique source of information on the worst crimes."

And this morning, as the rising sun radiates withering heat into the lobby of the Palace of Ashes, Kiernan is waiting to interview Xanana Gusmao, who was often the voice of Radio Fretilin in the Timorese mountains and who is one of the few people alive who can be aptly compared to Nelson Mandela.

Finally, a small caravan of SUVs pulls up to the door. The guards at the desk leap to attention, and order the waiting guests do the same. Then the president strides through the burned-out lobby, nodding to his people.

President Gusmao, whom the Indonesians incarcerated for years, has an office strangely reminiscent of a prison cell. It's a stark cement room with bare floors. The sole window, a small one near the ceiling, lets in almost no natural light. As a gesture to the room's status, the walls have been painted; they are pale blue. On them hang recent pictures of Gusmao with the leaders of countries that once regarded him as an enemy: George W. Bush, Jacques Chirac, and Indonesian president Megawati Sukarnoputri.

When Kiernan enters the room, the president rises, flashes a smile, and embraces him, slapping his back. "Great to see you! How have you been?" he says, in richly accented English. The two men met in March 2001, when Kiernan headed a delegation of Yale's East Timor Project to Dili, and then a month later when Gusmao delivered an address at Yale. (The East Timor Project is an assistance program initiated by the late Episcopalian bishop Paul Moore Jr. '41, a longtime fellow of the Yale Corporation. In 1989, Moore, one of the first Westerners allowed to visit East Timor since the Indonesians invaded in 1975, was so shocked by what he saw that he vowed to help the East Timorese.)

In the president's office, we sit around a simple coffee table. Gusmao is pleased to hear that Kiernan has been producing scholarly work about his country. He needs foreigners, he says, scholars like Kiernan with ironclad reputations, to make the world understand what happened here. Kiernan just delivered two lectures on East Timor in Australia, and an essay by another scholar is included in a recent book he co-edited, *The Specter of Genocide*. The essay's author,

Professor John Taylor of South Bank University in London, has been a visiting fellow at the Genocide Studies Program.

Kiernan tells the president that he is researching the East Timorese resistance —"Genocide scholarship hasn't paid much attention to attempts to oppose genocidal regimes," he explains. Gusmao is eager to fill him in on the details. So while guests wait in the mounting heat of the lobby, for the next two hours the president of East Timor relives, in halting but heartfelt English, the years of the occupation.

Before independence, Gusmao spent years on the run as a revolutionary in the mountains. When East Timor's resistance was badly splintered, he unified it and rebuilt it into a spectacularly tenacious movement. Gusmao was known to deliver passionate speeches to inspire his people, his body sweating and trembling, his words bursting out like machine gun fire. Today, in an open-collared, steel-gray shirt and black dress trousers, his thick salt-and-pepper beard trimmed, the president cuts a more genteel figure. But as he talks, he keeps shifting uncomfortably in his chair. He chain-smokes, crushing the butts in an ashtray that quickly overflows.

For 450 years, East Timor was a Portuguese colony, a trading post for sandalwood on the fringe of the archipelago that became the Dutch East Indies. In 1949, the Dutch were ousted and the islands were unified as Indonesia—except for East Timor, which remained Portuguese. Then in 1974, a coup in Portugal ushered in a leftist government that was sympathetic to the colonies' aspirations for freedom. An independence movement blossomed. Its acronym, Fretilin, stands for Revolutionary Front for Independent East Timor. The East Timorese dreamed of self-rule.

However, the Indonesian government of President Suharto had other plans. Suharto sought, first by charm and then by force, to annex East Timor. Japan, Australia, the United States, and other Western nations largely sided with Indonesia, because Suharto controlled vast natural resources and was a staunch anti-Communist ally. Moreover, the U.S. military was eager to safeguard its access to the extremely deep straits off East Timor, where nuclear submarines could slip undetected between the Pacific and Indian oceans.

Despite the international opposition, Fretilin declared independence on November 28, 1975. Little more than a week later, Gerald Ford and Henry Kissinger indicated to Suharto that they would not oppose an invasion. The next day, troops poured in from the sea, land, and sky.

As John Taylor describes in his book *East Timor: The Price of Freedom,* the atrocities began within the first hours of the war. The invading troops rounded up hundreds of civilians and executed them at the wharfs in the center of the city; they forced onlookers, including the next victims, to count as they dumped the bodies one by one into the harbor. Soldiers pried terrified children from their mothers' arms before shooting the women.

In the coming twenty-four years, while the West remained mute, the Indonesian military inflicted a nightmare on East Timor. The troops deprived villagers of food for months, bombing fields so crops couldn't be harvested. Some soldiers treated the East Timorese like playthings. According to a dispatch by Radio Fretilin, troops forced women to work in the fields, pulling plows like water buffaloes. Other testimony, submitted to the Australian senate, describes soldiers at a beach near Dili throwing children through the air before smashing their heads on rocks. Near the same picturesque beach, troops tied rocks to the legs of horrified East Timorese and dropped them from helicopters into the sea. By 1981, about 170,000 people—a quarter of the population—had been killed.

For a week and a half in Australia and East Timor, in taxis, over meals, on a three-hour bus ride, and, once, even before the morning's first latte, Kiernan and I discuss mass murder. We talk about the history, geopolitics, and trends common to a phenomenon that has killed over 30 million people in the twentieth century. He is just as conversant with the Roman destruction of Carthage as he is with the atrocities in Europe in the 1940s. The Roman and Nazi genocides, he says, have a lot in common, "including a cultural prejudice, a militaristic expansionism, and an idealization of agricultural society. Both the Romans and the Nazis were driven, in part, by a contempt and fear of their urban entrepreneurial opponents, the Carthaginians and the Jews."

One of the characteristics of genocides, Kiernan argues, is that powerful nations often deny, disbelieve, or show indifference to them. "When the Nazis embarked on the conquest of Poland and the extermination of millions of Jews, Poles, Roma, and other 'undesirables,' Adolf Hitler asked a revealing question: 'Who ever heard of the Armenians?'" Kiernan says. The answer, of course, was no one. "Yet only a generation earlier, the Young Turks had killed two-thirds of the Armenian population. Hitler believed that the world would let him commit genocide with impunity." Likewise, Kiernan points out that in Rwanda in 1994, Hutu leaders watched the world's indifference to genocidal crimes in Bosnia and concluded that they too could get away with murdering their ethnic rivals, the Tutsi.

"While perpetrators of genocide seem to have benefited from their own comparative analysis of the potential and possibilities for genocide in the modern era," Kiernan has written, "the rest of humanity has so far failed to learn all the lessons from the past that could lead to meaningful intervention in such catastrophes." He founded the Yale Genocide Studies Program to support scholarship that would elicit these lessons: research and documentation, but with a mission. "Genocide is one of the most pressing human issues," he tells me. "The GSP contributes to the prevention of genocide."

The program began in 1998, with a grant from the Andrew W. Mellon Foundation, as a series of weekly seminars. Although it continues to sponsor lectures—more than a hundred to date, by intellectuals from all over the world—it has grown into an interdisciplinary research center, with projects in partnership with Yale's law, medical, divinity, and other schools. The GSP (and its precursor, the Cambodian Genocide Program, which Kiernan founded in 1994) regularly assists foreign nationals from countries afflicted by genocide; its experts have trained dozens of Cambodians, East Timorese, and Rwandans to create databases for evidence. It has a project underway to compile digital satellite maps, with a grant from the Yale Institute for Biospheric Studies, showing the "before" and "after" of genocides in Bosnia, Guatemala, Sudan, and elsewhere.

Most of its scholarship, however, falls into one of three categories. One of these is the effort to discern long-term factors like poverty, war, and trauma that may contribute to the rise of genocidal regimes. For example, says Kiernan, "Trauma often repeats itself from generation to generation. In Yugoslavia, the traumas of many Serbs who were victimized during World War II produced the second-generation traumas of Bosnia in the 1990s. Researchers are exploring whether trauma is transmitted from parents to children by their behavior, so that children subconsciously relive or re-enact the violence to which their parents were subjected. Slobodan Milosevic may be an extraordinary example of this. Both of his parents committed suicide."

A second area of research is on methods to punish perpetrators and help survivors recover. One project, run by psychiatry professor and GSP deputy director Dori Laub, is exploring ways to help Holocaust survivors in Israeli psychiatric hospitals. Because society provided them with no opportunity to share their ordeal, Laub writes, "their traumatic experiences remain encapsulated, causing the survivor to lead a double life: a robot-like semblance to normality with incessant haunting by nightmares and flashbacks." Laub—who has vivid memories of his own internment in a World War II labor camp, Cariera de Piatra, where his father perished—is testing whether the illness can be treated by creating "an ongoing, videotaped testimonial dialogue between the patients and caregivers."

Some of Kiernan's own scholarship focuses on the GSP's third research category: searching for the early warning signs of potentially genocidal movements. "I identify the common characteristics of genocidal regimes, and compare them to emerging political groups to see if they might have genocidal tendencies," he explains. In theory, "if you find evidence of a particular sect or faction that exhibits the ideological elements that are already identified in previous genocides, you could have a way of predicting or anticipating a genocide should this particular group come to power. The racial rhetoric of the Hutu regime, for example, foreshadowed the 1994 bloodshed by a year or more."

When the young Ben Kiernan chose to write his undergraduate honors thesis at Monash University on Cambodian history, he had no idea that the decision would lead him to spend his life studying genocide. He had planned to be a schoolteacher. The son of a Catholic solicitor and a part-Jewish full-time mother, Kiernan was the oldest of seven children born and raised in Melbourne. He learned from his father the importance of tolerance and human rights. His maternal grandfather, Abraham Gershon Silk, was a Polish Jew born in Australia. In the last year of Silk's life, he told his grandson Ben, who was then sixteen, that he regretted not trying to help his relatives in Europe during the Holocaust. He had never heard from them afterward. "They are probably all dead," he said.

After graduating from college in 1975 and working briefly as a tutor, Kiernan won a government scholarship for doctoral work at Monash. Again he focused on Cambodia, which by then was in the grip of the Khmer Rouge's brutal Maoist revolution, led by Pol Pot. The outside world knew little about it. Western journalists and academics had learned immediately that they were not immune to the regime's blood quest, and the United States and other Western nations were not eager to jeopardize their warming relations with China, a close ally of Cambodia.

For his PhD research, Kiernan got as close as he could to the atrocities, interviewing refugees in France and on the Thai border. In 1979, the Vietnamese overthrew Pol Pot, and Kiernan spent eight months in Cambodia over the next two years gathering victims' testimony. Out of this research came the books *How Pol Pot Came to Power* (1985) and *The Pol Pot Regime* (1996). Both were extensively cited by the UN commission that eventually recommended an international tribunal on the Cambodian genocide.

The Reagan and first Bush administrations, however, continued to recognize the deposed regime—which was waging guerrilla warfare from the jungles of northwest Cambodia—rather than the Vietnam-backed socialist government that held power in Phnom Penh. Thanks to Washington's backing, throughout the 1980s Pol Pot's deputies occupied Cambodia's seat at the UN, a situation Kiernan found appalling. He lobbied against it from every available podium. "Diplomats and politicians would try anything to make me go away," he recalls. The U.S. government changed its position during the 1990s. In 1994, Congress passed the Cambodia Genocide Justice Act, mandating the administration to seek the evidence necessary to try the Khmer Rouge.

When the State Department contracted Kiernan for the job, he found himself suddenly provided with money, an office, and a staff in Phnom Penh. But many who had supported the Khmer Rouge, including the Heritage Foundation and Senators Jesse Helms and Trent Lott, attacked the investigation and Kiernan's personal character. Someone dug up an article that Kiernan had written in an undergraduate magazine before he entered graduate school (an article he had long ago retracted) and used it to tar him as a communist and a Khmer Rouge sympathizer. (At the same time, he noted in *Human Rights Review*, the Khmer Rouge were calling him an "arch war criminal" and an "accessory executioner of the U.S. imperialists.")

Nevertheless, within months, Kiernan had established the Cambodian Documentation Center in Phnom Penh to gather and catalogue evidence. Among tens of thousands of other documents, he and his staff found the smoking gun that Congress sought: the 50,000-page Santebal archive, which showed that Pol Pot and other senior leaders had directly supervised the mass killings.

That there would be a jackpot like the Santebal archive, Kiernan explains, is a consistent trait of genocides. "The paper trail is usually extensive," he says.

"The orders have to be written down, acknowledged with another piece of paper, and the results recorded with another. To destroy so many people is a massive bureaucratic operation."

In East Timor, the evidence-collecting role is being led by a UN-sponsored committee: the Commission on Reception, Truth, and Reconciliation. Kiernan is following its progress and helping with documentation where he can. Before his audience with President Gusmao, he takes me to hearings organized by the commission.

The hearings take place in the courtyard of a former Indonesian prison. Several cells have been preserved, including miniscule, lightless solitary-confinement chambers and one cell whose doorway is partly blocked with concrete. A truth commission official tells me that the Indonesians used to fill the cell with water, forcing prisoners to stand for hours or days at a time.

We walk in past photographs of famine victims—children squatting in the dirt, their skin clinging to their bones and the submissive look of starvation in their eyes—and take seats in plastic chairs, huddling up with interpreters. The witnesses sit behind a banquet table, protected from the sun by a canopy. All day, amplifiers blast their solemn words to the crowd, and cameras broadcast them across the country. There is, however, no sign of international press.

Today, the topic is the late 1970s, when civilians were indiscriminately driven from villages, detained in camps, and later resettled in the lowlands in an effort to deny aid to Fretilin fighters. A soft-spoken man, Francisco Soares Pinto, tells about life in the camps. There was no food, so the 6,000 inmates quickly exhausted the coconuts that grew on the grounds. Some ate banana stalks, which made them sick. Many succumbed to beriberi and cholera. Others starved. As many as fifty people died each week. Later, Soares was thrown into prison—the very prison where the hearings are being held--because his family remained in the mountains, where they might aid the rebels. The guards forced him to strip, he says, and crawl all day back and forth across the same courtyard where he now sits testifying, until his hands and knees wore literally to the bone.

Another witness, Maria Josa da Costa, a neatly dressed woman with a troubled face, recounts her experience during the "encirclement and annihilation" campaigns. These began in late 1977, after the United States, France, and Great Britain provided planes and ammunition that bolstered Indonesia's "counter-insurgency" capabilities. In 1978 the military attacked da Costa's village. "Warships fired from the sea, warplanes attacked from the air," she recalls. Soldiers doused the brush with gasoline, then torched it before marching in. The scene recurred all over East Timor. Da Costa, who was a teenager at the time, watched her grandmother scream for water as the flames swallowed her.

In the Palace of Ashes, Gusmao lights another cigarette and tells Kiernan about Fretilin's struggle to alert the world to the Indonesian violence. In May 1981, the Indonesians had begun using a new tactic against Fretilin (and its armed wing, called Falintil). They forced some 80,000 East Timorese men and boys to join arms and form human chains across the island, and then marched this "fence of legs" through the mountains to flush out revolutionaries. Fretilin, vastly outnumbered from the start, was soon demoralized and its troops drastically reduced.

It was in this grim time that Gusmao took command. He resuscitated Fretilin, unifying its splintered factions and taking it underground to more effectively oppose the Indonesians, who by now had near-total control of the island. He became a legend to the shattered populace. From their hideouts in the rugged, sun-parched mountains of East Timor, the resistance fighters had only one channel of communication: a Wagner fifty-watt single sideband transceiver. They kept the transmissions short, because the Indonesian troops shelling them from below could trace their position from the radio signal. When the broadcast was over, they ran. The biggest problem was that the battery that powered the radio was extremely heavy. "We had a very strong man to carry the battery," Gusmao says. "His nom de guerre was Hadomi." After six months Hadomi could barely handle the load. Gusmao's men struggled to keep the transmissions going, but the Indonesians killed Hadomi and eventually Radio Fretilin was silenced.

Gusmao agrees with Kiernan that an archive of Radio Fretilin transmissions would be a key historic record today. But he isn't convinced that it was worth the cost at the time. "We tried to denounce the atrocities," he says. "But the world was indifferent."

In 1992, Indonesian soldiers captured Gusmao in a hideout near Dili. Fortunately for him, East Timor was finally drawing some international attention. The Pope had visited in 1989, and in 1991 an undercover British journalist had filmed Indonesian troops opening fire on a funeral procession. The Indonesians couldn't simply dispose of the Fretilin leader in a remote ravine, as they had done with his predecessor, Nicolau Lobato. Gusmao was given a life sentence (later commuted to twenty years) and imprisoned in Jakarta. But he was able to smuggle messages out regularly, and some scholars believe that he was even more effective in captivity, as a symbol of the struggle, than he had been as an outgunned guerrilla.

In 1997, the East Timorese got a break from an unexpected quarter: the Asian financial collapse. The economic crisis in Indonesia triggered street riots, bloodshed, and, within a year, the fall of Suharto. His successor, President B. J. Habibie, desperately needed multilateral loans to stanch the chaos. To court international support, he proposed a referendum in which the East Timorese would choose either autonomy within Indonesia or independence. But while Habibie made headlines by cooperating with the United Nations, Indonesian generals were secretly recruiting and arming thousands of East Timorese to form pro-Indonesia militias. Militia violence mounted throughout 1999 and climaxed after the August 30 vote. They raped women and murdered more than 1,000 people. They slaughtered villagers' livestock and burned their homes. In one incident, they opened fire and lobbed grenades into a church in Suai, killing three priests and a hundred women and children who had fled inside for safety. UN officials overseeing the referendum—with neither the means nor the mandate to restore order—watched helplessly before fleeing to save their own lives.

The generals hoped that the militia violence would incite full-scale civil war in East Timor, so that Indonesia could step in, cancel the referendum, and impose martial law. But Gusmao, who had been released to house arrest in Jakarta and was exercising his influence over the resistance fighters by phone and fax, urged his troops to stay quiet—to let the carnage go unchecked.

It was a costly gamble, but it stymied the generals' plan. Dozens of foreign journalists who had arrived for the referendum witnessed and reported on the Indonesia-backed atrocities. News programs around the world broadcast footage of the murders and arson. Finally, after hundreds of thousands of Timorese had fled to the mountains and 70 percent of the country's buildings had been destroyed, Australian troops arrived under the UN banner to quell the mayhem. In late 1999, as the last cinders stopped smoldering, East Timor emerged with its freedom.

For the past few years, life has been relatively peaceful in East Timor. In the hills and along the beautiful coastline, villagers are rebuilding their communities. In the capital, the air is fresh, the pace of life relaxed.

On a street not far from Gusmao's Palace of Ashes, skinny children gather near a cluster of cafes that serve the peacekeepers and the relief workers, who still perform many of the country's basic services. The kids stand less than navel-high and wear only shorts, their flesh suntanned the color of a muddy river. When I see them, I can't help but think of the starving children in the photos at the truth commission hearings. Life is better for these kids. They smile and often joke with the foreigners. They run barefoot along the street, offering to wipe dust from the Land Cruisers to earn some pocket change for their families, if they have them, or for their next meal. Late in the day, as the heat subsides, some head for the beach to play soccer.

But four in ten of East Timor's citizens live below the poverty line, and many war orphans and children conceived by rape during the 1999 violence are cared for by the government or charities. Although the country has its independence, it has little else. Schools and hospitals have been burned. Many of the educated elite are dead. In the capital there is an acute shortage of skilled workers, yet half the population is unemployed. Poverty is rampant. Alcoholism is high. And there remains uneasiness about the future. Many former independence fighters are unemployed and disaffected; some are suspected of instigating a recent riot in which the prime minister's house was burned. Across the border in Indonesia, thousands of militia members—perpetrators of the 1999 violence—remain in refugee camps, perhaps counting the days until mid-2004, when the UN peacekeepers depart.

With so many problems to address, with so much at stake for the young nation's future, Gusmao spends all morning talking with Kiernan about the past.

He wants help coming up with a precise death toll. He hopes to create a museum. He's seeking assistance in gathering documents from around the world.

Why is Xanana Gusmao obsessed with history? He gives three reasons. "First, it is something that we owe to the people"—the "small people" of East Timor, who suffered terrible oppression and still prevailed. Another reason he illustrates with an anecdote: "Two days ago, an old man came to me and said, 'I am dying. How can I tell the experience of our resistance? I am dying!' The old people, above 50 years old, are only between 7 to 10 percent of the population. If we delay, many people will die." And the deeds of the resistance will never be known.

Finally, Gusmao believes that history must record the brutalities his people endured. At one point during our meeting, in the midst of a technical discussion over whether the killing fits within the legal definition of genocide, his mind wanders. He stares into the distance, takes a drag from his cigarette, and suddenly exclaims in a hushed, forceful voice: "They crucified people." The words and the tone take us by surprise. "They crucified people. They cut the ear off of the husband—alive—and gave it to the wife. They cut the penis off men. They crucified people! Horrible, horrible!"

It's not every day that historians of genocide meet with heads of state. The heavy lifting for Kiernan usually involves interviewing witnesses, hunting for documents, and sorting through papers. In Canberra, he takes me to the National Library of Australia, where he leafs through an archive recently bequeathed by a member of the Australian group that received and tried to publicize the Radio Fretilin broadcasts. Most of the pages are filled with blocks of seemingly meaningless letters and numbers; they are in code, but the archive includes the encryption key.

Kiernan holds up one document, written in Portuguese. It contains the text of an intercepted telegram. "This was written by Fretilin's information minister, obviously passed on by an opponent of his, who labels him a traitor," he says. Halfway down the page, there's a list of senior Fretilin leadership. Kiernan looks at the date on the telegram. "Five or six of the names I recognize on this list were killed in the following year," he says.

This is one of only two occasions when I will see Kiernan visibly stirred. The other is when he tells me about visiting the infamous Khmer Rouge killing fields of Choeng Ek in 1980, just as the bodies were being exhumed. The site is now a morbid tourist attraction, with a glass-walled memorial stupa containing skulls of the murdered. Kiernan has visited Cambodia many times since 1979, but has never returned to Choeng Ek. "I understand it's a moving memorial. I haven't seen it. I can't really do it very easily," he says, and hesitates, grimacing. "I don't want to go back there."

But most of the time, Kiernan is matter-of-fact, discussing brutalities with the historian's enthusiasm for dry, precise detail. Over the days we spend together, I find myself perplexed by his bottomless capacity to contemplate atrocity. He seems neither obsessed nor traumatized, and it's hard to figure out how he copes. He hasn't cultivated the morbid sense of humor associated with members of other terminally grim professions—cancer surgeons, say, or undertakers. Instead, the historian of carnage is a well-balanced family man, fun to be around. He seems happy. I try to probe him about how a quarter century spent investigating barbarity has affected him. Does it depress him? Does he ever want out? He says only, "I think it's important work worth doing, and I'm glad I've done it."

I'm not the first person to be struck by Kiernan's serenity. A reviewer for the newspaper *The Scotsman,* critiquing *The Pol Pot Regime*, wrote, "Professor Kiernan has acquired superhuman qualities of detachment." Gregory Stanton, a close friend of Kiernan's and president of Genocide Watch, offers another explanation. "There's no way you can avoid becoming angry doing this type of work," he says. "Many people get depressed. They go under. Ben has reacted by channeling this into an extraordinary outpouring of extremely useful scholarship." Kiernan's wife, Glenda Gilmore, the Peter V. and C. Vann Woodward Professor of History at Yale, agrees. "He researches and writes on tragedies," she e-mails me, "but it would be much more tragic to him if genocide happened and no one knew about it or took action. So, in a difficult way, his work uplifts him because he knows that he is making those lost lives count for more."

Youk Chhang, the director of the Cambodian Documentation Center (which Kiernan has turned over to its Cambodian staff), is one of the most immediate beneficiaries of his work. "I was a child who grew up during war, lived during genocide, and was suppressed by the communist ideology," he tells me. "So what's most important to me is freedom and independence. Ben Kiernan gave me the freedom and independence to combat genocide. The UN tribunal will not bring back 1.7 million lives. But it will serve as a very important resource to help Cambodians leave their past behind and move on with their lives, and it can be a source where our kids can learn from what happened. That to me is the meaning of justice."

For Kiernan, the East Timor trip has a personal meaning. He visited here as a student in 1972, when the island was still a Portuguese colony, and that first foray into Asia cemented his professional interest in the continent. This time around, he wants to show the countryside to his son Derry. The two have traveled through Europe and Asia together and last year backpacked a section of the Appalachian Trail.

We rent a jeep and drive out into the mountains. Just ten minutes out of town, the road is sinuous and steep, a constant series of hairpin turns that snake up through tawny dry-season grasses. We pass thatched shacks and the carcasses of dwellings destroyed in 1999. But the country is clearly rebounding. Barefoot children play in the street. Workers with shovels and pickaxes are repairing the tarmac.

Kiernan reminisces about the decades he spent campaigning for justice for Cambodia. He remembers well the cool reception to his message when he arrived in the United States in 1990, when the Khmer Rouge flag was still flying at the United Nations. "Imagine the swastika flying in New York in the 1950s, with the Nazis still maintaining an army on the border of Europe and threatening to return to power," says Kiernan. He swerves to avoid a large pig crossing the road.

He's pleased with the trip. In meetings here he has finally traced the owner of a garage in Sydney he's been hearing rumors about, which holds a major archive of materials from Radio Fretilin. When he returns to Australia, he'll make arrangements to have it photocopied. Then the documents will have to be catalogued and analyzed. The archive probably doesn't hold anything comparable to the Santebal records; it won't likely implicate Indonesian generals. But it could make a significant contribution to the academic understanding of genocide, or it could tell a story that will finally capture the world's imagination and bring East Timor into international public consciousness. Or it could simply help the East Timorese remember their history. "True documented history is our reminder of human cruelty," Xanana Gusmao once said. "It is the lighthouse that forever flashes a warning to our succeeding generations."

Introduction

"You should also tell the Cambodians that we will be friends with them. They are murderous thugs, but we won't let that stand in our way. We are prepared to improve relations with them." Here U.S. Secretary of State Henry Kissinger was addressing the Thai Foreign Minister, Chatichai Choonhavan. They were meeting in Washington on November 26, 1975, seven months after the Khmer Rouge regime had taken over Cambodia, Thailand's neighbor.[1] The closest Khmer Rouge ally was Mao's China, and U.S. President Gerald Ford was about to leave for a visit to Beijing. Afterwards Ford and Kissinger went to Jakarta to meet Indonesia's President, General Suharto, on December 6. There Ford told Suharto that in China, "we made it clear that we are opposed to the expansion of any nation." He added: "The unification of Vietnam has come more quickly than we anticipated. There is, however, resistance in Cambodia to the influence of Hanoi. We are willing to move slowly in our relations with Cambodia, hoping perhaps to slow down the North Vietnamese influence although we find the Cambodian government very difficult." Kissinger then explained Beijing's similar strategy: "the Chinese want to use Cambodia to balance off Vietnam.... We don't like Cambodia, for the government in many ways is worse than Vietnam, but we would like it to be independent. We don't discourage Thailand or China from drawing closer to Cambodia."[2]

Later in this conversation, Suharto raised what he called "another problem, Timor." Jakarta had plans to invade that small Portuguese colony the next day. Suharto told the Americans: "We want your understanding if we deem it necessary to take rapid or drastic action." Ford replied: "We will understand and will not press you on the issue." Kissinger added: "You appreciate that the use of U.S.-made arms could create problems.... It depends on how we construe it; whether it is in self-defense or is a foreign operation. It is important that

---

1. Memorandum of Conversation, "Secretary's Meeting with Foreign Minister Chatichai of Thailand," Nov. 26, 1975, declassified July 27, 2004, p. 8: www. gwu.edu/~nsarchiv/NSAEBB/NSAEBB193/HAK-11-26-75.pdf (accessed Dec. 12, 2006).
2. Text of Ford-Kissinger-Suharto discussion, US Embassy Jakarta Telegram 1579 to Secretary State, 6 December 1975, in *East Timor Revisited: Ford, Kissinger and the Indonesian Invasion, 1975-76*, National Security Archive Electronic Briefing Book No. 62, William Burr and Michael L. Evans, eds., December 6, 2001. Online at www. gwu.edu/~nsarchiv/NSAEBB/NSAEBB62/doc4.pdf (accessed Dec. 12, 2006)

whatever you do succeeds quickly. We would be able to influence the reaction in America if whatever happens happens after we return. This way there would be less chance of people talking in an unauthorized way.... We understand your problem and the need to move quickly. . . Whatever you do, however, we will try to handle in the best way possible.... If you have made plans, we will do our best to keep everyone quiet until the President returns home."[3]

In this way, two outbreaks of genocide and extermination that began in Southeast Asia in the same year both did so with powerful foreign acquiescence. Any indigenous force seeking militarily to contest either Khmer Rouge rule in Cambodia or Indonesia's occupation of East Timor was likely to meet major international inertia. It was in this diplomatic climate that Pol Pot's Communist Party ruled Cambodia for nearly four years, from 1975 to 1979, and Indonesian military forces occupied East Timor for a quarter century, until 1999. Even after the Vietnamese army's overthrow of the Khmer Rouge in 1979, Washington voted in the United Nations for the exiled genocidists to continue to represent Cambodia there until the early 1990s, and the U.S. supported Indonesia's occupation of East Timor until the late 1990s. During their rule, the two perpetrator regimes inflicted massive casualties in similar proportions, causing the deaths of about one fifth of the population of each nation, or a mortality of approximately 1.7 million in Cambodia and possibly 170,000 in East Timor. In both cases, most of the deaths occurred in the period 1975-1980. Both regimes exterminated ethnic minorities, including local Chinese in each case, as well as political dissidents. Yet the ideological fuel that ignited each of these conflagrations was quite different. Jakarta pursued anti-communism; the Khmer Rouge were communists. In East Timor, the major Indonesian goal was conquest. In Cambodia, the Khmer Rouge goal was revolution.

The identification of genocidal ideologies is an important element in genocide prevention, a field of study that has been gaining significant attention from scholars and policymakers in recent years.[4] In 2004, the United Nations established an Office of the Special Adviser for the Prevention of Genocide.[5] But these efforts have not yet been able to prevent new outbreaks, like the genocide raging in Darfur since 2003. Studying how to bring an end to mass murder once in progress remains as important as ever.

Modern genocides have been stopped in various ways. The Nazi Holocaust during World War II ended only in the face of a massive external military onslaught mounted on two fronts, by both the Allies and the Soviet Union. Jewish and Soviet partisans, and resistance movements in Poland, Yugoslavia, Czecho-

---

3.   Text of Ford-Kissinger-Suharto discussion, US Embassy Jakarta Telegram 1579 to Secretary State, 6 December 1975, in *East Timor Revisited*: www.gwu. edu/~nsarchiv/NSAEBB/NSAEBB62/doc4.pdf (accessed Dec. 12, 2006).

4.   See for instance the *Journal of Genocide Research,* and the new journal of The International Association of Genocide Scholars, *Genocide Studies and Prevention.*

5.   www.un.org/Depts/dpa/prev_genocide

slovakia, Norway, Italy, Greece, and France all inflicted significant casualties on Nazi forces, in some cases causing substantial losses, but such indigenous opposition played a secondary role in the defeat of the Hitler regime.[6] This is not surprising, because genocidal regimes also tend to be aggressively expansionist, and frequently create international crises or provoke external cross-border retaliation. Yet domestic opposition can also be important. In Bangladesh in 1971, local guerrilla forces resisted the Pakistani army's genocidal repression until an invading Indian army ended it. In Rwanda in 1994, it was left to an externally-trained but indigenous, predominantly Tutsi insurgent army, the Rwandan Patriotic Front, to overthrow the Hutu Power regime and halt its genocide of Tutsis.

The two perpetrator regimes examined in this book finally collapsed or withdrew in the face of substantial international intervention or pressure: a full-scale Vietnamese invasion in the case of Cambodia in 1979, and a United Nations peacekeeping force in East Timor in 1999. Yet Cambodia and East Timor both also produced significant indigenous resistance movements, which challenged the genocidal regimes with military force that proved inferior though not ineffectual. Resistance forces were able to draw upon or muster important indigenous political support that contributed to the eventual defeat of the two perpetrator regimes. The factors that led them to take action merit study.

Although the two genocidal dictatorships, communist and militarist, came from opposite ends of the political spectrum, and the motives of the rebel leaders who confronted them varied, in these two Southeast Asian cases both of the resistance movements originated in radical leftist political parties. National independence was a major goal of the Fretilin guerrilla movement in East Timor, and Maoist ideology was an additional influence on some of its leaders. Along with indigenous racism, Maoism was also a major element of the ideology of Pol Pot's Cambodian regime, but Mao's thinking initially also influenced the Khmer Rouge cadres who rebelled against that regime. In both Cambodia and East Timor, however, the leading resistance forces, though they began as radical organizations, also became more moderate over time in the face of genocide and extermination.

Resistance movements that inflict casualties on perpetrator regimes, such as those examined here, are of course not the only forms of resistance worth studying. In various cases, organized non-violent or passive resistance has also obstructed mass repression and rescued targeted victims.[7] At an individual level, more everyday forms of resistance have also enabled victims to sur-

---

6. See for instance Yitzhak Arad, "The Armed Jewish Resistance in Eastern Europe: Its Unique Conditions and its Relations with the Jewish Councils (Judenrate) in the Ghettoes," in *The Holocaust and History: The Known, the Unknown, the Disputed, and the Re-examined*, ed. Michael Berenbaum and Abraham J. Peck, Bloomington: Indiana University Press, 1998, 591-600.

7. See for instance Jacques Semelin, *Unarmed against Hitler: Civilian Resistance in Europe, 1939-1943*, Westport, CT: Praeger, 1993.

vive, including by enabling them to maintain their dignity and self-respect.[8] These other kinds of resistance are not the focus of this book, but deserve equal attention.

The first part of the book offers analytical essays on aspects of the genocide, extermination and resistance in Cambodia and East Timor, followed in each case by new documentary sources on the resistance movements. The second part traces the cumulative documentation of the crimes committed, efforts to bring the perpetrators to justice, and obstacles that had to be overcome. The third part of the book includes some of my contemporary reporting from the Thai-Cambodian border and from Cambodia itself, in the aftermath of the genocide there.

---

8.   James C. Scott, *Weapons of the Weak: Everyday Forms of Peasant Resistance*, New Haven, CT: Yale University Press, 1985; Scott, *Domination and the Arts of Resistance: Hidden Transcripts*, New Haven, CT, Yale University Press, 1990; Ben Kiernan, *The Pol Pot Regime: Race, Power and Genocide in Cambodia under the Khmer Rouge, 1975-1979*, 2nd ed., New Haven, CT: Yale University Press, 2002, 246-50.

Part 1

Genocide and Resistance

1

Wild Chickens, Farm Chickens, and Cormorants: Cambodia's Eastern Zone under Pol Pot[1]*

In his 1981 memoir of life in Pol Pot's Democratic Kampuchea, entitled *Cambodia: 1,360 Days!*, Ping Ling described the newly victorious Khmer Rouge as they forcibly emptied Phnom Penh, capital of the defeated Lon Nol regime, of its two million residents. From the viewpoint of a civilian evacuee, Ping Ling provided a glimpse of the contrasting roles of the different Khmer Rouge units that occupied the western and eastern banks of the Tonle Sap River:

> *30 April, 1975*: No fresh news at the temple today, except rumors spread by the blackshirts themselves that the blackshirts on the other side of the river are worse than those on this side…. We really don't know what to believe, no one dared ask. *1 May, 1975*: The embankment going down to the boat was steep and far, with only a wooden plank a foot wide between the boat and the wet mud bank. Extraordinary how everything did go across that plank, even pigs; except for one incident where a pregnant woman, carrying a baby in one hand, her basket containing food in the other, and a bundle of clothing on top of her head, suddenly seemed to lose her equilibrium…she let go of the basket of food and that bundle on her head toppled into the river. But she did keep the baby in her other hand. A number of blackshirts were nearby, looking calmly on without lending a hand. One good thing, though; they didn't laugh.

> Two hours later, we arrived at a small wharf. 'Greenshirts' instead of blackshirts could be seen on this side of the river. They were at the end of the planks where the passengers were descending, helping everyone who was overloaded with things in their arms. Carrying babies for the mothers, they even helped to carry the invalid ashore. So much for those blackshirts' propaganda on the other side. They even tried to steady me by holding on to my arms loaded with bundles. They were helpful…good commie soldiers.

* This chapter appeared in David P. Chandler and Ben Kiernan, eds., *Revolution and Its Aftermath in Kampuchea*, New Haven, Yale Council on Southeast Asia Studies, 1983. A grant from the Christopher Reynolds Foundation made possible my research for it in Cambodia in 1980.

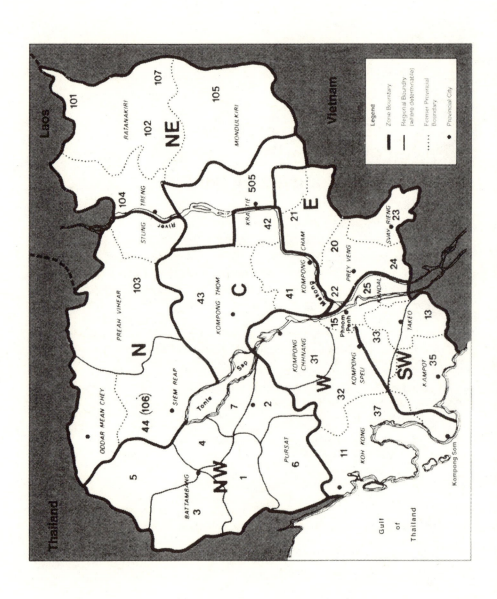

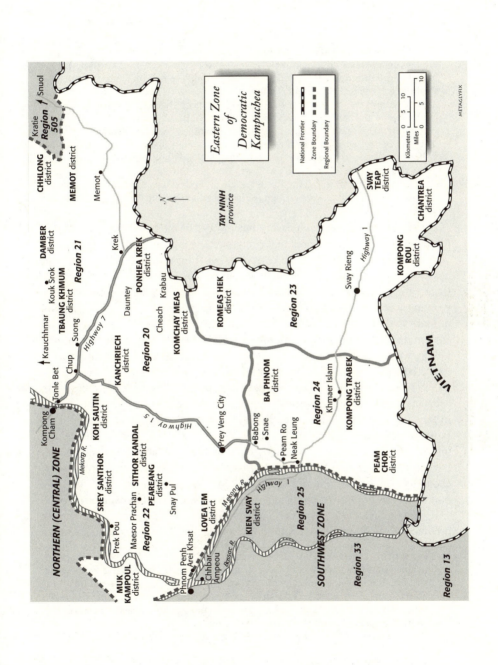

Eastern Zone
of
Democratic Kampuchea

In September 1975, the former customs officer Sok Sopha crossed the Mekong to the Eastern Zone and also found what "seemed like another world." Sopha recalled:

> I was met by local people and militia who each gave me a tin or two of milled rice, 25 kgs. in all. They all asked me what things were like back there.... I knew these people were different but I dared not say so. I could see that [defeated] former Lon Nol soldiers were still alive and was told that even generals had been spared here. The people were only working three days per week and could search for dispersed friends and relatives and barter for goods on the other days. Buddhist monks took part in the Pchum Ben festival in September. Very large canals had been dug, the rice crops were big, and there was a good deal of palm sugar and pig-raising. Nurses visited from village to village to tend to the sick. The people liked the Eastern Zone cadre, they were united as one. There were no classes as in the Pol Pot areas: everybody was a soldier for the revolution. If the Eastern Zone group had won control throughout the country in 1977, things would not have happened as they did.

Sopha made several such visits, but always to the same village, and his idyllic picture of the large area that comprised the Eastern Zone of Democratic Kampuchea (DK) in 1975 is an extrapolation from that. Although other witnesses confirm that urban evacuees in the East were accorded considerable liberty to search for relatives and friends,[1] no other evidence exists that the working week was limited to three days; some executions of former Lon Nol military and others did occur there; there was even starvation in one or two eastern districts in the first six months after April 1975; and the last remaining monks were all defrocked by the end of 1976. But the contrast which Sopha draws between the two sides of the Mekong was nevertheless real, and so was the 1977 turning point which he identifies. In 1975-76, at least, there were substantial differences between the Eastern Zone and other zones of Cambodia, in terms of living conditions and the implementation of revolutionary policy. In the words of a Communist Party of Kampuchea (CPK) "Center" (*mocchim*) internal report, dated 20 December 1976: "In 1976 the labor force was feeble. It was only in the East that it was not feeble."[2] In a detailed study of the DK economy, Marie Martin has noted that in Prey Veng and Kompong Cham, the major eastern provinces, engineers evacuated from the cities were employed to design the irrigation projects built there. In Prey Veng and the other eastern province, Svay Rieng, pre-revolutionary projects and project designs formed

1.   For instance, during the last eight months of 1975, a former Lon Nol military policeman travelled widely in Regions 22 and 24, which he called "somewhat loose, still free Regions to some extent. . . People could travel and forage and there was no starvation." He added, "I did not hear of any killings, only arrests of Lon Nol officers," and corroborated Sopha's picture in most other respects. [See also Ben Kiernan, *The Pol Pot Regime: Race, Power and Genocide in Cambodia under the Khmer Rouge, 1975-1979*, New Haven, Yale University Press, 2nd ed., 2002, 205-10.]
2.   *Report on the Activities of the Party Center: Political Tasks*, 1976, 58 pp.

the basis for successful post-1975 irrigation schemes.[3] This was not the case for other Zones, whose leaders tended to reject non-revolutionary "experts."

In this essay I have tried to piece together the story of the main segment of Pol Pot's "internal opposition" – largely a loyal, even unwitting opposition at first, but one that by May 1978 was driven to outright rebellion. By then or beforehand, the Pol Pot group or CPK Center had decided that the Eastern Zone cadres and population possessed "Khmer bodies with Vietnamese minds" (*khluon khmaer khuo kbal yuon*), and it began a large-scale program to eliminate them. Over 100,000 perished in the next six months – the worst single atrocity of the DK period. Paradoxically then, the area almost universally considered by Khmers as the safest place to live in DK until 1977, became by far the most dangerous in 1978. Further, the two key themes of regional variation and the centralization of control can both be found in the history of the Eastern Zone, and it is there that tension between them was most evident. It was the culmination of a process of Center intervention in the Zone that began in earnest around mid-1976 and nearly annihilated the veteran Eastern Communists, although they had the last say in 1979 when their remnants, led by Heng Samrin and Chea Sim, and backed by the Vietnamese army, returned to positions of power. Study of the Eastern Zone is therefore useful for an understanding of contemporary Khmer politics. It also fills gaps in our knowledge resulting from the fact that until 1979-80, few refugees from the Zone reached the distant Thai border to make their experiences known to the Western world.

My research in this chapter is based on eighty-seven interviews conducted in the period 1979-81, with people who had lived in all five Regions (numbered twenty to twenty-four) of the Eastern Zone between 1975 and 1979. They include forty "base people" (*neak moultanh*, i.e., those, mostly peasants, who had lived in CPK-held areas during the 1970-75 civil war), twenty-seven "new people" (*neak thmei*, those evacuated in April 1975 from the towns, held until the end of the war by the Lon Nol regime), and twenty revolutionary cadre. Thirty-three of the base people I interviewed were peasants, and twenty-three of the eighty-seven interviewees were women.[4] In the absence of a more sub-

---

3. Marie Martin, "La riziculture et la maîtrise de l'eau dans le Kampuchéa démocratique," *Etudes rurales* 83 (juillet-septembre 1981), 28, 34.

4. Eighty-two of the eighty-seven were interviewed separately, the others in two group sessions. None were married to one another. The youngest interviewee was fifteen years old, the oldest sixty-seven; the rest were all between twenty and sixty-five, with a slight majority in the thirty to fifty age range. All were ethnic Khmer apart from three Cham (one base person, one new person, one cadre) and three ethnic Chinese new people. Nine of the interviewees were refugees in Australia or France; the rest were interviewed in or near their homes or work places in Cambodia itself. There seem no significant divergences between the accounts of those interviewed in different countries. None of the interviews were conducted in refugee camps. Of those conducted in Cambodia, there seem no significant divergences between the ones attended by a 28-year-old guide from the Ministry of Information and Culture, and those conducted privately. The eighty-seven interviewees were almost evenly

stantial survey, a conclusive appraisal of social conditions in the East cannot
be attempted. In what follows I will summarize the evidence available to me as
of 1981, and illustrate it with some verbatim accounts. I will discuss at greater
length the political struggles that took place there, including local resistance to
the genocide. What we know of these suggests that the reasons for the differences between the Eastern Zone and elsewhere in DK were indeed political, at
least in part, and it throws some light on the moderate socialist policies adopted
by the Heng Samrin government after 1979.

For over a decade, however, Heng Samrin and Chea Sim both declined my
requests for interviews. Chapter 2 reproduces my 1991-92 interviews with
them.

Executions and Starvation in the Eastern Zone: Summary of Data

1975-76

Of the sixty-seven interviewees who were not Khmer Rouge cadre, ten
mentioned specific victims of killings by Eastern Zone cadre in the years 1975
and 1976, numbering over 190 victims in all. At least five of the ten were not
eyewitnesses to the killings they mentioned, so there is no certainty about all of
them. On the other hand, thirteen interviewees also reported people disappearing
after being taken away "to study"; and from the testimony of five or six such
people I interviewed, some of those apprehended in this way were executed.
(Most were released – especially in the southern Regions 22, 23 and 24[5] – and

divided between residents of the five Regions that made up the Eastern Zone of
Democratic Kampuchea. Except where specifically stated, I have not taken into
account the interviews with revolutionary cadres in the discussion of living conditions, or of executions. Those interviews were conducted in order to gain insight
into the internal politics and aims of the Communist movement, and I draw on them
extensively for that purpose only.

5. In *Region 22*, 1,000 new people were arrested in May 1975 in Koh Sautin district.
    Twenty "civil servants and merchants" were released almost immediately; four
    hundred more Lon Nol officials were "given permission to rejoin their families"
    in July; and of the other 580 who were Lon Nol military personnel, "junior of-
    ficers and soldiers returned in great numbers" to the villages in September. The
    officers, however, had not returned by December 1975. One of those released, Kong
    Samrach, said that the prison regime was harsh but "nobody had any intention of
    escaping" at that stage. (Testimony at the "Cambodia Hearing," Oslo, April 1978,
    typescript.) Another new person, Thun, 22, who lived in Srey Santhor district from
    April 1975 to December 1976, told me that the revolutionaries there "did not perse-
    cute the people, and there were no killings." "They genuinely re-educated a lot of
    new people. There were schools [for them] and the teachers were well-qualified."
    (Interview with author.) In *Region 23*, over 600 people, including 300 teachers,
    were imprisoned in Svay Rieng district in 1975 and then released, apparently in
    1976. (Interview with author.) In Svay Teap district, 193 prisoners were sent back
    to their villages in March 1976. Towards the end of the year, however, presumably

large-scale deaths among those who remained in detention do not appear to
have taken place before late 1976.)

Of the 190 reported victims, thirty were reported from a single district:
Chantrea, in Svay Rieng province of Region 23.[6] Another eight to ten deaths
occurred during an abortive uprising led by former Lon Nol regime figures,
in Region 22 in November 1975. About 130 of the reported executions were
dated at mid- to late 1976. For the sixteen months after April 1975, then, spe-

---

in connection with the purge of local cadre at that time, the prisoners began to be
recalled and most were subsequently executed (Katuiti Honda, *Journey to Cambodia* (Tokyo, 1981), 90.) In *Region 24*, Song Van, 52, a base peasant from Peam
Ro district imprisoned in 1973, was released in April 1975 along with 170 others.
He estimates that seventy percent of all prisoners in the seven Region jails were
released at that time. A Region-level meeting of cadres decided on the releases, Van
says. "Chhouk and [his deputies] Thuch and Chey were not harsh people. If they
were as bad as the leaders who took their place, the people would not have believed
in them." After Van got back to his village, a number of new people, and even the
chief monk, were imprisoned, but there were no executions, he says, until late 1976,
after Chhouk himself had been arrested. (Interview with author.) Sokhun, a former
chauffeur for the French embassy, was imprisoned for three months' "re-education"
along with 100 other new people who arrived in Kompong Trabek district. Then
they were released and given "normal" work in the fields. He said that "Lon Nol
soldiers, government officials, intelligence agents and customs officers disappeared,"
perhaps were killed, in 1975, but there were "no killings" in 1976 until, again, late
in the year when former government officials and alleged "servants of foreigners" were sought out and killed. (Interview with author, 11 September 1981.) An
officer of the U.S. embassy in Thailand provided more information in an official
report dated 21 September 1976 and declassified in 1978. He wrote: "One person
who came from eastern Cambodia claimed that executions are much fewer [there]
because the more sympathetic Khmer Rumdos are in control there. He noted that
they have generally required only that former [Lon Nol] officers from the rank of
second lieutenant upward shave their heads and do forced labor." Another refugee
from the east who arrived in Thailand in late July 1976 said that the Khmer Rumdos
"continue to allow Buddhism to flourish, execute people rarely, make people work
only a normal working day, and let them eat and dress better [than in other Zones]."
("Cambodia Today: Life Inside Cambodia," 13 pp., at 4, 13.) These two accounts
provide the only glimpses of the Eastern Zone in sixty-one pages of declassified
reports on DK by U.S. embassy personnel from the 1975-76 period. For discussion
of the "Khmer Rumdos," see the section on "Political Struggles" below.

6.   According to one account, Chantrea, alone among the Zone's thirty-two districts
      – perhaps because of its strategic location, at the tip of the "Parrot's Beak" and
      surrounded on three sides by Vietnamese territory – was said to have been taken
      over in 1975-76 by the Southwest Zone cadre, who were more closely allied to
      the Center. Bunni, 55, a Phnom Penh woman evacuated to Chantrea, told me: "In
      1975-76, Southwestern cadres arrived in vehicles and motorcycles and took control
      of most subdistricts ..." Chantrea was also the scene of the only reported mass
      execution in the Eastern Zone in 1975-76. In late 1975, as many as one thousand
      Khmer refugees who had fled to Vietnam were sent back to Kampuchea in several
      groups, in exchange for ethnic Vietnamese leaving the country. They are said to
      have been killed as soon as they were some distance from the Vietnamese border.

cific executions reported by the sixty-seven non-cadre interviewees outside of Chantrea district numbered about twenty, to which must be added seven victims of a self-confessed executioner whom I also interviewed. There were, obviously, more executions in the hundreds of Eastern villages not covered by this sample and these probably numbered in the thousands. Six interviewees mentioned in general terms the types of people liable to execution in that period: "intellectuals and Lon Nol officers;" "most military, officials, and rich people;" "many Lon Nol officers;" "only well-educated people;" "one or two who refused orders or were lazy;" and "not many like in 1977," when there were fewer again than in 1978. However, twenty-nine of the non-cadre interviewees asserted that there were "no killings" of people from their villages in 1975-76; another ten mentioned none; ten described uncertain circumstances that may have led to executions, and two others mentioned executions limited to revolutionary cadre.

Starvation took a heavy toll in two of the interviewees' villages in the year 1975 – twenty deaths were reported in one Chantrea village, fifty in a village in Memut (Region 21). Apart from these cases, however, all accounts agree that rations distributed and food available were adequate for basic nutrition in 1975 and 1976.

Most of the interviewees who reported executions or starvation in their villages in 1975-76 described the revolution and their conditions of life at that time as "no good." Of the other fifty-five non-cadre interviewees, eleven expressed no opinions on the subject. Among the remaining forty-four, a range of views was expressed, usually quite complex and nuanced. Seven described the revolution and conditions of life in that period as "no good" primarily because of hard work and low rations but reported no executions or starvation. Another seven described them as something between (or, in different respects, both) "no good" and "tolerable" (*kuo som*) or "all right" (*kron bao*). Twenty-one described them in terms such as "tolerable" or "all right," and nine in terms such as "good" (*la'o*) or "not a problem" (*ot ey te*). Further, ten of the new people who did not hold such a view themselves, expressed the conviction that in 1975-76 the base people (i.e., the local peasants) in their village were supporters of the revolution.

There are several reasons for these relatively favorable reports. One is that the next two years were far worse, and made previously imposed hardship seem like benevolence. This applies particularly to Chantrea and to Region 21, and to the experiences of the seven informants whose descriptions of conditions in 1975-76 fall in the middle of the range of opinions expressed. For the thirty whose accounts were more positive, and in the other four Regions, this factor also applies but is affected by two others. Many peasants had supported the revolution during the 1970-75 war, and the combination of peace and victory raised morale considerably among the population at large as well as among cadres. Anticipating that life would greatly improve in the long term, where rations fell and working hours increased, many saw (probably correctly) a short-term sacrifice as necessary for post-war economic recovery. Even violence or mistreatment of the population by cadres was expected to decrease as tensions, and the system itself, gradually settled down. Finally, for many peasants in the East, there was little deterioration in conditions in any case. Relations with revolutionary cadres (if they were not indeed relatives) were often good, sometimes excellent, and the arrival of the new people, at least where the latter were treated as outsiders and inferiors, frequently served to strengthen these relations. Thus, while in the case of many informants the description of 1975-76 as "tolerable" or "good" simply means "not as bad as in 1977-78," in others it was a view genuinely held at the time. The evidence suggests a rather close relationship between many cadres and peasants that was to persist until the deaths of both at the hands of another group of outsiders from Phnom Penh.

1977-78

Beyond several descriptions of the year 1977 and the early part of 1978, none of the interviewees expressed the opinion that the revolution and the conditions they lived under for the second two-year period were "good" or even "tolerable." All mentioned large-scale executions in 1977-78, as well as continued (or usually, increased) heavy work demands and continued low (or usually, reduced) food consumption. Around the end of 1976, most reported that rations were reduced and in a number of places, private foraging for food – even outside of the long working hours – was prohibited. As a result, there was serious starvation in some villages and widespread malnutrition. There was a detectable deterioration in conditions from 1976 to 1977,[7] when the war with Vietnam began, and a very sharp, dramatic and brutal deterioration after May 1978.

There are some parallels between what happened in the Eastern Zone in 1975-76 and events a decade before in parts of Indonesia during another kind of social upheaval. On the island of Bali in 1965-66, 40,000 to 100,000 people out of a population of 1.8 million were killed.[8] In the Eastern Zone of Democratic Kampuchea, whose population after the evacuation of Phnom Penh numbered

7.   The report of an Eastern Zone Party Congress on 17 July 1977 adds: "from the end of May up to now, the living standards of the population have worsened; it is impossible to achieve the levels fixed by the Party because some regions are very poor (*denuées*).... The poverty of these regions was more serious, especially in the districts of Krauchhmar, Peamchileang, Koh Sautin and Muk Kampoul, and living standards were lower than in 1976, to the point where the population has had nothing to eat but gruel." The report described the situation as one of "famine" and "general exhaustion." *Trial of Pol Pot and Ieng Sary,* People's Republic of Kampuchea (Phnom Penh, August 1979), Document no. 2.5.13.
8.   John Hughes, *The End of Sukarno* (London, 1968), 177, 188.

1.8 million,[9] the executions in 1975-76 were somewhat fewer, probably well under 10,000. But in 1977-78, deaths among residents of the Zone exceeded 100,000. This is despite the fact that recriminations and economic hardship might have been expected to occur in the aftermath of such a devastating civil war as that from 1970-75, but to cease or decrease (as they did, temporarily, in 1976) as the new regime consolidated itself. Other forces were at work and the time lag before the largest massacres, particularly those of 1978 in Cambodia's Eastern Zone, gives them a decidedly more deliberate and premeditated character.

Social Conditions

One theme which emerges from the interviews is that very few people approved of communal eating, introduced with high-level cooperativization in the latter half of 1976 in some areas, and in early 1977 elsewhere. The generalized resentment stemmed not just from the concomitant reduction in food rations. It was, certainly, a method of population control and of state economizing; but it was also an ideological attack on what was called "privateness" (*kar aekachun*), and as such it was repugnant to many peasants, especially when combined with prohibitions on family (or personal) gardening and foraging. As we shall see later, this was a crucial issue for Eastern cadre such as Chhouk, CPK chief of Region 24, who seems to have been committed more to a "peasant revolution," an upheaval that would raise the material and social conditions of the rural mass, rather than to an ideological "revolution from above."

Even if Eastern Communists attempted "re-education" in most cases, and released thousands of new people after short periods in prison, they were not averse to executing elite new people (including some religious leaders) on the basis of their class origins, or others whom they considered "enemies." They were also prepared to implement directives from above urging them to prohibit religious practice, abolish conventional education, and limit freedom of movement. In no way can these actions be described as enlightened or benign. But cadre like Chhouk and, if to a lesser extent, the Zone chief So Phim, seem to have sensed that to lower the living standards or threaten the basic lifestyle of their peasant constituents would deprive the revolution of the moral force they believed it could command. Ruthless, with as much blood on their hands as all pre-1975 Cambodian political groupings, they nevertheless saw themselves as acting primarily in the interests of the mass of the peasantry, and not of a Colossus state or a demanding ideology. They were much closer to the village people

---

9.   *Kumrung Pankar Buon Chhnam Khosang Sangkum Niyum Krup Phnaek Rebos Pak, 1977-80* [The Party's Four-Year Plan to Build Socialism in All Fields, 1977-80], 110 pp., dated July-August, 1976. Table 1 at p. 13 gives a figure of 1.7 million for the population of the Eastern Zone in mid-1976. However, in late 1975, perhaps 100,000 new people in Region 22 had been (again) evacuated, to the Northern – later renamed the Central – Zone. Kong Samrach (see note 5 above) says 35,000 were evacuated from Koh Sautin district alone.

than the remote Pol Pot group (the Party Center) or the far more militaristic Zone leaders, Mok and Pauk, of the Southwest and North.

On May 10, 1978, two weeks before the Center-sponsored suppression of the East with the aid of Pauk and Mok, Phnom Penh Radio warned of the need to "purify...the masses of the people."[10] Such a process, now to take the form of a vast massacre, had in fact begun at the end of 1976 with the nation-wide attempt to remold people's way of thinking and acting, mainly through "tempering" them (*lot dam*) and abolishing "privateness." Reduction of rations two years after victory, the enforcement of communal eating, the prohibition on foraging – were not what So Phim, Chhouk and their comrades fought, killed and died for. As Phim is reported by a member of the Center armed forces to have remarked in this period, the aim of the revolution was improvement in the standard of living, not the enforcement of poverty or misery in order to teach people what it was like to be poor.[11] It was Phim's failure to appreciate until too late that the Center and its "blackshirt" cadres seriously if silently disagreed with him, which was to prove fatal for the Easterners. What follows are the accounts of five base people and five new people who lived in all five Regions of the Eastern Zone. It should be noted at this point that new people made up less than one-third of the Zone's population in 1975.

Region 20

1. Ek, 58, a base peasant whom I selected at random for an interview, said that in his village there was no starvation, and "no killings from 1975 to 1977." On further questioning, he said that at some stage before 1978 three people, including two former teachers, had been taken away by security forces and had not returned.

> I saw them taken away but we were not very interested because the Khmer Rouge were only looking for their enemies [and] did not kill ordinary people in those years...
>
> In the period when So Phim was still alive, from 1975 right up to 25 May 1978, there were no problems. The cadres and people were on good terms, and would invite each other to meals in their homes. Conditions in the village were good, and the leadership was good, close to the people.
>
> The people had no say in what work they did, and so production was relatively low, and they feared the cadres to a small extent, [but] they believed them. From 1974 to

---

10. Phnom Penh Radio, 10 May 1978. *BBC Summary of World Broadcasts,* 15 May 1978, FE/5813/A3/4. The same broadcast also said: "[Each] One of us must kill thirty Vietnamese...so far, we have succeeded in implementing this slogan of one against thirty.... We need only two million troops to crush the fifty million Vietnamese, and we would still have six million people left."

11. Manuscript of a forthcoming book by Michael Vickery [*Cambodia 1975-1982*, Boston, South End, 1984], quoting a former member of a communications unit in a Center Division stationed in the East.

1977 there were meetings in which they explained politics to us, educated us, led us. They told us to love one another, not to quarrel, and to work together to increase production. We worked enthusiastically; people were happy and chatted casually, visiting one another from house to house in the evenings. We could travel to nearby villages or go fishing; so long as we just asked permission first, they would let us go.

But then in 1978, in the Pol Pot period [sic] we were too afraid to move around like that; it was prohibited. You needed a letter from the district office. The deep fear began in 1978 when the killings started. From May 1978 when the Southwest Zone forces arrived, there were no more political meetings and we had less food to eat than before. Then in November the evacuations started. They took over forty people from my village, people they were not happy with. I just kept quiet and never said anything, so they did not evacuate me.

2. Hor, 30, a former university student evacuated from Phnom Penh with his family to their native village in Komchay Meas district, spent the next eighteen months in prison. Apart from a three-month stint breaking rocks in Region 21, where life was "very tough" and two of his group of forty prisoners were accused of being rebels and executed, the first year was "not very hard" because "we grew rice with the people" and "lived with the people who would secretly give us supplies" at the risk of being reprimanded. Finally, around April 1976, Hor was transferred to an official jail where "all the prisoners from all over" the district, 120 people in all, were sent. There they worked a thirteen-hour day with very little food, particularly in the final months of the year before the harvest. During October, eighty prisoners died of starvation or exhaustion. The next month, the forty survivors were released and Hor went back to his native village.

There he found that the seven members of his family were "healthy but having a tough time" because new people were regarded with contempt by the authorities and the 500 other villagers, all base people. "When I first arrived I could see that the base people really believed in and liked the revolution because it had just been victorious. They had defeated the United States. And also in 1976 the food situation was still all right and meals were eaten at home. In 1975-76 the cadres did not make the people suffer greatly. They gave people three tins of rice per day instead of one."

Hor even expressed approval of some of the district level cadre. However, at the end of 1976, new cadre arrived and over the ensuing months executed many of the old ones, including "all the educated ones." Around March 1977 cooperatives were formed, communal eating instituted which people resented, and rations became inadequate. In Hor's view: "These difficulties following a period of ease meant that the people became unhappy with the revolution. They changed their minds about it because life was so tough in 1977-78-79."

Communal weddings, involving twenty couples in a single ceremony, also began in early 1977, and the following year thirty-five forced marriages took place in the village. In May 1978 cadre from the Southwest Zone rounded up all local officials from village chief upwards, and executed them. About a month later, when the Eastern Zone rebellion was in full swing, evacuations began, provoking a demonstration of "150 villagers, including all the men," in November, according to Hor. "Then the Southwest forces fired two shells at the crowd, killing about seven people. I saw this and my brothers and I immediately ran to get our things ready to move."

Region 21

3. Nal, 43, a former rubber plantation worker who took to rice farming in Tbaung Khmum district in 1970, said: "From 1975 the Khmer Rouge did not yet do many bad things; they just arrested and jailed some people and took away the harvests. In 1976-77, they killed intellectuals evacuated from Phnom Penh, and there were also some deaths from starvation. Everyone, base people and new people, now ate only gruel and salt."

In 1977, Nal said, his mother died of starvation, and his brother, sister, and thirty other relatives also perished. Then generalized "killing of the people" began with the Phnom Penh government's military suppression of the Eastern Zone in May 1978. In his words: "They killed all the Eastern Zone cadres and ordinary people who committed the most minor offenses, such as talking about family problems at night. Every day they would take away three to five families for execution...we would hear them screaming for help."

4. Dara, 26, a law student evacuated from Phnom Penh with his brother and a friend, arrived in Chhlong district in June 1975. Within a month, over 100 former Lon Nol soldiers and a number of teachers were "taken away for re-education, and disappeared." Dara said he was "very afraid of the base people," who numbered 1,700 out of 2,000 in his village: "We were told to keep quiet if we wanted to survive, and I went along with this." Nevertheless, "at first there were no problems; there was plenty of food." Rations consisted of "all rice" until the end of 1976 and meals were still eaten at home. For a full year, ten Buddhist monks continued to beg for food in the traditional way; there was a "lavish" Khmer New Year festival in April 1976. Dara found that attitudes to the system varied:

> The new people mostly knew what was happening and did not like it. At first the base people supported the revolution, but as it got harsher and harsher.... In 1977 they became disillusioned when gruel was introduced in the communal eating halls – one meal per day of gruel and one of rice. In 1976 they had been told that the Organization was leading them towards three meals of rice per day, and sweets for 1977. But when rations were reduced to gruel instead, they lost confidence in the system.

Also in 1977, two members of the district committee, who Dara said had been "good to me when I met them," were executed. "The killings began in that year when they killed cadre, although there had been one or two killings in 1976 of people who refused orders or were lazy." In 1977 again, children over the age of seven were taken from their homes to live in separate groups, and for the first time Dara heard cadre mention an apparently foreign "enemy." In 1978 rations were reduced again until "there was only gruel, and for some meals we got nothing at all; we ate lizards and insects." In mid-1978, Dara and ten families were sent to a "jungle village." Elsewhere, his brother and friend were both executed. Soon after, however, the village committee and most of the base people "ran into the jungle in opposition to the Organization. The Center troops came searching everywhere for them and executed the subdistrict committee. The Center troops were not violent to us, but they supervised us at our work with guns, which had not happened before."

Region 22

5. Nhek Davi, 32, and her husband, a former senior Foreign Ministry official, reached Lovea Em district from Phnom Penh in May 1975 and lived there for six months. Rations were low "because of flooding," but the new people exchanged goods for food with peasants who had "plenty of rice." No one starved at first, and there were no killings or disappearances. "They were just educating us, calling us to meetings, and so on. They did not force us to work very hard." She approved of the subdistrict chief because he was "educated."

However, in late October 1975, Davi and her husband were taken off to prison in Srey Santhor district. She was released after "the women who questioned me agreed that I had done nothing wrong," but in January 1976 her husband and fifty of the 1,000 prisoners were taken to Phnom Penh, where he was executed five months later in Tuol Sleng (the national prison run by the CPK Center's Security force, the *Santebal*).[12] Davi spent the next two years in three separate locations in Srey Santhor and Peareang districts without knowing her husband's fate. She reported hard work, fairly low rations, but no starvation or executions, although six or seven people, mostly former soldiers and police, were arrested in the first two villages. In the third, she noted that

> The base people really liked the revolutionaries who trusted them, although the people had not dared to protest when communal eating, which they did not like much, was introduced. The serious killings began in 1978. In midyear, cadre executed two families of people from our village considered to be part-Vietnamese, then three or four families of new people were taken away, followed by three families of the Cham minority. They said the Cham nationality was 'rebellious' and had to be 'abolished.' There was also killing in nearby villages.

> The Center and Southwest forces arrived at this point and said the Eastern Zone was traitorous, and killed the local cadre and their families. At first ordinary base people were not touched, but they were certainly frightened by the change of cadre.

12. In 1979, Davi went to Tuol Sleng prison where she saw her husband's photograph and name on an execution list dated 25 May 1976.

In November-December 1978, the entire subdistricts of Kanchum and Prey Sralet were evacuated to the north. We were saved because the Vietnamese attacked in time. On the way, a village cadre had told me we would all be killed on arrival in Tonle Bet.

6. Sang, 43, a base peasant from 0 Reang Au district, said he approved of the revolution until 1975 and that the mutual aid teams it sponsored brought "real prosperity." The establishment of cooperatives after victory was unpopular however, and brought shortages but no starvation. Methods of punishment included hard labor and low rations but not execution or imprisonment. Although rations were divided equally among the population, there were a number of deaths from "disease caused by malnutrition." The first arrests he knew of took place in 1977, and some people died in prison; but he claims that in the second half of 1978, the newly arrived Southwestern cadre "killed five people from my village and 700 from the rest of the subdistrict." Sang said that about one-third of the village population "continued to believe in the system until May 1978, when some of them were massacred along with the rest."

Region 23

7. The impact of the introduction of communal eating in 1977 is clear in the following record of part of my conversation with Poeu, 42, a base peasant woman from Svay Rieng, and the interruptions from other locals who had gathered around.

B.K.: When did you first meet the Pol Pot people?

Poeu: 1977.

Interruption: No, that's later; it started in 1970.

Poeu: 1970.

B.K.: What did they do at that time?

Poeu: They came and collected pots and pans and all goods, put them in a communal warehouse, and started communal eating.

B.K.: From 1970?

Interruption: Talk about 1970.

Poeu: Communal eating.

Interruption: No, in 1970, 1972 there was no communal eating.

Poeu: Base people like me can't think of 1970 or 1972 or whatever. In 1975-76 they did not persecute us, but then from 1977 they did.

B.K.: How ?

Poeu: Communal eating. Not enough to eat. We had to work harder than in 1975-76. Ten people had to work one hectare [per day]. We had to try very hard.

In 1976, Poeu's peasant husband went off "to study" but came home again after two months. A year later he was taken away and never returned. Her mother and father had been imprisoned in 1973 because three of their sons were in the Lon Nol army (one was an officer). In April 1975, the mother was released but these three were arrested. In October the father was released, followed by his three sons in July 1976. Then in 1977, according to Poeu's mother, forty village base people were executed for allegedly being rebels. In 1978, Poeu's brothers were taken away, never to return.

8. Lay was evacuated from Phnom Penh with her six children to her native village in a neighboring subdistrict. She said that starvation was absent throughout, and there were no deaths in her own family. However, there were "many killings" of Lon Nol officers in 1975; apart from these, "only people who resisted orders or protested at conditions" were executed. In 1976 things settled down; there were no killings and conditions became "loose" (*thuu*). The base people, the majority of the village population, were supporters of the revolution; one member of the district committee, "a former Issarak [anti-French independence fighter] well-known to all the local people, [was] a good man who did not make us go short of food." Nor, she said, did he starve the numerous new people who were in prison.

In late 1976 communal eating was introduced, rations fell, and the base people became disillusioned. In 1977, killings began again with a change of cadre; both the dismissed cadre and the imprisoned new people were victims. The worst killings began in late 1978, when the Southwest cadre arrived in Lay's village, and like so many people from the Eastern Zone, she attributed her personal survival to the arrival of the Vietnamese army.

Region 24

9. Schoolteacher Nuon Chan, 56, was evacuated from Phnom Penh to his family's village in Kompong Trabek district. At first he was put to work building canals and dams, but then "they saw I was an old man, so they let me stay in the village and plough the land. The rations were all right, not a problem; we were still eating rice in 1975-76. It was tolerable [*kuo som*]." There were no killings in those two years, he says, but a total of ten former Lon Nol soldiers, teachers, doctors and even some locals whose thinking was "non-revolutionary" were imprisoned in early 1976. In the second half of that year, things began to change. Mutual aid teams were amalgamated into "high-level production cooperatives," and enforced communization of goods and communal eating began.

> In late 1976 early 1977 it became hard. In 1977-78 we ate only thin gruel with banana stalks and salt.... In late 1976 they took away the wives of the soldiers, doctors and others who had been jailed. Only one of the ten originally imprisoned was released. Large-scale killings began in 1977, when they killed local people accused of having a non-revolutionary attitude, and foreigners like Vietnamese who had Khmer wives.

10. Chan Theng, a base peasant from Peam Ro district, recalled that "persecution began in 1976." Late in that year the "adequate" food rations ("all rice") were reduced, and from then on people ate only gruel for nine months of the year. The 1,200 base people in the village, he asserts, "continued to believe in the revolution until the introduction of communal eating in 1977."

Three hundred urban evacuees had arrived in Theng's village in 1975, and fifty or sixty of them, whom he said were "leading officials of the Lon Nol and Sihanouk regimes and ex-soldiers," were arrested, some as "CIA agents," over the next two years. In late 1976 and 1977, children over the age of six were taken from their parents to live in groups. General arrests and executions then began, of "everyone," including two former Buddhist monks, schoolteachers, and a number of entire families. The year 1978 was even harsher. By late in the year, a total of "277 new people" had been executed, as well as a number of base peasants now accused of being "KGB agents." The 1977-78 period also saw the first mention of Vietnam as an enemy.

Political Struggles

Cambodia's Communist movement first emerged in the late 1940s among the anti-colonial "Issaraks" cooperating with the Vietnamese Communists during the common struggle against the French.[13] By independence in 1954, the Khmer People's Revolutionary Party had about 1,800 members, up to half of them in the eastern provinces near Vietnam – Kompong Cham, Prey Veng and Svay Rieng.

After the Geneva Conference over 1,000 Issaraks, including over 500 Party members, withdrew to North Vietnam. Many others then gave up political activity and a few were imprisoned or killed by the Norodom Sihanouk regime, which inherited state authority from the French and whose crackdowns were facilitated by the defection of the then communist party secretary, Sieu Heng. Heng was replaced at a Party Congress in 1960 by Tou Samouth, while Saloth Sar (later to be known as Pol Pot), who had returned from studies in France seven years before, assumed the No. 3 position, after Nuon Chea. Pol Pot claims to have been elected Deputy Secretary in 1961, but gives no indication of how or why. The next year Samouth disappeared, probably betrayed to the police and executed, and Pot became acting Secretary. A 1963 Congress confirmed him in this post. Forty-year old So Phim, who as No. 4 in the 1954 hierarchy was probably the most senior active communist in the country, stood against Pot but was defeated, "not

---

13. Ben Kiernan, "Origins of Khmer Communism," *Southeast Asian Affairs 1981*, Singapore, Institute of Southeast Asian Studies, 1981, 163-181. [And *How Pol Pot Came to Power: Colonialism, Nationalism and Communism in Cambodia, 1930-1975*, New Haven, Yale University Press, 2nd ed., 2004.]

by a vote but by opinion."[14] It would seem that poorly-educated and rural-based cadre like Phim, and even former Bangkok law student Nuon Chea, deferred with characteristic peasant reticence to the dynamism and self-confidence of French-educated intellectuals from well-off backgrounds. Phim gained No. 4 position in the five-person Politburo, and two others with French education, Ieng Sary and Vorn Vet, were ranked third and fifth.

The Party began reorganizing its activities. Phim was appointed Party Secretary of the Eastern Zone, the only Politburo member given a specified geographic responsibility. The other four assumed general control of national activities, and effectively came to make up the Party "Center." In 1964-65, Pol Pot visited Vietnam and then China on the eve of the Cultural Revolution; he formed a close relationship with Beijing, with the common aim of undermining Vietnamese influence in the Party.

The eastern organization which So Phim built up in the late 1960s was very largely made up of veteran Communists who, like himself, had worked closely with the Vietnamese during the First Indochina War. For the most part, they did not want to be dependent on the Vietnamese, and after 1965 were not prepared to restrain their opposition to Sihanouk as Hanoi would have liked. But they saw little reason to be hostile to the Vietnamese, or to Communism as practiced in Vietnam. Although Phim reportedly "never forgot" Vietnam's refusal to give him guns until 1970, during the same period he and many of his subordinates benefited from sanctuary and training facilities in NLF-controlled zones of South Vietnam. According to firsthand accounts, in 1968 Phim ran Party schools in the jungles of the Eastern Zone, in which he lectured cadres like Chhouk on politics, military strategy and tactics, emphasized cooperation with the Vietnamese against U.S. imperialism, and displayed portraits of Marx, Lenin, and Ho Chi Minh.[15]

According to one of the few survivors of that period, Tea Sabun:

> The armed struggle began in 1968. At first we had only a few soldiers; Phuong, Chan and myself had thirty men in Damber and Kauk Srok [Region 21], and So Phim ninety in Krabau and Bos [Region 20]. The Vietnamese Communists did not aid us at all. We went to ask for help and they said: "You should not be struggling or asking for arms. Wait until we have liberated Vietnam. Then we will fight." But we went after guns.

> By 1969 my forces numbered over 100. However, we were driven out of Damber and had run out of food and medicine. We all fled into Vietnam through Memut that year.... At the border the Sihanouk forces fired on us, and so did the Vietnamese

---

14. Author's interview with Tea Sabun, former Issarak chief of Tbaung Khmum district and Party Central Committee member, Phnom Penh, 23 August 1980; Kiernan, "Origins of Khmer Communism," 176, 178.
15. Author's interview with Yim Seun, who joined the communist party in 1954 and attended these jungle schools in 1968, Kandol Chrum, 28 July 1980. Also Tea Sabun, ibid.

Communists. But then we made contact and smoothed things over, and they let us into Vietnam, deep in so as not to let Sihanouk know; they were in touch with Sihanouk and were buying supplies from Kampuchea, and they did not want to disturb the relationship.

So we moved about fifty or sixty kilometers inside Vietnam; there they gave us rice and pork to eat, shoes to wear, etc. After three or four days' rest, they escorted us south, inside Vietnamese territory, and we met up with So Phim at his place, at Thnaot, a kilometer from the Kampuchean border. He had 100 soldiers there, and in all there were 300 revolutionary troops, three companies, in the Eastern Zone.

In 1970 when Lon Nol carried out the coup, I was with So Phim at Thnaot. We were in the middle of a meeting of about 100 cadre from all Regions and districts of the Eastern Zone, when we heard the news. We sent out twenty messengers to instruct all cadres on the spot to organize an offensive; meanwhile, Sihanouk arrived in Peking and confessed, and called on the people to rise up against Lon Nol. Everyone joined the resistance.

The Vietnamese Communists moved into Kampuchea to fight Lon Nol, and liberated a lot of territory. They met with So Phim and asked him first, but in the beginning we did not agree, because it was our country. We just asked them to give us guns. However, they said that if we did not agree it would be harmful to their country, and they would go in anyway. They said that without their help, we would not be able to liberate our country. From then on we were very close to the Vietnamese, we went everywhere with them, getting the guns they seized, for our soldiers. We raised whole divisions.

A relationship, it seems, rich in nuance and complexity. The Khmer Communists, harassed by Sihanouk, failed to share the Vietnamese view that temporal coordination of strategy was imperative, given the much greater threat to the Vietnamese revolution, posed by the massive U.S. presence in Vietnam. The Vietnamese no doubt considered their own interests paramount. But in the circumstances, the Khmer revolutionaries, as well as the Vietnamese, would have been in even deeper trouble had the latter provoked Sihanouk by supporting armed rebellion against him. The Prince's fierce independence kept the U.S. and the war out of Cambodia, and protected the Vietnamese against attack from the rear. His failure to pursue serious domestic reforms, and their Party leaders' determination to work for his overthrow, meant that the Eastern Zone Communists saw little use for Sihanouk, and were prepared to struggle on, alone if necessary; even so, they needed sanctuary in Vietnam in 1969, and in 1970 accepted what fell into their lap – territory, arms and support from Sihanouk – all products of past and current Vietnamese policies more than their own. But there is no sign in this period, of Khmer dependence on the Vietnamese, nor of any Khmer hostility to them. The political relationship seems to have been one of mutual advantage, even though the Khmer were clearly the weaker party.

Thus in March-April 1970, So Phim, Chhouk, and other Eastern Zone Communists came back into Cambodia to establish their administration on the heels of the Vietnamese Communist armies. This was not the case for the leaders of other Zones.

During the five-year war that followed, the Executive of the Eastern Zone Party Committee was headed by So Phim and his deputy Phuong, who had been deputy chief of Komchay Meas district (Region 20, Prey Veng province) during the Issarak period, and it included Chhouk, Party Secretary of Region 24. Five others completed the Eastern Zone Party Committee. These were: Kev Samnang, later Zone military commander; So, Secretary of Region 23; Chhien (a former Issarak and a Phnom Penh teacher), Secretary of Region 22; Chan, Secretary of Region 21; and Peam, head of the Zone Office and thus in charge of day-to-day administrative affairs. Of these eight Eastern Zone leaders, only Chan was to retain the trust of the Center until 1979; in the meantime, his position in the Party, and Peam's in the administration, were to prove crucial.

Peam had studied in France with Pol Pot in the early 1950s and was quite possibly a Center appointment as head of the Eastern Zone Office. He seems to have taken to the jungle around the same time as Pol Pot (1963) and soon after was instructing former Issaraks distributing literature in the east about "anti-imperialist people's war," apparently his term for the struggle against Sihanouk. One of his peasant students at the time, Chum Sambor, seems to regard him as something of a fanatic: "He was an intellectual, a teacher. He didn't wear normal clothes; he wore very old ones, and a scarf.[16] When he ran into the forest, he planted cucumbers, gourds and vegetables of all kinds, and when he had to move on for fear of discovery, he carried them all with him on shoulder poles. He was a very hard struggler." Peam was apparently not one of those who sought refuge in Vietnamese territory in 1969-70. Chan, a villager of local extraction, was. However, according to Ouch Bun Chhoeun: "Ever since the period of political struggle [1954-67], Chan had been close to Pol Pot. Pol Pot and Nuon Chea had been in contact with Chan, staying in his house and giving him political instruction. They trusted Chan more than So Phim." It is possible, too, that Chan, and to a lesser extent Phuong and other Region cadre whose border crossing came later and was more difficult, reacted more bitterly than Phim and Chhouk did to the strains of the pre-1970 relationship with the Vietnamese, and less enthusiastically to the joint victories won after 1970. This would have made Chan a natural ally of the Center, and it may have been why he was given prominence by being included in a 1974 delegation to China, Vietnam, and North Korea. Nevertheless, shared experiences, successes and a common desire not to be dependent on the Vietnamese, whether they regarded them as friends or enemies, kept these Easterners united for a long time.

---

16. Interestingly, Hu Nim wrote in his Tuol Sleng "confession" dated 28 May 1977, that Peam "had studied tailoring in France and made clothes in the 'capitalist style, Paris type.'"

In the early 1970s, a new generation of Khmer military cadre was trained in the East by the Vietnamese Communists and by former Issaraks who had themselves been trained in Hanoi since 1954, returning home in 1970. Among the latter were several nephews of So Phim, including a specialist in heavy artillery named Kim Teng. Teng trained a former high school student named Hun Sen, who became a battalion political commissar in 1973. The Eastern Zone troops, commanded by a former monk named Chan Chakrey, soon became distinguishable from the black-clad Khmer Rouge "cormorants" (*ka'ek tik*) dominant in other Zones, by their "green" fatigue uniforms and their more politicized, Vietnamese-style guerrilla tactics.[17] They referred to themselves (as did more scattered units trained by the Vietnamese Communists in other Zones) as *Khmer Rumdos* ("Khmer Liberation"), whereas the black-shirted "cormorants" were known as *Khmer Krohom* ("Red Khmers").[18] The former have usually been regarded simply as "Sihanoukists," but *rumdos* is a direct translation of the Vietnamese term *giai phong* (liberation), used by the Vietnamese Communists.[19] (The "Khmer *giai phong*" policy of alliance with Prince Sihanouk did not mean they were under non-Communist leadership.)

In June 1970, Pol Pot arrived back in Cambodia from Beijing via the Ho Chi Minh Trail.[20] Not until six months later was he followed by the one thousand former Issaraks who had long been undergoing training in Hanoi.[21] A possible

---

17. Chhin Phoeun, then a fifteen year-old member of a Southwestern Brigade, described what he called "the different military tactics of the Eastern Zone troops," as follows: "We would attack and then dig trenches. They would use trees as trenches and then move up to attack." Before and after 1975, black-clad "cormorants" became known for their preference for conventional, large-unit military campaigns, often involving pitched battles and trench warfare, rather than "fish in water" guerrilla actions. (See note 65 below.) It is noteworthy that in most other Zones, the military commander, in alliance with the Center, sooner or later took power from the Zone Party chief. In the Southwest, Mok eclipsed Chou Chet in 1973; Chet was made Secretary of the Western Zone in 1975, but seems to have held less power than the Zone military commander, Pech Soeung, who eventually arrested Chet in 1978; in the Northern Zone, Ke Pauk similarly triumphed over Koy Thuon, who was arrested in January 1977. No such "Zone coup d'état" occurred in the East, whose leaders eventually had to be eliminated by outside military forces at the Center.

18. See, in particular, Kenneth Quinn, "Political Change in Wartime: The Khmer Krohom Revolution in Southern Cambodia, 1970-74," *Naval War College Review* (Spring 1976).

19. I became aware of this during a late 1980 visit to Vietnam where ethnic Khmer refer to the Vietnamese Communist soldiers as "Rumdos."

20. *Livre Noir: Faits et Preuves Des Actes D'Agression et D'Annexation du Vietnam Contre le Kampuchéa,* Ministry of Foreign Affairs of Democratic Kampuchea (Phnom Penh: September 1978), 54, 70.

21. "Khmer Rouge Rallier Keoum Kun," unclassified airgram from U.S. Embassy, Phnom Penh to Department of State, 13 January 1972, 4. Kun was one of the returnees.

explanation for the delay is that Pol Pot had used the time to organize against them. On their arrival, the returnees were assigned relatively junior rank in the Party throughout the country. Within four years most of them had been selectively assassinated by special units of the Party Center's security forces, prefiguring the key role of such forces after victory, in the resolution of political conflict and the attempt to erase Vietnamese influence in the Cambodian Party.

Yos Por, then a member of the Kampot province committee in the Southwest Zone, recalls that in September 1974:

> One evening six armed men came to visit me at home…I asked them: "What do you want with me?" "We have been ordered to arrest you." "Why?" "Because you are a reactionary, a revisionist…a lackey of Vietnam. All your ilk must be liquidated before independence." They took me 500 meters from the village, beyond the salt pans, and into a small wood. One man stayed at its edge. The others made me undress and tied my hands behind my back with nylon. "You won't need any clothes to go where you are going," they said…

Por managed a miraculous escape, but his comrades were not so lucky. Over a hundred Khmers from Hanoi had been assigned to the Southwest Zone, he says. By 1975, Por and four others had fled to South Vietnam, six were in a prison in the Cardamom mountains, and the rest had been murdered; seven men and women were shot in public in front of their houses, according to Por.[22]

The situation was slightly different in the East. Hem Samin was one of seventy-one Hanoi-trained cadre assembled for "a study course" in Chhlong district, Region 21 in August 1974. They were all "violently abused," Samin recalls, especially by a young district chief called Ouch Bun Chhoeun but also by Chan and other Region 21 cadre. Political lectures included claims that the anti-French struggle had been "meaningless" because "we were just following the Vietnamese," and reprimands for having sought safety in Vietnam while Sihanouk persecuted the revolutionaries who had remained behind. Phuong then informed the group that they were in detention, and had "to stay where we were in order to be self-reliant…until the Organization came up with a solution so that [we] could go back to work." Ten of the prisoners soon disappeared, allegedly taken "to carry out duties somewhere else," in fact quite possibly executed. The other sixty-one, including Samin, were put to work in the fields under close supervision.[23]

In Region 20 in the same period, there was also opposition to the Vietnamese and the Khmers they had trained, of whom local cadres said that "the wild chickens are trying to scatter the farm chickens" (*moan prei chong komchay moan*

---

22. "Déclaration de Li Yang Duc (Yos Por)," *Problèmes politiques et sociaux* 373 (Paris, 12 Oct. 1979): 5-6.
23. Author's interview with Hem Samin, Phnom Penh, 28 September 1980. Also Stephen Heder's interview with Samin, 8 July 1981.

srok).[24] This was an expression of independence; but it also suggests a certain defensiveness on the part of cadre whose positions may have been threatened by their more senior and better-trained "wild" cousins.

According to Stephen Heder, "for the most part, the identification and liquidation of victims seems to have been the special and exclusive task of the 'State Security' branch of the Party,"[25] known as *Santebal.* The Eastern Zone leaders seemed to have preferred the dismissal and incarceration of Hanoi-trained cadre, with the likely exception of the ten who disappeared in Region 21 in late 1974, possible victims of Zone or Regional security units (*Santesok*). In the same period, perhaps another thirty or more of their comrades were quietly murdered elsewhere in the East by *Santebal* units. One of these victims was So Phim's nephew, Kim Teng. His fate suggests that neither the initiative for the purges nor effective opposition to them came from Phim.

Hem Samin recalls that in November 1973, at a political study session in Koh Sautin district, "we started to hear about people with so-called 'Khmer bodies and Vietnamese minds.'" Kim Teng, who had become a brigade commander, then raised the issue with So Phim, expressing his fear that he would be "squeezed dry like a lemon and then thrown away." Phim asked: "What makes you say that?" The reply was, "If you don't believe me, wait and see." According to Hun Sen, who was also present, "So Phim was very unhappy but could not reply. There was silence."[26] Within a year, Teng was dead.

Kim Teng's early death in this period contrasts with the fate of Yun Soeun, who had studied in France with Pol Pot in the early 1950s and then went to Hanoi. On his return to Cambodia in 1970, he became deputy Secretary of Region 22 under Siet Chhe. In 1972, the two men published textbooks and drew up plans to open a junior high school in Region 22; but as Hu Nim wrote in his 1977 confession, the project was quashed "mercilessly" by the Party. According to Bun Chhoeun, Nuon Chea presided over a Zone Assembly devoted to the question; he was "worried about" the school "and did not allow it." Soeun was then demoted and made Chief of Zone Artisanry: "he survived because he and

24. Yim Seun interview, note 15 above. Seun claimed, however, that So Phim "did not say this." "He was in close contact with the Khmers from Hanoi, sharing everything in the fight against the Americans." Hu Nim wrote in his confession that by 1974 "I already knew brother Phim's concepts and standpoint, especially his stand towards the Vietnamese and his concept of employing and trusting cadres who have been to study in north Vietnam…[Phim] said: '… we do not agree with the Politburo about the policy towards Vietnam...[we] must accept aid from every country.'"
25. Stephen Heder, "From Pol Pot to Pen Sovan to the Villages," Asian Institute, Chulalongkorn University, Bangkok, May 1980, 6. Heder says that the Security forces were known as *Nokorbal*, but no cadre I interviewed used that term. They used *Santesok*. According to Tuol Sleng documents, the Center branch was called *Santebal*, a secretive organization indeed. See also note 41 below.
26. Author's interviews with Hem Samin (note 23 above) and Hun Sen, Phnom Penh, 21 October 1980.

Pol Pot returned from France together in 1953, so Pol Pot forgave and spared him," at least for the time being.

In September 1973, the Eastern Zone's "military political service" published a *Party History*[27] which several times acknowledged the "firm support" of the Vietnamese Communists in the Party's 1951 founding and expressed views about socialism which were strikingly similar to those of the Vietnamese. It also explicitly acknowledged, in discussion of the 1960s, the authority of the Hanoi-based Khmers (the "Committee of Liberation"), as well as that of the Pol Pot-led internal wing (the "Central Committee").[28] At the same time, it rejected the "game of negotiations" with the Lon Nol regime, a policy then favored by Hanoi and its Khmer supporters, in this context describing the latter as an "obstacle" because "they tended to split our country's political forces in three or four directions" (testimony, incidentally, to their local base). It was therefore a compromise position, but also a coherent one, stressing a desire to go it alone, while showing none of the signs of generalized hostility to Vietnam already characteristic of the Pol Pot group. There is no trace here of a 1971 Center decision that the Vietnamese were the long-term "acute enemy" of the Kampuchean revolution.[29] This does not mean that the Eastern cadres shared the ideology or the domestic program of the Vietnam Workers' Party. They usually accepted the authority and the independence of their own Party Center. But their implementation of its directives was to a large extent informed by the political style of the Vietnamese Communists with whom they had had such a long-standing relationship. For this reason, perhaps, short-term imprisonment rather than execution was the fate of most members of the defeated Lon Nol forces in the East in 1975.

Unity among Eastern cadre also resulted, as their *Party History* quoted above also says, from the Vietnamese Communist withdrawal from Cambodia in 1973, both in implementation of the Paris Agreement and in response to pressure from the CPK. The Vietnamese, unable to get Pol Pot to agree to a ceasefire with Lon Nol and confronted by the killings of Hanoi-trained cadres, most likely concluded that they would have to accept Pol Pot's supremacy in the Communist Party of Kampuchea. They would have informed dissident Cambodian

---

27. *Summary of Annotated Party History.* Copy in the Echols collection at Cornell University's Olin Library.
28. Ibid., 1. (See also Kiernan, "Origins of Khmer Communism," 178.) All these references were carefully deleted in a version of *Party History* distributed by Ieng Sary in 1974 [Kiernan, *How Pol Pot*, 364-67].
29. Heder, "From Pol Pot," 4. Heder says this was a resolution passed by the Party Congress at that time, but that is contradicted by Tea Sabun, who attended the Congress, and Ouch Bun Chhoeun, who was told much about it (and given twelve books of documents produced at the Congress) by Phuong, who also attended. Author's interviews with Sabun (note 14 above) and Chhoeun, Phnom Penh, 30 September 1980. It is probable, though, that the Party Center made some decision of this kind during or after the Congress and then claimed its imprimatur.

Communists that support for a rival faction would not be forthcoming, forcing the latter to reach some accommodation with the Center.

In 1975 the Eastern Zone leadership remained intact and cohesive in contrast to that of other Zones. In 1973-74 in the Southwest, for example, the Zone Chairman Chou Chet had been eclipsed by its party secretary, Mok; and the deputy secretary, Prasith, and the fourth member of the Zone Committee, Sangha Hoeun, had been executed by Vorn Veth and Mok. These conflicts seem to have resulted from the refusal by the three men, none of whom were returnees from Vietnam, to go along with the Center's and Mok's anti-Vietnamese and anti-Sihanouk policies, and the practice of executing Lon Nol soldiers who defected or surrendered. In the East all three would likely have retained their posts. However, the purges, even though still limited to those actually trained in Vietnam, no doubt impressed on everyone the dangers of political dissidence.

The common ground in the East was to crumble only from late 1976, when Center policies, backed locally by Chan, demanded: (1) massive primitive accumulation, necessarily at the expense of peasant living conditions, to build a state that would have no need for trade or other relations with Vietnam and could, in fact, sustain a war with it; (2) execution of leading cadre considered too close to the Vietnamese, such as Chhouk and So, whose downfalls angered So Phim,[30] and (3) repetitive planned attacks across the Vietnamese border, and rejection of proposals for negotiations.

These Center initiatives backed So Phim into a corner. The man known for his "broad solidarity,"[31] who enjoyed universal respect among Eastern cadre could no longer unite them around himself, and his authority began to dissolve. So did the Zone itself, of course, but for the short period of stability and autonomy that remained, the major beneficiary was the Center's protégé, Chan.

The first Center move came in late 1975 when the Zone Party Committee was revamped. So Phim remained Zone Secretary, but Phuong, who in April 1976 became Minister of Rubber Plantations, was replaced by Chan. So Phim's own choice for his deputy was apparently former ICP member Men Chhan, then on the Zone Economics Standing Committee and head of the Zone Transport Service. The Center not only over-ruled Phim on this, but Men Chhan was dropped from his two positions and given a less influential one.[32]

So Phim accepted the changes and appears to have had full confidence in Chan. According to Hu Nim's "confession," Phim was to say in 1976: "Com-

---

30. Author's interview with Mat Ly, Phnom Penh, 13 August 1980. See also the section on Region 24, below.
31. In his confession, Hu Nim wrote: "I respect brother Phim; he has broad solidarity, he is mature and stable, and is also close to me." Chhouk gave a similar description of Phim (see the section below on Region 24) as did surviving cadre in interviews with me.
32. Men Chhan says he became Director of Zone Agriculture, a post involving supervision of a number of work sites at Zone level, but nevertheless lost his position on the Zone Economics Standing Committee. Interview with author, 25 September 1980, Phnom Penh.

rade Chan's standpoint is in total accord with mine. [He] speaks well of Korea constantly. Friend Chan could replace my own eyes and nose."[33] Ironically, Chan was to do just that in May 1978. In the meantime, however, Chan was to replace the eyes and nose of Chhouk, now dropped from the Zone Executive to become an ordinary member of the Zone Committee. Chhouk's replacements on the Executive were Chhien from Region 21, and Peam. Within eighteen months, both Chhouk and So would be dead and their Regions 23 and 24 under the direct control of Chan.

Like so many key DK cadres, Chan appears to have enjoyed much more rapid promotion than his revolutionary seniority would seem to justify. In the Issarak period, Chan was a member of the thirty-strong Tbaung Khmum guerrilla force led by district chief Tea Sabun. While Sabun held the same position twenty-five years later, and had meanwhile been dropped from his position on the Party Central Committee, Chan had risen two ranks above him, to deputy Secretary of the Zone Executive and also (from 1975) candidate member of the Central Committee. In the same period Chan had also leapfrogged over Veng Ky, chief of Memut district in the Issarak period, who remained in that post for twenty years. In the 1960s, Chan was already deputy party secretary of Region 21, under Phuong (who was deputy zone secretary as well) and it was only in 1971, when Phuong became head of the Eastern Zone Economics Standing Committee and Chan assumed leadership of Region 21, that Veng Ky rose to the post of deputy region secretary. As secretary of Region 21 from 1971 to late 1975, Chan had presided over a period of brutality towards the Cham minority living along the Mekong River in Krauchhmar district, and discrimination against them in other parts of the Region.

Policy towards the Cham, I believe, is an important indicator of the political worldview of the DK regime. In the Southwest Zone, for instance, cadres told members of this Muslim minority (descendants of inhabitants of the Champa kingdom conquered by Vietnam in the fifteenth century) in 1977: "... The Chams are hopeless. They abandoned their country to others. They just shouldered their fishing nets and walked off, letting the Vietnamese take over their country."[34] The Chams as an autonomous racial group were considered a weak point in the state. The authorities dispersed the inhabitants of Cham villages among the majority of Khmer population, with whom it was hoped they would soon assimilate.

This policy had begun to be implemented in Region 21 under Chan in 1974. Late in that year, a Cham rebellion is reported to have taken place in one

---

33. Hu Nim's confession, 28 May 1977. [Text translated in D. Chandler, B. Kiernan, and C. Boua, eds., *Pol Pot Plans the Future: Confidential Leadership Documents from Democratic Kampuchea, 1976-77*, New Haven, Yale Council on Southeast Asia Studies, 1988.]
34. Author's interview with Nao Gha, 45, a Cham woman in Smong village, Treang, Takeo, 26 August 1980.

Krauchhmar village, and another rebellious village nearby is said to have been razed and many of its people killed a few months after April 1975. Although Phuong and So Phim sanctioned suppression of these revolts,[35] it is noteworthy that they broke out in Region 21. From around this time, cadres there, unlike in other eastern Regions, are almost always described as "fierce" (*khlang*), even if they did not resort to violence. Outside Krauchhmar district, the assimilation still took a non-violent form: in October 1975 at least one Cham village in Tbaung Khmum district was dispersed, and in 1976 Chams who had joined the revolution and become village chiefs or officials there were dismissed from their posts. Interestingly, one Cham member of the Tbaung Khmum district committee, Mat Ly, retained his post, but Ouch Bun Chhoeun, then deputy chief of Region 21, remarks that, "from what we could see he was like a phantom—he had no freedom."

Mat Ly's father, Sos Man, had been minister of religious affairs in the insurgent Issarak government before 1954. Sos Man spent the years 1954-70 in North Vietnam, then returned to Cambodia to become president of the Communist-sponsored "Eastern Zone Islamic Movement" from 1971 until 1974, when it was disbanded. According to Tea Sabun, "when Sos Man first came back So Phim trusted him; later he obeyed Pol Pot and withdrew confidence, but built a house in which Sos Man would live quietly." Man was told he was "too old" and confined to a Region 21 village on Highway 7. However, according to Mat Ly, in September 1975 two strangers arrived on a motorcycle and offered Man "medicine." Man took it and died that night; Mat Ly claims he was fooled into taking poison.

It is probable that Cham communities in the Eastern Zone, having been organized by the Hanoi-trained Sos Man from 1971-74, were regarded by Chan and his Center backers as politically (as well as racially) tainted. Some further connection is possible between Chan's late 1975 rise to the post of deputy Zone Secretary and the penetration of the enforced assimilation policy into Regions other than 21. El, 50, a Cham from the outskirts of Phnom Penh, was evacuated to Peareang district of Region 22, where he said two leading Cham dignitaries were soon executed.[36] However, he went on: "In 1975 they used persuasion to some extent. But in January or February 1976, the cadre said: 'Chams who eat pork, raise pigs, and dare to slaughter pigs, will be spared.' They said no religious beliefs were allowed, and we were not allowed to speak Cham."

Consistent with reports for 1976 from elsewhere in the East (and for 1975 outside of Krauchhmar), El did not report racially selective violence against

35. Stephen Heder's interview with Hem Samin, 8 July 1981.
36. One of those he named, Toun Srong Yusos, is said by Muslim officials in the Ministry of Religious Affairs of the People's Republic of Kampuchea to have been executed in that locality, but in the next year, 1976 (see below). Author's interview with Ibrahim, Phnom Penh, 19 September 1980. Two other Muslim dignitaries, according to Ibrahim, were executed in Krauchhmar in 1976, and another at Speu in the Northern Zone in the same year.

Cham populations in Peareang district in that period. But the already emerging assimilation policy was a relatively early manifestation of the racial-chauvinist ideology which was to lead to such tremendous violence later, for instance in 1977 when, according to many accounts, Cham and Vietnamese families were selectively murdered, and in 1978 when the entire Eastern Zone population was accused of having "Khmer bodies with Vietnamese minds."

Another event perhaps also resulting from the revamping of the Zone Executive was the execution at the end of 1975 of fourteen more[37] of the sixty-one Hanoi-trained cadre imprisoned in Region 21. Two others had died suddenly not long before when they contracted dysentery and were given as a remedy what was in fact "a very strong poison" – an incident reminiscent of the death of Sos Man in same period. In the ensuing months however, relative freedom of movement was allowed the forty-five survivors. In August 1976, Hem Samin and a fellow detainee (saying, "Do we have to wait until they put us in irons before we say we're in prison?") slipped away and managed to cross into Vietnam.[38] It is not known when the remaining forty-three Hanoi-trained cadre there were executed. It may have been in mid-1978, when their six colleagues in the Southwest were finally ordered killed. The much larger number who survived in the East until then is noteworthy. In the words of Hem Samin, "If I had been taken to a jail in Phnom Penh, I wouldn't have survived."[39] But his two years of imprisonment and the deaths of his sixteen comrades engendered considerable bitterness, especially towards So Phim for his failure to protect them. "If [he] had been a correct and loyal revolutionary, the compatriots who had gone to study in the north would never have been in danger," Samin says.[40]

The 1975 elevation of Chan and Peam was not the only portent of the future. At the same time, the Eastern Zone Security force was disbanded.[41] Only regional

---

37. Author's taped interview with Hem Samin (note 23 above). Stephen Heder's typescript of his later interview with Samin gives the figure as twenty-four rather than fourteen (note 23 above).
38. Interviews with Samin, ibid.
39. Author's interview with Samin, ibid.
40. Heder's interview with Samin (note 23 above). However, in 1978, when a real chance for overthrowing Pol Pot presented itself, Samin put aside the past: "All of us pin our hopes on So Phim, the dissident leader who had taken part in the Nine-Year Resistance [1946-54]. News concerning him is vague and even contradictory. In any event, if So Phim is not at the head of the movement as we had hoped, if he is dead, one of his peers will emerge," in *Kampuchea Dossier,* vol. II (Hanoi: Ministry of Affairs, 1978), 68-69.
41. Author's interviews with Hun Sen and Men Chhan, ns 26 and 32 above. Chhan also said, however, that in 1977 a man called Nat came from the Central Zone and was made chief of Eastern Zone Security forces (*protean santesok Bophea*). (He said the word *Nokorbal* was used only for the Center Security forces; see note 25.) Ouch Bun Chhoeun, for his part, said that a man named Tem was chief of the Zone Security forces, but if he retained his post after 1975, he does not seem to have played a significant part in the purges. He was executed by Center forces in May 1978.

and district security units remained, and Yin Sophi, a former subdistrict clerk who had joined the revolution in 1970,[42] was appointed chief of the Security forces of Region 21, the key Region in a Zone now without Zone-level Security forces. Over the next two years and particularly during 1977, Yin Sophi hacked away relentlessly at the base of the Eastern Zone Communist Party branch, arresting cadres and veterans at the district, subdistrict and village levels in most Regions, and even Regional and Zone level cadres outside the Party Committees.[43]

According to Ouch Bun Chhoeun, "Yin Sophi had general powers," and could make arrests not only in Region 21 but throughout the Eastern Zone. How was this possible for a Region Security Chief ? "It was the Zone which gave him his authority – as a mere regional official he would have had no power to make the arrests," even of district chiefs. According to Men Chhan, "the only one who could sign" such authority over to Yin Sophi was Peam, in his administrative capacity as head of the Zone office.

The Peam-Yin Sophi purges which laid the political groundwork for the May 1978 military takeover of the East were certainly extensive. Men Chhan claims that Yin Sophi was responsible for the arrest of "500 to 1,000" Eastern cadres in 1976 and 1977. His victims no doubt included Bun Sani, a former high-ranking Issarak who was Director of the Zone Rubber Plantations (arrested 10/7/76), Bun Sani's replacement Sok San (8/9/77) and the Directors of the Zone Artisanry Service, Yun Soeun (4/11/76) who was trained in Hanoi, the Zone Commercial Service, Uy San (4/11/76), the Zone Rubber Transport Service, Pech Phoan (2/3/77) and his replacement, former deputy Party Secretary of Region 21, Veng Ky (1/6/77).[44]

But it was at the lower levels of the Party that the greatest damage was probably done. During 1977, after the arrests of Chhouk (August 1976) and So (March 1977), the purges of their Regions 23 and 24 completely overturned the administration there down to the village level. In Region 22 in the year 1978, the party secretaries of five of the eight districts were arrested. So were two members

42. According to one local informant, Yin Sophi joined the revolution only in 1970, and owed his rise through the movement's ranks to the fact that, as a government official in Kor subdistrict, he had mobilized people there to participate in the 1970 demonstrations protesting the overthrow of Prince Sihanouk. He apparently married Phuong's daughter. Another source has it that he could "summon a Zone assembly —only he dared to do so" among Region cadre.
43. The arrests of Region chiefs such as Chhouk and So, and members of Region Party Committees, may also have been the work of Yin Sophi's security squads, but such people were handed over to the Center's *Santebal* and taken to its interrogation and execution camp S-21, better known as Tuol Sleng, in Phnom Penh.
44. "Important culprits," a list of 262 revolutionary cadres arrested by the Pol Pot regime between April 1976 and 1978. The document was found at Tuol Sleng in 1979 and copies of translations distributed at the "Genocide Trial" *in absentia* of Pol Pot and Ieng Sary, Phnom Penh, August 1979, as Document no. 2.5.24.

of the four-person Region Party Committee, including its deputy secretary. In Region 21 in the same period, at least three of eight district party secretaries, including one member of the Region Party Committee, were arrested, and probably another two district secretaries, named as "traitors" in confessions extracted under torture in Tuol Sleng prison at this time. In Region 20, the secretaries of Prey Veng, Mesan, and Kanchriech districts were arrested and killed in 1975, 1976, and 1977 respectively, and the remaining two district chiefs, Chea Sim of Ponhea Krek and the secretary of Komchay Meas, were in fact named as members of Chhouk's "traitorous" forces in Hu Nim's "confession" dated 28 May 1977.[45] These two managed to escape to Vietnam in 1978 and a year later assumed leading roles in the People's Republic of Kampuchea.

Ouch Bun Chhoeun, who became deputy to Sos, Secretary of Region 21 after Chan's elevation in 1975, explained the political mechanics of these purges:

> When they interrogated people in Phnom Penh, the names of all the Eastern Zone cadres from subdistrict committees upwards were mentioned. Whether Pol Pot forced people to write what they did or whether they wrote it of their own accord, I don't know. [The list] was then sent to So Phim for him to take action on it himself in Regions 20, 21 and 22. All the military cadres were mentioned. My name was there too, on a list of "traitor chiefs of the network in Region 21."

> So Phim thought it over and said that those people, including Chhien, Sos, myself and Sin, were not a problem. He didn't arrest us. So Pol Pot no longer trusted So Phim.

> [Meanwhile] Pol Pot had called in Chan, the Zone deputy Party Secretary, for education and instruction. After that Chan was made Secretary of the twin Regions, 23 and 24, in order to arrest the people there whose names were on the list. So after his instruction Chan ordered the arrest of the entire Region [administrations]. And who did they bring in to make the arrests? Yin Sophi. Then Pol Pot got Chan and Mok together and got them to agree to bring in Mok's Southwest Zone cadres to replace the Eastern Zone cadres there...

> They said So Phim was protecting traitors, and were in conflict with him from mid-1977 to early 1978, and then in 1978 it became serious. They put Chan in Regions 23 and 24 to use them as a base from which to attack the other three Regions.

But before this could be done, the Eastern Zone military apparatus had to be at least partially dismantled.

During the 1970-75 war, the Eastern Zone leaders had built up five brigades or divisions (*kong pul*) of troops. In July 1975 the Center assumed direct control of the largest two of these which were transferred to Phnom Penh and became the 170th and 108th Divisions. Chan Chakrey retained his command of the former, however, and was also appointed deputy chief of the general staff un-

---

45. For an analysis of this confession, see B. Kiernan, C. Boua and A. Barnett, "Bureaucracy of Death," *New Statesman* (2 May 1980), 669-76.

der Defense Minister Son Sen. The 3rd, 4th and 5th Brigades remained under the command of the Eastern Zone Staff, and a regimental commander named Heng Samrin became political commissar of the 4th. The Eastern Zone's fatigue uniforms were now discarded in favor of the black pajamas worn by troops of the Center and all the other Zones.

According to Ouch Bun Chhoeun: "In 1975-76, the Zone brigades were engaged in agricultural production. Frontier defense was the task of regional and district forces." These included five more brigades, one in each Region. However, there was little if any border fighting in the 1975-76 period. Liaison committees from border provinces in both countries still held joint meetings. In 1976, according to Chhoeun, an Eastern Zone delegation was even sent to Ho Chi Minh City "for a meeting about the frontier." It included Chan, Peam, the district chief of Memut, and a member of the Region 20 Party Committee. In the same year So Phim's wife, Kiro, spent three weeks in hospital in the south Vietnamese capital.[46]

However, in May 1976, Chakrey, two members of his Divisional Staff and one of his regimental commanders were arrested in Phnom Penh and taken to Tuol Sleng prison. They were said to have "exploded grenades behind the Royal Palace and fired on the National Museum" nearby,[47] in what was possibly an attempt on the life of Pol Pot. There is no evidence of any plans for a general uprising, but the Center seized the opportunity for a much wider purge. Under torture, Chakrey allegedly implicated Ly Phen, political commissar of the Eastern Zone forces, who had been educated for a time in the United States, in a coordinated plot involving seizure of the towns of Prey Veng and Svay Rieng by the 3rd and 4th Brigades while Chakrey took Phnom Penh.[48]

Ly Phen was arrested in July. At the end of the year, according to a former member of the 3rd Brigade, its commander, Hak, was taken away, "followed by about 200 officers of the brigade, including the platoon commanders, who were all killed." Hak's political commissar, Pen Cheap, was incarcerated in Tuol Sleng in March 1977, according to the prison's records. "The rank and file were dispersed, and replaced mostly by Central Zone troops in a newly constituted 3rd Brigade."

The same soldier said that officers of the 4th and 5th Brigades were also arrested, and troops from other Zones joined easterners in these brigades, but they were not disbanded and reconstituted as the 3rd Brigade was. Phan, political commissar of the 4th, was arrested, but Heng Samrin, who had become its commander in 1976, and a sufficient number of other leading easterners retained their posts in the 4th and 5th to make them less pliable instruments of the Party Center than the 3rd.

---

46. Author's interviews with Men Chhan, Ouch Bun Chhoeun and Tea Sabun.
47. *Ompi Pankar Ruom Chong Kraoy* [On the Last Joint Plan], written by Tuol Sleng officials in early 1978, 24 pp.
48. Author's interview with Hun Sen, note 26 above.

In March 1977, according to Ouch Bun Chhoeun, the Eastern Zone brigades were ordered withdrawn from their production areas and sent straight to the border. When fighting began, "Eastern Zone troops attacked Vietnam first and soon after Center and Central Zone troops arrived to help them." There is agreement in all accounts, including many eyewitness ones, that the hostilities were initiated by the Kampuchean side.[49] By mid-1977, four Divisions had been sent to the Eastern border – three Center Divisions, including one former Eastern Division, and one from the Central Zone. Early in the year Chan had visited Mesan district in Region 20, where according to a witness, he spoke publicly of a struggle "to recapture Kampuchea Krom" (the Mekong Delta) and even "Prey Nokor" (Ho Chi Minh City) from Vietnam. Chan is the only Eastern Zone leader known to have ever spoken in such terms. Controversy over the military buildup in the East may have been a factor leading to the arrest at the end of April of Siet Chhe, former Party Secretary of Region 22, who had become a member of the General Staff of the Revolutionary Army of Kampuchea.[50] No matter how much the Eastern cadre disliked the Vietnamese – and opinions about this varied – most (apart from Chan) thought it pointless if not extremely dangerous to mount unprovoked military incursions into Vietnamese territory, let alone attempt to "recapture" Kampuchea Krom.

Hun Sen, then a regimental commander responsible for the border between Region 21 and Vietnam, also gives March 1977 as the date when he received instructions to attack Vietnamese territory. Ordered to move against the village of Or Lu in Loc Ninh province, Sen says that he, his political commissar Sok Sat, and Sat's deputy Chum Sei, refused to do so. However, over the next four months, according to Sen, more than 200 military cadres were arrested in eastern Kompong Cham alone. Sat and Sei were executed. Resistance appeared hopeless, and in July Sen fled across the border into Vietnam.[51]

The Center had established a new command structure in the East at the beginning of 1977. On the "Highway 1 Front," comprising the "twin Regions" (*damban phluoh*) 23 and 24, both now under Chan's administration, direct military command was assumed by Chief of the General Staff Son Sen. On Highway 7 which passes from Kompong Cham City in the Central Zone through Eastern Regions 22, 21, and 20 to the frontier, So Phim became "President of the Front Committee," and Pauk (Ke Vin), Party Secretary of the Central Zone, Deputy President. Minister of the Economy Vorn Vet arrived in Kompong Cham and assumed control of supply and logistics along Highway

49. See Ben Kiernan, "New Light on the Origins of the Vietnam-Kampuchea Conflict," *Bulletin of Concerned Asian Scholars* 12:4 (1980): 61-65, which is based on material gathered before my 1980 visit to Cambodia, where numerous further interviews with eyewitnesses and participants confirmed this.
50. "Important culprits," see note 44 above.
51. Author's interview with Hun Sen, see note 26 above.

7.[52] Pauk moved to the East with a Division of Central Zone troops and set up his headquarters near Kandol Chrum in Region 21.

It was in this atmosphere that an "Eastern Zone Conference" was held on July 17, 1977. It is not known who convened the meeting, but an official report of the proceedings was sent to Heng Samrin as commander of the 4th Brigade. It predicted a large-scale border conflict in which Vietnam would have "to strain to stop us." It went on: "We must also be prepared to go into enemy territory to collect intelligence...in order to prepare for victorious attacks."[53] However, Southwest Zone forces had begun such attacks on Vietnam in March; greater reluctance by some in the Eastern Zone may explain the document's understated foreshadowing of the offensive, to occur "if the enemy commits aggression." Further, there was not complete agreement on the offensive: "We must first generalize our unity." In the context of what it said were Vietnamese designs on Kampuchea, the report noted: "How can we solve this question? Do we think we can solve it in accordance with the line of our Party or must we solve it according to the cowardly position of a group of traitors who kneel down and work as lackeys of the Vietnamese ?"[54]

Whether or not Heng Samrin belonged to this alleged category of cadre, within a few months he had been transferred from his brigade command and appointed Deputy Chief of Kev Samnang's Eastern Zone Staff, now a largely redundant body in view of the new command structure.

According to many sources who were in close touch with So Phim during this period, he exhibited only vague signs of hostility to the Center before 1978, but throughout 1977 lacked enthusiasm for the fighting with Vietnam. He was also suspicious of the turn events had taken, and set up a secret base for himself in the border subdistrict of Cheach, in Komchay Meas.[55] He was also ill for much of the year. This meant that Pauk increasingly assumed effective control of the Highway 7 Front, and with Son Sen in command on Highway 1, military affairs throughout the Eastern Zone passed into outside hands. In August-September 1977, according to Bun Chhoeun, So Phim actually spent more than two months in Beijing undergoing medical treatment. It was at this stage that the war against Vietnam began in earnest. On the night of 24 September 1977, elements of the reconstituted 3rd Brigade under the general command of Son

52. Ouch Bun Chhoeun, see note 29 above.
53. *Kampuchea Dossier*, II (note 40 above), photograph 1, reproduces some of the text of this document which has been translated in part by Stephen Heder, who regards it as an authentic Pol Pot regime internal document (see *The Call*, Chicago, 5 March 1979).
54. For a translation of this part of the document, I am grateful to Gareth Porter.
55. Author's interview with Daok Narin, Kompong Chhnang, 4 September 1980. Narin, who was born in Cheach, said that in January or February 1978, Phim "feared for his security and established a secret second headquarters on an island surrounded by a forest of bamboo in the middle of a plain."

Sen,[56] crossed into Vietnam's Tay Ninh province and massacred nearly 300 civilians in the villages of Tan Lap and Ben Cau districts. Taken by surprise, Vietnamese units only re-occupied the area a week later, by which time they were also confronting the 5th (Eastern) and 18th (Central) Brigades.

Several days after the 24 September attack, a Central Zone company commander returning from the scene remarked with sadness, according to a witness, that "he had never expected the revolution to come to what he had just seen and done." Having written a brief suicide note, he shot himself. His fellow officers later broke down in tears on reading the note, said the witness, who did not know what it said.

It was at this point, September 1977, according to escapee Yos Por, that because "so many Khmer refugees had crossed into Vietnam, the Vietnamese called me away from farming to look after these refugees."[57] And perhaps, to begin organizing them; there is no prior evidence of any Vietnamese preparation for an invasion.

The border war continued for several months until the first Vietnamese invasion of December 1977. Nil Sa'unn who was then working in the fields near Kandol Chrum, recalls: "On 22 December two Vietnamese tanks drove into Kandol Chrum township in an attempt to contact So Phim. Then they turned back towards the border." Inside them, it seems, were several Khmer revolutionaries who had previously fled to Vietnam. Hun Sen, Hem Samin and eight others accompanied the Vietnamese forces on this offensive across different sections of the border. That some of them came in tanks is an indication of the complete breakdown in communication since the Cambodian withdrawal from the border liaison committees and the hostile military buildup. Hem Samin managed to penetrate into Svay Rieng province dressed in black with a squad of ten bodyguards. He heard the grievances of the people, but leading cadre were nowhere to be seen: "We tried to make contact...but no way; we couldn't make any contact." Nevertheless, these small Vietnamese-sponsored joint operations by a handful of "wild chickens" and "farm chickens" signaled that, with or without So Phim, solidarity between the two groups was capable of resurrection.

Nil Sa'unn continues: "On 31 December [1977], Vietnamese tanks and infantry appeared again and we all ran away. On 6 January they returned to Vietnamese territory." Over 100,000 Khmers from all sections of the border took the opportunity to escape to Vietnam with them.[58]

---

56. During a visit to Tan Lap and Xa Mat in 1980, locals told us that the 24 September 1977 attack had been carried out by the 3rd Eastern Brigade.
57. Author's interview with Por, Phnom Penh, 11 September 1980. Por may have meant December 1977, since it was then that the Vietnamese invasion gave tens of thousands the opportunity to flee Cambodia.
58. *Age*, Melbourne, 10 June 1978, quoting the United Nations High Commission for Refugees.

The 4th and 5th Eastern Zone Brigades, and the 6th (Region 20) Brigade, retreated immediately when the first Vietnamese crossed the border. Kim Y, then a district-level cooperative cadre in Ponhea Krek, takes up the story. "When the Vietnamese pushed back in retaliation at the end of 1977, the Kampuchean troops, both Central Zone and Eastern Zone, all ran away to the west. When the Vietnamese withdrew of their own accord, our side did not know about it. We came to see if they had gone or not and then we moved back." In the meantime, the army was in disarray: "...no one knew who was in command of what or who was where, and troops looted a great deal of goods and produce from the people. After the Vietnamese had left, some said it was they who had caused the destruction, some said it was the Eastern Zone troops, and some blamed the Central Zone forces. There was a big dispute over this." But the major cause of the dispute might have been different. On 29 December, in Damber district fifteen kilometers from the highway, Yin Sophi and twelve members of his Security forces, driving a truck along a forest road, met up with Sareth, military commander of the 4th Eastern Brigade, traveling on a motorcycle with two bodyguards. Both vehicles stopped, and the two cadres got out and shook hands. Yin Sophi then drew a gun and shot Sareth dead. Sareth's bodyguards immediately opened fire, killing Sophi and all twelve of his men.[59]

It may well have been this incident which finally convinced Pol Pot and his colleagues that despite everything, the Eastern Zone could not be taken over from within. According to one analysis, So Phim was dropped from the Party's Politburo in December. Vorn Veth moved into Phim's No. 4 position, and Son Sen was promoted to the Politburo.[60] Preparations now began for outright suppression of the Zone.

Region 24: The Lotus in the Sea of Fire

During his experience as a young guerrilla medic in So Phim's Issarak unit, Chhouk ("The Lotus") had learned to speak Vietnamese. Although of peasant background, he later obtained a high-school education and in the early 1960s

59. I was told of this incident by two former Eastern Zone cadre now working in different parts of the country; the first in Kompong Cham on 26 July 1980, and the second in Santuk, Kompong Thom, on 16 October 1980. The details given were consistent.
60. This is S. Thion's analysis of diplomatic reports at the time. See his "Chronologie du mouvement communiste cambodgien," in *Khmers Rouges !* (Paris, Albin Michel, 1981), 291. This is confirmed by Lonh, a participant in the 5th Congress of the Communist Party of Kampuchea in August 1978. He told Stephen Heder in 1980 that at the Congress the Politburo "remained the same" and named its seven members as Pol Pot, Nuon Chea, Mok, Ieng Sary, Vorn Veth, Son Sen and Keu; if Phim's death in June had not altered the Politburo membership, he was presumably already outside it.

became a teacher at Phnom Penh's Lycee Kambuboth, a center of radicalism of which Hou Yuon, the school's director, was the best-known leader. In 1965, according to his widow, Chhouk was approached by a government agent and asked to spy on Hou Yuon. Already a Party member, he was naturally unwilling to do this, so he informed Hou Yuon what had happened and asked permission to leave. Chhouk was then nominated underground chief of Region 24 and slipped into the countryside.[61] For the next five years he was constantly on the run, but managed to build up a network of former Issaraks and a number of younger people. A front-type Youth Association was established clandestinely in Region 24, as well as branches of the ultra-secret Communist Youth League. Sin Song, who joined the latter organization in Peam Chor in 1965, estimates that 80 percent of the young men of the district were recruited into the Youth Association, "especially in the 1966-68 period." Monks were also active in the movement, in particular at Stung Slaut monastery at Neak Leung, "a struggle movement monastery" under the influence of a Buddhist dignitary named Achar El. When Sin Song and six others were arrested in 1966 for their opposition to a corrupt subdistrict chief in Peam Chor, a popular demonstration outside the district office and a letter to Prince Sihanouk by some of the local population effected their release after only three months.[62]

Nevertheless, in the ensuing years government harassment forced Chhouk to seek sanctuary in the NLF zone across the border where he was joined by Chan Chakrey, a former monk from Phnom Penh's Langka Pagoda.[63] After their return to Cambodia in 1970, Chhouk established his headquarters at a low range of hills known as Ba Phnom, once a site of mystical significance where two nineteenth-century anti-French rebel leaders, Pou Kombo and Si Votha, had ceremonially proclaimed the legitimacy of their struggles, in 1866 and 1877. Chhouk and Chakrey were now joined by Chan Saman, former leader of the Issarak Youth Movement, who had been in Hanoi since 1954. In 1972 Saman took charge of the Peam Chor battlefront; just across the Mekong were "blackshirt" troops of the CPK's Southwest Zone. In an early account of their differences, Kenneth Quinn wrote that in this area by November 1973, "the two factions were at each others' throats:"

On November 3, the KK [Khmer Krohom, i.e., forces loyal to the Party Center] kidnapped three KR [Khmer Rumdos, i.e., the pro-Vietnamese "Liberation" forces]

61. Author's interview with Chhouk's widow Suas Samon, Phnom Penh, 12 August 1980. Chhouk's real name was Suas Nau.
62. Author's interview with Sin Song, Phnom Penh, 12 August 1980.
63. Hu Nim's confession, 28 May 1977. Nim says intriguingly: "Chakrey is a proud, swaggering type, sizzling and impetuous. He placed a higher value on himself than on other people. So he revealed to me: 'I do not hang around, waiting for this and that.... Whenever an opportunity arises I will attack the Communist Party of Kampuchea.'" This conversation allegedly took place in 1976 before Chakrey's arrest.

near Angkor Borei mountain who have not been seen since and were presumably executed. One day later, KK cadre in Region 25 [Kandal province] met with KR cadre from Region 24 [Prey Veng province] at Rokar Chuor hamlet on the west bank of the Mekong river; the KK demanded that the KR [who control the Khmer Communist movement in Prey Veng] terminate their policy of cooperating with the Vietcong and North Vietnamese in Region 24. The KR refused, the discussion grew heated, and a firefight ensued. The KR, supported by a nearby VC/NVA unit, killed forty-two KK and drove the rest off. Since that time the KK and KR have conducted raids across the Mekong into each other's territory.[64]

The "KR" in this case were presumably led by Chan Saman, and it may have been these incidents and resultant pressure from the Center that led to his arrest by the Region 24 Security (*Santesok*) forces, ironically probably saving him from assassination by the *Santebal*. But the fighting across the Mekong did not cease even after the withdrawal of the Vietnamese to the border. Further north, in July and August 1974, troops of the Southwest's 11th Brigade clashed with Chakrey's 1st Eastern Brigade based in Region 24. Phoeun, then a member of the 11th, recalls:

They wore green, not black like us, with different caps, and they called us "cormorants." Each side thought themselves tougher than the other. They shot two of us in a boat on the river, and after that there were constant reprisal raids back and forth, day and night. The conflict lasted right through to liberation when the troops were reconciled. As for the leaders, I don't know…[65]

Until then, however, both sides directed their greatest efforts against the Lon Nol regime and its U.S. backers, reaping political as well as military successes. One Region 24 peasant told me how from 1970-75, "the people believed in the Khmer Rouge…because of their propaganda, their talk about resisting the imperialists." Did the people know what an imperialist was? I asked.

They were angry because bombs were dropped on the village. Three or four people were killed, and four houses burned down by napalm in 1973. In the same year, F-111s dropped bombs in the middle of a village two kilometers away, killing over twenty people. Over sixty people from our village, out of anger at this, then joined the revolutionary army. Chhouk and [his local cadre] were good people; they pursued the interests of the people who supported the movement. Everyone was against Lon Nol – there was no disagreement about that.

According to a former schoolteacher from another district:

…the peasants believed in Chhouk. He organized the people to improve their work; if there was a shortage of lemon-grass or mint, he got it planted, or would even plant it himself.

64. Kenneth Quinn, "The Khmer Krohom Program to Create a Couuuunist Society in Southern Cambodia; 1971-74," unclassified airgram to Department of State from U.S. Consulate, Can Tho, 20 February 1974.
65. Chhin Phoeun, interview with the author, Kong Pisei, 17 September 1980.

If the people's houses were unsanitary, he would clean them out. This was at the time when the Vietnamese were here with him. He organized work in the fields according to the socialist system and implemented it in a genuinely good way. At a time when we were not familiar with it, he taught us, and the people appreciated this. And in particular, he was appreciated because he got rid of thieves; he refused to tolerate them at all.

A good number of peasants in Region 24, as elsewhere in the Eastern Zone, were looking forward to victory.

Sin Song became a regimental political commissar in Region 24 in 1974-75, and then a Regional economics cadre. According to him:

Immediately upon liberation on 17 April 1975, there was a Special Center Assembly for Cabinet Ministers and all Zone and Region Secretaries. Eight points were made at the Assembly, by Pol Pot:

1. Evacuate people from all towns.

2. Abolish all markets.

3. Abolish Lon Nol regime currency and withhold the revolutionary currency that had been printed.

4. Defrock all Buddhist monks and put them to work growing rice.

5. Execute all leaders of the Lon Nol regime beginning with the top leaders.

6. Establish high-level cooperatives through out the country, with communal eating.

7. Expel the entire Vietnamese minority population.

8. Dispatch troops to the borders, particularly the Vietnamese border.

There was some disagreement with these points at the Assembly, especially over the creation of high-level cooperatives because three million city people and others were not familiar with revolutionary politics. And also, the country had just emerged from a war, so there were great shortages and a lack of capital and facilities. Communal eating cooperatives throughout the country was not a feasible proposition. Hou Yuon, for one, said that this was just not possible, Chhouk reported to me afterwards. After that, Hou Yuon was sacked from the Cabinet.

Some people also disagreed with the policy of execution, preferring re-education so that the victims could then play a useful role. And there was disagreement with the abolition of money and markets.

Chhouk and the Secretary of the Northeast Zone, Ney Sarann, were among the main dissidents. When he came back, Chhouk called a meeting of over thirty Region 24 cadres, including myself. He told us he disagreed with these policies and if the Party went ahead along this road, he would not yet follow, especially as far as communal eating cooperatives were concerned, because there was a great shortage of food and rice in Region 24 after the war.

As a result, according to Sin Song, communal eating was not introduced in Region 24 while Chhouk was still in command there. Production cooperatives were organized, but the crop was distributed among the members and meals eaten at home. In this way adequate living conditions were maintained, in Song's view. He says executions were minimized as well, although there were some.

This was their general project, in particular to kill the people politically associated with Lon Nol's regime.... Chhouk struggled politically over the line adopted—he didn't regard Pol Pot as an enemy. He just had different ideas, and implemented some policies and not the ones he disagreed with. He ordered the abolition of markets and money, and the defrocking of monks, but disagreed most strongly on the establishment of communal eating cooperatives throughout the country. Chhouk understood what was happening and thought that Pol Pot was on the wrong road, although he didn't often say so. He wanted to struggle against this politically, from the inside.

According to Nem, a member of the Information Service of Ba Phnom district in 1976:

High-ranking cadres told me a little about this. One of them, Vung, deputy secretary of Ba Phnom district, had close relations with Chhouk; another was Chhim, Chhouk's deputy and head of the Region 24 Information and Culture Service.

In 1976 Vung took some of us to work with him digging canals, and one day we had a meal together on an island. There had not been much to eat that year, and he mentioned how the work was tiring and proper rations necessary. He gave us plenty to eat, and said, 'life is hard if you can't eat your fill.'

We suspected he was probably a revisionist [*sao reu*], and were happy with him because things had got so tough. He told us that we were not alone, the little people; the chief of Region 24 was struggling for freedom rights and that it was up to the people who had fought the war but had encountered great difficulties once Pol Pot got control. So Chhouk wanted to establish revisionism throughout the Eastern Zone. All the officials in Region 24 were in agreement about revisionism, but all we heard was that Chhouk was in favor of freedom rights and prosperity—he kept everything very quiet.

Sin Song added that as far as foreign relations were concerned:

Chhouk maintained frequent contact with Vietnamese across the border in order to solve problems in a framework of cooperation. Meetings were held, with the Vietnamese sometimes coming to Region 24, and Chhouk sometimes going to Vietnam. In early 1976 there were still such contacts. In 1975-76, when it began to be said that Vietnam was a strategic enemy, there was as yet no such change of line in Region 24.

Nem also told me he heard no mention of Vietnam as an enemy before 1977. Sin Song said that Chhouk, whose widow in an interview with me made the same point, "had criticisms of Vietnam but regarded such problems as normal, capable of being solved by meetings and discussion." Chhouk "kept very quiet" his lack of hostility towards the Vietnamese – he even seems to have feigned hostility for the benefit of visitors from Phnom Penh, including at one point Pol Pot himself.[66] Kun, an interpreter for the North Korean advisors sent to the Region, recalled with a hesitancy which seemed born of doubt that Chhouk's associates had given him the right impression: "I know Chhouk, I used to eat with him. But I don't know what he was like. He spoke well of the revolution. It seemed like...well...people would say repeatedly that he really hated the Vietnamese. He spoke Vietnamese. I was told everybody was scared of him, especially the Vietnamese."[67] In Region 21, battalion commander Hun Sen says he received a circular from Chhouk in early 1976 which referred to Vietnam as an "enemy." "But others I trust say that Chhouk was a friend of Vietnam so he may have been deliberately hiding his views at that time."

Around the very same time Chhouk was saying quite different things to cadres in his own Region. Sor Van Thuon, chief of the Economics Service in Kompong Trabek district from 1971 to May 1975, claims that early in 1976 Chhouk visited the Kansom Ak subdistrict office and in his presence told the district chief, Suon Voreach, and five district and subdistrict officials: "Our revolution seems to be not authentic, a fraud—we must collect our forces and send them to Vietnam." Thuon thinks that Chhouk was arrested because he was preparing to dispatch troops and civilians to safety there. Corroborating the two accounts from other districts mentioned above, Thuon says that Chhouk "secretly disagreed with the cooperatives, with their communal eating and so on."[68]

Kang Khlouk, 58, a politicized base peasant from the border subdistrict of Peam Montea, said that in his experience, "Chhouk did not persecute the people." Meals were eaten privately until 1977. Nor was Chhouk hostile to Vietnam in Khlouk's view: "The reason the fighting started was that Chhouk disappeared in late 1976. Then it started."

Meas Chhum, 49, a base peasant who had been jailed in Region 24 for five months in 1973, worked from May 1975 as a mechanic in the eighty-member Region 24 Transport Service. From the beginning meals were eaten collectively

66. Interview with Kun, Paris, 1 February 1980. Kun's superior responsible for the North Koreans in Region 24 was a hill tribesman from Preah Vihear with close links to Ieng Sary.
67. Ibid.
68. Thuon added: "Chhouk was a real patriot. He did not go along with Pol Pot, so he was arrested." Interview with the author, Kompong Trabek, 8 October 1980.

in such organized work units, he said, but not in the villages. He met Chhouk on a number of occasions in 1975 and 1976.

> He never insulted or bothered me. He would speak to us in normal tones, neither cruel nor very lenient. Living conditions were middling, not that bad. Our rations were normal; there was enough to eat. We ate rice, not gruel. We worked eight hours a day, never in the evenings. We were just told to work hard and carefully, for the Organization.

> New people and base people in our unit were treated equally. None of us was taken away or disappeared. Our families were all in the villages; if we wanted to visit them for two or three days, we only had to ask permission from the head of the service. If your wife was sick or there was some problem with your children, you could get one or two weeks' leave. I saw my family every four to six weeks.

Then (on 28 August 1976) Chhouk disappeared and his subordinates were gradually replaced by new cadres who were "tougher in terms of rations and in terms of working conditions."

> Rations fell continuously. In February 1977, communal eating was introduced in the villages. Sometimes we had to work until 11 P.M. The new cadres told us to forget about "familyism" (*kruosaa niyum*) and not to miss our wives and children, whom we were now allowed to visit for only three days every three months. Two members of our work unit were taken away to prison and never returned.

According to veteran local cadre Neang Samnang, Chhouk had Chan Saman released from confinement just before his own arrest. (Saman then disappeared, probably recaptured by Pol Pot's forces and killed along with Chhouk.)

It was around the same time, on 6 August, that Deuch, chief of the Center Security (*Santebal*) apparatus, completed a report on Chakrey, Ly Phen and other dissidents in the Party, outlining their activities such as the distribution of leaflets and the explosion of grenades in various parts of the capital. In connection with this alleged conspiracy, and on the basis of the dissidents' confessions, Chhouk was mentioned as one of a number of cadres involved in collecting "200 kilograms of gold, and millions of dollars," presumably thought to have been confiscated from wealthy urban evacuees.

> The gold is not in the form of jewelry, it is gold leaf and bars [*dom*].... According to a very clear analysis, [the gold and money] has definitely not fallen into the hands of the Eastern Zone organization; even though some opinion has it that it was taken [there] in June 1975, the majority opinion is that it was taken [there] in September 1975. [sic] Some say brother Chhouk has it, some say it was taken to Vietnam...[69]

This "very clear analysis," contradicted by "majority opinion," seems an attempt to isolate Chhouk by connecting him with Vietnam, and at the same time hinting that he was in some way a link between Vietnam and "the Eastern

69. Deuch [Kang Khek Iev], *Sekkdey sorop damnaer ruang pi mun* [Summary Report on Previous Events], S-21, 6 August 1976, 6 pp.

Zone organization," itself implicated but not yet targeted. It first had to be undermined.

In Tuol Sleng, on 1 September, Chhouk wrote out his first "confession." Ignoring the accusation about gold and money, it began: "With respect, my name is Chhouk. I would like to inform the Center Political Standing Committee...." But it was unlikely that all formal members of this body which still included So Phim would be "informed." Chhouk described his relationship with Phim: "I have respected and learned a great deal from him, especially his intelligent, mature, steady and non-impetuous standpoints. In particular, his moral standpoint is a good model. Further, since the beginning, I have personally feared him." The last sentence may also be a cryptic reference to the frightening situation Chhouk found himself in, a context for his expression of loyalty to the Center. (A short note he had written the previous day reveals that he was aware of his ultimate fate. It ended: "I die under the red revolutionary flag!") Chhouk then confessed to "shortcomings": "My standpoint on the offensive to interrogate traitors in order to clean up [the enemy] was not fierce. I left them time to enable them to escape. Prisoners were continually getting away."[70] Moreover, in the early 1970s: "In establishing the armed forces I did not [just] bring in base people. People such as outcasts and Khmer Serei, etc., were buried [inside the forces]. I am not sure of their background. In establishing the administration I liked theorists who could talk and write...."

The confession ends, after sixteen pages: "Finally I would like to ask the Party to forgive me and spare my life.... I would like to express my wholehearted loyalty to the Party.... And if the Party decides to expel me or to imprison me, I am prepared to accept what the Party does. Let the Party just forgive me." A note across the top written by prison chief Deuch records that the confession and a photocopy of it were sent to "the Organization" the next day. Eleven weeks later, on 13 November, Chhouk signed his thirty-second confession, "A list of names of traitors in the network of IX" (i.e., of fellow dissident Ney Sarann), and disappeared into history.

Three weeks after Chhouk's arrest, a letter was sent to Region 24 by the "Vietnam-Kampuchea Liaison Committee" of neighboring Dong Thap province in Vietnam. It began: "Recently the Liaison Committee in Dong Thap sent a letter inviting the Region and district officials to a meeting on 15 September 1976 at the border...but we do not know if the comrades received our letter or not. There has been no reply...."[71]

---

70. Chhouk [Suas Nau], *Chamlaiy Suas Nau leuk ti muoy* [The First Reply of Suas Nau], dated 1 September 1976. A Phnom Penh woman evacuated to Region 24 in 1975 told me that before his arrest Chhouk had organized the release from prison of several "truckloads" of well-educated people, and that he had advised them to flee to Vietnam, saying: "You are many and I am alone. You will survive and I will die."
71. This document was found in the file of S-21 confessions written by Non Suon.

There was to be none. The letter was sent on to Tuol Sleng for use in interrogations while the entire Region 24 administration was purged. Chhouk's deputy in the Party branch, Nau Chey, was temporarily put at ease by his appointment as Chhouk's successor, while Center Security forces carried out a vast round-up of veteran local cadres. Those arrested in the next few months included the chiefs of the Region Information, Economics, Transport, Agriculture and Health Services; Vung, Suon Voreach, Sin Song, Achar El and over five hundred regional, district, subdistrict and village officials. On 9 July 1977, large numbers of them were executed; Sin Song and two others escaped and made their way to Vietnam by night. Three days later Nau Chey was arrested. The purge had already spread to Region 23 with the arrest of So, its Secretary, on 17 March. Supported by Mok's Southwest forces and those of the Center, Chan consolidated direct control over the "twin Regions." The sea of fire had enveloped the Lotus, but the smoke did not go unnoticed elsewhere in the Zone. According to Kim Y, then building houses for a "model cooperative" in Ponhea Krek:

> At the time he heard of the arrest of Chhouk, So Phim denounced him as a traitor in accordance with the information he had received from above, from the Center. But a month or so later, at the end of 1976, he observed [the situation] and said: 'It seems that Chhouk and all those people are not traitors,' referring to Chakrey and other high-ranking cadres. Phim complained a lot at the end of 1976 and early 1977....

The End

The 1977 purge of about half of the district and regional-level administrative cadre in Regions 20, 21 and 22, discussed above, paralleled an even more massive elimination campaign in other Zones. Then in February 1978, according to a Chinese government source, Phnom Penh "acted to strengthen the discipline of its armed forces."[72] Partly in response to all this, the Party Secretary of the Western Zone, Chou Chet, who from all accounts shared So Phim's lack of enthusiasm for the war with Vietnam, planned a military uprising. This was aborted in late March when he and his co-conspirators were arrested and taken to Tuol Sleng. The Center certainly considered So Phim to have been involved in the affair, but if he was, Chet's failure seems to have dissuaded him from making another attempt. According to a woman who was then working in the Ponhea Krek district office:

> So Phim just knew that the situation kept changing. But he did not dare [do anything]. He was being watched very closely by Pol Pot's people. Of course he knew but he couldn't get away.

> He called a secret meeting in Pha-Au in March 1978. I was serving the food for the leading cadres there, but I went in close and heard what was being said. Phim told

---

72. "Geng Biao's Report on the Situation of the Indochinese Peninsula," in *Journal of Contemporary Asia* 11:3 (1981), 382.

them that the situation had now changed considerably, and the comrades should all take an interest. He reminded the regional and district cadres of this standpoint because at that time regional, district and military cadres were being taken away one after another, everywhere. When he noted this, he said that those arrested were loyal servants of the people, his friends, not traitors. He told everyone to watch out, to be careful.[73]

It was pathetically inadequate advice. Tuol Sleng prison records show that by 19 April 1978, Eastern Zone personnel being held there numbered 409; the largest number from any other Zone was only forty-eight, from the Northwest. The twenty-eight prisoners who arrived the next day were all from the East.[74]

The commanders of two Center Divisions stationed in the East were also arrested in April. Both men were reportedly close to So Phim. One of them was Heng Thal, younger brother of Heng Samrin and commander of the 290th Division, formerly Chakrey's 1st Division of the Eastern Zone. (His political commissar, Ke San, had been arrested on 4 March.) The other was Et Samon, also an easterner by background, commander of the 280th Division and Deputy Chief of the General Staff of the Revolutionary Army of Kampuchea. According to a relative, Samon committed suicide in custody soon after his arrest.

In the first three weeks of May, Ke Pauk summoned the commanders and political commissars of the three Eastern Zone brigades and five Regional brigades to "meetings" at his headquarters in Sra village north of Highway 7. As they arrived they were all disarmed, arrested and executed. The first victims included Sarun, commander of the Region 20 Brigade, and his deputy Be. They were followed by Kun Ybol, a member of the brigade committee, Chhoeun, new commander of the 5th Zone Brigade, Kim, Heng Samrin's replacement as commander of the 4th and a member of the Zone Staff, and even Kry, new commander of the reconstituted 3rd Brigade. Next came Keo Samnang, Chief of the Zone Staff and member of the Zone Executive; Chhien, Secretary of Region 22 and also a member; Chen Sos, Secretary of Region 21, and Sin, Secretary of Region 20. By 22 May, their subordinates in all regional and district committees, and military officers right down to platoon commanders and chiefs of the youth militia, were also being called in. The executions numbered in the hundreds.

Phim was apparently ill at this point and certainly unaware of the extent of the massacre. But even when, after the event, he learned of the arrests of Heng Thal and Et Samon, he had been able to do little more than express his anger. He was hamstrung by a sense of Party discipline, and by his belief that these events could not reflect the nature of the revolution. An excellent underground leader and military commander, Phim had had only two years of high school education and seems to have lacked the political acuity to cope with the developments that were about to overtake him. Just as in 1963 when his bid for

73. Prok Sary, interview with the author, Prey Veng, 12 July 1980.
74. This document is reproduced in Kiernan, Boua and Barnett, "Bureaucracy of Death," 674.

Party leadership failed "not by a vote but by opinion," just as in 1970 when the Vietnamese disregarded his reluctance to ask their troops to intervene, just as in 1976 when he had at first failed to back his own judgment of Chhouk, so again in 1978 he was powerless in the face of a revolutionary *fait accompli*. Whether or not they worked in his own favor, what he saw as the inexorable laws and hierarchy of history and the omnipotence and discipline of the Party stripped him of political initiative. When the inevitable "invitation" from Pauk arrived for him, Phim could only exclaim: "I am the President of the [Highway 7] Front. What right does the Deputy President have to call me to a meeting? It should be the reverse. What does this mean ?"[75]

He must have known, of course. But the closer he came to a full realization, the greater his inertia – as chief of the Zone he would have seen at least more clearly than any of his comrades, that the elements of a successful armed resistance had almost been swept away. Remarking cryptically that "security" for such a meeting was better at his own base than at Pauk's,[76] he sent Mey, one of his bodyguards, to assess Pauk's activities. Mey was arrested and executed. Another message arrived and another bodyguard set off, meeting the same fate. A third "invitation" caused Phim to send his nephew Chhoeun to investigate the disappearance of the bodyguards. Chhoeun, too, was killed. Finally, on 23 May, Phim sent Peam to represent him at Pauk's headquarters. Despite his own role in the purges of Eastern cadre, this seems to have been the kiss of death for Peam, who was arrested and sent off to Tuol Sleng.

Long suspicious, now shocked, and more importantly, his channels of communication with the local level suddenly smashed or totally disrupted, Phim could not accept that history was no longer leading the revolution (and himself) by the hand as it seemed to have done during so many years of struggle. Just as he saw Pauk as his subordinate, so he saw Pol Pot as his superior. If this destruction of the revolutionary world he knew was the work of the Party leadership, then they were indeed traitors to be resisted, but while regional warlordism remained a possibility, for him to attack the Party would be a fatal confrontation with history. Treason must and would be defeated; of that alone Phim was sure.

On 25 May, Pauk struck. Two more brigades of Central Zone troops, one of them an armored brigade of ten amphibious tanks, crossed the Mekong and moved swiftly down Highway 7. Remnants of the Eastern Zone army put up stiff, spontaneous resistance. Phim proclaimed that Pauk and Son Sen were traitors, and tried several times to make radio contact with Phnom Penh, "to protest about the killing," according to Puk Soum. There was no reply. "He called a meeting at his headquarters, and asked everybody to wait while he went to meet the Center to find out what this was all about. He said he would return if he was unsuccessful, for then he would know that it was the work of the Center."

---

75. Ouch Bun Chhoeun, see note 29 above.
76. Ibid. The account that follows is compiled from information gathered in interviews with ten or more Eastern Zone cadre.

Accompanied only by his family and a few bodyguards, Phim climbed into a jeep and drove off to meet Pol Pot.

Ouch Bun Chhoeun had decided to take to the jungle. He went to see his former superior, Phuong, now minister of rubber plantations, but found him even more immobilized by revolutionary fatalism than Phim. "You will never defeat the Party," was Phuong's reaction. The two wished one another well and Chhoeun slipped away. Phuong seems to have played no part at all in subsequent events and was arrested and taken to Tuol Sleng on 6 June.

This combination of loyalty and despair was telling. In Chhoeun's words: "Some of our cadres were the same. They said: 'I am not a traitor. I will not betray the people, the nation, the Party. If the Party kills me while I remain loyal, I will die a patriot.'"

> One group of more than twenty youths aged about fifteen was arrested. They did not try to run away. They just said: "I am faithful to the Party. I obey the Party. If I die I die faithful to the Party and loving it." And all those youngsters were executed. The Party was more than a god to them.

Others, however, were determined to resist. Tea Sabun in Tbaung Khmum was the first to take up arms.

> I had sent my people and troops to those meetings and they had all been arrested, and their motorcycles seized. Anyone who was a revolutionary was arrested. And they were all killed. If we wanted to survive, we had to make a revolution. I called in the militia forces from Vihear Luong, Chong Kraung, Anchaeum, Sralap, Lo Ngieng and Kor subdistricts. There were about three to four thousand of us in the forest. We had the contents of So Phim's Eastern Zone arsenals – tens of thousands of guns including all the B-40s and B-69s. We didn't have enough trucks to cart everything away so we had to blow up the rest. We hit them east of Suong at three in the morning of the 26th. There was fierce, close-in fighting for three days and three nights. We fell back and regrouped, then attacked again and drove them out of Suong. Then they recaptured it. They had two brigades to our force of approximately one regiment. We killed many of them and blew up five or six tanks and many vehicles by mining the roads. They would take a village and then we would push them out again the next day. If defeated, we would run into the jungle and then return and attack them.

Avoiding the northward advance of Mok's forces from Region 24, So Phim drove through the ricelands of Region 22 and reached the Tonle Tauch river at Peareang. He sent a courier to Phnom Penh in another attempt to make contact with Pol Pot, and apparently succeeded, for he spent a week waiting at Prek Pou. On 3 June, two ferries pulled in, loaded with Center troops. As they closed in on him, so did despair. He told Daok Samol and Yi Yaun, district chiefs of Peareang and Sithor Kandal: "You must rise up and struggle. They are traitors. You keep up the struggle; I can't solve this. We are alone. I don't know what will happen. I can't find a solution." Samol and Yaun left for the jungle. Just after sunset, Phim drew a pistol and shot himself in the chest. A second bullet through the mouth proved necessary – it was not physical courage that he lacked. His bodyguards went to a nearby village, drank themselves into a stupor with home-made alcohol, and then scattered. At 9 P.M., Phim's wife and children were massacred on the river bank as they prepared his body for burial.

A traditional Khmer saying has it: *Khmaer men caol kbuon, Yuon men caol put* (The Khmer adhere to regulations, the Vietnamese adhere to deception). It is doubly ironic that this axiom applies rather to So Phim's relationship with Pol Pot's Party Center who, in these terms, fitted better than he did their description of "Khmer bodies with Vietnamese minds."

The Beginning

Phim's suicide was not meaningless, for by this action he avoided ending his days as a tortured informer in Tuol Sleng. But he had failed to take a public stand, and his enemies were able to cheat him in death as they had in life. Back in Kandol Chrum, Pauk was parading the body of Kim, commander of the 4th Zone Brigade, whose features resembled those of his chief, along Highway 7 on the back of a truck. Villagers were shown the corpse of "the contemptible Phim, the traitorous chieftain" (*A-Phim mékbot*). In several places crowds gathered to witness evidence of the new power of the revolution, unaware that the hopelessness which marked Phim's actual end was an even more eloquent testimony.

Most ironic of all, perhaps, was the looting of Phim's Zone treasury of gold and dollars at Suong. It was presumably the hoard Deuch had suggested Chhouk may have sent to Vietnam, although it was indeed in the form of jewelry. A fabricated suspicion had justified the first of the widespread purges that had led ineluctably to Phim's downfall.

But resistance grew, and the ensuing struggle laid much of the political basis for the overthrow of the Pol Pot regime. Heng Samrin, aided by Daok Samol, led an unknown number of regular units into battle south of Highway 7. Militia units were also mobilized: a force of 3,000 took to the jungle in the border subdistrict of Krabau, in Komchay Meas district, under the command of Chum Sambor. Across the Highway in Region 21, a *maquis* of similar size was formed in Tramoung district, and most of the Memut district committee were also organizing resistance. According to Kim Y, in Region 20:

> We all fought the coup at first for two or three days, in some places two weeks. But then the fighting subsided, and airplanes dropped leaflets [signed by Chan] which said: "Compatriots, please put down your arms. Please pool your forces with us and participate with us. Let us exterminate the enemy together, namely So Phim, the traitor chieftain in the Eastern Zone." Our youths and cadres thought hard. Some kept quiet; others in small squads put down their arms and went in to save their lives by confessing, and some even took their guns in with them. But most of us took our guns into the forest. That was when it all started.

The most important battles were nevertheless being fought in Tbaung Khmum, where Region 21 troops led by Tea Sabun, Mat Ly, Ouch Bun Chhoeun and So Phim's former courier Mau Phok temporarily tied down the bulk of Ke Pauk's forces at the western end of Highway 7, giving the rebels closer to the Vietnamese border valuable time to regroup and organize. Fierce fighting continued throughout June and July. In Stung Trang district of the Central Zone, fifteen kilometers across the Mekong, one informant recalls that in this period "we could hear guns firing every day."[77] The rebels destroyed more than twenty military vehicles, but they took heavy casualties as the superior numbers of the combined forces of Pauk, Son Sen and Mok began to tell. At the same time, massacres of surrendering rebels and of the inhabitants of villages suspected of harboring "traitors" drove tens of thousands of peasants into the jungle during July, destroying any remaining possibility of political consolidation of the Zone by the Center. According to Kun, the interpreter for the North Korean technical advisors in Regions 23 and 24:

> After So Phim's death the people in Region 22 and in Komchay Meas rebelled in anger.... The people had long wanted the private system back again instead of the Party's communitarian system, and they supported the rebellion. They stopped eating communally and were distributing ox-carts and other things among themselves. Cadres still faithful to the Party line were afraid to remain in place for fear that the people would kill them, and they fled to Region 24 where I met them. The army could not go into Region 22....

But the Center recovered in July and the massacres of the population followed. By August it was clear that despite the exodus into the jungle, the rebels were unable to hold territory, and, starved and exhausted, they began a tortuous retreat towards the heavily mined and patrolled Vietnamese border.

Along the way, at meetings held in jungle clearings, the narrowing options were discussed. According to one source, "some Region 21 cadre" who had committed themselves to an overtly anti-Vietnamese stance in the past were still unwilling to solicit Vietnamese aid. They and many ordinary rebels feared they would not be well-received in Vietnam because the two countries were at war. Those easterners and some of the apparently numerous defectors from the Center's 280th and 290th Divisions who had witnessed or participated in massacres of Vietnamese civilians or fighting with troops across the border were naturally most concerned about the possibility of Vietnamese revenge. (There may also have been a fear that Vietnam, which had been calling for negotiations with the Pol Pot regime, might eventually reach an accommodation with it, under the terms of which the rebels might even be handed back to the Democratic Kampuchea authorities.) Further, Heng Samrin and others who addressed these meetings denied the Pol Pot accusations that they were traitorous agents in the

---

77.   Author's interview with Chhil Channo, Tuol, France, 28 October 1979.

pay of the Vietnamese – their rebellion sprang rather from murderous and trai- torous policies on the part of Pol Pot and Son Sen, they said, not to mention the danger posed to their own lives. By way of illustration, Heng Samrin pointed out that he had participated in border attacks on Vietnam. In this context of rebutting Center propaganda, these were not necessarily anti-Vietnamese statements. The rebel leaders knew that Phnom Penh was responsible for the war with Vietnam whether or not they had themselves implemented its orders to go into battle, and that it had little to do with "independence and self-reliance." The general position of the Eastern cadre was one of preparedness to resist the Vietnamese army should it cross the border without their agreement,[78] but they were already stressing to their followers that such an agreement with the Vietnamese would not make them "lackeys" or "puppets." At a meeting in Krabau forest, Heng Samrin finally said: "We have no mastery of the situation. We cannot solve the livelihood problems of our people. We have only to contact the Vietnamese again for the Kampuchean people to survive."[79]

Chim Chin was not far away in the same expanse of forest. "At this point we heard the voices of our friends who had been taken away for execution but had escaped and crossed into Vietnam. They were still alive. They held meetings and interviews which were broadcast over Vietnamese radio. When we heard this, we decided to go there as well." Tith Sou was chosen to cross the border on behalf of Heng Samrin and Chea Sim. As acting secretary of Komchay Meas district in 1977, Sou, a 62-year-old former Issarak, had refused to carry out orders from the Center to, as he put it, "kill and make enemies of our friends alongside whom we have struggled against the imperialists for generations."[80]

In September 1978, Sou led a force of 600 into Vietnam south of Highway 7, losing twenty dead as they crossed fifty meter-wide minefields at the border. They arrived at Thnaot, So Phim's old base camp of 1969-70. Sou "smoothed things over with the Vietnamese," as Phim had done in 1969, and told them: "If you don't help us we are finished." This time the Vietnamese were willing to provide more than mere sanctuary. They guaranteed aid to the rebels and word was sent back to Chea Sim and Heng Samrin. Chea Sim brought a group of three hundred, mainly cadre, across the border in October. Another group of seven hundred, mostly civilian base people, was attacked four times by Center

78. Such sentiments were reported by an informant who said he was told this by Region 22 troops in 1975. At the same time, the troops said they were "not happy with the system being established from Phnom Penh," and had had skirmishes with forces from other Zones. Author's interview with Sisavoun, 30 November 1979, Paris.
79. Author's interview with Chum Sambor, Prey Veng, 12 July 1980. I found no evidence for Stephen Heder's statement: "It had become necessary, he [Samrin] decided, to sacrifice Kampuchea's independence in order to save its people." Heder, "Kampuchea 1980: Anatomy of a Crisis," *Southeast Asia Chronicle* 77 (February 1981), 6. Few of those involved seem to have seen the issue in such mechanistic terms.
80. Author's interview with Tith Sou, Prey Veng, 12 July 1980.

troops on the way; forty people were killed.[81] Vietnamese troops then struck into Cambodia and escorted Heng Samrin and a group of two to three thousand back across the border. As many as fourteen thousand others who had fled into Krabau forest from Komchay Meas, Ponhea Krek and Kanchriech soon followed. A small force of one hundred, commanded by Chun Sambor, stayed to fight on in Krabau.

Meanwhile, north of Highway 7, Tea Sabun's Region 21 forces had concentrated and arrived at the border via Damber; they now numbered about 3,000. Ouch Bun Chhoeun, for his part, had resisted moves to contact the Vietnamese, but Sabun was in contact with Chea Sim and had agreed with his policy. "We were out of supplies and ammunition, food, medicine, clothing.... We were sleeping on leaves. We had no bases to retreat to, and we realized that we could never defeat Pol Pot even if we won in the East. I said it was all right. I had known the Vietnamese since the Issarak period. They would not kill us whatever we did." He, too, chose former Issarak veterans as couriers.

> I sent them off while we were still fighting at I-ai. When contact was made we would go to Vietnam. They crossed over, and then the Vietnamese came in to open the way for us, protecting us from Pol Pot. Some of us were still afraid of the Vietnamese at first, but when we got together and all shook hands, everyone relaxed. They welcomed us and gave us rice, clothes, took our sick to hospitals nearby. We went on to Ta Tong in Tay Ninh, where Chea Sim's people were. The leaders went off to a meeting with the Vietnamese.

It was Sabun's second such traumatic border crossing in ten years, and resulted in his third alliance with the Vietnamese Communists. "The leaders" now included not only earlier defectors to Vietnam, such as Hun Sen and Hem Samin, but also former Issaraks like Pen Sovan who had gone to Hanoi in 1954 and had never returned to join the revolution. Fighting continued between Kampuchean and Vietnamese troops along the border over the next month, and the Vietnamese invested the Snuol rubber plantations in Kratie. On 2 December, about seventy Kampuchean rebel leaders gathered there and founded the Kampuchean United Front for National Salvation.[82]

The human cost of the Center's suppression of the Eastern Zone will never be accurately known. Apart from the executions of cadre – reported in almost all districts, subdistricts and villages – a number of entire villages were massacred, including all 120 families in So Phim's base village of Bos in Ponhea Krek,[83]

---

81. According to many participants' reports, the losses were far higher, around forty percent on each crossing. *Kampuchea Dossier* II (note 40 above), 62-63, cites a column of 1,200 people who all disappeared on the Cambodian side of the border. "'They must have been massacred, all of them,' said old Tith Sou."
82. Tea Sabun, see note 14 above.
83. Author's interview with Lim Thi, Takhmau, 15 August 1980. Thi, a native of Dauntey subdistrict, said that "only one person survived" in Bos out of a population of 700.

and killings in other villages were widespread.[84] Perhaps a third or more of the Zone's population was evacuated to other Zones, where most perished through a policy of selective killing and starvation. At least 100,000 died between May and December 1978. In Komchay Meas district alone, the toll exceeded 6,000 of a population of 60,000.[85] This account by a former Party member from Region 20, who ceased political activity in 1973 due to illness and now lives the life of a peasant, is not atypical.

> 1978 was the worst period for killings - of cadres, soldiers, everyone. People were taken away in truckloads, fifty at a time. After the May 1978 coup, some people were killed on the spot: one hundred in my village, including all the teenagers in the work brigades and the Youth Association, and many Party members. Four of my six children were executed.

> Then from July 1978 came the evacuations of the ordinary people to the west, to be killed there. Of 1,330 in the village, about 600 were evacuated in November. Only half of the 600 returned [in 1979-80]. They were preparing to evacuate the rest of us but they ran out of time.

In 1979, Pol Pot cadres retreating into the mountains of western Cambodia continued the massacres of troops and civilians whom they had driven there from the East, and claimed that when victory over the Vietnamese invaders had been won, they would "leave nothing but ashes in the Eastern Zone."[86] Two years later Hun Sen responded to criticism of Heng Samrin and others, for their failure to take action against Pol Pot until May 1978, by saying that when the rebellion did occur, "it saved hundreds of thousands of lives."[87] The criticism seems unanswerable, but so does the reply.

On 7 January 1979, Vietnamese forces captured Phnom Penh, ending nearly four years of Pol Pot rule. The Salvation Front immediately proclaimed the

---

84. In 1980 Honda Katuiti investigated the fate of the inhabitants of two hamlets in Svay Rieng. Of a total of 182 people, sixty-nine were executed in 1978. One died of hunger in the same year. By comparison, one had been executed in 1975, and one perished in jail and two died of hunger in 1977. (Katuiti Honda, *Journey to Cambodia* [Tokyo, 1981], chapter 3.) I obtained similar accounts from many informants throughout the Eastern Zone. See also Michael Vickery, "Democratic Kampuchea: CIA to the Rescue," draft article prepared for the *Bulletin of Concerned Asian Scholars*, for similar accounts obtained from different sources.

85. According to local officials interviewed by the author at Kranhoung on 9 August 1980, 7,000 people out of the district's population of over 60,000 "disappeared" during the Pol Pot period. This figure is not inconsistent with information gathered by independent sources (see note 84), which indicate also that "disappearances" during 1975-77 would number 1,000 at a maximum, probably far less. According to Hor, who was jailed in Komchay Meas in 1976, "all the prisoners from all over the district" then numbered 120. See the section on "Social Conditions" above, Interviewee no. 2.

86. Author's interview with two new people who were forced into the mountains by retreating Pol Pot forces in early 1979. Kompong Chhnang, 5 September 1980.

87. Press conference, Phnom Penh, 23 September 1981.

People's Republic of Kampuchea, headed by Heng Samrin. Chea Sim became Minister of the Interior. As of 1982, other Ministerial posts were held by such Eastern Zone cadre as Hun Sen (Foreign Affairs), Tea Sabun (Social Action), Ouch Bun Chhoeun (Justice), Mat Ly (Vice-Minister of Agriculture), and Sin Song (Vice-Minister of the Interior). Long-suffering new people were ministers of education, agriculture, health and information. Hanoi-trained cadre like Hem Samin (chief of Kandal province) and Yos Por (secretary-general of the Front) probably held greater power; however, when one of them, Pen Sovan, was replaced by Heng Samrin as secretary of the newly formed People's Revolutionary Party (in December 1981), reconciliation may have gained an edge over bitter memories.[88] Farm chickens and wild chickens triumphed against the cormorants, but only by their unity, by returning to their tradition of solidarity with Vietnam, and by their adoption of a more humane attitude towards the "new people" whose skills Pol Pot's tragic experiment had shown were indispensable to the country's progress.

---

88. See Kiernan, "The New Political Structure in Kampuchea," *Dyason House Papers,* Melbourne, 8:2 (Dec. 1981). Also "Kampuchea 1979-81: National Rehabilitation in the Eye of an International Storm," *Southeast Asian Affairs 1982,* Institute of Southeast Asian Studies (Singapore: Heinemann, 1982). At the local level, too, surviving Eastern Zone cadre returned to positions of power in 1979. In Kraol Ko subdistrict, Svay Rieng, a former chief of the district Economics Service, purged in 1977, was elected deputy subdistrict chief in "general elections in which everybody except children could vote," according to a refugee from the area interviewed by Stephen Heder in 1980. The same informant said that in 1979 a former subdistrict cadre, purged in 1978, became a village chief there, "not selected by the Vietnamese but by the people themselves." (Interview in Camp 007, 24 March 1980.)

As of 1982, Pol Pot remained Commander-in-Chief of the Democratic Kampuchea armed forces on the Thai border; Mok was Chief of the General Staff, and Ke Pauk, undersecretary-general.

2

Rebel Revolutionaries:
Interviews with Chea Sim and Heng Samrin

Introductory Note

Chea Sim and Heng Samrin led the Khmer Rouge mutiny against Pol Pot's Democratic Kampuchea regime (DK) described in chapter 1. It was a regional rebellion in the Eastern Zone, a response to massive repression by regular troops from the Party Center and DK's Central and Southwest Zones. Killing most of the Eastern Zone CPK leaders within a week, the Center's murder machine quickly turned on the Zone's civilian population of about 1.7 million, massacring over 100,000 easterners, possibly as many as 250,000 by December 1978.[1]

These two surviving party and military officers, both then in their mid-forties and with two decades of membership in the local CPK branch, became the most senior leaders of the armed resistance to Pol Pot's most extensive killings. Since 1970, Chea Sim, a former Buddhist monk of peasant background, had run the rice-growing district of Ponhea Krek, home of more than 30,000 Khmer villagers in Region 20, one of the five regions of the Eastern Zone. By 1978, Sim had also become a junior member of the CPK administration of Region 20, which had a population of over 200,000. Heng Samrin, another former peasant and veteran communist from Ponhea Krek district, had risen through the military ranks to become commander of the 7,000-strong 4th Eastern Zone Division. In 1976, his command brought him additional responsibilities as deputy chief of staff of the Eastern Zone army, which maintained three infantry divisions, and he also became the fifth-ranking member of the Eastern Zone CPK committee.

Neither Chea Sim nor Heng Samrin was a member of the CPK Central Committee or its powerful Standing Committee. But after the 1975 victory, both men attended national political meetings in Phnom Penh. Orders received

---

1.   Further details may be found in Ben Kiernan, *The Pol Pot Regime: Race, Power and Genocide in Cambodia under the Khmer Rouge, 1975-1979*, 2nd ed., New Haven, 2002, 403-23.

there before May 1978, or their local authority in the Eastern Zone, may have led them to commit crimes there, which they inconclusively denied or evaded in these interviews.[2] Their influential regional roles also gave them a significant local following to call upon during the 1978 crisis, and from that point at least, contributed to the eventual resistance to the Pol Pot regime.

After the Vietnamese invasion and overthrow of the Pol Pot regime on January 7, 1979, Heng Samrin and Chea Sim became leaders of the new People's Republic of Kampuchea. Despite my repeated requests, commencing the next year, they long refused to grant interviews. Therefore chapter 1, detailing some of the history of the Eastern Zone resistance, was written a decade before either of them had given an extended account of those events. They did not agree to do so until after the 1991 Paris Peace Agreement on Cambodia. To my knowledge, they committed their stories to record for the first time only in the 1991-92 interviews I have translated here. I was able to interview the two men separately in Phnom Penh on December 2 and 3, 1991, and I re-interviewed Heng Samrin a year later, on December 7, 1992. Their answers to my questions, which I have attempted to arrange here in chronological and thematic order, comprise a primary source on the origins, outbreak, and course of the 1978 revolt, as they recalled it thirteen years afterwards. Each of the men first describes his family background and early political career, then his first-hand observations of CPK Center leaders Pol Pot, Nuon Chea and Son Sen, and of the oppressive and genocidal policies of their regime. Finally, each details his role in the 1978 uprising against it. Their accounts tell us something about the communist discipline and terror that such men were long prepared and obliged to impose and endure, and also about what finally drove them to rebellion, and therefore, about some of the ways in which a genocide may begin and end.

The Eastern Zone rebellion was the largest, but not the only anti-Khmer Rouge opposition movement. In the west, from the Thai side of the border, rightist remnants of the Lon Nol regime and army, and leftist ethnic Thai guerrillas from Cambodia, mounted separate, sporadic operations against Pol Pot troops inside the country, beginning as early as 1974. And in the hills of the northeast, five thousand Cambodian refugees of various ethnic groups who had risen up against Khmer Rouge rule in 1973-75, continued to hold out across the Lao border, joined by 15,000 later arrivals.[3] Local rebellions also broke out in the Cambodian interior.[4] Despite the brutality and unpopularity of the

2.   On the Eastern Zone up to 1978, see also Kiernan, *The Pol Pot Regime*, 14-15, 65-68, 205-10.
3.   Justin Corfield, *A history of the Cambodian non-Communist resistance, 1975-1983*, Monash University Centre of Southeast Asian Studies, Clayton, Vic., Australia, 1991; Kiernan, *Pol Pot Regime*, 68-86, 307.
4.   Margaret Slocomb, "Chikreng Rebellion: Coup and Its Aftermath in Democratic Kampuchea," *Journal of the Royal Asiatic Society*, Series 3, 16:1 (2006), 59-72; Kiernan, *Pol Pot Regime*, 340-48.

Table 2.1
The Democratic Kampuchea Military Chain of Command

Center ('Office 870,' Phnom Penh)

1	Saloth Sar alias Pol Pot	Commander-in-Chief; chair of the Military Commission of the Standing Committee of the Central Committee (CC) of the Communist Party of Kampuchea (CPK)	
2	Son Sen	Deputy Prime Minister, Defence Minister, and member of the CC Standing Committee responsible for Defence and Security	
3	Chhit Choeun alias Mok	Chief of the General Staff, Revolutionary Armed Forces of Democratic Kampuchea (RADK); Commander-in-Chief, Southwest Zone Army	
4	Chan Chakrei	Deputy Chief of the General Staff, RADK; former commander, 1st Eastern Division	arrested May 1976
5	Ke Vin alias Pauk	Deputy Chief of the General Staff, RADK; Commander-in Chief, Central/Northern Zone Army	
6	Ni Kon alias Tith Nath	Deputy Chief of the General Staff, RADK; former commander, 12th Special Zone Division; nephew of Son Sen	
7	Siet Chhe alias Tum	Member of the General Staff, RADK; former CPK Secretary, Region 22, Eastern Zone	arrested April 1977

Eastern Zone Military Command

1	So Phim	CPK Zone Secretary, Commander Zone Army	killed June 1978
2	Seng Hong alias Chan	Zone Deputy Secretary, Zone Deputy Commander	executed 1979
3	Kev Samnang	Chief of the Zone Military Staff	executed 1978
4	Ly Phen	Chief Political Commissar, Zone Armed Forces	executed 1976
5	Heng Samrin	1st Deputy Chief, Zone Military Staff	rebelled 1978
6	Pol Saroeun	2nd Deputy Chief, Zone Military Staff	rebelled 1978
7	Poeu Hak	Commander, 3rd Zone Division	executed 1976
8	Kry	Commander, 3rd Zone Division	executed 1978
9	Phan	Political commissar, 4th Zone Division	executed 1976
10	Heng Kim	CPK Secretary, 4th Zone Division	executed 1978
11	Paen Cheuan	CPK Secretary, 5th Zone Division	executed 1978

Center 'Divisions' (or Brigades):
    164th (ex-3rd Southwest Zone); 170th; 310th (ex-Northern); 450th (ex-Northern); 280th (ex-1st Eastern); 290th (ex-2nd Eastern); 502nd; 703rd; 801st; 920th; 108th (formed 1977 or 1978)
    Regiments: 75th, 152nd, 377th, 488th; 'Battalion for Guarding Office 870' (CPK Center)

Zone Level
    The Zone Command included several battalions of marines and a company of two tanks.

Region Level
    By 1978, each of the five Eastern Regions (numbered 20-24) had one kong pul (division or brigade—three or more regiments), except Region 22 which had one regiment only.

Pol Pot regime, the lightning Vietnamese invasion that overthrew it in December-January 1978-79 could not have progressed so rapidly across Cambodia without the contribution of indigenous rebels and allies who had prepared the political ground.[5]

Interviews with Chea Sim and Heng Samrin

Chea Sim (CS): I was born [November 15, 1932] in Svay Rieng province, in Romeas Hek district, Ampil subdistrict. My parents are dead. My father was Yin Sau, my mother was Pen Nou. We were five brothers and sisters. The oldest was Yin Nu, a sister; the second was my brother Yin Son, who was killed by Pol Pot in 1978; then me, the third; then two other children, Yin Phon, who was also killed by Pol Pot in 1978, and the youngest brother Yin Phun, who was also killed by Pol Pot in 1978. They had been officials in the Pol Pot period.

My parents had five hectares [of farmland] in Svay Rieng. But they came to live [in Krabau subdistrict, in Ponhea Krek district of Kompong Cham province], where my father had six hectares. In all, eleven hectares…. In the 1940s, he had many draft animals; six or eight head of cattle, and as many buffaloes.

Heng Samrin (HS): I am from a peasant family in the countryside, from Ponhea Krek district in Kompong Cham province. My father's name was Song Hém [1882-1954]. My mother was Heng Seng [1912-1992]. I lived in Anlong Chrey village, Kâk subdistrict, in Ponhea Krek district of Kompong Cham. We lived by farming riceland and other cropland. We were peasants without much land. We just cultivated over one hectare, that's all, with a pair of buffalo, a cart, and household belongings. We were poor peasants. I was born [in 1934,]

---

5.   For an analysis of the successful Vietnamese military campaign to overthrow the Pol Pot regime, see Merle L. Pribbenow II, "A Tale of Five Generals: Vietnam's Invasion of Cambodia," *Journal of Military History* 70 (January 2006), 459-86.

the third of eight siblings, four brothers and four sisters. The eldest was Heng Samkai, then Heng Som Uon, then me, then Heng Thal, then my sisters: Heng Suon, Heng Seng, Heng Son, then Heng Khân. I use my mother's surname [Heng].

My parents and relatives joined in the struggle against the French colonialists, supporting the Khmer Issarak ["independent Khmers"]. This was a liberated zone in the time of the struggle against the French imperialists, a zone of the revolutionary bases. My family participated in helping the struggle against the French colonialists. My father was not a soldier, an ordinary civilian, but he helped in the revolutionary struggle.... He died of disease in 1954, a few months after the peace. He was 72.... My mother just died last month, aged 80, on 27 October 1992.

Six siblings are still alive. Two are dead: Heng Thal, who joined the struggle against the U.S. imperialists, and then after liberation became a division commander in the Pol Pot period. But he was arrested and killed by the Pol Pot group. His whole family was also killed, his wife and five children. It's not certain that he was killed in Tuol Sleng prison [S-21, in Phnom Penh]. He was arrested at the front in 1977. My other sibling died of disease, the youngest, Khân, in 1959.... My other younger sisters' husbands were taken and killed in 1977. Only my sisters and their children are left. I lost two brothers-in-law. Their names were Chen Sot, husband of Heng Seng and Region 21 party secretary; his father was called Chen. Heng Son's husband, also dead, was Iv Hot, a soldier. Heng Suon's husband is still alive.

Political Career to 1970

CS: I joined the revolution in 1948 [aged 16], as a messenger in the eastern region. In 1949, I became a monk, until 1954. First I was in Svay Rieng, then I went to study in Kompong Cham, and then came to study at [the leading Phnom Penh monastery] Wat Unnalom, from 1952 to 1954.... During the [independence] struggle in the East; I met [the leaders] Tou Samouth and Chea Soth, with whom I lived and struggled before 1954. I was a monk, but still involved in the movement. Taing Saroeum was another involved in the East. Kim Yin and I were together, and Nuon Sareth, we struggled together. Others were [later] all killed by Pol Pot. I met all these people before I became a monk in 1949.

After the Geneva Conference [in 1954], I stayed in the struggle movement in Phnom Penh. I joined the [Khmer People's Revolutionary] Party in 1959, after a six-month candidacy... I joined the Party in Krabau subdistrict (*khum*), in Komchay Meas district (*srok*) of Prey Veng province. The man who recruited me, Puth Sun, is dead. Heng Samrin joined up in a different place. All four of those with whom I joined are dead.

During the secret struggle in the 1960s – at first [1959-60?] I was party secretary of Kalaing Chreou village (*phum*), the secretary of the party cell of the village. After 1960, I was party secretary of Krabau subdistrict. The subdistrict party branch had fifty members, with cells in each of the eight villages.

The armed struggle began in 1968, I don't remember the month, mid-1968. The orders came from the Center to take up arms. I took to the forest in 1968, 1969–1970. [After] the coup of 18 March [1970] when Lon Nol overthrew Sihanouk and the forces of the struggle movement grew strong, the armed forces also were strong and liberated a majority of the territory in the East and the Northeast. In 1970 I came out of the forest. I lived in Komchay Meas district as before, in Krabau. At that time there were as many as seventy party members in the subdistrict, over 100 in the district. At that time I don't know how many party members there were in the Eastern Zone. I was in charge of one area. I was with [Eastern Zone CPK Secretary] So Phim. I had met him in the struggle before 1954, and after 1954 we also met from time to time.

(What did So Phim think of Vietnam in the 1960s and 1970?) He never had any thoughts with Vietnam, just good contact with it. The struggle was always linked to and supported by the Vietnamese Communist Party. He received a small number of guns from Vietnam from 1968 from the armed struggle. (How many?) Few. At that time our [insurgent] forces were few. In the Eastern Zone in 1968 at the time of the armed struggle there was only one *ko* (company). In 1970 the army grew a great deal, forming battalions, then regiments. At the time of the [March 1970] coup there was still only one company in the Eastern Zone army. The forces grew after that.

In 1970 I became party secretary of Ponhea Krek district, [a position I held] from 1970 to 1978. In the 1960s, there were 100 party members [in the district]; in 1970, 180; in 1975, over 200; and in 1978, 350, of whom fifty were candidate members, and 300 were full rights members. Usually most were full rights, and a minority, candidate members.

HS: I joined the revolution and worked for it from 1959. At that time I was a combatant in the secret [underground], the leader of a struggle group in the bases. I was appointed to the cell committee in a base, leader of the cell. The subdistrict cell had ten-twenty people. In the village, there were more. Later, in 1961, I was made deputy chief of a technical liaison group, to lead people between the Center and the base. There were over ten in the group. The chief in 1961 was *mit* (friend) Pich whose name in the base was Bai, who was also administrative secretary of the Eastern Zone. He was in charge of the technical side, and of the technical courier cell. He lived in the revolutionary base. The Eastern Zone office was mobile; at that time it was in Anlong Kres.

So Phim was tall, stocky, big and strong. About 1.8m. high, dark, with straight black hair....He spoke curtly. He was a soldier from the beginning, since the [1945-54 war]. His background was as a French soldier, a medic for the French. He left to join the resistance. Later as an adult he lived along the Vietnamese border. He came from Prasaut district. During the nine-year struggle he went to Vietnam before everyone else . . .

I joined the Party in 1961. As a poor peasant, I was a candidate member for three months. Middle peasants did six months' candidacy and rich peasants twelve months, according to the Party's statutes. Then it was called the Khmer People's Revolutionary Party.... It did not yet have the [later] name. It was called the Pak Kop, Pak Khop. [Khop] meant the Khmer People's Party; [Kop] the Kampuchean Revolutionary Party, meaning the *Pak Kommunis Kampuchea* [CPK, so named by Pol Pot in 1966]. It had not yet publicized the name Communist Party or People's Party. It was still in the middle, undecided what its name would be. Because at that time there was a party in exile outside the country [Issarak "regroupees" in Hanoi since 1954], and inside the country, they were requesting opinions for a Congress and had not yet fixed the name of the Party. So they used *Pak Khop* and *Pak Kop* after the Second Congress in 1960. The name Khmer People's Revolutionary Party was no longer used.... It was not yet clearly called the Communist Party. From 1961, they appointed something called *Angkar* (the Organization). That meant the vanguard party.

I met Pol Pot in 1962-63. I came to Phnom Penh to take him to the bases, to the regional meeting place for a [party] Congress. For every annual Center congress he went to the base in the region I lived in. All of them, Nuon Chea, Ieng Sary. I came and brought them to every Center meeting, to the base. It was a resistance base and we could assure security there. (Elsewhere) they couldn't have congresses, so they brought (representatives from) every Zone. I was the technical courier, to guide the people from every Zone into this region. So if Pol Pot had any prominence he would have gone, with me as a guide. From here [Phnom Penh] we didn't guide, just rode in the car or whatever ...just a matter of noticing, the car number, road number, the house, such as a house with a sign, there were signs. On arrival at the house we saw each other's faces but didn't speak. Then the car number, on arrival we got in the car, didn't know what kind of a car it was, until we got to the fixed place and got out right there. They got out, we got out, and we led them along the forest tracks. As we walked we got to know one another and they followed our directions. I even gave directions to Pol Pot. We commanded the security, how to walk. We generally walked at night. On arrival at the Region they had the congress; one, two or three months later they'd be finished and I'd take them back.

We didn't even know yet who was the leader; just the collective leadership committee, the collective organization. We didn't know that Pol Pot was the very top leader. We only knew when we created the government and [he became] General Secretary of the Party, in 1975–76. We only knew the Organization, and the names 'Brother No. 1' and 'Brother No 2.' We knew this, but we didn't know what kind of brothers they were. They called this the Organization. It was *very* secretive. Pol Pot was secretary. So at that time he didn't use the name 'Pol Pot,' he used the name 'Pol,' but in the time of political struggle [pre-1967] he didn't use that name, he used a Vietnamese name, 'Hai,' and so on. So they all, the wife of Pol Pot, the wife of Ieng Sary, the wife of Son Sen, Mrs. [Yun] Yat, they came to stay in my Region and lived there.

Later, after the coup [of March 1970], Pol Pot used the name 'Pol,' just that. Nuon Chea used the name 'Nuon.' But my group usually didn't use these names. We called Nuon Chea 'Ta Prahok.' We'd say, 'Eh, I met Ta Prahok', and so on, and they'd know, because the old man ate a lot of *prahok* [Cambodian fish paste]. And they also called him 'Ta Polep Polop.' The old man spoke unclearly, like a Thai, like Ta Sae [Sae Phuthang]. He didn't speak Khmer clearly. But he spoke Thai. That was Nuon Chea.

I don't know what code names Ieng Thirith and Mrs. Yat used, but they all lived in the Region. And this Region, after the coup [of May 25, 1978] they took away and killed all the people in those villages: Bos and Bos Rokar. . .

Right up until 1968 when I took to the forest, I was active between the Center and the Zone bases. I took to the forest because of heavy destruction by [Prince] Sihanouk's Popular Socialist Community (*Sangkum Reas Niyum*) government. [Leftist parliamentarians] Hou Yuon and Hu Nim also took to the forest [in 1967]. The government of Prince Sihanouk was destroying a lot and killing many people. We couldn't keep living in the bases, and had to take to the forest. We received orders from the Zone, saying we couldn't stay because of the destruction, (we had to) go into the jungle. Later it was decided to adopt for the struggle of the whole country, taking to the jungle, to adopt 20th [March] as the day of the commencement of semi-legal combat, of combined armed struggle and political struggle. Taking to the jungle meant taking up arms – bows and arrows, knives, etc. – combined with weapons that we could get by theft from the enemy on a small scale, and take them up, combined with politics. Those who could stay legally in the bases still carried out politics. Those whose cover had been blown, and couldn't live in the bases with the people, took to the jungle to do both politics and armed combat.

On March 20, 1968, we were ordered to go into the forest, after Samlaut. (There was no revolt in the East in 1967 at the time of the Samlaut revolt in the Northwest). At first some 300–400 people took to the forest together, because in the bases, many were uncovered. I was in the base, carrying out revolution-ary political struggle and also legally, I was in the Prince Papa (regime) of the Sangkum Reas Niyum. I was commander of a (government) militia (*chivapol*) division. I had many rifles, in every base. But at the time of the flight into the jungle, they invited me to Ponhea Krek district office, at Krek military base. [Major] Thach Suon wrote a letter to invite me to go to the district office and to Krek base, but I did not. I knew then that to go would be to get arrested. Thach Suon was the major at Banteay Krek. I don't recall who was district chief; they didn't dare come to get me. At that time I had many rifles, over thirty in the vil-lage. Then one month, they sent me a circular to have the village militia send their guns to the district office. But at that time, grasping the general situation at the higher level, I commanded the militia who bore rifles to take them all to the district office. We didn't take the guns into the forest. We didn't dare, for fear that [the government forces] would wreak destruction and persecute the people in the bases. So I gathered all the rifles and had them sent to the district office. But I personally didn't go. Then after the guns had been taken away, I took to the forest. I didn't go far from the village of my birth, but to clearings in the forest, in order to listen. Three days after we'd disarmed, three truckloads of soldiers came to my house to get me and my group. But I was already in the forest; only my wife remained. They asked her, but she replied: "One day a letter came from the district office inviting him to go there. Then he went to the district office and still has not come back." So they didn't have any excuse to mistreat my wife, because the letter had come from the district office inviting me, and she had not seen me since. Thus we threw the accusation back on them. So at that time I escaped into the forest. From then I never dared come back. My wife stayed there in the village throughout. Until then, I had been head of the village militia.

Ten days later they came again to the village. This time they burnt down my house, but did not mistreat my wife. They just burnt down the house, the pair of draught animals, the rice barn with a little rice inside. And then they arrested three young men in the village, killed them, and threw them in a well. And then the anger of the struggle raged, and other youths took to the jungle: six or eight more youths from the village.

The 1970-75 War

CS: (When did you start to realize what Pol Pot's policies were?) We just knew progressively; we were just interested but not deeply aware. Starting in 1972, 1973 we knew something. We could see the arrests of cadres and them disappearing one after another; we considered that there was killing going on. We didn't know what were the reasons. Each of us just thought and worried what day we would be arrested as well. We thought like this all the time.

There was no chance to rebel, just to think. When someone was arrested, we didn't know what they had done wrong. They just disappeared like that. They were said to be going off to study, and would disappear for good. Pol Pot had many tactics to kill people, many legal tactics. Because at that time there were only legal tactics...By calling [people to meetings?] Right up to 1975, when it became increasingly tight.

HS: After the Lon Nol coup [of March 1970], I became a soldier. Before the coup, I was in the office responsible for the [Eastern] Zone hospital. But I was not a technician nor an expert, so I asked to command troops. Before the coup, in 1968, in late 1968 or early 1969, I became chief of a platoon belonging to Region 20, which was then called Section 6. I was Party Secretary of the platoon, of over thirty men. We were active in propagandizing the people in the Region's bases, going from village to village, guarding the propagandists in the bases. Then after the coup I was put in charge of troops formed into an army. I became commander of a company, then commander of the 12th Battalion, in late 1971 and early 1972. Then, in 1973, I became chief of the 126th Regiment of the Zone.

At that time the 126th Regiment was active in Region 25 on the Bassac River, from Prek Eng right downriver. The 1st Division had three regiments: the 126th, 173rd and 160th. The 1st Division had not yet been formed, it was the Front Committee of Region 25. Chakrey was the Front's president. I was deputy president of the Front, and direct commander of the 126th. Chakrey was president and direct commander of the 173rd Regiment. And Saphoeun who commanded the 160th was a member of the Front Committee, as was Chhouk Sau, who was Party Secretary in the regiment, the younger brother of sister Chhouk Chhim...

The Eastern Zone and the Southwest Zone troops wore different uniforms until after [the April 1975] liberation. After liberation, the troops wore different uniforms, khaki, horse-shit color, [provided as] Chinese aid after 1975, in 1976. But before [liberation?], only the East wore them; the other Zones refused to wear military uniforms, they wore all black. Both East and Southwest wore black trousers but the East wore mixed, according to availability. Whatever they had, they wore. In fact my troops wore military uniforms, khaki, mixed with camouflage uniforms that we could get hold of. Wherever they went my troops wore uniforms. But go into the Southwest Zone, and they wore all black.

There was conflict and division between the Eastern Zone and the Southwest Zone since 1973. There was division over Region 25. Prey Krabas district was in the Southwest, and Sa'ang district was in the East, in Region 25. At that time my troops went to climb Mt. Chisor to find traditional medicine to cure troops who had malaria. In 1973, the Southwesterners arrested twelve of my troops and took them away and killed them. I assigned a representative to go and struggle with Mok, the [Southwest] Zone Secretary. There was a confrontation. I had So Phim write a letter to get them to release the troops, but Mok resisted and said he didn't know anything about it, and there was even conflict between Ta Mok and Ta Phim. This was in late 1973. We requested a meeting of representatives of the Zones, for negotiations between the Eastern Zone and the Southwest. They didn't accept or recognize [the issue] and said they didn't know [what happened because] that region was a rebellious region. So when our forces went in, they didn't know whether it was their troops or others who had arrested them. We said it doesn't matter whether they had arrested them or not, but we asked for them to be released and allowed to come back. They said they hadn't released them, but took them away and they disappeared. This meant they'd been taken to be killed. And they disappeared forever. From that time on, my troops who [had been] stationed in Region 25 and in the Southwest Zone, never again crossed the boundary. And they even brought up guns and set up artillery facing us on the border of Region 25 and the Southwest. There was conflict between us. Not fighting but threatening each other. There was even struggle – at that time the Region 25 Secretary was Ta Chey, formerly called Non Suon of the *Pracheachon* newspaper. He worked with my group, no problem, but he was not in accord with their side. Mok and Chey were not very friendly.

Before the liberation [of Phnom Penh on April 17, 1975], there was a plan meeting of the Center. I didn't go personally to the meeting to hear the plan. Chakrey went. At the meeting the plan was announced to attack and liberate Phnom Penh, and then to evacuate the people out of Phnom Penh temporarily. So it was not yet official but [the plan was] to evacuate the people temporarily from Phnom Penh. This meeting was three days after the liberation of Neak Leung [April 1]. Chakrey went to receive the plan. I don't know where the Center had accepted the plan; this was the Zone (level). And at that time, according to information that was reported, Hou Yuon, during the time of the [earlier] Center meeting when the plan was announced to evacuate the people, Hou Yuon struggled against it, got up and said it was not the right situation to evacuate the people from the cities. Then Pol Pot accused Hou Yuon of not agreeing to implement the plan of the Center. That was a few days after the liberation of Neak Leung [that I heard about it?]. From that time on, Hou Yuon disappeared forever. And immediately after the liberation of Neak Leung, Hou Yuon [also] made a report in support of the troops who had liberated Neak Leung. That was right afterwards. But later, from when we received the plan from the Center to liberate Phnom Penh, Hou Yuon disappeared from that time. Chakrey told me about this when he came back to the front from the meeting. He didn't say this openly, but secretly.

The 1st Division fought hardest and drove deeply, in the Highway 1 region and along the Mekong downriver right to the border, and was very active… The liberation of Neak Leung involved this Division, and my 126th Regiment fought and liberated Neak Leung from east and west and on the water, to liberate it on April 1, 1975. I liberated Neak Leung from the east and the west. Then I was ordered to send my troops to go and fight into Phnom Penh, but that did not involve strong fighting. At that time the Lon Nol soldiers rallied to us, and let the troops go through.

On 17 April at 9 A.M., I arrived at the Independence Movement [in Phnom Penh]. After liberation there was a division of responsibility among three divisions from the East. There was my 1st Division, my younger brother's [Heng Thal's] 2nd, and Chhien's 3rd Division, who fought up to Chrui Changvar with marines. The 2nd Division fought its way up to opposite Arey Khsat, and my 1st Division, along Highway 1 and the road from Takhmau, into Phnom Penh. These were the three thrusts from the East.

After liberation the responsibility for guarding the big road was divided: from Wat Phnom right this way along the white line, the Eastern divisions were on that side, Ta [Mey?] Chhôn on that. Because at that time there was the Special Zone, a Special Zone with Vorn Vet as Secretary and Son Sen as Deputy Secretary. It had two divisions: Nath's 12th Division (Nath was later called [Ni] Kon), and Saroeun's 11th. The 12th, Nath's division, was all women. [The capital] was divided between us, and on their side, only women stood guard. And my troops on that side crossed over the white line to the west, their territory, and they would stop us. If we insisted they would arrest us. I worked to get releases, to bargain and resolve this; they took many of my group. So on that side of the road, you couldn't come to this side. It was divided up right from that time on.

Relations with Vietnamese Communists, 1970-75

CS: We heard it said that Vietnam was an enemy, all over the place, bit by bit. From 1971. Pol Pot said it. In 1971 Pol Pot's language reached that level. He said there was conflict between Cambodia and Vietnam. But at that time the conflict was not yet antagonistic. It was [labeled] an internal conflict between Cambodia and Vietnam. It was only Pol Pot and Nuon Chea who said this, in speeches to political schools. From 1970 on. In 1970 I studied at the Sen River, in the Northern Zone, for a month. It was a national school for district and Region [party] secretaries.

In 1971, 1972, 1973, and 1974, I studied [at the Sen River] for a month each year… Usually I went each November, near the end of the year. Pol Pot gave his view of the situation of relations with Vietnam. In 1970 and 1971, he spoke of conflict between Cambodia and Vietnam, but that conflict was one that could be resolved; it had not yet become an antagonistic conflict. Then in 1973, Pol Pot explained that the conflict between Cambodia and Vietnam was increasing. From 1970 to 1973 the conflict was increasing but had not yet become antagonistic. In 1975, it was said to have become antagonistic.Because at that time the Vietnamese residents were expelled from Cambodian territory. So it became antagonistic.

HS: In 1973, Pol Pot was not happy with Vietnam signing the Agreement to End the War in South Vietnam, at the Paris Conference [January 27, 1973]. He accused Vietnam of taking the opportunity to weaken the Cambodian revolution at that time. He stirred up anger against Vietnam from then, saying that it did not want the Cambodian revolution to liberate [the country, and that it] slowed its struggle activities. So they talked about the struggle movement, they spoke about and stirred up anger between Vietnam and Kampuchea in history, from [the early nineteenth-century story,] "Don't Spill the Master's Tea." They started talking about that from 1973, about Vietnam as the hereditary enemy (*setrew sourpouch*), but they just educated internally about this, not yet educating deeply among the people. After the signature [of the Paris Agreement], other Zones attacked Vietnam, most importantly the Southwest. The East did not find fault with Vietnam. Vietnam withdrew [its troops from Cambodia] in 1973. But in 1973 and 1974 there was fighting with Vietnam in the Southwest and in some Zones. And there was also struggle from 1974 on. We inside Cambodia were struggling, we saw that Pol Pot had [given] a sign that he was not in agreement with the struggle of the Cambodian revolution at that time. So there was struggle in certain places. Most important, the earliest struggle to resist Pol Pot was in 1974 in Koh Kong [province] in the Southwest, where [Center forces] arrested and killed cadres from 1973 and 1974. They arrested and killed the leaders in the Southwest Zone. In 1973 [Eastern Zone CPK Secretary] So Phim didn't say anything (about Vietnam); he just said that he still had contact [with the Vietnamese] because Vietnam still had advisers in the Zone, right up to 1973-74…

[Pol Pot] had talked about carefully screening internal agents in the Party, who had come into the CPK from all backgrounds, from America, France, Thailand, and Vietnam. They had mixed in… It was in 1973 when he said this. He said we were most interested in the Party members who came from Vietnam, among the Khmer party members from foreign countries. Khmers who lived abroad and joined the Thai party, came [back] from Thailand. There was a party from France, and one from America. And there was a party from Vietnam, and a party inside the country. So they were counted together as one party with a congress to establish a party leadership. Of those from abroad, of most interest were those who came from Vietnam. Especially those troops mustered in 1954 to regroup north [to North Vietnam]. Pol Pot said this in documents. I was not there myself. I read them myself in *Tung Padevat* ["Revolutionary Flags," the CPK monthly internal magazine]. I was still in the army fighting. There were *Tung Padevat,* and *Tung Yuvachon* and *Renaksei* ["Youth Flag" and "The Front"].

The May 20, 1975 Meeting in Phnom Penh

HS: Immediately after the liberation there was a meeting in order to receive the plan distributed from the Center…. It was for the whole country, not just for one division. It included both military and civil (officials). At the time [representatives of] all Zones from throughout the country came to the meeting to receive the plan from the Center, from Pol Pot. That was on 20 May [1975], which we commemorate now as the Day of Hatred, the day the Pol Pot plan was fixed for general distribution, to implement the political plan inside and outside the country at the time Pol Pot announced it. So we have now taken May 20 as the Day of Hatred, as history.

The meeting was in Phnom Penh, at the Sports Stadium. To receive the plan for implementing the policies, not to circulate money, don't do that, evacuate the people from the cities. At that time, immediately after liberation it was declared that the people were to be evacuated temporarily, for fear that American planes would drop bombs. So the people were evacuated into the environs of the city, not yet to distant regions. Then after receiving the plan on [May] 20th, the people were evacuated to the remote countryside, out of the cities. From that time on, they were evacuated forever, not allowed to live in cities again. From the time that the plan was received on the 20th, the people were evacuated further again. It was Pol Pot who personally distributed this plan at the meeting for representatives of cadres from the entire country, at the Sports Stadium. He said don't use money, don't let the people live in the cities, and various political standpoints. There were many political standpoints: don't allow people to do anything at all, evacuate all the various [foreign] embassies, gather them up and remove them, don't let them be here, the ambassadors that were in Phnom Penh before liberation, such as the French, etc, many [others]. And after receiving the announced plan they evacuated all the ambassadors so that there were none in the country, none stationed in Cambodia any more…

On 20 May (1975) it was the general plan. There were Pol Pot and Nuon Chea who made speeches about the documents, and put the plan to the national meeting. They held this conference in order to distribute the plan. It was Pol Pot and Nuon Chea who did the speaking about the plan. There were many people in the audience, representatives from all over the country. Thousands of people, from all districts and regions, district and region [party] secretaries came from all over the country. And representatives from all armed forces and units and regions. So there were thousands… It was a conference in order to distribute and plan, after liberation, and then implement the plan. There was no mention of closing schools and hospitals. They spoke of the plan. Importantly, they said: "Our system here does not have money in circulation." At first there was money, provisionally. But then when they had put out the plan not to circulate money, they threw money away. This was the plan, the big plan, not to circulate money. But they didn't talk of closing schools.

[Buddhist] monks, they said, were to be disbanded, put aside as "special class." At first in the struggle they divided (society) into classes; peasants, the petty bourgeoisie, capitalists, feudalists. There were five classes. And the special class were the monks, the most important to fight. They had to be wiped out (*lup bombat*). Pol Pot and Nuon Chea said this, (before and) on the day of May 20, when they were distributing the plan for general implementation after liberation. I heard Pol Pot say this myself at the general meeting....He said no monks were to be allowed, no festivals were to be allowed any more, meaning "wipe out religion" (*lup sasana*). Religion was not to be allowed, meaning that communists did not allow religion. This was Pol Pot's view of communism. They would wipe it out and not allow any religion. So they caught all the monks and disrobed them. In every *wat* there were no monks. Pol Pot and Nuon Chea had no differences about this. Clearly the same, no difference. Mostly Nuon Chea did the talking. Nuon Chea was the one who did the consciousness work, the propaganda, all the documents and so on; only the very special documents would be introduced by Pol Pot, any document that was special. But beside those, it was Nuon Chea who spoke on all the documents. The consciousness work was Nuon Chea's alone.

In general Pol Pot spoke little, and [only] about big general principles. Important things were disseminated by Nuon Chea, whether about monks, that wats would not be allowed, about the need to evacuate Vietnamese residents from Cambodia back to their country and so on, and that the circulation of money was not allowed. All these views were mostly distributed by Nuon Chea. While he was speaking, the two of them were right there together presiding side by side, but only Nuon Chea spoke about the documents. Pol Pot was the listener. Pol Pot did not have many personal opinions, only about any special documents that were important, then Pol Pot spoke; apart from them, Nuon Chea was the one.

The special questions were principles, big questions of the line, principles, lines, vanguard views, the path to socialism, great leaps forward, great whatevers, these were big general principles. So in the case of a document, Nuon Chea was the one who opened it up. As to what methods were to be used, it was Nuon Chea who announced this.

They didn't say kill [the defeated Lon Nol regime's leaders]. They said scatter (*komchat*) the former government officials. Scatter them away, don't allow them to remain in the framework; it doesn't mean "smash" (*komtec*). Nuon Chea used this phrase. *Komtec* means "kill" but they used the general word, *komchat*. Nuon Chea talked of wiping out markets, not allowing money. If there were markets and money, there was property. The important, heavy pressure was against property. If there was money there were markets, and if there were markets there would be people with money, and those people would have property. So they wanted to wipe out property. Not allow private property to exist.

They spoke a little about minorities. They spoke in categories. The Vietnamese foreign residents were not allowed in Kampuchean territory. This was a general principle, not just after the day of liberation, but since 1973. After Vietnam had signed the Agreement at the Paris Conference, they [the CPK] had already gathered up Vietnamese residents who lived in Cambodia and sent them away to Vietnam. After the liberation [of 1975], those who remained had to (go). Even those who stayed the longest of all, Vietnamese wives of Khmer husbands, had to go. Those who did not go were killed. They even killed them. They started to kill them in 1976. It was not Pol Pot and Nuon Chea who ordered this, it was [cadres at] the implementing level who said this. They even ordered husbands to kill their own wives who were Vietnamese. This happened, but it happened little. Some who were quick, decided that when they were evacuating they couldn't be separated from their children and wives, so they all went together. They were themselves Khmer but went with their wives out of sentiment. Because if they didn't go there would be difficulty. If the wife stayed she would be killed, and if they killed the wife and children it would be hard for the husband to live with. And they even went so far as to kill those of us who were attached to their wives and children.

So at that time there was very strong consciousness. This was what they (*puok via*, i.e. the CPK Center) commanded. Concerning other nationalities, or Khmers who had been living abroad, they were clearly divided up on the basis of their tendencies, and [Khmer] people who came from every place and from the important countries, France, America, Thailand, and Vietnam. And the important ones whom they looked after most of all: the ones who came from Vietnam. (Who said this?) Pol Pot and Nuon Chea said this. On the 20th [May 1975] and before, they said this. They divided people up. After liberation every category [of?] the CPK, every category of the people that joined to work in the struggle, they divided up into those who came from France, America, Canada, international countries, from Thailand, etc., and from Vietnam. And it was important to look after Vietnam or those who came from Vietnam. (What did "look after" mean?) "Have to look after" means, so that they killed all the people who came from the north [Vietnam], who had gone to study in the north and come back. "Look after" means kill them. "Look after this group" means a group that resists their Communist Party. The ones from the north, meaning the ones from Vietnam, when we Khmer [Issarak resistance fighters] were disbanded after the [1954] Geneva Conference, some went to study in Vietnam. And so now when these came back [after 1970], they [*puok via*] killed them all. The only survivors were those who did not come and those who escaped back [to Vietnam]. All the ones who stayed within the country were killed. Like the leaders from that [Issarak] period, Keo Meas, Keo Moni etc., they were all killed. They were accused of being spies for Vietnam and the KGB, meaning Soviet, they had to be looked after with interest. Anyone with Soviet and Vietnamese tendencies, they were interested in killing.

[1992: Last year you said that on 20 May 1975 there was a meeting in Phnom Penh. Where was it?] In the Sports Stadium in Phnom Penh. Not in the Assembly. A number of days after the liberation, they declared the 20th [May] a Center meeting. I was there. I was living in Phnom Penh at the time. Chea Sim had come from his district, and didn't know Phnom Penh so well, and he was still a civilian. It was only the army that prepared things. So the meeting was definitely at the Olympic Stadium, and the school was opened at the Olympic Stadium.

CS: It was a national meeting. The secretaries of every district, the secretaries of every Region and Zone [attended]. I can't remember how many people but there were hundreds… Every district secretary from the Eastern Zone was there.

I came from Ponhea Krek the day before the meeting. From Tonle Bet we took a ferry [across the Mekong and on to Phnom Penh]… The night before, I slept at the [former Khméro-Soviet] Technical University, on the road west to Tuol Kork…. There are two buildings, with a walkway linking them. There is a meeting hall there. That's where we slept, hundreds of us. On 20 May the proceedings began at 8 A.M. The program lasted five days, ending on May 25.

The meeting took place at the Techno, in the meeting hall. Nuon Chea spoke first, on the first day, then Pol Pot on the second day.

At first [Nuon Chea] spoke about the line and principles of building social-ism in Kampuchea. Nuon Chea said that building socialism in Kampuchea consisted of two parts, agriculture and industry. Agriculture he said would be modernized in ten to fifteen years by means of scientific methods by preparing irrigation dams and canals all over the country. And these dams and canals had to be started in the coming year, 1976. Industry would be modernized in a similar period of ten to fifteen years.

And the second question: in order to achieve the construction of socialism progressively and advance all together towards modernization in the period set, we must take care to carefully screen internal agents in the Party, in the armed forces, in the various organizations and ministries, in the government, and among the masses of the people. We have to carefully screen them. Nuon Chea said this. He spoke of "the line of carefully screening internal agents to make them good and pure, in order to implement the line of building socialism so that it advances to modernization by new scientific technology in the period that we mentioned." In 1976, start to build irrigation dams and canals throughout the country. This was a big offensive, concerted, simultaneous, and nationwide.

The concerted action was to start on January 1, 1976, the start of the offen-sive to raise earthworks. At that time the people were harvesting, or in some places had completed the harvest. They started. In general, immediately after the harvest, the offensive to raise earthworks began throughout the country. In Ponhea Krek district where I was in charge, we had 15,000 hectares to make into a checkerboard. Each ricefield was to be a one hectare square.

At the time of Nuon Chea's speech [on May 20, 1975], the people had all been evacuated from Phnom Penh. (Temporarily?) After the 17th April, the orders from the Center were to evacuate the people temporarily. After liberation, they said it was for fear that American planes would come and bomb, creating danger for the people who were in the city. It was for a short period. Then the people would be allowed back. This was declared on the radio.

Later they just sent people on and distributed them permanently. They didn't announce it, but just sent people on. And during the departure from Phnom Penh, they started to kill, step by step. Any family that protested a little, they would take them and kill them. These were the orders. From after 17 April when they were evacuating people from Phnom Penh, their killings began bit by bit. They considered that protest like that, meant that the people were determined not to agree to implement the orders. They killed them.

(Mr. Mat Ly told me that when Pol Pot and Nuon Chea spoke on 20 May, they made eight points.) That's right, eight points. Earlier I spoke to you very briefly just about generalities, about the big principles, that's all. Because Mr. Mat Ly was there too, that day. (I spoke with Mr. Sin Song. He was not there. He told me that there were eight points. Mat Ly has eight points too, but they are slightly different.) Yes, because some things have been forgotten. Please read the 8 points to me. (Mr. Sin Song said [the eight points were]:

1. Evacuate the people from the cities
2. Close markets
3. Abolish money
4. Defrock all monks
5. Kill the leaders of the Lon Nol government
6. Create high-level cooperatives
7. Expel the Vietnamese minority
8. Send troops to the borders.)

Yes, that's right there were many issues. Before I just mentioned the big principles, [which] were in order to do these things....This number of points was the same.

(Did they talk about closing the schools?) Closing markets (schools [too]?) Schools were still teaching, but they were as a rule used for different purposes, for warehouses etc.... There was learning, but only a little. Not much education. (Were hospitals closed too?) The hospitals were still in Phnom Penh, but all closed. Only one here (was open).

At first Nuon Chea spoke, then Pol Pot. Pol Pot spoke like Nuon Chea, just similar. Pol Pot spoke a lot about the question of Vietnam. He stressed the importance of the issue of evacuating all of the Vietnamese people out of Cambodian territory. Just like the point mentioned above. But I spoke earlier about the big lines and principles: this was a specific concrete question of theirs that had to be done. Something that came from their socialist line that had to be carried out. How to resolve certain problems was within the list of eight points. The eight points are authentic.

(Did Pol Pot speak of killing people, or did he never use the word "kill"?). Concerning Pol Pot, it is difficult for us to understand. We saw Pol Pot's behavior and heard his words, and he did not seem to us to be a killer. He seemed kindly.... He did not speak very much, just smiled and smiled. He spoke little. And his words were light, not strong. In general, you would estimate that Pol Pot was a kindly person, simple, with a mass view. But his methods were confrontational – just a killer. Nuon Chea's behavior was somewhat coarse, different from Pol Pot's. People say he is a little [more] cruel; his behavior is stronger. And Pol Pot, people [would] praise him as the kindliest person of all...

I met Khieu Samphan. People considered Khieu Samphan as a kindly person. But seeing that he killed people, they say he is strong. He was a kind person, but his orders to kill people were strong ! He was considered kindly! Because these orders all came from Pol Pot. Whatever anyone did, it was on orders.

The orders came in sections. For instance, from the Center an order went to the Zone. And the Zone gave orders on.... The document [with the orders] from the Center stayed with the Zone. The East put out its order, and so on. ("Circular 870"?) I received some of these circulars progressively. There were some orders that I received. The important orders were in the economic field – three tonnes [of rice per hectare], six tonnes, etc.

We saw that the aim at that time was the line of careful screening (of people). This was a very important order to kill. Because their careful screening was to take all measures so that people had purity (*peap borisot*). The line laid down had to be followed at all costs.... If (people) could not do it they would be taken away and killed. This was called the line of careful screening. It came out in concrete specifics in the eight points mentioned by Mr. Mat Ly. These came from the big lines, the strategic principles. Socialist construction can only succeed under the line of careful screening of internal agents. These words "carefully screen" were the killing principle. (When did you start to hear those words?) "Careful screening" was said strongly on May 20 [1975] at the school, which put out the line of careful screening. It was to be done.

(Did you ever meet Pol Pot's wife [Khieu Ponnary]?) I never met her, but Pol Pot's wife studied in 1975 at the Olympic Stadium, she came to study as well. Ieng Sary's and Son Sen's wives [Ieng Thirith and Yun Yat] studied there too. (After 1975 did you ever meet Pol Pot's wife again?) After 1975 we didn't meet during study sessions, we met occasionally, passing each other in Phnom Penh, we met once in a while at places of work. In 1976, she seemed a little silly. She had no children or grandchildren. There is some scattered information, I don't know if it's true or not, just heard it all over through others, that his wife resisted Pol Pot.... She had no children. And she was a lot older than Pol Pot. She was old, with white hair. Don't know if she is dead or not. My memory is not as good as documents.

(Have you ever heard Pol Pot speak about retaking the territory of Kampuchea Krom ["Lower Cambodia," i.e. the Mekong Delta of Vietnam]?) I didn't hear clearly, just through others. In his speeches he didn't speak clearly about Kampuchea Krom. He didn't go as far as talking about taking back the territory. He just said that the territory of Kampuchea Krom was Cambodian territory. He started to say this a lot from 1975. At the meeting on 20 May 1975, he spoke about this but not much. He said it had been Cambodian territory in the past. Pol Pot said this personally. I didn't hear it again, just through others.

(At that time did they talk of sending troops to the borders to attack Vietnam, or not yet?) Not yet. That was a separate order. (In what year?) Late 1976, 1977. The end of 1976. (Did you see the order?) There was an order. An order to attack in the Southwest, to attack Vietnam. The order came through the Eastern Zone. When I saw this order I was in Ponhea Krek. I was in Ponhea Krek right up until the coup of 25 May 1978.

After 1975

CS: I came to Phnom Penh for big meetings and to study. So from 1975, I came to study in Phnom Penh in 1975, 1976, 1977, three times, 1½ months each time. (And the first time was May 1975?) That was a meeting. And I also studied in 1975, at a school for the [party] secretaries of all districts throughout the country. The teachers were Nuon Chea and Pol Pot. It was in November, at the end of the year. That was at the Olympic Stadium. 700 people were there. The documents were not different from the 20th of May. The important points were the move to construction of cooperatives, from low-level to high-level cooperatives. They talked a lot about that. I was there for 1½ months. In 1976 I came only for one month, at the Sports Stadium. In 1977, it was also for one month, November, at the Sports Stadium. They said the same things. Nuon Chea and Pol Pot were always in agreement. As one; a single principle.

The November 1975 (school) was for district secretaries from all districts in the country, and Region secretaries. For the structure included districts, Regions, Zones and the Center. Four levels. Apart from them there were only subdistricts and villages. They did not come. Only district secretaries or higher came: district secretaries, Region secretaries, members of Zone (committees).

The year 1976 was tight. In 1977 when I went to study at the Sports Stadium, we were frisked even down to our pens. They turned them around and inspected them. They even took out the insides, everything. So in 1977 they didn't trust us, and checked us very firmly. And when I went to study in 1977, I just worried if I would ever get back [to Ponhea Krek]. Or would I be kept here this time? On arriving back I was so happy. But I still worried what day.... Sometimes my close friends would be arrested and disappear. And I would just wonder if they would connect them to me or not? Oh, our private thoughts went around and around. We didn't know where we dared to go. We just went.

I was secretary of Ponhea Krek district until 1978, and a member of the Region (20) Committee, [though] not a member of the Region Standing Committee. The following were members: Sun, Region Secretary, who was killed by Pol Pot in 1978. Not Puth Sun, just Sun. His original name was *Khim*. A former student, born in Kampot, he went to the Eastern Zone in 1966. The Region deputy secretary was Kuong Sokun, also called Tui, now dead. The third member is still alive: Keo Sin, in Kompong Chhnang. The fourth is dead, I forget his name. These were the four members of the Standing Committee [of Region 20]. There were five other members of the (Region) Committee. I was a full rights member and the other district secretaries were candidate members: the district secretaries of Kanchriech, Komchay Meas, Mesang and Prey Veng. And Sim Ka, a Region cadre, who was a member of the Region committee. He was head of the Region office. I don't know the population of Region 20.

HS: About three days [after the meeting in May 1975?] I received orders from higher up in the Zone, to withdraw two divisions, the 3rd and 2nd, back to the East, to the rear. This left only the 1st Division, just mine, still guarding [the capital] from Wat Phnom right to Chbar Ampeou down to Prek Eng. Then after staying three months they [also] had my division leave the Division command for Chbar Ampeou, and the troops went to Prek Eng, to grow rice at

Beng Snao. And of all the equipment in Phnom Penh, they did not allow the division to take any at all, except hoes. Even the division combatants who had carried monosodium glutamate or even toothpaste, anything over two bundles, they took one away and let you take only one. As for hoeheads, if you had ten, they would praise you, saying "that's good, go ahead." They were so strict then. They wouldn't allow the troops to take anything at all from Phnom Penh. So my troops withdrew on their own, to go and grow rice…. As for me personally, after three months I had to withdraw back to the East. In that three months I did a lot of work. . .

After liberation they reassigned that Front Committee as the 1st Division. At that time I was still with Son Sen. He had meetings, and divided us into groups. I took part in activities with Son Sen. He didn't say much. [To me] he just spoke about education, about building the army, technical military matters. Because I was in the army, not in the state authority. This was important, but I was aware only of the general principles and general plans, and I knew in detail only about the military. The building of the army, making the army tough and strong in order to defend the country and the motherland. He didn't yet talk about sending troops to the borders.

[Two Eastern divisions were] reassigned to the Center. Reassigned were Chakrey, Chhouk Sau, and another whose name I forget, from the 1st Division committee. The 1st, which had fought into Phnom Penh, became the 280th. Later the 2nd changed its name to the 290th. These became Center divisions, belonging to Pol Pot directly. These divisions were not equal in size, not full, meaning the framework of a division, with all equipment; they were just infantry divisions. They had no motorized equipment then. In a division there were three regiments, each of three battalions. There were 1,500-2,000 men per regiment. Some divisions comprised 7–8,000 men, with 5–6,000 combat-ready. [There should] be vehicles, artillery, everything – a division would number 10,000 forces on paper. But in fact they were less; then we had no vehicles, tanks, or artillery, only infantry… The 2nd [290th] Division's base remained at Neak Leung, its command post, in 1975-77. The command post of the 1st [280th] was at Chbar Ampeou.

Then after three months in Phnom Penh here, following liberation, I was sent back to the East…. The Center did not take me. The three they rejected were me, Kry and Kim, from the [1st] Division. The Center did not take us and sent us back to the Eastern Zone…. Then after I got back to the East, the 1st Division was destroyed, [its officers, including Chakrei] arrested. If I had still been in that division, I don't know what would have become of me…. And it was this 1st Division that Pol Pot [had] praised highly, in the fighting…

I left Phnom Penh in June 1975, for Prey Veng city. After I returned to the bases,… at first I was chief of the [3rd?] Division…. Right after liberation, after the Center took the two others, only one Eastern division remained, the 3rd, comprising 5–6,000 troops. It was about the same size as the 1st and 2nd; the

1st had the most, 6,000–7,000 men…. Later, in the East they created two more divisions, the 4th and 5th…. These were not called *kong pul thom* (division) or *kong pul touc* (brigade), just *kong pul*…. They were not new, [but] assembled from independent battalions, and from district and province forces. First the 4th division was created, with 8,000 men, in early 1976. I commanded that division myself…. In early 1976 I went to command the 4th along Highway 7, at Krek, the 4th Division's command base. It was responsible for all of Highway 7. From early 1976 to 1978 I was at Krek, not Prey Veng. The division patrolled Highway 7.

In the 4th Division there were three regiments, plus a heavy artillery regiment to make up the division. The fourth was a support regiment, with intelligence, artillery, even tanks. But at that time we had no tanks. We had 105mm. [artillery pieces], two or three of them. We had whatever we could get after the victory. The 4th Division had the most. Its regiments were called the 65th, 67th, and 68th. The support regiment was the 50- somethingth. A regiment's strength at that time was 1,500-2,000, up to 2,000 men. A battalion had 400 to 500…. My [4th] Division had only infantry and artillery, no tanks, and only one 105mm. artillery,… According to the plan [division strength] was fixed at 10,000… but it had only 6-8,000 combat-ready troops.

In early 1976, after the creation of the 4th Division, I [also] became deputy chief of the Eastern Zone military staff. The Zone congress selected me and also brought me into the leading [CPK] Zone Committee…. At that time the Zone organizations were responsible for both political and military matters. As a military (official) I was also a member of the Zone Committee, as well as deputy chief of the Zone military staff and chief of the 4th Division…. Later, in early 1977, another Division was created, the 5th, with only about 5,000 [eastern] troops; the other [two] divisions were all easterners…Kim, deputy chief of the 4th Division, took command of the 5th. Kry became deputy chief of the 4th…. These were the Zone forces, three divisions under direct (Zone) command…

The Eastern Zone had had tanks since early 1976. The 4th Division had none. [Tanks were deployed] at the Zone level only. There were twenty tanks, all booty from the U.S.: M-113's, with tracks, small tanks. They had been taken from Lon Nol's army, and sent from Phnom Penh to the provinces [in early 1976]…. The Zone had only 105 mm. artillery… [and] few trucks, even Chinese ones. They were mostly booty, U.S. GMC's. The 4th Division had only five GMC trucks, the 3rd and 5th about the same. But the 5th was created later and had no booty trucks, only new Chinese ones. At most, five trucks. . .

Then there were the Region (*damban*) forces. There were five Regions, 20 to 24. Some had two regiments, some had two incomplete regiments. The smallest force was that of Region 22, which had two incomplete regiments, over one regiment…. The Region regiments had 1,500 to 2,000 men. They were numbered. I can't remember the numbers, e.g. 500th. Then there were the district (*srok*) forces. A district had two companies. One district company had at most 115–130 [troops]. In some districts they had only 70-80, but the official strength was 130. Some districts had two companies, some one; I don't recall which. The subdistricts (*khum*) had militia, just ten—twenty troops. The security forces (*santesok*) were separate. These were for guarding the villages. Villages had no militia because we already had cooperatives at subdistrict level [from 1977].

The Zone forces comprised three divisions of 8,000, 6,000, and 5,000, for a total of 20,000, and the Regions had up to two regiments each (some under strength) for a total of 15,000. Regular troops consisted of the Zone and Region forces only.

Districts had two companies averaging 100 troops, i.e. 200 for each of the thirty districts [in the Eastern Zone], for a total of 6,000.... District forces had no salary or support...like [the population of] the cooperatives. They were not in the armed forces, [but] part of the cooperatives. Subdistrict troops were not a standing army; they had no guns, but were just sentries.

(How many Party members were in the Eastern Zone army?) Many, but I can't say how many. At that time there was a divisional party committee, cells, committees down to the bases, cells in each company, and sub-cells in each platoon. The Party led.... If you wanted to know who was a cadre, slightly cleaner clothes was a sign. And a pistol. A pistol was worn in a sling by cadres from company commander up. So if you want to know if someone was a cadre, they just had to have a pistol.... And officers from battalion commander up were called *Ta* (elder, or grandfather). When they called someone 'Ta,' he was high-ranking. Even if younger, his elders still called him 'Ta.'

The task of the army was to defend security in the frontier bases, especially to defend the frontier and the bases. At that time we received plans from the Center, from high levels, just to engage in production after liberation, to grow rice, to support ourselves and under no circumstances to ask the population for anything. The army had to support itself. Work hard to grow rice and plant other crops to support itself. This was the orders to the army. So we worked hard and in my division we planted crops and vegetables and gave some to the people to eat as well. But when the people grew rice collectively, the Center fixed to take the rice from the people. The people went without.

The Rural Cooperatives

CS: Ponhea Krek district had a population of over 30,000 by 1970. In 1975, evacuees came from both Phnom Penh and Kompong Cham city. Over 10,000 [urban] people came to live in Ponhea Krek district, [making a] total of over 40,000. The people evacuated in 1975, wherever they came from, were all called "new people" (*pracheachon thmei*). Sometimes they were called "the 17 April" [1975] people. The locals were called the "old people" (*pracheachon cas*). (Later there were three divisions?) Yes. Later they established full-fledged cooperatives throughout the country.

That was called cooperativization. Cooperatives were first established in 1974 before liberation of the whole country, when there were (still) only liberated zones. These cooperatives were of two types: big and small. Sometimes they were called low-level, and other times, big and small cooperatives. There were many stages. I can explain a little. They established [only] low-level cooperatives at first. These had ten to fifteen families, of people who joined the low-level cooperatives. As for the family's farmland that went into the cooperative, it did not all go into the low-level cooperatives. If a family had three hectares (ha.), two ha went into the cooperative, leaving one ha private. This was called a low-level cooperative. Or if there was two ha, 1 ha went into the cooperative, leaving 1 ha as private property.

Then with liberation in 1975, there were both low-level and high-level co-operatives. They started to create high-level cooperatives with twenty to thirty families each. And all the land went in, with none left over as private property. All land and draft animals went into the cooperative.

There were still some low-level cooperatives. I want to talk about the low-level cooperatives a bit. The land left to private property was (still) all for the private interests. But as for the land put into the cooperative, part of the production was kept for the cooperative, and part was divided up for family property. This was in the low-level cooperatives…. At that time there was not yet communal eating; produce was distributed daily to each person as rations.

In 1976, all the low-level cooperatives were transformed into high-level ones, big cooperatives…All the land went in, all the cattle and buffaloes went in. And the production of the cooperative all stayed in the communal granary, under the control of the cooperative…. Each village or subdistrict became a single cooperative. There were some subdistrict-sized cooperatives, but in general they were village-sized. In these all the people ate collectively. Pots and pans were all collected, and the cattle, buffaloes and land were all in the cooperative. This happened in 1976. The whole country consisted of high-level cooperatives with communal eating. Everything was communal. Small villages had one communal kitchen; large villages had two. At mealtime they beat a gong. When they were collecting all the pots and pans to put into the collective, people said one day this goes, the next that goes. There was simply less and less. The people fell into poverty bit by bit…

When the high-level cooperatives were established, the people were divided into three categories: full rights, candidates, and deportees (*pracheachon phni-aer*)…The full rights people were the old people who had lived in the villages and bases since before [April 1975]. And the candidates were people who had been in the [defeated] government, had been subdistrict chiefs, district chiefs or soldiers and had left [the government side] since 1970, and also lived in the bases. These were called candidates. And the deportees were the people who left the cities on 17 April…

Ponhea Krek district had 15,000 ha. [of farmland]. The orders from the Center were to divide the land into two categories, that which could produce six tonnes [of rice] per hectare, and land which could produce 3 tonnes. Therefore the slogan was "from 3 to 6 tonnes." This was repeated constantly from 1976. On this land of six tonnes (productivity per ha.), we had to gather mobile work brigades (*kong chalat*) comprising the young men and women, and establish camps to grow rice at yields fixed at six tonnes per hectare. A district could have one to three camps, depending on whether it was big or small.

The six-tonne land comprised about 30 percent (of the 15,000 ha in Ponhea Krek district). The three-tonne land made up 70 percent. But we could not get six and three tonnes per hectare! On some land we got 1.3 tonnes, on good land in some places we got three tonnes, and some land produced 2.3 tonnes, but the majority got 1.2 to 1.3 tonnes.

There is some land in Cambodia that without fertilizer or many inputs can produce six tonnes in normal times, because there is a lot of good land in Cambodia. But in what was fixed in 1976 in the Pol Pot period, land fixed as having to produce six tonnes, sometimes this land did not have that capacity. So there was real compulsion. Because some land was not of the quality to ensure six tonnes per ha even when adequate fertilizer was used. But in Cambodia there is some land that is naturally rich enough, fed by river water so that six tonnes can be produced on one hectare. There is. [But] in all of Komchay Meas district, there is probably not any land that can produce six tonnes. Ponhea Krek district is similar. Some land can produce three tonnes. But this is not general. In some places you can get three tonnes. In some it is tough.

The principle for each district's rice production was to leave only enough for consumption. That was the Center's plan. Everything else had to be collected and taken away. At that time there was no money in circulation. The state only let you have little. So they collected from the cooperatives. And from higher up [in the administration] they just sent cloth and so on, just clothes, all black cloth, that's all. Per year you would get two meters of black cloth. And scarves. Salt. There was enough salt sent to support the life of the people. No shortage. Cambodia has plenty of salt.

In late 1976–early 1977, the collection of rice from the cooperatives increased. Because of the annual production, they left [people] enough to eat for only six months. They collected all the rest. The collectors said: "Leave only 6 months supply in the barns." This was the order from the Center. (A document?) It was a principle: leave (enough for) six months. How did they expect the people to stay alive? They reasoned that in six months' time there would be a new harvest. We had to grow a new crop. That was their thinking. When we had eaten the six months' supply, there would be new rice available. We would have planted and grown a new crop. That's what they thought.

(Was it true that the people were growing two harvests each year?) In each year there was only one crop. But if you think about the period after the completion of the [main January-February] harvest, you must extend the transplanting; there is a period of six months before the next harvest. So they said they calculated to allow enough food for those six months after the harvest. In that six-month period, people started transplanting and getting a crop of light rice which takes three months to mature. This crop came in and the next began.

The people worked hard to produce a lot.... But they ate less [than?] in 1975 and 1976. They started to eat [only rice] porridge, on a large scale. All over Battambang province [in the Northwest Zone], people ate mere porridge. [Even] right after the harvest they were eating porridge. In Ponhea Krek it began in late 1976. In 1977 and 1978 people ate only porridge. Before that they ate rice. But the situation only worsened...from porridge with many nutrients, to watery gruel. Living conditions did not improve, they fell.... In Ponkea Krek district, few people died of starvation. But they mostly ate gruel. Some fourteen to twenty people died of starvation in those years...

When the Center came to collect the harvest, as I said, they left only enough for food, and for seed. They took the rest. (What percentage?) Of the production, as I said earlier, it depended on the period. In 1975 and 1976, they left enough for a full twelve months' food, plus seed. After that, they collected and took everything, because (we were then) in the cooperatives. There was no set percentage. I can't calculate that. Not clear. They took more than they left. In 1977 and 1978 they said just leave enough for six months' food until the next crop. They took the rest. From that time, the people starved, increasingly seriously. Like in Battambang, where many died. [People] ate gruel with one or two spoons (of rice) and mostly water, because of the cut (in rations)...

Before [May 1978] Ponhea Krek district had [only] three trucks. Some districts had two trucks, some none. In the Pol Pot period, Komchay Meas district had no trucks, and Mesang had none either. The others did have one or two. Ponhea Krek had three, trucks for transport. The district is on Highway 7 and the rice is stored in warehouses there. The production was sent to Ponhea Krek district for transit, and warehoused there. Contact by district and subdistrict was by radio or courier. The district had a group of twelve couriers and the subdistrict had couriers too. The district couriers are all dead now...

Chinese advisors came to the Eastern Zone. I saw them. They were mostly military advisors for tanks and artillery, sent from the Center. They were with a Center unit sent to help in the Eastern Zone. Most of their aid was their expertise on tanks and artillery. Besides that, there were advisors in economics and agriculture. In that field there were also North Korean advisors, in hydrology and irrigation. They came to Ponhea Krek district, to inspect the construction of canals, etc. But they did not yet do anything.

(Chim Chin told me that Chinese advisors came to inspect the troops and Pol Pot told the troops to hide their new weapons so that the Chinese would think they only had old ones. Is that true?) It was a strategy for requesting arms. It did happen to some extent. After 1975, when (Chinese advisors) reached the Eastern Zone. But the Chinese advisors were with the tank units, as experts in training in the use of tanks. I don't remember how many tanks the Zone had. Perhaps a company.

HS: [In 1975] they implemented the plan for the reconstruction of the country. They did not yet talk about communal eating ["high-level"] cooperatives. Just at that time of the announcement of national reconstruction, cooperatives were also mentioned, but medium-level cooperatives. At that time they divided the people into categories: "full rights" were those people liberated before the 1975 liberation, who lived in the liberated zones. But the people who had just been evacuated here were called "candidates" (*pracheachon triem*). They were divided thus. The deportees (*pracheachon phniaer*) were among the candidates. But later there were many new divisions. So later there was a division of the people into three new categories...the people living in the liberated zones from before the date of the [March 1970?] coup; and the *triem* were the people living there after liberation, after the coup, who were separated out as candidates, and the people [liberated] after 7th January [*sic*, 17th April] were the deportees (*pracheachon phniaer*). This was done later, but at first there were two divisions, then three categories.

At the time of the construction of cooperatives there were only low-level and medium-level ones. I would like to tell you that this was because the bases were autonomous, at that time they let.... But in the implementation the bases that were old wanted to build high-level cooperatives. When they did, the higher-levels would make this the plan. In the beginning, it was autonomy, to be one's own master, as regions, as individual bases. But when this was done, the high-level would put forward the plan. They put the plan in 1977 to create communal cooperatives (*sahakor ruom*). (1977?) 1976. Early 1976, communal eating; at the time they established the new government of Democratic Kampuchea with Pol Pot appointed as Prime Minister, at that time [April 14, 1976]. And there was an election, but only in form, an election to choose people's representatives [March 20]. An election in the work sites for dams and canals, wherever they were working on dams and canals a lot, they had elections. These were not national elections. The peasants in the countryside knew nothing about the election, they didn't...

(Why was the Eastern Zone different?) It went back even to different uniforms...

The East was different as far as tight control and oppression of the people were concerned. The Eastern Zone framework was looser. The different frameworks in the Zones depended on those in charge. So the tightest of all were the Southwest...

During the struggle in the liberated zones, they created cooperatives, but they were both light and high-level, low level. So the Eastern cooperatives were just at the level of mutual aid teams. In the documents cooperatives were called high-, medium- and low-level. Three. The East formed cooperatives from the beginning, but mostly low-level, mutual aid and solidarity groups, still private. Then later when cooperatives were to be built at medium- and high-level, mostly high-level, in the East most remained medium. This was because there was a principle, but most depended on those implementing it. Those who from any province or Zone wanted to be famous, to rise high and be praised, they worked hard to make high-level (cooperatives) in order to be the first and get the credit. The Eastern Zone did it according to the possibilities, only when the people understood well. It was a matter of cadres.

So in the Zone there were some Regions that did it *chril* too. Some strong districts and Regions that experimented with eating communally before everyone. But they…. like Ponhea Krek, Suong, Tbaung Khmum. They did it but not generally, like in one Region, a model was not successful.

In 1977 they came in strongly, pushing especially the construction of irrigation canals, with "learn from Ta Chai" as a model. The East did not yet do so. They studied but didn't yet do it. Some places ate communally, most did not. So Phim was not a great follower of the Chinese line. As far as parties were concerned, he was under Vietnamese influence, because he had joined the Indochina Communist Party.

Family Life

(What orders did you receive about families?) **CS**: This was raised all the time, in every document. They said "Don't encourage familyism, cliquism"… generally. (Families meaning parents and children?) Yes. That was familyism (*kruosaaniyum*). They also considered sentiment between one spouse (*kruosaa*) and another, closeness, as familyism. Even cases of leading cadres, such as district and Region secretaries, husbands who brought their wives to live with them, they considered that as familyism too. They raised this (problem). So each cadre was always uneasy. Not many had their wives living with them. Most lived separately, worked and lived in different places. Once in a while they could greet their spouse; apart from that they lived separately. If you lived together, they considered that as familyism.

HS: We knew clearly that they were changing history, and the truth. Before that, we could only suspect, it was not clear. But when we suspected, we did not dare speak deeply with anyone, because each of us would dare to speak only with very close friends. We didn't speak. Apart from close friends, we all suspected each other, we couldn't trust anyone. They made a powerful consciousness, so that children could kill their fathers. It was hard. They could [change people's] consciousness.

Killings

CS: The killings began before 1970. There were more and more after 1970. In 1975 they kept on increasing more and more. They were cumulative. In 1978 they became strong (*khlang*). It became an offensive…. The killings were done through the network of an established organization called the Security Organization (*angkar santesok*). There was a Zone, Region and district *santesok*. The head of the [Eastern] Zone *santesok* is dead...I forget his name. It was not Kev Somnang. He was in the army, that was separate. Kev Somnang was sought, arrested and killed by the *santesok*. There was another *santesok* who arrested and killed people in turn, incessantly.

The Center *santesok* gave orders to the Zone *santesok*. The orders came through the Zone, both the *santesok* and the Zone [headquarters]. To the Zone first, and the Zone gave orders to the *santesok*. And it also happened that [members of] the Center *santesok* went down to the Eastern Zone for direct contact. They went to sort out work issues...

(The northern regroupees who came back from Hanoi [in 1970-71] held positions until when?) In general, until 1976. Then they were killed. In mid-1976 they started to clean them out; they used the term "clean out" at that time. It meant kill. The only fraternal cadres who had regrouped to the north and come back and are still alive are the ones who went back to Vietnamese territory. They survived. Those who worked in the radio station, who knew and grasped that the situation was not good, and went back, survived. Like Taing Saroeum; Kim Yin also [worked] on the radio. (In the Northeast Zone?) Yes, and after 1970 there was a mobile radio at Sen River, a little mobile radio. They were there.

...In 1977 and 1978 there were a lot of killings. Many. I have forgotten a lot of the details but I can tell you some things. There is one village in Ponhea Krek district that had 150 families; it was a village that had been through the struggle; in the period after 1954. Pol Pot had taken shelter in that place. The people had hidden him during the struggle. This was Bos village. In 1978 Pol Pot ordered the whole village slaughtered. Only one family survived, only one family still remains there. All the rest were killed. It was May 1978. About ten days after the coup [of May 25, 1978]. The troops who did the killing were mostly sent from the Northern Zone, the Zone secretary had come to take charge in the Eastern Zone: [Ke] Pauk.

HS: Security forces (*santesok*) existed only at Region and minimally at the district levels. Security forces in a Region comprised fewer than 100 men. They were not called a company or any unit, just security units, not organized into battalions or regiments or any thing. At district level, security forces numbered at most ten–twenty people, not many. The important forces were the army.

At the Zone level, the *Santesok* forces were also few. Not like now, when they have police (*nokorbal*); they were called *santesok*. They wore plain clothes. You couldn't tell who was security and who was military, all wore the same clothes, black. And you wouldn't know who was a cadre or commander of any level, because they wore the same clothes without insignia or badges of rank. They all wore black shirts.

The Eastern Zone security chief was Yin Sophi.... Originally he was an agent of the Khmer Serei ["Free Khmer"] network, those they call the Kbal Sor

["White Turbans"], who were active along the border. After the 1970 coup, when that group were defeated, Yin Sophi came to live in the bases and later [Region 21 secretary] Chan Seng Hong brought him to be chief of district security at Chhlong, Memot. Later he was made security chief of Region 21, then later of the Zone, under Chan Seng Hong. That's all I know.

Yin Sophi killed one of my soldiers, a regimental commander. He was riding a motorcycle with two bodyguards on motorcycles. Yin Sophi came along in a car and met my friend. They got out of the car, six of them. Sareth, the son of grandmother Hân, had two young courier-bodyguards. They dismounted. Sareth stayed on his motorcycle. But the two bodyguards armed with two rifles got off their motorcycles. Yin Sophi got out and shook hands. While they were shaking hands, he took out a pistol and shot Sareth dead. He fired and hit him with several bullets. Then the bodyguards opened fire and cut them all down, killed them all, Yin Sophi first. There were two left wounded. We took them to hospital and they later died. After that I don't know whether a [new] Zone security chief [replaced Yin Sophi]. We were considered to be already in rebellion. I don't know who it was.

(When did you start to protest, to think and say that what Pol Pot was doing was bad?) We had the principle to speak up but did not dare to. We thought so after liberation in 1975, [when] we knew clearly that the [ruling] principles were not good. And as for Pol Pot, we didn't know what he was like. Thus straight after liberation they abolished the Special Zone, and moved Region 25 [originally in the East] into the Southwest Zone. They withdrew Ta Chey, alias Non Suon, to the Center. All the district chiefs [in Region 25], of the districts of Kien Svay, Leuk Dek, Sa'ang, etc., were taken by the Southwest, and the Southwest killed them all immediately, right at that time. After liberation they started killing them. I knew about this clearly, but I did not dare say anything, because if I said anything I would be in danger myself. We just knew ourselves and talked about it with friends who knew...

In 1976-77, we had a struggle but a secret one. Things were tight and cramped. There was no opportunity to rise up and struggle. Even Ta Phim was concerned about testing the conditions for a struggle. He used to say: "We will have further bloodshed" (*yeung ning mian kar bongho chhiem khnia tiet*). But there was no opportunity. The opportunity for us to struggle came when they saw us change to some extent, so they made a coup first in order to destroy us. When they did that, we seized the opportunity to rise up and struggle. But because Ta Phim was sick...before that he was sent to China for medical treatment [May-August 1976]. When he was in Beijing they arrested Ta Chhouk, secretary of Region 24.

The Cham Muslim Minority

(What did Pol Pot say about the Cham people?) **HS**: Just to force the Cham people to act according to the principles like normal Khmers. So they forced them to eat pork, to stop believing in religion, they forced them, and anyone who resisted was killed, like on the island [Koh Phol, site of the mid-1975 Cham revolt on the Mekong in Kompong Cham]. They killed them because they forced them to disrespect religion.... Speaking the Cham language was one thing...we won't go into that, but the important thing was, they had them eat pork, had them raise pigs. Pol Pot said this. I'm not sure when, from before liberation. I did not receive direct orders from Pol Pot on this, but the people he ordered directly said it was "the high organization." He didn't say it on the 20th [May 1975], but even earlier. They said it was the high organization who had said this. So they started to force Chams to raise pigs and eat pork. So the Cham people of the island in Kompong Cham rose in rebellion. After attacking and killing the Cham people on that island, they evacuated the people to malarial zones and they died...

My troops did not go and get involved in the repression of the Chams. That was the Security (*santesok*) of the bases, subdistrict, village, district. That island was in a newly created district, Peamchileang, next to Krauchhmar. The troops didn't [do it].... After liberation the troops were not active in anything. The *santesok* even arrested troops, took them from the army and killed them. That happened. When we saw the *santesok* had entered the army's domain, the army didn't have any authority.... The *santesok* were soldiers too. There was no separation like today between the police, the army, what we now call the military police. When they come along, the soldiers are scared...

CS: At that time the Cham people were considered as a national (minority) among the various nationalities throughout Cambodia, like other various national groups. And they were all killed together. Whether the minority groups were Cham or others, they were killed.

Rewriting the Party's History

HS: In 1976, Pol Pot changed the Party statutes about the party's anniversary, to erase the early [pre-1960] history of the struggle, and even wipe out the struggle of the combatants and cadres who had fought against the imperialists...the history of the struggle and the founding anniversary of the Party in 1951. They didn't accept the year 1951, they kept the same day [but] they took 30 September 1960 [as the founding date]... So we saw clearly the change, and the treason of Pol Pot bit by bit. They changed the history of the people's struggle. Kampucheans who had struggled earlier [were not recognized,] only those from when Pol Pot joined the Second Party Congress in 1960, as the birthday and anniversary of the Party in 1960. They wiped out the period before he had joined the Party leadership. Later they killed, disappeared [party founder] Tou Samouth in 1962. Two years after Tou Samouth had attended the Congress, he disappeared...

Every year the birthday of the Party, which was then called the Communist Party of Kampuchea, was taken as 30 September 1951. Every year there was a festival, since 1951. From 1961 when we joined the Party, the festival was for 30-9-51, as the day of the anniversary of the birth of the Party. Every year until 1976, [when] on the day of the festival, we had prepared the festival, the gathering, the food, cattle and pigs for the feast, for the festival for the troops. Then when it was all done, at about 12 midnight we received a telegram from the Center, [to me as?] commander of my Division at Krek, to postpone the festival of the Party's anniversary. "Wait until you receive a circular later." So it was midnight already, we couldn't tell any of the units. Only the division command did not go ahead. Whatever food had been prepared, we all ate it, but did not have a festival. But every regiment and battalion went ahead.

The telegram from the Center came from the East which received it directly from the Center, '870' as it was then called. Pol Pot. The Eastern Zone passed it on with another telegram to the divisions. We received it on the night before the festival that was to be held the next morning, on the 29th [September, 1976] at midnight. "The festival must wait for a circular which will decide later." We waited and later found that the statutes of the Party had been changed, the anniversary of the Party's birthday had the same day and month but the year [of the Party's foundation] was now 1960. In October the circular arrived about this, nearly two weeks later when the party statutes went out. There would be no festival that year for those who had received the circular to hold it off. Those who hadn't received it, in every place, base, village, subdistrict, people did it...

In 1977, Pol Pot came out and officially declared it. It was not yet an open Party, still secret, called "Angkar," not the Communist Party of Kampuchea, neither by the party nor the people. Pol Pot was known as the leader but the form of the Party was not yet public. Then in 1977, on 30 September, it was openly declared as a Communist Party. Its birthday was officially in 1960. We knew from October 1976, but it was now official.

Attacking Vietnam, 1977-1978

HS: After liberation in 1975, the Vietnamese all left. Contact continued. The solidarity in struggle between Vietnam and the Eastern Zone really did break off, but there was still mutual contact by courier; relations existed, but not close. Just contact back and forth between them, mutual solidarity, no conflict or interference in the Eastern Zone...Eastern Zone cadres had contact (with Vietnam) only along the frontier, they didn't go to Ho Chi Minh City. But people like Ta [So] Phim did have contact, such as goodwill messages from Vietnam. They used to live alongside one another, sending medicine, etc., right up to 1976 or so. But it was not official. This was for fear of the Center who had declared [the break], though the East was not concerned. In the East it never became an inimical and angry conflict (with Vietnam). But along the border, between the people on one side of the border and the other, there was conflict concerning the borders, violations back and forth, as normal. They made it so there was conflict between one another, arguing, fighting, moving flags back and forth, there was that. It started in 1976, 1977 on a small scale along the border. But higher up there was not yet any conflict. Only in the Southwest and other Zones…

[In 1975-76], there were no Center troops in the East. In 1977, there were, because of the confrontation. They brought Center divisions to be stationed in the East, many forces. My [former] division, the 1st, and the 2nd Division. The 1st was [now] commanded by Tath, an easterner; all its personnel were from the East. Tath came from the 290th Division, the former 2nd. The 2nd Division commander was Heng Thal, my younger brother, who had been in it since the 1970 coup and commander since 1975.

The Center sent in the [former] Eastern 1st and 2nd Divisions because they knew the geography… There were two fronts in the East: the Highway 7 Front and the Highway 1 Front. Highway 1 was Son Sen's responsibility. Son Sen's command headquarters was in Svay Rieng. Beside Son Sen there was [his nephew Tith] Nath, now called Ni Kon, deputy chief of the General Staff. I used to know him when we were fighting the U.S. and Lon Nol. He was stationed in the Special Zone under Von Vet and Son Sen. Nath was commander of the 12th Division. After liberation they dissolved the Special Zone which came under Center command, and Nath joined the general staff, as deputy chief under Son Sen. On Highway 1 was the [former Eastern] 2nd Division, [now called] the 290th. On Highway 7 was [Ke] Pauk, with the [former Eastern] 1st Division, the 280th Center Division.

On Highway 1 were Son Sen, Nath, the 290th Division, and Chinese tanks. One such tank unit had over ten tanks, not many. In all, the Center sent twenty to twenty-five Chinese tanks to the East, in early 1977 after the war with Vietnam started.… The Chinese tanks were all amphibious.… They were not attached to the Eastern units but were separate, directly commanded by the Center. The 1st and 2nd Divisions did not have the Center tanks [either], which were not attached to the Divisions. They sent the tanks in separate tank units, as support units for specific battles. Under direct command.… And the Center's representatives on Highway 1 were Son Sen himself, and Nath, who was based at Svay Rieng. Son Sen had a mobile command post. He went up and down to Svay Rieng on Highway 1.

And on Highway 7, at first there was So Phim, and then they sent Pauk there, with 10 Chinese tanks under Center command. I don't know who their commander was; they didn't let us know each other. They were not under So Phim, nor Pauk, nor Von Vet. He was not the military commander, only Son Sen [had that authority]. Under Son Sen there was only Ta [So] Phim, who could command the tanks, and so could Pauk.

The 7th Division from the Southwest [was also deployed into the East]. I don't know its strength, 5,000–7,000.… The 7th was commanded by Van, from the Southwest, but it too was under Pauk.… Also a division from 304 [the Central, formerly Northern Zone], then came to attack Vietnam [via the East. It was] directly commanded by Pauk, but also had its own division commander.... There were many [command structure] changes, in quick succession.

The attacks on Vietnam had started and they didn't trust the Eastern divisions, so they sent in these divisions...in early 1977. The Center sent in four divisions, with artillery and...Chinese tanks to the Eastern Zone, I don't know how many, and 130 mm. artillery. The Northern Zone division that came in had only 105 mm. artillery. The 1st and 2nd Divisions had no tanks either. Only the Zone and the Center did...

The same day that they declared (the Party) publicly, they attacked Vietnam. On September 30, 1977 they declared attacks into Vietnam all along the frontier. [So what did Mr. Phim think about that?] So Phim did not yet have any thoughts on it. He just knew that the revolutionary situation at that time was changing ...At that time he was not often in the area either. He was sick. He was taken for treatment in China [early May-August 1976]. When he came home after treatment in China, they had arrested Chhouk from Region 24, and others. He didn't know what to do so he didn't protest, he couldn't protest... So Phim didn't believe Chhouk was a traitor, and he did. A little each way, half and half. So that's why it happened. If he hadn't believed it, he wouldn't have died.... He had many resources, divisions that he could command and would all follow him, even Center troops. But he believed in the Party. He believed in Pol Pot...

So Phim didn't even protest. I never saw him protest. But at that time it was hard to say. He was accused of having plans to stage a coup against Pol Pot. But in fact he had no important problems (with Pol Pot). But he said some things. He said: "Our country will have to struggle again." That's all he said. With me personally and other close aides whom he knew well and who worked with him, he just raised the point that, "Our country, if things continue like this, we will have a war, and another struggle." That's all he said. That was in Prey Veng. He lived in the Zone base at Suong. He came to Prey Veng in early 1977 and stayed three or four days only. He said we shouldn't attack friends, but should follow orders "for a period." He didn't specify a short or a long period.

...Villagers would contact and meet one another, troops too, civilians as well, to meet to discuss problems between people beating one another or quarreling, between Khmer and Vietnamese people along the border. We made contact through these messengers. The messengers made contact at the level of their province or district in Vietnam. They met and discussed things. There were still discussions. At that time it was Chea Sim, in a committee to resolve the border (problems), as [CPK] secretary of the district in Region 20 on the border. He was in regular contact. And there was still contact between the armed forces, they met normally right up until 30 September 1977, when they were sent to fight.

I received the order to attack Vietnam at that time, from the Zone, from both So Phim and [Ke] Pauk. At the time they had sent Pauk and the Northerners there. Both men sent it; it was signed by Ta Phim. It said to attack as instructed from above [using] the troops that were already there. The 4th Division, [elements of] all regiments – the 65th, 67th, 68th – went together. But not all, only a force to attack, about 500 troops or less. The attacks occurred all along the border, as the day of victory of the birth, of the public face of the Communist Party. All parts of the Vietnamese border were attacked that day.

I didn't receive orders to kill Vietnamese civilians. There were such orders, but we didn't receive them. These were their secret internal orders. 870 [the CPK Center] sent them directly only to the command(s), because at that time they had lost trust in the East, lost trust in Phim. So they sent in reinforcements to Phim. That is, [they sent Ke] Pauk. Because at that time Phim was not there because he was very ill, in hospital, (etc). So they sent Pauk as a reinforcement to be stationed there in the Eastern Zone. And Pauk received his orders from above. He sent the order (out) to every Division, because they had already created a Front Command (Committee), and Pauk was deputy president.

I received the orders from Pauk, who was in direct command of the whole Front. Phim was not in direct command, he was [away]. So there was just Pauk, at the time of the attack. Pauk called a meeting of all the Division commands and gave the order to attack Vietnam. On killing Vietnamese people, he just said that "wherever you strike to, burn and destroy." That's all.

The 4th Division did not do anything strong. We did attack, but we attacked from this side and that, within the framework of our orders. We didn't kill civilians. Later they didn't trust the 4th Division, the Zone divisions, and they withdrew them. In March or April 1977 [sic, 1978?], and sent them to the rear, and sent the Center divisions and the Southwest and Northern divisions up front. Then those people went and attacked and killed. This was after 30 September 1977. On 30 September we only attacked along the border. We did not go into [Vietnamese?] territory. To tell the truth it was like this. At that time there was a lot of quarrelling and disputes between the people on both sides of the border. Vietnamese people encroached and came to establish villages and posts in Khmer territory. And we Khmer went to establish villages in places that they used to go to make a living before [inside Vietnam?]. So the militia and security forces, there are many in Vietnam, came with the people, in order to guard them. That created conflict at that time, [but] just between the people. When the army was ordered to go, the army was only to clean up along the border, the Eastern units attacked the Vietnamese there. It was not like in the Southwest Zone where they attacked in deeply, up to the province capitals, [like] An Giang, fighting and burning.

The attack on Vietnam was carried out by the 3rd Division, and the Center's 1st and 2nd Divisions, as well as the 4th. The Southwest and Northern Zone divisions attacked about two weeks later. We didn't yet have artillery then. After Vietnam had been attacking [back?] for about two weeks, the Center sent artillery and tanks. At first, only the infantry attacked along the border, without tanks or artillery. The Southwest had attacked long before, six months before, but the East still had contact with Vietnam, with no fighting. If there were disputes we would send a delegate to resolve them. On September 30, the casualties on our side were in the hundreds, of easterners. And forces sent from here died in large numbers. Many Vietnamese were also killed. At that time we had the idea to resolve the problem.

At that time the courier stationed on the border was Heng Samkai, my older brother, who was head of the couriers stationed on the Vietnamese border at Smach. There was still contact between Vietnam and Khmer when the orders came from the high level to break it off, and three days later (new) orders came to attack. And after a period of attacking, they accused the East of joining up with Vietnam and thus not defeating Vietnam, because the troops were on Vietnam's side. That's why [in 1978] they carried out a coup against Ta Phim, accusing him, including me, of joining up with Vietnam.

(Did you also attack?) At that time, they ordered me, it was normal [to do so]. I was under orders. (If you didn't go?) If you didn't go, they'd attack and kill you. At that time, no one dared argue the case. They would become suspicious. If we just did something a little wrong, they'd say we were "pacification agents" (*santec sampoan*). That accusation meant certain death. They would certainly kill you, whether you were in the army or a civilian. If you did anything against their principles, they'd accuse you.

(After the 20th May 1975, did you ever see Pol Pot again?) Of course. Only once. He came in [Jan. 1978] to have a big meeting at Suong. After Vietnam attacked into Svay Rieng and withdrew again, he had a meeting at Suong, at Wat Taung, near the rubber plantation. The people and the troops were called to this big meeting. At that time I was in the army, and I attended. There was Pol Pot, who gave the address, and also Son Sen, Ta [So] Phim, [and Ke] Pauk. Pot Pot just spoke about fighting Vietnam. For one Cambodian, he said, fight thirty Vietnamese in order to move forward to liberate, to fight strongly in order to take southern Vietnam back. He entrusted the army with this; he created that movement. Pol Pot said this personally, in his report. Nuon Chea was not at the meeting, just Son Sen, Pol Pot, and on the Eastern side there was Ta Phim, and from the Northern Zone "304," Pauk. And I was there as a representative of the [Eastern Zone], in charge of the army.

(Did Pol Pot talk about retaking Kampuchea Krom? ["Lower Cambodia," i.e., the Mekong Delta]) Yes. He said we would liberate it. A movement to rebel, to have the people of the south rebel and overthrow Vietnam and take the south. He said this. He said to encourage the Khmer people who live in southern Vietnam, the Khmer Krom, to rise up in rebellion. "Don't be self-centered. Act in combination with the army's attacks." That's what Pol Pot said clearly. And there would be victory. Each Kampuchean soldier would undertake to kill thirty Vietnamese. Thirty is a lot, too. That was the goal fixed by Pol Pot when he spoke at the big meeting.... It was fixed that each Khmer should kill ten, no, thirty Vietnamese. (Was this about the troops...? or the general population?) The whole, everyone. Both troops and civilians. Each Khmer had to kill thirty Vietnamese. Pol Pot said that directly. It was certain that he was not talking just about the troops. He said, "We have to attack the Yuon [Vietnamese]. Attack and kill the Yuon; as a target each Khmer has to kill 30 Yuon, in order to win victory." He also said many other things. Secondly, [he referred to] "the struggle between the enemy Vietnam, national hatred for Vietnam, a life-or-death enemy of the people." This was the first time I had heard him say this...

That was after January 6, 1978, the day of victory in driving back the Vietnamese. The meeting was a few days later. After Vietnam withdrew, there was the meeting at Suong. Apart from that, I did not meet Pol Pot again...

Later they didn't let me stay with the Division any longer. The Zone, Ta Phim, withdrew me, in 1978, on May 18th 1978, from the 4th Division. He had me come to Suong, to meet him at the Zone command and then gave me the task to go to stay in Prey Veng, to be responsible for the Zone military command. To look after the men in the Zone (HQ) office in Prey Veng city. I got to Prey Veng that day. The coup occurred on the 25th.

At Prey Veng there were no divisions, all of which were at the front. I had three or four battalions under my command. Two battalions of marines, the 5th and 6th. In all the Zone had only three battalions of marines, the 5th and 6th, and the 8th, which had its headquarters at Peam Chor. Each battalion had about 200 men. Besides those, at Prey Veng there was only the military school, with 300–400 soldiers. And two tanks. No artillery. That belonged to the Zone but it was not at Prey Veng, it was at the command center at Thnal Totung, at Chup, the artillery and tanks. At Prey Veng I had two tanks.

The Region forces were not at Prey Veng, nor were the district forces. The Prey Veng command was a Zone area. For the Zone military, there were no civilians. The people had all been evacuated; there were none living in the whole province capital. Troops were sent in. The 3rd Division was sent into Svay Rieng town, the people all sent away. And Prey Veng was the command centre of the Zone army. Every Ministry was there, no civilians. I was still deputy chief of the Zone armed forces, but I had no command. I had command only of the marines, but I could send commands by telegram to every division even though I was in Prey Veng.

CS: (In 1975 did they talk of sending troops to the borders to attack Vietnam, or not yet?) Not yet. That was a separate order. (In what year?) Late 1976, 1977. The end of 1976. (Did you see the order?) There was an order. An order to attack in the Southwest, to attack Vietnam. The order came through the Eastern Zone. When I saw this order I was in Ponhea Krek. I was in Ponhea Krek right up until the coup of 25 May 1978...

The main reason that So Phim died is that he scarcely respected, scarcely carried out the instructions that came from Pol Pot. Because he was still in good contact with Vietnam, throughout. Because he personally, from the beginning, he still had a positive attitude towards Vietnam. Ta So Phim was not someone who was angry with Vietnam. That's why the Pol Pot group killed him.

When [Northern Zone Secretary, Ke] Pauk came to the Eastern Zone [in 1977] in order to attack Vietnam, the cooperation between them was not very close. There was constant conflict, over the army's attacks on Vietnam. Because So Phim was more lenient on attacking Vietnam. And Pauk was strongly active. So they had different views, and there was conflict.

I don't remember what month Pauk came, but it was early 1977. They established a Front with So Phim as Chairman and Pauk as his deputy. Pauk was *not* later elevated to Chairman over So Phim. But this deputy [Pauk] gave some orders over the head of the Chairman. So at the end in 1978, Pauk arranged to arrest Ta So Phim, by inviting him to a meeting. But So Phim knew what was coming, and didn't go to the meeting…. The meeting was in early May [1978]; he knew that if he went, he would be arrested.

(But did he order troops to attack Vietnam, or did he refuse?). He did give some such orders. It's not that he didn't. He did order troops to attack Vietnam. Eastern Zone troops went. Both Northern Zone and Eastern Zone troops attacked Vietnam. Because this was an absolute order from Pol Pot. If you didn't do it you couldn't live. But I want to speak of the views. Ta So Phim did not want to attack Vietnam, but this was an order from Pol Pot. But as for Pauk…. He did. If So Phim had not agreed to attack Vietnam, at that time he would have been immediately arrested. That is the truth.

The May 25, 1978 "Coup"

CS: Then in 1978 when the enemy changed…we understood the causes from before, and drew our conclusions. It was not that certain people were being killed. Everyone was to be killed. So we had to choose a road, for if we did not resist we would die. So that is why we had to rise up and resist, lead a people's movement, encourage all the troops to join us, in order to rise up. Because the troops were being killed. From the division level, at first from the division level right down to the battalion level, the first wave after 24th-25th May on. From the division level down, the battalion level up. The second wave, from the company level, they were arrested one by one, in general. My son was arrested with the secretary of Region 20, on the same day. He was in the army.

(Did you take to the jungle straight after the coup?) It started on the 24th. They set a trap to catch the cadres. On Highway 7. I was there too. I knew the situation there. On 24th and 25th I got out, into the forest. There were many of us. Sim Ka was with me, Mat Ly and Heng Samrin, [Heng] Samkai too. And many others. We were separated. North and South of Highway 7. South of the Highway we were in groups, separate from each other. Before the coup and the slaughter, we were all suspicious. Then on 24th May it was clear, we knew that they were going to kill the Eastern Zone cadres.

HS: We had no warning of a coup. But we suspected their activities and resisted their measures starting from 1976 when we knew Pol Pot was a traitor. But we sought methods to resist their measures; we didn't yet have the capacity to resist, or the opportunity. The time was not yet ripe...

(At the time of the coup, did you know So Phim was preparing for rebellion, or not?) I didn't. I just knew that when he had returned from Beijing, he came here, and they tried to get him to go to Kompong Cham to recover. But he was still sick and did not agree to go. He stayed where he was, in his base. At that time their plan was to call a meeting. Pauk called a meeting. [Phim] didn't go. He had Ta Peam go. Peam was chief of the Zone office. He disappeared. When he saw that [Peam] didn't come back, [Phim] was suspicious. So he had me in Prey Veng come and get him. He was sick and went to hide with his wife's relatives in Srei Santhor district. I was with him before the coup...

The Resistance

CS: So we took measures to resist and struggle against the enemy, to raise forces to struggle and fight Pol Pot. We had various military forces who had broken away from Pol Pot and joined together. We had many troops, a battalion at first, 500 men. Most were quartered in Ponhea Krek, because it is forested. They started to fight the Pol Potists along Highway 7. This was considered a Region battalion, stationed in Region (20). And there was another Region north of the Highway, Region 21, and it had forces that fought hard.

The Regions fought simultaneously, in concert. (Was there premeditation?) That was the time that we all began to realize, and then rose up together. It was not until June that we were in contact by messenger with Sabun and Ouch Bun Chhoeun. Because Highway 7 was so tightly (patrolled). The enemy was dug in there, very strongly. It was hard to cross back and forth. Then in June we were able to cross and make contact with Sabun and Ouch Bun Chhoeun. There was no radio contact...

The number of people who took to the forest [after the May 1978 "coup"] south of the Highway, in the forest of Ponhea Krek but from other districts as well – there were over 10,000 in the forest. I don't recall how many there were north of the Highway. There, they were mostly troops. I don't know how many.

The troops in the forest were Eastern Zone troops, and a company of Center troops, from the 280th Division of the Center. This company was a good fighting unit, because it was a spearhead unit. The company's commander is dead, I don't remember his name, but many of his troops survive. It was not a Northern Zone unit, but a Center unit mostly made up of former Eastern troops. It was initially from Heng Samrin's 1st Division, which had fought along Highway 1 [against the Lon Nol regime]. After liberation in 1975, Heng Samrin went back to the East, and the Division was transferred to the Center. It was reassigned as the 280th Division. It was stationed in the East, because its troops were Easterners. And there was also the 290th, in the Eastern Zone. The commander was the younger brother of Mr. Heng Samrin, Heng Thal.

HS: (When did the rebellion begin?) On the 25th, the day of the coup. At that time I was in Prey Veng city. I attacked from Prey Veng city...

The Divisions at the front reported to me...I knew as soon as the coup had taken place. I sent telegrams to every division to report in. They reported that they had been called to a meeting by Pauk, on Highway 7. All officers from the battalions, regiments and divisions, at the front.

When they disappeared [at Pauk's meeting], I called a meeting. I invited a number of district (officials) to a meeting in Prey Veng once I knew the situation. First I went to get Ta Phim. Phim was not at Prey Veng. He was at Tuol Preap, about less than 20 km. away. From Prey Veng through O Reang Au, Kong Chey up to Tuol Preap, on the border of Kanchriech and Ponhea Krek districts. I went to get him and bring him to the meeting in Prey Veng, to observe the situation of the events along Highway 7 and Highway 1. There were many at the meeting. From the districts there were Chea Sim from Ponhea Krek; there was Ta Tui, the deputy secretary of Region [20]; from Peam Ro, Komchay Meas, and Prey Veng districts, two people from each, the district secretary and deputy secretary. Chea Sim came to the meeting in Prey Veng town. After the meeting we worked out a plan. We saw that there had been a coup at that time. We declared that we would fight back. It was clear. So Phim knew what was happening now...

There were twenty people at the meeting, district secretaries and military commanders, mostly military: Pol Saroeun, who was also [2nd] deputy chief of the Zone military, in charge of equipment, the ammunition factory which he had taken over from Hem Samin, a technical factory which made grenades and shells at Koh Sautin. He came to Prey Veng city for the meeting, which took place on 27 May...

Let me tell you more about the meeting, when I drew up the plan. It is true that [Phim] didn't believe what I said, but he offered the opinion that: "If we resist, the resistance has to rely on support. If we resist, we need support. This support is our old friends. There are only our old friends. We have to go seek out our friends for support." He said this clearly. "We have to find our friends for support. If we don't seek out our friends, we will not get any support." Because the "friends" were, frankly, Vietnam. "It is true that we have been in conflict for a short time but we have a custom of common resistance; the conflict is only recent. Our friends will not abandon us. If we resist we have to run find our friends."

At this meeting there were others too. The secretary wrote it down, Ta Tor here, Khim Phan, Chea Sim, Heng Samrin, Pol Saroeun, So Phim, and Ta Tui and brother Run, who is the chauffeur for [the Buddhist Patriarch, Venerable] Tep Vong. I forget the others' names. Not Daok Samol. The commanders of the marine battalions, the 5th and 6th were both there. And Song Niet...[My brother] Heng Samkai was not at the meeting [on 27 May]. At that time he was in O Reang Au. His base was at Suong but he had moved to O Reang Au. So he didn't attend the meeting...At that time we drew up the plan to fight. To fight to open the road to Prey Totoeng-Chup. To open the road to contact...

There were few of us at the meeting. Not every district was represented, only some. It lasted two hours. We discussed resolving the general situation, the events. In general Tal Phim was still ambivalent at that time. And he didn't believe me. Had he believed me at that time he would have survived. He still believed Pol Pot. He said the coup was the work of Son Sen, who carried it out to overthrow Pol Pot. But I said that it was not Son Sen; it was a policy of Pol Pot. It was very clear that Pol Pot had a policy of screening out internal agents in the party. We had read documents talking of internal agents. So it was clear. They had already done this in every Zone but the Eastern Zone. This was the last. At that time the final action of Pol Pot was to use the machinery of a coup. I told Phim this, but he didn't believe me. He said he still had hope in "Brother No. 1." ...He said that Pol Pot was faithful, good, and that the coup was the work of Son Sen. He went to resolve things with Pol Pot.

So while we were fighting hard against Pol Pot at that time, [Phim] had us hold off for a time, while he went to Phnom Penh. As he was heading to Phnom Penh, he had a discussion with me. He said to let him go alone, with his five or six bodyguards. If we didn't see him back in three days' time, we should start to fight back again. But if he did come back in three days, we should wait to talk to him.

He was gone only two days. He got to Arey Khsat and sent a messenger [across the Mekong to Phnom Penh] to take a letter to the place of the messenger of brother [name inaudible – Chey Sangkream?], in front of Wat Unnalom. Then the messenger returned to Arey Khsat. Phim waited a long time, about an hour, over an hour, then he saw forces setting out [across the Mekong], marines. He said maybe they were coming to get him. But when they arrived, they didn't pick him up. They surrounded him and shot at him. He ran off, abandoning his jeep and everything at Arey Khsat. He went up to the Arey Khsat subdistrict office, took the subdistrict chief's horse-cart and drove it to Prek Tral, to Wat Prek Pra...to Prek Champa.

[Meanwhile] They had already arrested all the leaders of the 4th Division, there were none [left]. I took various units from here and there, consolidated them, took a regiment of marines from Neak Leung, the 6th Battalion; and the 75th artillery battalion and other units from the Armed Training School and combatants from some units from the 4th Division whom we won over, led by Song Niet.

I commanded Song Niet to take a squad to fight along Route 15 to Chup and Peam and open the road and cross to the north of Highway 7 and make their way to Memot, in order to muster the forces of the 4th [Division]. I sent him with about seven men to contact the 4th Division. I couldn't contact them...

And Pol Saroeun led three companies of 300 men, Zone support troops for the artillery units. When they abandoned the artillery they took up rifles to fight. This was the 75th regiment, but with only 300 men. They went to fight, along Highway [15] to Thnal Totoeng, Chup, then to Peam as far as Suong. They fought their way there, and when they took it, they took their troops through Suong and up to the north of Highway 7. This was Pol Saroeun.

Another force was led, now I remember, by Hem Bo, another person. They went to resist, at the resistance front near Krabau, in Komchay Meas, to attack from the east. Hem Bo had been at the [27 May] meeting. He took his district troops. He was then secretary of Komchay Meas district. So he fought...

And I went to command the fighting along National Highway 15...In the morning I got [to Lor Khdach?]. I slept the night there and organized forces to go and meet the Pol Pot forces...I was in command but our forces were few and Pol Pot had twelve tanks attacking my forces, and I had two tanks. Heh ! ... Twelve tanks and many planes which flew over and machine-gunned us at Lor Khdach. They attacked and scattered my forces.... So they fought their way into Prey Veng. We blew up two or three of their tanks. Many of their forces died...They took three days to get into Prey Veng ! I had no forces there, we had all left, but they did not dare go in, saying that they were afraid of Prey Veng, because in Prey Veng I had killed very many of them, set fire to many tanks, and so on .... My forces did not suffer many causalities. They were marines. They dug in and shot the enemy as they approached in the open. We lost few. I don't know how many we killed but a large number. One side can't claim to have counted.... After the battle I abandoned my two tanks at Prey Snguot...

We fought hardest and blew them up when they attacked from Highway 1, at Peam Banan, near Snae. We destroyed many of them there.... We fought along Snae Reservoir, they attacked and came on, they attacked and when they got through it was along Highway 15 into Prey Veng. I got out at Lor Kdach in the direction of Lor Ut. I was commanding from there. They attacked early in the morning, they pounded me with artillery, and I left for Prek Thbal. I stayed among the people, took off my uniform, mixed with the people. And when they entered Prey Veng I left and walked east ...

This was before So Phim came back. He had had us wait for him [in Prey Veng, but] the enemy attacked and took Prey Veng.... When three days were up, I went after him. He had disappeared so I followed him ...I came to meet him [at Prek Champa]. He had been shot by Pol Pot and was ill with diarrhea, and bleeding.... I saw him, wounded, in the wat. I met him in the wat, don't know its name, at Kiep dam, on the road from Srei Santhor ...to Peareang district.

Above Kompong Ampil. Across from there is a banyan tree, called Prek Pra. It is far from Prey Veng, near Srey Santhor district.

So we met again. There was Ta Phim, Ta Véng, Ta Chhien the secretary of Region 22, and Ta Chum Sarun, head of Eastern Zone commerce and uncle of Pol Saroeun. When we arrived and met him, he just said "Goodbye." He said: "I can't go anywhere. I'm finished. I'm staying here. You friends go ahead and fight on. Fight on, I can't go on." He had alcohol. He was wounded and bleeding from the stomach. He drank the alcohol. We begged him to come along. But he insisted on staying. But I arranged for Srey Santhor district troops, 300 men, three companies, and Yi Yaun the district secretary, to take him into the forest of Srey Santhor district and guard him. He sent me away. It was only 4 P.M. when I left the place where he was. He sent me away to look after the troops...

I was with him when he gave his order to fight back against Pol Pot. It was clear. He gave the order, and I was the person who issued the order directly to the military. So I attacked, and I took him there to hide temporarily, so that when we had a chance to fight we would withdraw him back to the east, because they had already seized Prey Veng city.

We couldn't take him with us. We left him there in Srei Santhor district with the bodyguard force to defend him...Then without resting I called in all the commanders, from Prey Veng and everywhere, to prepare a plan. The plan was to take Ta Phim to the east, in order to get him out to Vietnam...[However] the enemy aircraft distributed leaflets accusing So Phim, saying that So Phim was a traitor, and the deputy secretary of Srei Santhor picked one up and then took it and ordered troops to attack and kill him. After they had killed him they took his body to make terror propaganda, to show the people that the accusations were true and that he was dead.... These were Yi Yaun's forces, but if you ask Yi Yaun, he says he had already left. His deputy was still there, a traitor. I can't remember his name...The unit that I had arranged to guard [So Phim], 300 district troops, killed him. Srei Santhor district troops killed So Phim ...The deputy secretary of the district betrayed Ta Phim.

When I left Prey Veng I went east into the forest. We were all scattered far and wide. Chea Sim, Hem Bo, Heng Samkai, Ros Chhun, and many others... In the forest, we had many Divisions, around 2,000 troops. From various units and the 280th Division. We gathered in some companies from the 280th, over 200 men. Their commander was Sieng Hai, deputy commander of the 280th Division. He joined us with over 200 men...We fought, but at that time in the forest we had no bases to depend upon, no medicine, no food in reserve, [so] we dispersed to some extent...

Over the next months we fought Pol Pot many times. We fought and smashed them and seized their ammunition by the truckload on many occasions. We destroyed three or four trucks. We seized and drove one into the forest until we had no gas. We attacked hard north of Highway 7. That was done by the 4th Division and various mixed units like Pol Saroeun's artillery support forces.

We had many forces. South of Highway 7 we had many. We had 200 men just from the 280th alone. Then there were district and Region forces that joined us, 3-400 district forces and around 100-200 Region troops. The total north and south was nearly 2,000 troops, almost a brigade.

The commanders of the forces north of the highway were Pol Saroeun, Song Niet, Mau Phok, So Nal. Ta Nya [Chum Sambor] was a civilian Region [20] official, in security, south of the highway. And battalions led by Sae Chhum and Sar Kheng. And north of the highway were cadre, Ta Chan Seng, Ta Mat Ly. Ouch Bun Chhoeun, Ta Mam Sabun, and a number of units. In all 2,000, scattered north and south. At most there were 100-200 in one place. In Memot, Niet had over 100 men, mustered from the 4th Division. And there were other forces in the districts, all separated. We met up in the liberated area at Memot. We met only two or three times. The first time was in Memot in September. The second was when we met to create the Front, in December [December 2, 1978]. We met before that to prepare the statutes and general structure of the Front, in November. Then in December we had a Congress.

The first time we met, in September, we talked about the plan to unite and create a Front. When we had made the preparations to create the Front, we went and made contact with Vietnam, and then we requested Vietnamese help. There were no Vietnamese representatives present at the September meeting in Memot. But it was close to the border. The meeting was in the factory. There were many at the first meeting. Chhuon, Phok, Meas, Pol Saroeun. Not Chea Sim, we had not yet met up with him. Later, at the second meeting, we met Chea Sim. A week later, we met up and had a meeting to draw up a plan for a Front program. In October. We met and raised the standpoint of a plan for a Front.

I crossed to the north of Highway 7 in August. At first I was on the south side, then in July I crossed from the south, to meet and make contact with people there and to find and make contact with Niet in Memot. Then in August I went back to the south, then at the end of August I went back to the north, and cut through to the meeting in Memot in September.

There were many civilians in the forest with the troops south of the Highway. Tens of thousands of evacuees, in the south and north. But they crossed over to Vietnam. Most were in the south, because it was forest, and from the forest it was hard to contact Vietnam, because there were mines. There were about 20,000 people in the south. Later when we had made contact with the Vietnamese, they helped us evacuate the people in the forest into Vietnam. Over 10,000 people crossed into Vietnam, and then some came back. They crossed into Vietnam in September. This was from the south. There were also many from the north, about 10,000 at that time.

During the months in the forest, we attacked the Pol Pot forces many times, but only in small guerilla attacks. We didn't attack on a large scale, because we didn't allow their forces to meet us. We eluded their forces, because we did not have the forces to fight them. We had neither food nor medicine. We would run away from them, but we still attacked them about ten times. We would attack with fifty–sixty troops each time, and the enemy would be in their bases. We attacked their bases, especially in Damber, at Chup, on the river bank at Krauchhmar. We didn't attack and overrun those bases, but attacked on the road and seized food supplies to eat. That's all. We didn't take over anything because our forces were few and they were many.

We killed many of them, three or four at a time. In all, maybe 100 during those months. We lost fewer because we attacked by surprise, guerilla-style. After attacking we ran away, didn't let them catch us. We would attack in the mornings; blow up their trucks, and escape. We also blew up two tanks north of the Highway. Not in Prey Veng, we blew up some there also. These were tanks, don't know if they were Chinese or not, after they'd been blown up!... At that time our technology was not very precise...

Crossing to Vietnam

HS: We contacted the Vietnamese authorities, and crossed the border in September, after establishing contact with Vietnam in Memot. It was very difficult to cross to Vietnam. At that time my troops numbered over 1,000. They were not fighting but journeying across towards the frontier. And at the frontier Pol Pot's forces ambushed us again. We separated, and my group of seven people were arrested by the Vietnamese. As we were separated, Pol Pot's force was on this side, my group in the middle, and Vietnamese were there, and attacked. After they attacked, the Pol Pot force was defeated and ran away, and my group was left. [Vietnamese] came and arrested us, and didn't harm us. They took us for interrogation, asked us questions and then recognized us. We all knew each other. The Vietnamese knew us. We made a detailed report. Because those Vietnamese had previously joined with us to struggle and fight against the American imperialists, so we knew each other...

I crossed the border in late September, from Memot into Vietnam. The people crossed over from September to November, in many groups. Forces would come from there to take the people across, then they could go. The people were in the area, if we wanted to go get the people, our forces had to come and guard the way for the people to go. Once 5,000 people [crossed the border], at another point 6,000, in various groups. They went in many groups. In all, about 30,000–40,000 people crossed the border.

CS: I crossed over into Vietnam with thousands of people in September. We all went together, after seeing that if we didn't we would be killed.

Final Reflections

(In the Democratic Kampuchea period, from 1975 to 1978, is there any thing else that you regret, that you think you should have done?) **HS:** They denied the people the victory…. They wiped out the people's struggle. They wiped out all the history of every period (too). So the struggle from 1951 on, they recognized only the struggle from 1960 when they themselves entered the leadership, in the second Party Congress…. They cut out the period from 1951 to 1960, and took [only] the period when they had roles in the Party leadership. They said the Party was only born when they were born into the Party.

(But you knew about this from 1976 but did not yet resist. Do you regret that?)

I didn't yet resist. I regret that, because I didn't observe and think clearly. I believed the Party, what they said…. As for the living conditions of the people, after liberation we knew about it. Before that the people's living conditions remained normal, they were private. Then after liberation they created cooperatives. The low-level cooperatives were all right, the mutual aid system. But by 1976, they created communal cooperatives. They divided up the people.

3

Genocide, Extermination and Resistance in East Timor, 1975-1999: Comparative Reflections on Cambodia

Cambodia, East Timor, and the USA

On July 5, 1975, two months after the communist victories in Cambodia and Vietnam, Indonesia's President Suharto visited Washington for his first meeting with U.S. President Gerald Ford and Secretary of State Henry Kissinger. The conversation ranged over Southeast Asian affairs. Suharto assessed the U.S. defeat in Vietnam: "It is not the military strength of the Communists but their fanaticism and ideology which is the principal element of their strength" – something he said Vietnam's anti-communists had not possessed. Suharto continued: "Despite their superiority of arms in fighting the Communists, the human factor was not there. They lacked this national ideology to rally the people to fight Communism." But Indonesia was different, he said: "We are fortunate we already have this national ideology [*Panca Sila*]. The question is, is it strong enough?"[1]

On December 6, Ford and Kissinger in turn called on Suharto in Jakarta. Ford told him that "despite the severe setback of Vietnam" seven months earlier, "The United States intends to continue a strong interest in and influence in the Pacific, Southeast Asia and Asia…we hope to expand this influence." Ford was returning from China, where, he said, "we made it clear that we are opposed to the expansion of any nation or combination of nations." The U.S. aimed this message not at China but at its rivals. Kissinger informed Suharto: "We believe that China does not have expansionist aims now… Their first concern is the Soviet Union and their second Vietnam." Ford agreed: "I had the impression of

---

1. Memorandum of Conversation between Ford, Suharto, and Kissinger, July 5, 1975, in W. Burr *et al.*, eds., *East Timor Revisited: Ford, Kissinger and the Indonesian Invasion,* National Security Archive, Electronic Briefing Book 62, Dec. 6, 2001 (www.gwu.edu/~nsarchiv/NSAEBB/NSAEBB62).

a restrained Chinese foreign policy." Suharto asked whether the U.S. believed that Cambodia, Laos and Vietnam would "be incorporated into one country." Ford noted the "resistance in Cambodia to the influence of Hanoi although we find the Cambodian government very difficult." Kissinger explained: "We don't like Cambodia, for the government in many ways is worse than Vietnam, but we would like it to be independent. We don't discourage Thailand or China from drawing closer to Cambodia."[2]

Even as Ford and Kissinger aimed to strengthen the independence of Pol Pot's Cambodian communist regime in the name of opposing Vietnamese expansion, another Southeast Asian humanitarian disaster was in the making, a result of Indonesian aggression. In that same December 1975 conversation, Suharto raised the "problem" of East Timor. He needed U.S. support, not condemnation, for planned Indonesian expansion into the small Portuguese colony. "We want your understanding if we deem it necessary to take rapid or drastic action." Ford replied: "We will understand and will not press you on the issue." Kissinger then added: "You appreciate that the use of U.S.-made arms could create problems.... It depends on how we construe it; whether it is in self-defense or is a foreign operation. It is important that whatever you do succeeds quickly. We would be able to influence the reaction in America if whatever happens happens after we return. This way there would be less chance of people talking in an unauthorized way.... We understand your prob- lem and the need to move quickly... Whatever you do, however, we will try to handle in the best way possible.... If you have made plans, we will do our best to keep everyone quiet until the President returns home."[3] Washington favored the independent existence of the Khmer Rouge regime, but not of East Timor. It was prepared to sacrifice Timorese independence to strengthen U.S. influence in Jakarta.

Suharto saw the green light, and Indonesian paratroopers landed in Dili the next day. The Cambodian genocide was underway, and the Timor tragedy now commenced. The death toll from the Indonesian invasion and occupation of East Timor from 1975 to 1999 would reach similar proportions, approximately a fifth of the territory's population.[4] As in Cambodia, an initial, small-scale civil war preceded the catastrophe and major international intervention. The two genocides that began in 1975 were also each in turn followed by extended foreign occupation, and finally by United Nations intervention.

War and Genocide in Cambodia and East Timor

The first Cambodian civil war, from 1967 to 1970, had pitted a few thousand insurgents of the Communist Party of Kampuchea (CPK, or "Khmer Rouge")

---

2.   Ford-Kissinger-Suharto discussion, Embassy Jakarta Telegram 1579, 6 Dec. 1975, in *East Timor Revisited*.
3.   Ibid.
4.   John G. Taylor, *East Timor: The Price of Freedom* (London: Pluto, 1999).

against the independent regime of Prince Sihanouk. After Lon Nol's coup of March 1970, the Vietnam War smashed across the border. Vietnamese communist and anti-communist forces, and U.S. ground troops and air fleets, turned Cambodia into a new battleground. Over 100,000 Khmer civilians were killed by U.S. B-52 bombardments alone.[5] Sihanouk joined forces with the now rapidly growing Khmer Rouge in a wider civil and international war. The Khmer Rouge defeated Lon Nol's Khmer Republic, entering Phnom Penh in April 1975, two weeks before the Vietnamese communists took Saigon.

Pol Pot's victorious Khmer Rouge immediately attacked into Vietnamese territory, only to be rebuffed there by the newly triumphant communists. In January 1977, Cambodia renewed its border attacks, escalating them over subsequent months.[6] Phnom Penh declared war at year's end, and rejected the Vietnamese offer of mutual pullback and negotiations. In December 1978, Vietnam invaded and quickly drove the Khmer Rouge army across the country to the Thai border. Hanoi's occupying forces established a new Cambodian government and army, headed from 1985 by Prime Minister Hun Sen. Khmer Rouge troops continued their attacks from sanctuaries in Thailand. Vietnam's withdrawal in 1989 was followed by the UN-sponsored elections of 1993. These brought to power an uneasy coalition of Hun Sen's People's Party and the royalist Funcinpec, led by Sihanouk's son Prince Ranariddh. This coalition, dominated by Hun Sen, finally defeated the Khmer Rouge insurgency in 1999.

Two months later, a UN-appointed Group of Experts concluded that the surviving Khmer Rouge leaders should be prosecuted by an International Tribunal "for crimes against humanity and genocide."[7] The events of 1975-1979, the legal experts reported, fit the definition of the crime outlawed by the UN Genocide Convention of 1948. In addition to committing "war crimes" against Vietnam and Thailand, the Khmer Rouge regime had also "subjected the people of Cambodia to almost all of the acts enumerated in the Convention." Did it carry out these acts with the requisite intent and against groups protected by the Convention?

In the view of the Group of Experts, the existing historical research justifies including genocide within the jurisdiction of a tribunal to prosecute Khmer Rouge leaders. In particular, evidence suggests the need for prosecutors to investigate the commission

---

5. Kiernan, "The Impact on Cambodia of the U.S. Intervention in Vietnam," in *The Vietnam War*, J. Werner et al., eds. (New York: M.E. Sharpe, 1993), 216-29; Taylor Owen and Ben Kiernan, "Bombs over Cambodia," *The Walrus* (Canada), October 2006, 62-69.

6. Ben Kiernan, *The Pol Pot Regime: Race, Power and Genocide in Cambodia under the Khmer Rouge, 1975-1979* (New Haven, CT: Yale University Press, 2002), 103-11, 357-68.

7. United Nations, AS, General Assembly, Security Council, A/53/850, S/1999/231, March 16, 1999, Annex, *Report of the Group of Experts for Cambodia established pursuant to General Assembly resolution 52/135*, 19-20, 23, 57.

of genocide against the Cham, Vietnamese and other minority groups, and the Buddhist monkhood. The Khmer Rouge subjected these groups to an especially harsh and extensive measure of the acts enumerated in the Convention. The requisite intent has support in direct and indirect evidence, including Khmer Rouge statements, eyewitness accounts and the nature and numbers of victims in each group, both in absolute terms and in proportion to each group's total population. These groups qualify as protected groups under the Convention: the Muslim Cham as an ethnic and religious group, the Vietnamese communities as an ethnic and, perhaps, a racial group; and the Buddhist monkhood as a religious group...

The UN legal experts added that "the intent to destroy the Cham and other ethnic minorities appears evidenced by such Khmer Rouge actions as their announced policy of homogenization, the total prohibition of these groups' distinctive cultural traits, their dispersal among the general population and the execution of their leadership."[8] Of the Cham population of 250,000, for example, approximately 90,000 perished in four years, many of them deliberately killed for their ethnicity. Under such conditions, combined with utopian Maoist forced labor programs and Stalinist exterminations of "class enemies" among the majority Khmer population, 1.7 million Cambodians perished.[9]

While recognizing these crimes against humanity, some legal experts doubt that the legal definition in the UN Genocide Convention – attempted destruction "in whole or in part" of "a national, ethnical, racial or religious group, as such" – covers either the Khmer Rouge mass murders of Cambodia's non-communist political groups and defeated officer class, or Indonesia's mass murder of political groups in East Timor from 1975 to 1999.[10] Objections to a legal interpretation protecting "political groups" also exclude the Indonesian army's mass extermination of its domestic Communist Party (PKI), over half a million of whose members were killed in 1965-66.[11] But the crimes committed a decade later in East Timor, with a toll of about 150,000 in a population of 650,000, clearly meet a range of sociological definitions of genocide used by most scholars of the phenomenon, who see both political and ethnic groups as possible victims of genocide.[12] The

8. *Report of the Group of Experts*, 19-20. Stephen Heder asserts that this *Report* "cautioned that it might be a 'difficult task' to prove that the CPK carried out acts 'with the requisite intent' to destroy such ethnic and religious groups 'as such.'" "Seven Candidates for Prosecution," American University, 2001, 14n24.
9. Kiernan, *Pol Pot Regime*, 458. See also chapter 9 below.
10. R. Clark, "Does the Genocide Convention Go Far Enough?," 8 *Ohio Northern L.J.* 321 (1981); B. Saul, "Was the Conflict in East Timor 'Genocide'?," *Melbourne J. International Law* 2 (2001): 477-522.
11. Robert Cribb, ed., *The Indonesian Killings, 1965-66* (Clayton: Monash Centre of Southeast Asian Studies, 1990).
12. Leo Kuper, *Genocide* (New Haven, CT: Yale University Press, 1981), 174-75, 186, 241; F. Chalk and K. Jonassohn, *History and Sociology of Genocide* (New Haven, CT: Yale University Press, 1990), 408-11; I. W. Charny, ed., *Encyclopedia of Genocide* (Oxford: ABC-Clio, 1999), 191-94; James Dunn, "East Timor," in G. Andreopoulos, ed., *Genocide* (Philadelphia: Univ. Pennsylvania Press, 1994), 171-190.

victims in East Timor not only included that substantial "part" of the Timorese "national group" targeted for destruction because of their resistance to Indonesian annexation – along with their relatives, as we shall see. The victims also included most members of the 20,000-strong ethnic Chinese minority prominent in the towns of East Timor, whom Indonesian forces singled out for destruction apparently because of their ethnicity "as such."

"Extermination" is a crime against humanity distinct from genocide. Its legal definition includes not only massacres but also "the intentional infliction of conditions of life, inter alia the deprivation of access to food and medicine, calculated to bring about the destruction of part of a population." Charges of crimes against humanity, unlike genocide, do not require proof of "intent to destroy" an ethnic group, or other group, "in whole or in part."[13] Both the Khmer Rouge and the Indonesian military committed crimes fitting this description of "extermination."

As in Cambodia, a small-scale civil war preceded the Timor tragedy. In mid-1975, a short conflict in the Portuguese colony led to unexpected victory for its independence movement, Fretilin. Jakarta's armed forces invaded the territory on December 7. Fullscale war raged until 1980. The occupation continued to take lives for another twenty years, even after a 1999 UN-organized referendum demonstrated that 79 percent of East Timorese wanted independence. Immediately, in a pre-planned operation, Indonesian occupation forces sacked the territory, destroying 80 percent of the homes, deporting hundreds of thousands of people to West Timor, and killing possibly one thousand. U.S. President Bill Clinton insisted that Indonesia "must invite" an international peacekeeping force to take over East Timor. Australian troops led in the UN forces as Indonesian soldiers left much of the territory in ruins. In UN-organized parliamentary elections in 2001, Fretilin won 57 percent of the vote. In the April 2002 presidential elections, Fretilin's former leader Xanana Gusmão won 79 percent, and its founding president, Xavier do Amaral, 17 percent.[14] On May 20, 2002, after over two years of transitional rule, the UN handed over responsibility to the new independent state of East Timor.

The two cases of genocide and extermination in Southeast Asia were in part products of international alliances and impositions. But they also reflected and provoked indigenous divisions, both ideological and regional. Were these divisions in both cases also ethnic? Domestic coalitions formed and ruptured over time. The CPK's Maoist ideology combined explosively with its virulent Khmer racism and expansionism to eliminate both political and ethnic enemies and to launch attacks on all neighboring states. Fretilin Maoists, on the other hand, fought Indonesian aggressors, but they also fell out with other Fretilin leaders, local elites, regional coalitions, and military profes-

---

13.   Chérif Bassiouni, "Crimes against Humanity," in *Crimes of War Project: www.crime-sofwar.org/thebook/crimes-against-humanity.html* (accessed Sept. 23, 2006).
14.   *New York Times*, April 17, 2002.

sionals. Was this in part for ethnic reasons, as in Cambodia? Regional and political differences plagued the Khmer Rouge too. The 1978 rebellion by the Eastern Zone CPK forces against the Party Center constituted the major armed resistance to the genocidal regime.[15] In East Timor from the start, political and regional divisions also debilitated the pro-Indonesian cause, not just the Fretilin resistance. But to fully understand the conditions in which these divisions emerged, and to what extent they were comparable, it is first necessary to examine the international forces that abetted both the Suharto and Pol Pot regimes.

Green Lights from Ford and Kissinger

Suharto had first raised the issue of the Portuguese decolonization of East Timor at his July 5, 1975 meeting with Ford and Kissinger at Camp David. Describing Indonesia as "a unified nation without any territorial ambition," which "will not commit aggression against other countries…[or] use force against the territory of other countries," Suharto nevertheless pointed out that for East Timor, "an independent country would hardly be viable," and "the only way is to integrate with Indonesia." However, "The problem is that those who want independence are those who are Communist-influenced." Suharto concluded that "Indonesia doesn't want to insert itself into Timor self-determination, but the problem is how to manage the self-determination process with a majority wanting unity with Indonesia."[16]

In this way, six months before ordering the December 1975 invasion, Suharto secured U.S. acquiescence in the territory's prospective incorporation by Indonesia. The expansionist impulse would simply be denied; the excuse, the communist threat. While the U.S. Department of State called the Timorese independence movement, Fretilin, "a vaguely leftist party,"[17] Kissinger would label Fretilin "a Communist government in the middle of Indonesia."[18] Suharto considered its members "almost Communists."[19] Jakarta saw a "Communist

---

15. On the Eastern Zone, 1970-78: Kiernan, *Pol Pot Regime*, 14-15, 46-47, 65-68, 205-10, 323-25, 369-76, 392-405; M. Vickery, *Cambodia 1975-1982* (Boston: South End, 1984), 131-39; Kiernan, *How Pol Pot Came to Power* (London: Verso, 1985), 270-84, 310-12, 320-21, 340-41, 358, 363-68; Kiernan, "Wild Chickens, Farm Chickens and Cormorants: Kampuchea's Eastern Zone," in Chandler et al., eds., *Revolution and Its Aftermath in Kampuchea* (New Haven, CT: Yale Southeast Asia Council, 1983), 136-211; Kiernan, *Cambodia: The Eastern Zone Massacres* (New York: Columbia Center for the Study of Human Rights, 1986); S. Heder, "Racism, Marxism, labelling and genocide," *Southeast Asia Research*, 5:2 (1997), 117-23.

16. Conversation between Ford, Suharto, and Kissinger, July 5, 1975, in *East Timor Revisited*.

17. Department of State, 'Indonesia and Portuguese Timor,' c. 21 November 1975, *East Timor Revisited*.

18. Memorandum of Conversation, December 18, 1975, Washington, DC, "Departmental Policy" (*www.etan.org/news/kissinger/secret.htm*).

19. Conversation between Ford, Suharto, and Kissinger, July 5, 1975, 6.

wing" of Fretilin in Timorese Maoist students educated in Lisbon during the 1974 revolution there.[20]

From March to July, 1975, the Portuguese authorities organized local village elections throughout East Timor. Fretilin won 50-55 percent of the vote.[21] Its main rival, the Timorese Democratic Union (UDT), favouring gradual progress towards independence, received slightly fewer votes. Apodeti, a small party favoring union with Indonesia, came a distant third. Fretilin had managed to bring a nationalist message to a population of 650,000 divided into possibly thirty ethnic groups speaking fourteen distinct languages.[22] This multicultural success, which included members of Dili's 1,000-strong Muslim Arab community in Fretilin's largely Catholic ranks, would remain one of the party's strengths.[23] Fretilin did remain suspicious of the local Chinese, a largely urban entrepreneurial community that failed to find a voice within Fretilin, which cited reasons of class but not race.

Suharto announced following his return from the U.S. on July 8, 1975, that East Timor lacked the economic basis for viable independence.[24] This was the backdrop to an attempted coup in Dili by Fretilin's rival UDT on 11 August.[25] In Washington the next morning, Philip Habib told Henry Kissinger that authorship of the coup was still unclear: "[I]f it is an Indonesian move, or the Indonesians move against it…we should just do nothing. It is quite clear that the Indonesians are not going to let any hostile element take over an island right in the midst of the Indonesian archipelago." Only if the coup proved to be a pro-independence move would the US act – i.e., against independence. Kissinger said: "[T]he Indonesians are going to take over the island sooner or later,' ensuring merely 'the disappearance of a vestige of colonialism." Habib added that "we should not get ourselves sucked into this one by having opinions."[26]

Civil War

In mid-June 1975, Fretilin forces led by a former Portuguese soldier, Hermenegildo Alves, had briefly seized power in Oecusse, a small enclave of

---

20. Jill Jolliffe, *East Timor: Nationalism and Colonialism* (St. Lucia, Univ. Qld Press), 1978, 84, 115; Xanana Gusmão, *To Resist Is To Win!* (Melbourne: Aurora, 2000), 28n51; Helen Hill, *Stirrings of Nationalism in East Timor: Fretilin 1974-1978* (Sydney: Otford, 2002), 66.
21. James Dunn, *Timor: A People Betrayed* (Milton, Qld: Jacaranda, 1983), 88; Taylor, *East Timor*, 45n52.
22. Dunn, *Timor*, 3; G. Gunn, *Timor Loro Sae* (Macau: Oriente, 1999), 40-41; R. Tanter, et al., eds., *Bitter Flowers, Sweet Flowers: East Timor, Indonesia and the World Community* (Lanham, MD: Rowman & Littlefield, 2001), 254-56.
23. Jolliffe, *East Timor*, 70, 220; Hill, *Stirrings*, 36, 133-35.
24. Dunn, *Timor*, 166.
25. UDT leader Joao Carrascalao acknowledged responsibility for the coup; Gusmão, *To Resist*, 23n36.
26. Department of State, "The Secretary's Principal's [sic] and Regional Staff Meeting, August 12, 1975," 2-4, in *East Timor Revisited*.

Portuguese territory within West Timor. Jill Jolliffe reports that "the Portuguese regained control after sending a negotiating force from Dili as a result of which Alves was jailed for twenty days and UDT and Fretilin agreed to rule jointly." This coalition prevailed in the Oecusse enclave for the next few months.[27]

However, within four days of their August 11 coup in the capital, UDT leaders arrested over eighty Fretilin members, including future leader Xanana Gusmão. UDT members killed a dozen Fretilin members in four locations. The victims included a founding member of Fretilin, and a brother of its vice president Nicolau Lobato.[28] Fretilin responded by appealing successfully to the Portuguese-trained East Timorese military units.[29] UDT's violent takeover thus provoked the three-week civil war, pitting its 1,500 troops against the 2,000 regular forces now led by Fretilin commanders.

By the end of August, UDT remnants were retreating towards the Indonesian border. A UDT group of 900 crossed into West Timor on 24 September, followed by more than a thousand others, leaving Fretilin in control of East Timor for the ensuing three months. The death toll in the civil war reportedly included 400 people killed in Dili and possibly 1,600 in the hills.[30] In the aftermath, "numerous UDT supporters were beaten and jailed" by the Fretilin victors.[31]

Indonesia stepped up its plans for invasion. In early September, as many as 200 special forces troops launched incursions, which were noted by U.S. intelligence, and in October, conventional military assaults followed.[32] Indonesian forces murdered five Australian journalists in the border town of Balibo on October 16.

In September, the leader of the pro-Indonesian Apodeti party, Osorio Soares, remained "freely able to move about,"[33] but as Indonesian incursions escalated, Fretilin took Soares and several hundred other Apodeti and UDT members into custody.[34] Political positions had hardened. Fretilin had begun as the Timorese Social Democratic Association, led by Jose Ramos Horta and former Jesuit seminarian Xavier do Amaral. Since the UDT coup, however, what Jolliffe calls "a discernible shift in power" had brought the ascendancy of a more "inward-turning" nationalist Fretilin faction led by Nicolau Lobato. They blended notions of "revolutionary African nationalism, pragmatism and conservative self-reliance," but, according to Jolliffe, "operated from a solely

27. Jolliffe, *East Timor*, 273.
28. Gusmão, *To Resist*, 29, 26.
29. Dunn, *Timor*, 177; Gusmão, *To Resist*, 22-31.
30. Dunn, *Timor*, 177-80, 321; Denis Freney, *Timor* (Spokesman, 1975), 24; Gusmão, *To Resist*, 30-31.
31. Sarah Niner, "A Long Journey of Resistance," in Tanter, *Bitter Flowers*, 17.
32. Dunn, *Timor*, 181-82.
33. Australian Senator Arthur Gietzelt reported meeting Apodeti Secretary-General, Fernando Osorio Soares, in Dili in September 1975 (Hansard, 7 April 1976, 1171). Fretilin killed Soares two weeks after the invasion (Dunn, *Timor*, 305).
34. Jolliffe, *East Timor*, 156.

nationalist framework with the stress on meeting local needs by whatever means necessary, whether socialization or foreign investment." Fretilin's left wing, too, "did not regard themselves as Marxists but as nationalists who believed they could draw on Marxism and adapt it to nationalist ends." As Jolliffe puts it, "The consequence of the marriage of these two streams was a Timorization of the leadership following the coup period, accompanied by an emphasis towards black nationalism rather than social democracy."[35] Helen Hill suggests this meant African-style politics rather than "black nationalism." Beyond an anti-Chinese or anti-capitalist undercurrent, evidence of indigenous racialist ideology is sparse.[36]

A full-scale Indonesian invasion loomed. Portugal had evacuated its officials offshore. Fretilin formally declared East Timor's independence on November 28, 1975, and a Fretilin Cabinet took office. Its eighteen members included a Portuguese and two Arabs, all members of the party's Central Committee (CC). Jolliffe writes of the new government's leadership, Xavier do Amaral, Nicolau Lobato, and Mari Alkatiri: "The two principal figures were practicing Catholics, the third a practicing Moslem."[37] There were no ethnic Chinese members.

Invasion, Genocide, and Resistance, 1975-1980

Political Turmoil and Division

Jakarta had secured the support of some of the defeated UDT leaders as well as the Apodeti party. Two East Timorese chiefs from the West Timor border area also proclaimed the support of their small Kota and Trabalhista parties for integration with Indonesia. Kota was a monarchist group established by a number of *liurai* (district rulers or "petty kings"), with several hundred members. It "appeared to be a racially pure satellite of Apodeti, based on an inner circle of tribal leaders with access to the mystical rites of the traditional culture." Trabalhista had "a dozen or so members, many of whom came from the same family."[38] This line-up enabled Suharto, in his talk with Ford and Kissinger on December 6, to claim the support of "four parties" from East Timor, adding: "The local kings are important...and they are on our side."[39]

Following the Indonesian invasion the next day, retreating Fretilin forces released a number of their Apodeti and UDT prisoners. But in the hills several weeks later, they summarily executed eighty Apodeti members, including the party's leader, Osorio Soares, and possibly seventy UDT prisoners, including

---

35. Jolliffe, *East Timor*, 152-53, 72.
36. Hill, *Stirrings*.
37. Jolliffe, *East Timor*, 219-20.
38. Jolliffe, *East Timor*, 67; Dunn, *Timor*, 75.
39. U.S. Embassy Jakarta Telegram 1579, 6 December 1975, in *East Timor Revisited*, paragraphs 39, 51.

Secretary-General Fernando Luz.[40] To compound the tragedy, as the Indonesians landed in Dili, according to James Dunn, "a large number of Apodeti supporters, who had just been released from internment by Fretilin, went out to greet their liberators, to be machine-gunned in the street for their trouble." Indonesian troops shot down thirty Apodeti supporters in cold blood. An Apodeti member "was shot while presenting his party identification card to a group of soldiers."[41] As we shall see, Indonesian force would soon also be turned against other non-Fretilin groups, such as the ethnic Chinese.

The Indonesians appointed the Kota leader, Jose Martins, son of a *liurai* from Ermera in western East Timor, to a prominent position. However, Jakarta's constituency even among anti-Fretilin Timorese quickly collapsed. During a March 1976 visit to the United Nations, Martins defected and criticized Jakarta's intervention.[42] Another initially pro-Indonesian Timorese official, UDT's founding President Mario Carrascalao, was placed under house arrest in West Timor and repatriated to Portugal in mid-1976. A third "pro-integration" Timorese official also defected to Portugal. Indonesia announced on January 31, 1976 that all Timorese political parties had now "dissolved themselves."[43] Just in case, Jakarta banned them on 3 February.[44] It then turned to traditional rulers from the western part of East Timor. After formal "integration" of the territory in mid-1976, the *liurai* of Atsabe became the Indonesian provincial governor, and the *liurai* of Maubara chaired the new province's legislature.[45] Thus, the strength of pro-Indonesian feeling was limited to traditional rulers in the west of the territory.

Differences quickly emerged in Fretilin ranks as well. On the morning of the Indonesian invasion, Fretilin's founding President, Xavier do Amaral, allegedly set out for the capital, telling his Cabinet minister Eduardo dos Anjos: "I am going to Dili to ask the Javanese why they [are] invading our homeland."[46] The next day dos Anjos told Fretilin Central Committee member Xanana Gusmão that do Amaral had threatened to "speak with the invaders to ask them to retreat

---

40. Gusmão, *To Resist*, 32; Dunn, *Timor*, 305; D. Ball and H. McDonald, *Death in Balibo* (Sydney: Allen & Unwin, 2000), 175; Paulino Gama (Mauk Muruk), "A Fretilin Commander Remembers," in P. Carey and G. C. Bentley, eds., *East Timor at the Crossroads* (New York: SSRC, 1995), 98-99; Niner, "Long Journey," 19.

41. Dunn, *Timor*, 283-85.

42. Dunn, *Timor*, 296; "Intervention of the Republic of Indonesia in the Life of Portuguese Timor," Kota internal document, 23/3/1976, cited in R. Tanter, "The Military Situation in East Timor," *Pacific Research*, VIII, 1977, 2:1-6; Jolliffe, *East Timor*, 282-87.

43. Dunn, *Timor*, 60, 296-97.

44. Taylor, *East Timor*, 72.

45. Dunn, *Timor*, 5.

46. "Full Text of Speech of Nicolau Lobato, Reading Statement of the Permanent Committee of Fretilin Central Committee on the High Treason of Xavier do Amaral, over Radio Maubere September 14, 1977," *East Timor News Agency* (*ETNA*), Sydney, September 17, 1977, 13 pp. typescript, 4.

immediately !" Xanana recalls that "Eduardo managed to convince him to stop such strange and daring behaviour !"[47] A month later, in January 1976, do Amaral approached Fretilin's vice president, Nicolau Lobato, suggesting they "ask the United Nations to hold a referendum on self-determination." Lobato and the chief-of-staff of Falintil (Fretilin's army) "categorically rejected" this proposal, arguing that the issue was now closed since independence was unilaterally proclaimed on November 28.[48]

The War

According to Australian intelligence, by April 1976 Indonesia had 32,000 troops engaged in East Timor, and another 10,000 in reserve in West Timor.[49] Against these Fretilin deployed 2,500 regular troops and 7,000 part-time militia, and could draw upon 10-20,000 reservists, all trained by the Portuguese.[50] Suharto acknowledged in August 1976 that "the Fretilin movement is still possessed of strength."[51] Indonesian intelligence reportedly estimated in September that Fretilin still fielded as many as 5,000 guerrillas.[52] Australian sources reported by late 1976 that Indonesia had lost 10,000 troops killed, wounded or missing.[53] In early 1977, a senior Indonesian officer conceded that Fretilin had inflicted up to 5,000 casualties.[54] But the invaders took a much greater toll on Fretilin forces, and by 1978 had also organized two Timorese battalions of their own.[55]

A discernible regional pattern began to emerge. Indonesia was able to count on *liurai* and other leaders from the northwestern part of East Timor. Within the resistance, as we shall see, moderate or conciliatory factions of Fretilin appeared strongest in the north-central sector. The Fretilin resistance would find its firmest support base in the remote eastern sector of the half-island.[56]

There were also ideological divisions. In 1984, Carmel Budiardjo and Liem Soei Liong described three major differences on issues that had divided Fretilin's resistance since 1975. These were: "compromise with the enemy, the nature

47. Gusmão, *To Resist*, 49; Carmel Budiardjo et al., *The War Against East Timor*, London: Zed, 1984, 61.
48. "Speech of Nicolau Lobato," 4-5.
49. Tanter, "Military Situation."
50. Taylor, *East Timor*, 70; Dunn, *Timor*, 291-92;
51. *Age* (Melbourne), August 26, 1976, in Tanter, "Military Situation."
52. Tanter, "Military Situation," citing Peter Monckton, ABC *AM* radio program, September 20, 1976, and *Sydney Morning Herald*.
53. Tanter, "Military Situation," citing *National Times*, September 27, *Australian*, September 20, 1976.
54. Dunn, *Timor*, 310.
55. Douglas Kammen, "The Trouble with Normal: The Indonesian Military, Paramilitaries, and the Final Solution in East Timor," in B. R. O'G. Anderson, ed., *Violence and the State in Suharto's Indonesia* (Ithaca, NY: Cornell Southeast Asia Program, 2001), 159.
56. Gusmão, *To Resist*, 29n.

of the war, and the implementation of Fretilin's social and political programs."
Firstly, from the start the majority of Fretilin's fifty-two-person Central Committee (CC) opposed negotiations or compromise with Indonesia.[57] But in early
1977, "the leadership split over the question," leading to do Amaral's dismissal.
The CC was committed to a Maoist-inspired self-reliant strategy for the achievement of independence. Secondly, there was further division over the nature of
people's war, a strategy Fretilin adopted at its national meeting at Soibada in
May-June 1976. Many of the professional army officers who joined Fretilin in
1975 had been trained by the Portuguese to keep the army out of politics. They
differed with those leftist Fretilin leaders who insisted that "the political line
prevail over the military line," and that peasant militia be trained. Army officers
also tended to resist overall military and political coordination, retreating into
and thus strengthening regionalism. Thirdly, Fretilin's political leaders emphasized rural development and egalitarian social policies that conflicted with local,
traditional, hierarchical structures in some communities and regions.[58]

In the first year and a half of the resistance war (1975-77), Fretilin president
Xavier do Amaral worked sporadically with his vice president and prime minister Nicolau Lobato. Both were reportedly shocked at the scale of Indonesian
brutality. As pressures escalated, however, differences between the two men
grew, and in September 1977, Lobato had his superior do Amaral arrested
for "high treason." In an extended denunciation speech broadcast by Fretilin
radio on 14 September 1977, Lobato acknowledged that "for over a year, the
Radio Dili of the Javanese invaders has spread the story that there is a serious
confrontation" between himself and do Amaral. "There was some truth in all
this," Lobato now announced.[59] As we shall see, divisions in Fretilin ranks were
not only regional and ideological, but also rather volatile, as circumstances and
opinions changed over time.

Fretilin's Minister of Information and National Security, Alarico Fernandes,
reflected this changing pattern in the different positions he adopted during
1975-78. A former meteorologist and non-communist social democrat, he had
originally seen Austria and Scandinavia as political models for Fretilin.[60] But
after the UDT's violent coup, Xanana Gusmão says, Fernandes became a "real
executioner" with "a frenzied thirst for vengeance." Before the Indonesian invasion, Fernandes announced: "I'll continue to stay [in] Fretilin but I will not
accept communism." Gusmão implies but does not clearly state that Fernandes
was responsible for the execution of the UDT prisoners after the invasion. As
the war against Indonesia ground on, Fernandes hoped for assistance from socialist countries, which never came.[61] In mid-1976 he aligned himself with the

57. Budiardjo, *War*, 60; Jolliffe, *East Timor*, 270.
58. Budiardjo, *War*, 60-65.
59. "Speech of Nicolau Lobato," 9-10.
60. Jolliffe, *East Timor*, 56, 72; Taylor, *East Timor*, 47.
61. Gusmão, *To Resist*, 22n31, 32, 39n68, 43; Budiardjo, *War*, 61.

professional military faction, but now also proclaimed: "I accept Marxism as the only way of liberating our people."[62] Initially opposed to negotiations, when Fernandes finally lost hope of international support in 1977-78, he "began to waver and slowly shifted" toward compromise with Indonesia.[63] By then internecine purges were escalating. The soldier Hermenegildo Alves, Second Deputy Secretary for Defence and, according to Gusmão, an "incorrigible drunk," had also become a "real executioner."[64] And the Maoist left wing of Fretilin, Gusmão later wrote, was itself responsible for "purging waves of massacres of nationalists" whom it "assassinated as reactionaries and traitors."[65]

Despite internal violence and instability, for the first years of the war Fretilin mounted a highly successful resistance to Indonesia.[66] About forty of its fifty-two CC members escaped death or capture during the initial invasion.[67] (Jose Ramos-Horta and Mari Alkatiri, who were abroad, took up the diplomatic struggle at the UN and elsewhere.) Nicolau Lobato's rambling speech of September 1977, revealing the intense political and regional differences, also conveys an impression of great mobility on the part of the Fretilin leaders, of often free movement of forces and units, of mass meetings and assemblies in the hills, and of large areas and populations under Fretilin administration, despite occasional serious harassment from the Indonesian occupiers.[68] A report from Indonesian Church sources in late 1976 estimated that "80 percent of the territory is not under the direct control of the Indonesian military forces."[69] A foreign diplomatic delegation, which visited East Timor in May 1977, reported that Indonesia still controlled only one-third of the territory, while Fretilin controlled a third and was able to move freely in the remaining third.[70] The next month, Alarico Fernandes claimed in a radio broadcast that Fretilin "control most parts of the country, 80 percent of the national soil, defeating the vandal Indonesian invaders on all fronts."[71] Nicolau Lobato added that "all over the country the resistance is still very strong despite the continuous raids deeply launched by the enemy to the large areas under our forces' control."[72] As James Dunn has pointed out, "an indication of the extent of Fretilin's control is that

---

62. Gusmão, *To Resist*, 42-43.
63. Budiardjo, *War*, 61.
64. Gusmão, *To Resist*, 32, 47; see Jolliffe, *East Timor*, 220, 154, 273.
65. Gusmão, *To Resist*, 134, statement dated 7 December 1987.
66. For accounts by priests living in Fretilin areas until 1979: Taylor, *East Timor*, 81-82.
67. Jolliffe, *East Timor*, 270.
68. "Speech of Nicolau Lobato," *passim*.
69. Tanter, "Military Situation," citing *Age*, November 19, 1976; Jolliffe, *East Timor*, 300-01; Dunn, *Timor*, 310.
70. Dunn, *Timor*, 307.
71. "Secretary for Information Answers Journalists' Questions," June 18, 1977, *ETNA*, June 21, 1977.
72. 'Prime Minister Nicolau Lobato Answers Questions,' June 30, 1977, *ETNA*, July 4, 1977.

it was able to hold the town of Remexio, only 15 kilometres from the capital, almost without interruption for more than three years."[73]

Of the territory's 1974 population of approximately 650,000,[74] an Indonesian attempted census in October 1978 returned a population estimate of only 329,000. Possibly 200,000 more may still have been living in Fretilin-held areas in the hills.[75] In the east, for instance, Indonesian officials later acknowledged that in 1975-76, "a large part of the population in this region fled to the mountains."[76] As late as November 1979, Indonesian foreign minister Mochtar conceded that only half of East Timor's pre-1975 population had been brought under Indonesian control.[77] Jakarta's hope of a quick victory had foundered. But Nicolau Lobato's prediction of triumph over "senile Javanese expansionism" was also premature.[78]

The Genocide

Indonesian massacres of Timorese began on the first day of the December 1975 landing. Dunn calls the assault on Dili "one of the most brutal operations of its kind in modern warfare. Hundreds of Timorese and Chinese were gunned down at random in the streets." The Bishop of Timor watched from his window as 150 people, including at least twenty women, were systematically shot on the town's jetty. Five hundred Chinese were killed on December 8 alone. About forty unarmed Timorese men were murdered in the south of the capital on 9 December. A priest reported that the invaders killed about 2,000 people in the first few days, including 700 Chinese.[79] John Taylor reports many testimonies "of entire families being shot for displaying Fretilin flags on their houses, of groups being shot for refusing to hand over their personal possessions, of grenades being rolled into packed houses, and of Fretilin sympathizers singled out for immediate execution."[80] The latter included the wife of Vice President Nicolau Lobato, shot dead on the dock. Her sister saved their infant son at the last minute.[81]

The massacres then spread to the coastal and hill towns. Dunn continues: "When they finally forced Fretilin to withdraw from Aileu, Indonesian troops, in

---

73. Dunn, 309. Indonesian forces attacked Remexio in June 1978; "Offensive near Dili," *East Timor News* 36, June 29, 1978, 1. From September 1977 Indonesian offensives began conquering wide areas. Budiardjo, *War*, 57-58, 63.
74. 1974 estimates are 635,000 (Jill Jolliffe, *Cover-Up*, Melbourne: Scribe, 2001, 46), and 689,000 (the Timorese church). Taylor, *East Timor*, 89-90, 98, 203.
75. Taylor, *East Timor*, 89-90.
76. Budiardjo, *War*, 201.
77. Taylor, *East Timor*, 201.
78. "Speech of Nicolau Lobato," 13.
79. Dunn, *Timor*, 283-85; Taylor, *East Timor*, 68-69.
80. Taylor, *East Timor*, 69.
81. Jolliffe, *East Timor*, 8.

a brutal public spectacle, machine-gunned the remaining population of the town, except for children under the age of four, who were sent back to Dili in trucks." The killings at Aileu even distressed Tomas Goncalves, son of the *liurai* of At-sabe, a leading supporter of integration with Indonesia.[82] Citing Dunn, Taylor reports that "in the villages of Remexio and Aileu, south of Dili, everyone over the age of three was shot." Taylor adds: 'When Indonesian troops entered Aileu in February 1976, it contained 5,000 people. When a group of Indonesian relief workers visited it in September 1976, only 1,000 remained – they were told that the remainder had moved to the mountains."[83] A visitor found no Timorese in Ainaro in late 1975. Of Baucau's population of 85,000, 32,000 met the arriving Indonesian troops on December 10, 1975, but by the end of February 1976 most had fled the exactions of the occupiers, leaving a population of only 9,646. In mid-1976, "When the towns of Liquica and Maubara were eventually wrested from Fretilin's control the Indonesians put to death nearly all members of their Chinese communities."[84] Twenty-six people were executed in Liquica in May 1976 alone. Some survivors did remain in these towns, while many others fled to Fretilin-held mountain areas. But the Indonesian massacres took a heavy toll. A Timorese guide for a senior Indonesian officer told Dunn that "in the early months of the fighting, as the Indonesian forces moved into the central regions, they killed most Timorese they encountered."[85]

Perhaps the worst massacre took place just inside Indonesian West Timor. At Lamaknan in June 1976, Dunn reports, "Indonesian troops who had been badly mauled by Fretilin units took their vengeance on a large refugee settlement which housed some 5,000 to 6,000 people." After setting fire to several houses, the troops fired at the refugees for several hours, "shooting down men, women and children." According to a Timorese truck driver for the Indonesian forces, about 2,000 people died.[86]

The president of the pro-Indonesian provisional government of East Timor, Lopes da Cruz, announced on 13 February 1976 that 60,000 people had been killed "in the six months of civil war in East Timor," suggesting a toll of over 55,000 in the two months since the invasion.[87] A late 1976 report from the Indonesian Catholic Church estimated that 60,000 to 100,000 Timorese had perished.[88] In March 1977, Indonesian Foreign Minister Adam Malik conceded that "50,000 people or perhaps 80,000 might have been killed during the war in Timor, but we saved 600,000 of them."[89] On 12 November 1979, Indonesia's

---

82. Dunn, *Timor*, 286, 303.
83. Taylor, *East Timor*, 70, 81.
84. Dunn, *Timor*, 293, 286; Taylor, *East Timor*, 80-81.
85. Dunn, *Timor*, 303, 293.
86. Dunn, *Timor*, 303.
87. Dunn, *Timor*, 302-3; Taylor, *East Timor*, 201; Jolliffe, *East Timor*, 278.
88. Dunn, *Timor*, 310, "Notes on East Timor," in his possession.
89. *Age*, 1 April 1977. See N. Chomsky and E. Herman, *The Political Economy of Human Rights*, I (Boston: South End, 1979), 175-76.

new Foreign Minister Mochtar Kusumaatmadja estimated that 120,000 Timorese had died since 1975.[90]

The pressures of full-scale invasion and ongoing genocide initially brought to the fore Fretilin's harshest and most radical elements, who began to predominate in the resistance. As we shall see, Indonesian military forces successfully targeted them for destruction in 1977-79, but still could not eliminate Fretilin, which soon reemerged and then rebuilt itself under Xanana Gusmão as the relatively moderate nationalist movement of its early years. In 1987, Xanana condemned the "senseless radicalism" that had "paid no attention to our concrete conditions" and "made us intolerably overbearing and led us to put many compatriots on the same footing as the criminal aggressor." But he also lamented that "humanity had closed its eyes to the extermination of the Maubere people, a genocide carried out by the assassinating forces of the Indonesian occupation."[91] Over $1 billion in military equipment, supplied to Indonesia mostly by the USA but also by Britain, France, and Australia, had made this genocide possible.[92]

The Resistance

How did resistance continue and function under conditions of Indonesian-imposed famine and genocide?[93] And how did moderate Fretilin leaders regain the initiative in a movement under such a siege? The primary evidence of internal Fretilin division, both regional and ideological, only underscores the remarkable persistence and survival of East Timorese nationalism, despite regional differences but with minimal ethnic conflict.

In his September 1977 denunciation, Nicolau Lobato claimed that do Amaral had "forged a racist theory, attributing the cause of the war to the *mesticos*."[94] Lobato's accusation of do Amaral's racism against those of part-Portuguese descent is a rare suggestion of a politics of ethnicity within Fretilin. It certainly betrays political animosities. With partial fairness, do Amaral may have complained of Fretilin being run by a small non-Chinese *mestico* elite rather than the indigenous Timorese majority. He may even have considered that Lobato's

---

90. Taylor, *East Timor*, 203.
91. Gusmão, *To Resist*, 132, statement of December 7, 1987.
92. Budiardjo, *War*, 8-11; Taylor, *East Timor*, 84, 133-34, 174-75, 203; Ball/McDonald, *Death*, 182; Tanter, *Bitter Flowers*, 135-36, 163-72; Geoffrey C. Gunn, *Complicity in Genocide: Report to the East Timor "Truth Commission" on International Actors* (Tipgrafia Macau Hung Heng, 2006); *Chega ! The Report of the Commission for Reception, Truth and Reconciliation in Timor-Leste* (CAVR), 2005.
93. See also *Generations of Resistance: East Timor*, with photographs by Steve Cox and a forty-five-page historical introduction by Peter Carey (Cassell, UK, 1995); and Carey, "East Timor under Indonesian Occupation, 1975-99," in *Handbook on Terrorism and Insurgency*, ed. Andrew Tan (Malvern, 2006).
94. "Speech of Nicolau Lobato," 4.

"black nationalist" posture was an educated pretention disguising undemocratic exclusiveness, and that Fretilin's multi-regional national identity was
urban in origin. But such political characteristics alone do not constitute racial
persecution. Do Amaral's complaint seems as much against top-down political
domination. Lobato, acknowledging and denying that complaint, in turn accused
do Amaral, son of a *liurai*,[95] of drawing upon regionalism, traditionalism, and
indigenous nativism to shore up his own political support. Such regionalism
would indeed pose a ready challenge to nationalist imposition.

As nominal resistance leader in 1975-77, according to Lobato, do Amaral
"never attempted to call a Fretilin Central Committee meeting." "He created
and fomented divisionism among Commands, among the rank-and-file,
among different zones, among the different ethnic groups." According to
Lobato, do Amaral's stronghold was an arc of territory in north-central East
Timor, from the mountains south of Dili to the coastal area to its west. "His
feudal fiefs were Turiscai-[Ainaro] – Remexio-Lekidoe – Manatuto and part
of Maubisse."[96]

What kind of regime prevailed in this north-central area run by do Amaral in
1976-77? Xanana recalls that during the war in early 1976, "We traveled through
Turiskai. Xavier was in his kingdom leading a carefree life under the feudalistic
care of his brother."[97] Lobato, claiming that do Amaral "installed his relatives
and friends," also faulted "his protection of feudal institutions, like the *rajahs*,
sucos [villages], *povoacaos*." "These chiefs, together with the secretaries, some
commanders and the major part of the other authorities [*sic*] are among his more
loyal followers." Do Amaral "spread through the mouths of his relatives and
feudal bosses, the wrong theory that Turiscai was the fount of politics in East
Timor." Lobato called all this "an authentic feudal authority."[98]

Locally, do Amaral seems to have made rather successful use of many of
the traditional techniques of *liurai* rule. Lobato accused him of the "recourse
to use of corporal punishment, trials by Councils of Elders, his support for the
feudal relations of parenthood, *balaques* (arranged marriages)," as well as *lulics*
(animist sacred objects) "and other superstitious practices." Do Amaral made
"visits to festivities with big noise and big banquets; long voyages in cavalcade
with the noise of numerous guards," and "big colonial-style dances lasting all
night and sometimes for a whole week."[99]

Significant political issues also emerge from these cross-currents of rivalry,
regionalism and traditional leadership. For his part, Lobato envisioned "a new
society, free from all forms of exploitation of man by man." He considered
"democratic centralism" to be "a fundamental principle…on which our politics

---

95. Dunn, *Timor*, 4, 63.
96. "Speech of Nicolau Lobato," 4-6.
97. Gusmão, *To Resist*, 40.
98. "Speech of Nicolau Lobato," 6-9.
99. Ibid., 7, 4, 6.

are based." He used the slogan, "Put Politics in Command," by which he meant: "Between a civilian and a soldier, no wall exists…easily in practice, a civilian can become a soldier and a soldier, a civilian. The civilian tasks as well as the military tasks, are all political tasks…all our acts must be oriented and directed to reach a political objective." The CC meeting in Soibada from May 20 to June 2, 1976, which adopted the people's war strategy, emphasized organizational as well as military tasks.[100] Budiardjo and Liong report: "It was concluded that it would be suicidal to continue to engage in frontal combat against the numerically superior and much better equipped Indonesian army units. As a result the leadership decided to switch to more appropriate guerrilla tactics."[101] Maoist influence was now on the rise. It may also have been at this meeting that the CC created the Supreme Council of Resistance to oversee a protracted people's war.

By contrast, Lobato said, do Amaral believed in separating the military struggle from the civilian sphere, giving the war precedence over state organization and economic tasks, and diverting scarce seed and human resources to the military on "the strange theory that in time of war there was no time to make politics," and "no place" even for military preparations. "Now, we have only to fight anyhow." Thus, Lobato claimed, many "disorganized soldiers…were put unprepared in the frontline around Turiscai and Maubisse." Do Amaral allegedly interpreted "Put Politics in Command" to mean placing his own civilian appointees in charge of the armed forces in his region. He turned his Zone Political Bureau into "a sort of mini-Central Committee, like little heads leading the people in the zone." This threatened Lobato's authority as Prime Minister, and the Supreme Council's overall control of Fretilin's still substantial territory. As Lobato put it, "only one vanguard exists: the Fretilin Central Committee – as in a person's body there is only one head."[102] This was clearly a political standoff.[103]

The rivals took their battle to Alarico Fernandes' radio transmitter. Do Amaral supposedly gave "erroneous orders" that broadcasts were "not to attack any further…imperialism and its lackeys." But Fernandes and Lobato broadcast that "the principal enemy of the people is imperialism." Then "do Amaral started and sustained a very sharp polemic" with Fernandes.[104] Meanwhile, Fretilin's Maoists also opposed do Amaral, as well as Fernandes and the military officers, who all wished to seek external support for their resistance. Xanana recalls hearing the anti-Soviet Maoist slogan: "'Imperialism [equals] social imperialism' was the reason the politicians gave for rejecting the request for help to the Soviet Union. 'I don't want to know if it is imperialism or social imperialism. I don't care if the help comes from America, the Soviet Union,

100. Ibid., 2, 13, 5, 7-8.
101. Budiardjo, *War*, 26.
102. "Speech of Nicolau Lobato," 6-8, 10.
103. Here we must rely largely on accounts of do Amaral's rivals and successors, not all of whom survived. Hopefully do Amaral will provide a memoir of 1974-77.
104. "Speech of Nicolau Lobato," 10.

China, or whatever. All I need is help. Isn't that what we need?' yelled Xavier, dazed and defeated."[105]

Strikingly, this partly political, partly regional internal conflict never became a racist crusade. In each political incarnation, the struggle remained nationalist and inclusive. The political divisions debilitated Fretilin, but did not prevent its eventual recovery across the territory, from a solid regional base in the east.

Implosion

Internecine conflict seems to first have broken out in March 1976, during a meeting of the CC Standing Committee at Fatu Berliu, the first of three Fretilin gatherings in the south-central sector. Fernandes "started to follow very closely the tracks of Xavier do Amaral." Then the CC rejected do Amaral's proposed candidates for membership.[106] In April, at a meeting in nearby Barique, civilian-military relations soured; "it became obvious that the military had an aversion towards those of us who were politicians.... Silence and an obvious dissatisfaction characterized the climate of argument...Outside the meetings, the soldiers avoided the politicians." However, "many" professional officers were promoted to the CC, "avoiding a rebellion of the soldiers."[107] Perhaps a deal had been struck to permit the establishment of the Supreme Council of Resistance.

At the CC meeting held at Soibada from May 20-June 2, 1976, initial ideological discussions turned to Marxist concepts of the state. Do Amaral declared the state to be "eternal, coming from God." In what Xanana calls "a revolutionary avalanche of minds," the CC adopted its strategy of people's war, with most favoring "self-reliance" – except the army officers.[108] Do Amaral left the meeting "after only attending three days of its work, with the excuse of the National Celebration of May 20." He planned "a big concentration of the masses in his feudal fief of Turiscai" in June. From then on, do Amaral allegedly "did not follow the resolution made in the May 1976 meeting." He asserted rather "that the organizational work must come after the war."[109] He may also have objected to being subordinated to the Supreme Council. Moreover, Alarico Fernandes "aligned himself with the soldiers" and also walked out on the Soibada meeting, taking the radio transmitter. "The soldiers did not indicate any consternation," which worried Xanana. "Xavier had lost control because he knew so little about politics. Nicolau was on the other side, the soldiers continued to form a separate nucleus, and the majority of us, the members of the FCC [Fretilin Central Committee], were unpoliticised."[110]

---

105. Gusmão, *To Resist*, 41-2.
106. "Speech of Nicolau Lobato," 11.
107. Gusmão, *To Resist*, 41-2.
108. Ibid., 42-3.
109. "Speech of Nicolau Lobato," 5, 11, 8.
110. Gusmão, *To Resist*, 43.

The Soibada meeting saw other divisions too. Some of the returned student leftists from Portugal, Xanana says, "tried to influence our thinking about 'free love,'" while others like Vicente Sahe advocated a life-style of "puritanism" that earned more popular trust. Sahe also gave Xanana a copy of *Historical Materialism*, "but I informed him I had already heard enough 'isms' in Barique."[111] More ominously, conflict continued between the CC majority and a group of Timorese sergeants led by Aquiles Soares, a *liurai* from the central eastern region. These conservative nationalists, professional soldiers, rejected national political oversight. Soares later reportedly disobeyed CC orders to provide food to other zones and transfer populations to more secure areas. He began moves to purge Fretilin nationalists from his region, and may have contacted Indonesian forces. In November 1976, Soares and three associates were arrested by neighboring Fretilin commanders, and subsequently executed.[112] One of them was a pro-Fretilin *liurai* in the central-east sector; several other local *liurai* were Apodeti members. According to Xanana: "Our commanders constantly arrested the Apodetis and I kept freeing them. Finally they got tired of arresting them…"[113]

The CC Standing Committee, which met on 20 September 1976, may have authorized the repression. It is not known if do Amaral attended. Again the ranks diverged. In mid-December, do Amaral allegedly met secretly with commanders in the absence of the local political cadres, and "tempted them to disobey" central directives.[114]

The ideological gap widened too. "At the end of 1976," Xanana recalls, "I managed to get hold of a copy of *The Thoughts of Chairman Mao*. I read and re-read it, trying to understand Mao's simple way of describing complex things." By May 1977, "In groups we studied the 'strategic questions' of Mao and a change of war theory. The theory excited us in the planning of ideas and in strategic thinking, but it was a theory that required a heavy loss of life."[115]

The internal divisions came to a head. Rejecting invitations from "all members" of the CC, President do Amaral boycotted the conference of the Supreme Council of Resistance of the CC Political Committee, held at Laline from 8 to 20 May 1977.[116] Xanana says that "Xavier was happy in his kingdom and did not want to go to any more meetings."[117] Despite his absence, "sharp debate centered on a proposal to declare Fretilin a Marxist movement." Xanana recalls that "we were still dazzled by a vision of a miraculous process of human

111. Ibid., 49, 42.
112. Taylor, *East Timor*, 95-96; Niner, "Long Journey," 19; Gusmão, *To Resist*, 42, 44-46, 50.
113. Ibid., 44.
114. "Speech of Nicolau Lobato," 8-9.
115. Gusmão, *To Resist*, 47, 49.
116. "Speech of Nicolau Lobato," 5.
117. Gusmão, *To Resist*, 47.

redemption."[118] At mealtimes between political discussions, Nicolau Lobato "stopped talking.... 'No one prays to thank God for this food that the people have sweated to collect,' Nicolau said." Xanana recalls: "I understood how he was upset because although he was a Marxist he continued to be a religious person.... Nicolau stopped going to the meetings. He said he was sick." He donated his family's coffee plantations to the state. Hermengildo Alves complained, "Any day now, the state will get my wife's gold earrings too," while the "inveterate bohemian" dos Anjos told "endless anti-revolutionary jokes, which did not amuse the Department of Political and Ideological Orientation." Finance Minster Sera Key "debated issues, making an effort to demonstrate his abilities as a political theorist. In fact he was the only one who livened up the meeting, until all the political commissars were told to sit around the same table and get organized. After that there was no more debate."[119]

As Fretilin leaders debated Marxism, heavy Indonesian aerial bombardments began. Debate was apparently unresolved when approaching Indonesian troops prevented ratification of the proposal.[120] According to Xanana, "Marxism was acclaimed," but apparently without formation of a revolutionary party.[121] Indonesian military pressure only widened Fretilin's internal divisions. The result was what Lobato would soon call a "profound crisis that has shaken our nation, hit our people, threatened our young state and undermined the unity of the Front."[122]

Heightening differences seem reflected in successive statements by do Amaral, Lobato, and Fernandes, all broadcast by Fretilin radio and recorded in northern Australia. On May 20, 1977, the third anniversary of Fretilin's foundation, do Amaral, absent from the Laline meeting, claimed that his government had "organised the people to defend their country, so that they were not bunched up to be captured, but were spread out to contain the invasion. They did very well with only guns, bows and arrows, and no heavy artillery. Today, the fight continues against colonialism and neo-colonialism."[123] Do Amaral thus emphasized the military and regional aspects of the struggle, and apparently avoided criticism of "imperialism." Nor did he mention the Maoist notion of Soviet "social-imperialism." By contrast, in a recorded interview broadcast the next month, Nicolau Lobato stated: "Always politics is [in] command. We don't make war by war. Our armed struggle has a deeply political form and sense." He called for "liberation of our people from the colonialists and imperialists."[124]

118. Niner, "Long Journey," 19.
119. Gusmão, *To Resist*, 47-8, 25n42; Jolliffe, *East Timor*, 219.
120. Gusmão, *To Resist*, 52n83; Niner, "Long Journey," 19.
121. Gusmão, *To Resist*, 47, 66.
122. "Speech of Nicolau Lobato," 11.
123. "President F. Xavier do Amaral on Radio Maubere May 20 1977," *ETNA*, June 8, 1977.
124. "Prime Minister Nicolau Lobato Answers Questions," June 30, *ETNA*, July 4, 1977.

This difference appears to have given rise to another issue, whether to seek negotiations. In successive interviews conducted by radio from Australia on June 18 and 19, 1977, Alarico Fernandes insisted on a slogan that may have required reaffirmation in recent debate: "negotiations with the corrupt Jakarta government, never," and "negotiations with the enemy, never."[125] Who had called for negotiations was still unclear.

Ideological discussions continued. In nightly meetings during August 1977, Vicente Sahe and Xanana prepared "for the time when a revolutionary party would be formed." Xanana recalled: "We would be Maoists. At least they were Maoists..." Sahe, who admired Albania and Cuba, asked Xanana if he would agree to join the Party. Xanana says he replied, "No."[126]

On 7 August 1977, "the traitor Domingoes Simoes" tried to assassinate Alarico Fernandes. Do Amaral got the blame, and on 7 September 1977, was arrested by Lobato and Fernandes, possibly after avoiding another Supreme Council meeting.[127] "In circumstances that are still far from clear, he had apparently sought to arrange a compromise with the occupying forces."[128] Lobato announced: "Against the mistakes of comrades, we use the weapon of criticism. Against the enemies, traitors and sellers of the homeland, we use the criticism of weapons. To do that we must strengthen the repressive apparatus of our State."[129] Attacking do Amaral's group as "loyal slaves of the Javanese expansionists," Lobato's faction expelled two CC members from central East Timor, and five cadres from the same region.[130] Other cadres and an alleged agent "infiltrated in the Department of Information and National Security," were arrested and "seriously interrogated." Lobato announced that confessions had been "dragged out of the prisoners," and that the Remexio Zone Secretary was "a traitor already under our control in a safe place."[131]

At a meeting of the CC Political Committee in Aikurus, Fretilin Education Minister Hamis Basserwan now assumed "responsibility for the ideological training of the Fretilin Central Committee members." Xanana Gusmão recalls Basserwan earlier confiding: "Don't think, Xanana, that we are well-versed in theory. In Lisbon, I spent most of my time with the Portuguese Communist Party painting slogans on the walls!"[132]

---

125. "Fretilin Secretary for Information Answers Journalists' Questions," June 18, *ETNA*, June 21, 1977; "Answers by Minister Alarico Fernandes..., June 19, 1977," *ETNA*, July 12, 1977.
126. Gusmão, *To Resist*, 66.
127. "Speech of Nicolau Lobato," 9, 3.
128. Niner, "Long Journey," 19.
129. "Speech of Nicolau Lobato," 11-12.
130. The CC members were from Manatuto and Lakular; the zone cadres were Laclo and Remexio secretaries and their deputies, and the Laklubar secretary. "Speech of Nicolau Lobato," 1, 3.
131. "Speech of Nicolau Lobato," 3, 11.
132. Gusmão, *To Resist*, 66, 47; Jolliffe, *East Timor*, says Basserwan was 'Hata' (219).

In the east, CC member Sera Key returned from Aikurus and told his subordinate Xanana of the purges and atrocities committed there. Confused but apparently convinced of the need for "revolutionary violence," Key launched an investigation of local "counter-revolutionaries." But at a meeting of four CC members, Xanana reports challenging him: "I cannot accept this violence. I cannot accept that a member of the Central Committee would inflict torture..." Xanana claims that he managed to persuade Key to let him conduct his own investigations, eventually freeing the prisoners.[133]

Despite the violent purge of his followers, do Amaral and his associate Arsenio Horta survived nearly a year in Fretilin custody. On August 30, 1978, they were captured by Indonesian troops during the battle for Remexio.[134] Do Amaral was taken to Dili, where he called on Fretilin to surrender.[135] (He spent the next twenty-two years in Bali and Jakarta.[136]) Then came the capture or surrender of his former rival, Information Minister Fernandes, on December 2, 1978.[137] One of Fernandes' last radio transmissions announced that he and several others had broken with the CC.[138] In turn, Fretilin now also accused him of plotting a coup with "a correlation of forces in the central-north sector."[139] That region had been Amaral's stronghold. Close to Dili and to the center of Indonesian power, in 1977-78 the north-central sector appears to have favored a succession of local and national leaders seeking compromise with Jakarta.

At his surrender, Fernandes named the six "intransigent" leaders of the continuing Fretilin resistance: President Lobato, the new Vice President and Justice Minister Mau Lear, National Political Commissioner Vicente Sahe, Education Minister Hamis Basserwan and Economy Vice Minister Helio Pina, and Commissioner Carlos Cesar.[140] One of their last bases was Mt. Matebian in the eastern zone, where 30,000 people were holding out against Indonesian encirclement.[141] Xanana arrived there with many others from the island's eastern tip in September 1978. He describes what he saw: "I visited all the front lines engaged in combat. There was no room for the people. There were bombardments, explosions, death, blood, smoke, dust, and interminable queues

---

133. Gusmão, *To Resist*, 49-52; Niner, "Long Journey," 19.
134. "Traitors Escape, Xavier Rescue," *East Timor News* (*ETNA*) 41, September 14, 1978, 1; Niner, "Long Journey," 19, 27n20.
135. Melbourne *Herald*, December 5, 1978; *East Timor News* 47, December 28, 1978.
136. Niner, "Long Journey," 27n20. In the 1990s, do Amaral joined a group favoring autonomy within Indonesia. He returned to East Timor in 2000.
137. Melbourne *Herald*, December 8, 1978; *East Timor News*, no. 47, December 28, 1978; Taylor, *East Timor*, 96.
138. Gusmão, *To Resist*, 58n91.
139. "Betrayal not end of Struggle," *Tribune* (Sydney), December 13, 1978; *East Timor News* 47, December 28, 1978; on fellow CC member Redentor, "Speech of Nicolau Lobato," 9.
140. *East Timor News* 48, January 18, 1979; Jolliffe, *East Timor*, 219-20.
141. Budiardjo, *War*, 33.

of people waiting for their turn to try to get a bit of water for the children....
There was total lack of control.... The fighter planes were sowing the seeds of
death all day long."[142]

The base fell to the Indonesian forces on 22 November 1978. That night
Xanana and some troops fought their way out to the east.[143] Others escaped west.
Fretilin was now unable to defend its even larger base area, the Natarbora plain,
with a population of 60,000 people near the south coast, commanded by Vice
President Mau Lear and Vincente Sahe. Indonesian forces occupied Natarbora
in December 1978.[144] Then, Nicolau Lobato was surrounded near Maubisse. On
December 31, the Fretilin President was killed after a six-hour battle with Indonesian
forces led by Suharto's future son-in-law, Prabowo. Twenty other Fretilin leaders
and troops fell with him, including Deputy Defence Minister Guido Soares.[145] Mau
Lear took his place as Fretilin president. Vicente Sahe took command of its military
wing, Falintil – after escaping the battlefield with Hamis Basserwan.[146] Mau Lear
was tracked down and executed on 2 February 1979. Later that month, pursuing
Indonesian troops wounded Sahe in the leg. He ordered his fleeing comrades to
leave him where he fell.[147] Basserwan, Pina and Cesar all disappeared.[148] In the
east, Xanana sent a young Falintil commander, Taur Matan Ruak, to the central
sector to "find the Resistance Executive," but his unit was betrayed and trapped
near Viqueque. Ruak surrendered on 31 March. He managed to escape after
twenty-three days, and would later become Falintil Deputy Chief of Staff.[149]

From September 1977 to February 1979, the Fretilin central command was
virtually destroyed. Only three of the 52 CC members survived, all in the eastern
zone: Minister of Finance and political commissar Sera Key, Xanana Gusmão (chief
of the eastern sector, Ponte Leste), and Mau Hunu (deputy secretary of the eastern
region command).[150] David Alex, who had commanded elite companies until the
fall of Mt. Matebian, also remained active in the east, his forces intact, including
fourteen troops from his native village there.[151] Budiardjo has written: "Although
losses suffered by Fretilin in the eastern sector were enormous, the resistance
movement there was in better shape than in the border and central regions."[152]

142. Gusmão, *To Resist*, 56.
143. Ibid., 57.
144. Budiardjo, *War*, 33, 66.
145. Gusmão, *To Resist*, 25n40; Dunn, *Timor*, 317; Budiardjo, *War*, 36; Jolliffe, *East
      Timor*, 220.
146. *East Timor News* 48 (18 January 1979), 3, citing Indonesian reports.
147. Dunn, *Timor*, 317; Taylor, *East Timor*, 97.
148. Xanana received a report that "Cesar Maulaka was in the South Centre region, in
      the area of Alas, but much of the information was contradictory" (*To Resist*, 63).
149. Gusmão, *To Resist*, 60, n94, 57n89.
150. Ibid., 25n42, 152, says Txay was the third surviving CC member; Budiardjo, *War*,
      67, 70, says Sera Key.
151. Gusmão, *To Resist*, 59n92, 60; Budiardjo, *War*, 196, 213.
152. Budiardjo, *War*, 67; Taylor, *East Timor*, 115; Gusmão, *To Resist*, 29n51.

It was here that Xanana now began the slow, painful process of rebuilding. In December 1978-January 1979, he recalls, "for a month and a half I traveled through the hamlets, making contact with the people." An Indonesian-appointed village official hosted a secret meeting with a former Fretilin CC member, Joao Branco, and they "settled a few ideas on the continuity of the struggle. In February 1979 I summoned Txay and Kilik so we could assess the situation." Also, "The Commanders who were supposed to be in the Centre Region joined me." They reported that the Centre was in "chaos," as was Viqueque Region, where the violent Hermengildo Alves had treated them with characteristic "suspicion." A CC member from the Centre-East, Solan, and his ill wife, as well as "Olo Kasa and his weak wife, and Sera Key and his wife," along with their escorts, were all "isolated from each other and abandoned by their forces. Sera Key recommended to his two commanders that the forces that had returned from the Centre Region, and those that could not get through, be put under my charge. He would go to the Centre to try to find the Resistance Executive." Xanana toured the east, locating bands led by Mau Hodu, Taur Matan Ruak, Mauk Moruk, David Alex, Lay Kana, Olo Gari, Fera Lafaek, and Sabica. But the Indonesians captured Solan and Olo Kasa. They massacred Lay Kana, "the best commander" in the east, with his company and other defectors.[153]

In March 1979, the top five surviving Fretilin military officers (Falintil operational commander Mauk Muruk, Kilik Wae Gae, Olo Gari, Nelo and Freddy) met with the five senior political leaders (Xanana, Mau Hunu, Mau Hodu, Bere Malay Laka, and Taxy) at Titilari-Laivai in the central eastern sector, "to analyse the causes and consequences of the military collapse, and to devise adequate measures for the reorganization of the resistance."[154]

Sera Key set out from the east in April to make contact with the remaining resistance bands in the central sector. He and his wife were soon captured, "sick, abandoned and betrayed by the last forces from the East Centre sector which had also surrendered." Indonesian troops reportedly took Sera Key to Dili by helicopter and dumped him in the sea. In July and December, Xanana and Mau Hunu sent out further missions, but both returned without encountering surviving resistance groups further west.[155] In May 1980, Xanana took half a company of sixty troops from the east to the western border and back. A Fretilin unit staged a spectacular attack on Dili TV station on June 10. By October Xanana had made contact with continuing resistance forces in Kablake near the border, and in the central sector. On Christmas Day, Falintil attacked Baucau, the territory's second city.[156]

Fretilin was eventually able to organize a national conference, from 1-8 March 1981, at Lacluta in the eastern central region. Xanana was elected presi-

---

153. Gusmão, *To Resist*, 51, 58-9.
154. Gama, "War in the Hills," 101.
155. Budiardjo, *War*, 67; Taylor, *East Timor*, 115; Gusmão, *To Resist*, 62, 25n42.
156. "Instruction Manual No. Juknis//05/I/1982: System of Security," trans. Budiardjo, *War*, 183; Taylor, *East Timor*, 115; Gusmão, *To Resist*, 64-65.

dent, Kilik Wae Gae became chief-of-staff, and Mau Hunu, deputy chief-of staff. Bere Malay Laka was named secretary of information. They reported to the conference that Fretilin had lost 79 percent of the members of its Supreme Command, 80 percent of its troops, 90 percent of its weapons, all its population bases, and all the channels of communication between its scattered groups and with the outside world.[157]

Famine and Mass Murder

According to Indonesian documents that Fretilin forces captured in 1982, "as a result of all the unrest, many village heads have been replaced, whilst many new villages have emerged." The experience of two eastern villages is instructive: "With the upheavals," the inhabitants "fled into the bush," returning only in May 1979, when they were "resettled" in a district town. "But this led to their being unable to grow food on their own land, so that food shortages have occurred."[158] Famine ravaged East Timor in 1979. Indonesian aerial bombardment of their homes and cultivated gardens in the hill areas had forced many Timorese to surrender in the lowlands, but food was scarce there. Indonesia's control eventually expanded, and its counts of the Timorese population rose from 329,000 to as many as 522,000 in mid-1979.[159] Over 120,000 Timorese remained missing, mostly victims of the famine and the continuing Indonesian-instigated massacres and repression. Taylor reports that on 23 November 1978, Indonesian troops shot 500 people who surrendered to them the day after the fall of Mt. Matebian; soon afterwards there was a similar massacre of 300 in Taipo, and in two further incidents in the east in April-May 1979, Indonesian forces murdered ninety-seven and 118 people, respectively.[160] Also in the east, Indonesians massacred Joao Branco and forty others at the end of 1979.[161] In a September 1981 massacre southeast of Dili, 400 people died, mostly women and children.[162] In August 1983, sixty men, women and children were tied up and bulldozed to death at Malim Luro near the south coast. On August 21-22, troops burned alive at least eighty people in the southern village of Kraras, and then made a "clean-sweep" of the neighbouring area in which another 500 died. Of East Timor's 20,000-strong ethnic Chinese minority, survivors numbered only "a few thousand" by 1985.[163]

As fighting continued, Indonesia's Special Forces worked to recruit Timorese paramilitary combat teams, predecessors of the militias responsible

157. Budiardjo, *War*, xii, 67-70.
158. Ibid., 201, 243, 212-13.
159. Taylor, *East Timor*, 98.
160. Taylor, *East Timor*, 88.
161. Gusmão, *To Resist*, 53-4, n89.
162. Taylor, *East Timor*, 101-2; Gama, "War in the Hills," 102.
163. Taylor, *East Timor*, 102-3, 142, 206, 68-70, 164, 207 (citing *Far Eastern Economic Review*, 8 September 1985).

for widespread massacres in the 1990s. In the first two months of 1982, the team Railakan I, comprising fifty-two troops, killed eight Falintil rebels and captured thirty-two. In an attack on Xanana's forces in September, Railakan I killed nine more Fretilin troops.[164]

Regional Resurgence

In the early 1980s, despite devastating blows, Timorese resistance still challenged Jakarta's forces, who termed Fretilin "gangs of security disruptors" (*Gerakan Pengacau Keamanan*, or GPK).[165] In 1982, Indonesian commanders in Dili acknowledged in confidential documents that "despite the heavy pressure and the disadvantageous conditions under which they operate, the GPK has nevertheless been able to hold out in the bush." For instance, from just six villages of the eastern zone, 293 inhabitants were "still in the bush." After seven years of occupation, Fretilin "support networks" still existed "in all settlements, the villages as well as the towns." These "underground networks are closely related to customs and to the family system." Jakarta aimed "to obliterate the classic GPK areas" and "crush the GPK remnants to their roots."[166] The conquered territory must "eventually be completely clean of the influence and presence of the guerrillas." Deportations continued; in one sector of the eastern zone, thirty more villages were resettled in 1982.[167]

The Indonesian commander in Dili, Colonel A. Sahala Rajagukguk, revealed to his officers that nine Fretilin bands continued to operate. Of four "small, unorganized groups," one even operated near West Timor and Dili, "in the border district of Ermera, and in the districts of Dili, Liquica, and Ailiu." Summarizing the activities of all these groups, Col. Rajagukguk concluded that "they can meet together at predetermined places... Meetings in the eastern region can be held in the regions of Koaliu, Matabean, Macadique or Builo. On such occasions there is a very sizeable concentration of forces in one place." He went on: "It is in the eastern sector that people's support is most militant and most difficult [for Indonesian forces] to expose. This is because of the very strong, close family ties and also because it has been possible for the GPK to consolidate its political leadership in this region for several years. This is also because a large part of the population in this region fled to the mountains and only came down to the new villages at the beginning of 1979. In such circumstances, the GPK has consciously chosen the eastern region as its hinterland and reserve base."[168]

---

164. Kammen, "Trouble," 159-60.
165. Captured Indonesian documents, trans. Budiardjo, *War*, 82.
166. Budiardjo, *War*, 176, 215, 222, 227, 194-96, 216, 242, 193.
167. Ibid., 242-3, 193, 228, 241, 213.
168. Ibid., 196, 201; Gusmão, *To Resist*, 29n51.

Normalizing the Occupation, 1983-99

In 1982 Indonesian intelligence knew of most of the surviving Fretilin leaders, naming Mauk Moruk, Mau Hunu, David Alex, Kilik, Txay, and Loro Timur Anan.[169] If Jakarta was as yet unaware of Xanana's leadership position, they learned of it within a year. A new Indonesian army commander, General Mohammed Yusuf, agreed to a ceasefire and negotiations with Fretilin. Xanana then held two days of talks with his Indonesian counterparts on 21 and 23 March 1983. Jakarta later abandoned the negotiations, but the ceasefire was a temporary acknowledgement of Fretilin's continuing military challenge. Fighting resumed, with Falintil estimated to be fielding up to 1,000 guerrillas in several areas. Indonesian reinforcements in 1984 brought troop levels back up to 14,000-20,000. Railakan I, a locally-recruited Special Forces paramilitary team, increased in size from 52 to 90 men. From March to December 1984 this team alone killed thirty-two Falintil rebels and captured twelve. As the war raged on, Suharto declared a state of emergency in East Timor on September 9, 1985.[170]

Douglas Kammen sees the 1983 ceasefire as Jakarta's "tentative, indeed abortive, first attempt" to normalize its control of East Timor and secure foreign recognition for its integration of the territory. However, this was accompanied by "alternative forms of violence," such as increasing Indonesian use of East Timorese combat "teams." Suharto made a second attempt in 1988, when he declared East Timor's "equal status" with Indonesia's other twenty-six provinces. Jakarta announced the "opening" of the territory and the introduction of "Operation Smile." The 1989 Papal visit followed. But, Kammen says, "greater openness was accompanied by the heightened use of covert operations and terror," especially against Fretilin's new strategy of non-violent urban protest, but also a new rural offensive aiming to capture Xanana, who moved secretly into Dili in February 1991.[171] In August 1991, Indonesian forces in East Timor totaled 20,700, including 11,000 "external" troops on rotation there from other provinces, 4,800 "territorial" or local troops, and other members of the Indonesian armed forces. Samuel Moore writes: "The East Timorese continued to live under one of the most intensive military occupations of modern history," with ten to fourteen troops stationed in each village and neighbourhood, a soldier for every thirty-eight civilians. In Dili on November 12, 1991, the army gunned down and bayoneted three hundred Timorese funeral marchers at the Santa Cruz cemetery, an event secretly filmed by a journalist, bringing East Timor to world attention. A year later, Xanana was discovered and arrested.[172] Still the resistance continued, and urban unrest mounted.

169. Budiardjo, *War*, 177, 196.
170. Taylor, *East Timor*, 136, 151, 206; Dunn, *Timor*, 319; Kammen, "Trouble," 159-60.
171. Kammen, "Trouble," 160-2; Samuel Moore, "The Indonesian Military's Last Years in East Timor: An Analysis of Its Secret Documents," *Indonesia* 72, October 2001, 9-44, at 14.
172. Kammen, "Trouble," 164-65; Moore, "Indonesian Military," table 2, 24-25.

In May 1990, Jakarta had replaced its combat Security Operations Command (*Koopskam*) with a new East Timor Operations Implementation Command (*Kolakops*). In response to international condemnation of the Santa Cruz massacre, external battalions began to be withdrawn and replaced by local territorial troops, and a third attempt at normalization was made with the liquidation of Kolakops, in April 1993. All security responsibilities, including command of the nine external battalions then on rotation in the territory, were now assigned to the local territorial command, Korem 164, headquartered in Dili but "entirely under the direction of non-East Timorese."[173] By April 1994, when the number of battalions under Korem 164 was reduced to seven, the military had begun forming paramilitary units such as the "Young Guards Upholding Integration" (*Gada Paksi*), which had 1,100 members by 1996. These militia forces expanded rapidly. By 1995 the former commander of the Railakan I paramilitary team headed a 300-strong militia. By 1997-98 there were twelve such paramilitary teams with 4,000-8,000 members. Also in 1997-98, the number of regular battalions under Korem 164 again increased, to thirteen.[174] By August 1998 the total number of Indonesian troops in the territory was 21,600, including 8,000 external troops.[175]

Suharto fell from power in May 1998, and pressure mounted on Jakarta to hold a referendum in the territory. This brought a sharp increase in militia activity. The army sponsored the creation of several new militia forces at the end of 1998.[176]

The Fretilin leadership had suffered major losses by the time of Suharto's fall. Falintil's Operational Commander Mauk Muruk, who had surrendered in July 1985, spent the next four years in the psychiatric isolation ward of a Jakarta military hospital.[177] In June 1990, Mau Hodu became Fretilin vice chairperson, but was captured in January 1992. After the arrest of Xanana in November the same year, David Alex became deputy chief of staff of Falintil. He was wounded and captured by Indonesian troops in June 1997 and is presumed dead. His successor Konis Santana, killed in an accident in March 1998, was replaced by Taur Matan Ruak, who had been deputy chief of staff in the mid-1980s.[178] But despite these setbacks, 600-900 veteran Fretilin troops fought on in the hills, joined by 600 recruits in 1998 alone. Taur Matan Ruak's force of 1,500 welcomed the United Nations peacekeepers when they arrived in the territory in September 1999.[179]

Despite its military losses, Fretilin had maintained a broad political base. In 1992, an Indonesian intelligence report entitled "Data on Disturbed Villages," categorized only 163 of East Timor's 442 villages as peaceful and secure. Seventy-nine villages were coded Red, meaning "disturbed" (possibly,

---

173. Kammen, 162-65; Moore, 28.
174. Kammen, "Trouble," 166, 168-69, 180, 174.
175. Moore, "Indonesian Military," 25, table 2.
176. Kammen, "Trouble," 182-83.
177. Gama, "War in the Hills," 103.
178. Gusmão, *To Resist*, 43-44, 57-60. Moore names other 1990s leaders: Sabica, Lere Anan Timur, Ular and Falur ("Indonesian Military," 14).
179. Moore, "Indonesian Military," 13.

Fretilin-controlled). In 1997, Korem 164 intelligence estimated that the GPK "clandestine front" had about 1,500 members in the capital, and in 1999, 6,000 members throughout the territory.[180]

In September 1998, in a historic reconciliation, all five East Timorese parties involved in the civil war of 1975 joined forces under the new umbrella organization CNRT, electing the political prisoner Xanana Gusmão as President.[181] A year later, 79 percent of Timorese voted for independence in the UN-organized referendum.

Genocidal Counterinsurgency

Jakarta was unable to achieve its goal of conquest. But what underlying ideology justified genocide in the attempt? In Remexio and Aileu, where "everyone over the age of three was shot" in early 1976, Indonesian forces explained that the local people had been "infected with the seeds of Fretilin." After the September 1981 Lacluta massacre, a soldier allegedly explained: "When you clean your field, don't you kill all the snakes, the small and large alike?" In 1984, a new territory-wide military campaign aimed at what one commander called the obliteration of Fretilin "to the fourth generation."[182] The mixture of biological and agricultural metaphors is common in genocidal regimes.[183] While the killings of over 500,000 communists in Indonesia in 1965-66 had not been accompanied by ethnic massacres targeting minorities, in the territorial expansion a decade later, Jakarta's repressive forces did single out the Chinese of East Timor for "selective killings."[184]

Indonesia's targeting of Fretilin as a multi-generational kinship group also resembles genocide. In early 1999, as the UN referendum approached, Indonesian military and militia commanders threatened to "liquidate...all the pro-independence people, parents, sons, daughters, and grandchildren."[185] At a meeting in Bali in February 1999, Indonesian commanders Adam Damiri and Mahidin Simbolon ordered militias "to eliminate all of the CNRT leaders and sympathizers."[186] On 16 February, meeting with militia leaders, Lieutenant-Colonel Yahyat Sudrajad called for the killing of pro-independence leaders, their

180. Ibid., 13-14, 16; a 1982 Indonesian document describes the "Red Zone" as areas of Fretilin control (Budiardjo, *War*, 203).
181. Kammen, "Trouble," 173.
182. Taylor, *East Timor*, 70, 102, 151.
183. Kiernan, "Genocide and 'Ethnic Cleansing'," in R. I. Wuthnow, ed., *Encyclopedia of Politics and Religion*, Washington, Congressional Quarterly, 1998, 294-299; Kiernan, *Blood and Soil: Genocide and Extermination in World History from Carthage to Darfur*, New Haven, CT, Yale University Press, 2007.
184. Taylor, East Timor, 69.
185. Andrew Fowler, "The Ties that Bind," Australian Broadcasting Corporation, 14 February 2000, quoted in N. Chomsky, *A New Generation Draws the Line: East Timor, Kosovo, and the Standards of the West*, London, 2000, 72; for details, A. Evans, "Revealed: the plot to crush Timor," *South China Morning Post*, September 16, 1999.
186. Quoted in Kammen, "Trouble," 183.

children and grandchildren. "Not a single member of their families was to be left alive, the colonel told the meeting."[187] Jakarta's governor of the territory, Abilio Soares, ordered that "priests and nuns should be killed."[188] (In 2002, Soares was convicted in a Jakarta court.) Militia leaders called on their followers to "conduct a cleansing of the traitors of integration. Capture them and kill them."[189] Tono Suratman, Korem 164 commander in Dili, warned: "if the pro-independents do win…all will be destroyed. It will be worse than 23 years ago."[190] A May 1999 Indonesian army document ordered that "massacres should be carried out from village to village after the announcement of the ballot if the pro-independence supporters win." The East Timorese independence movement "should be eliminated from its leadership down to its roots."[191]

The U.N.-sponsored Truth Commission concluded in 2005 that these policies amounted to "extermination as a crime against humanity committed against the East Timorese population."[192] Of the 1975 population of 628,000, possibly 150,000 people disappeared in the next four years.[193] According to the Truth Commission, Jakarta's extermination campaign included policies that caused between 100,000 and 180,000 Timorese deaths, including at least 84,000 under state-imposed famine conditions and over 12,000 murders of political opponents.

Maoist ideological influence on Fretilin in East Timor and on the Khmer Rouge in Cambodia produced political purges, repression and murder in both cases. Yet in the Cambodian case, Khmer Rouge military aggression against Vietnam, supported by China for geopolitical reasons, combined with a virulent Khmer Rouge racism that targeted foreigners and ethnic minorities for genocide. To the Maoist-influenced Fretilin regime, however, genocide came from without, in the name of anti-communism. East Timor did not attack Indonesia, but was the victim of aggression. Maoism functioned there within a multicultural nationalist party resisting foreign invasion and extermination. The political and geopolitical factors favoring genocide varied, and in each case regionalisms undercut the genocidists and the resistance, while racism and expansionism played major roles in both tragedies.

---

187. Evans, 'Revealed,' quoting Tomas Goncalves, 54, former head of the PPPI militia. Andrew Fowler reported that in early 1999, pro-Indonesia commanders threatened to "liquidate…all the pro-independence people, parents, sons, daughters, and grandchildren" (Chomsky, *New Generation*, 72).
188. Evans, "Revealed"; Kammen, "Trouble," 184.
189. Kammen, "Trouble," 184.
190. Brian Toohey, "Dangers of Timorese Whispers Capital Idea," *Australian Financial Review*, 14 August 1999; John Aglionby, *et al.*, "Revealed: army's plot," *Observer*, 12 September 1999.
191. Chomsky, *New Generation*, 74.
192. *Chega ! The Report of the Commission for Reception, Truth and Reconciliation in Timor-Leste* (CAVR), October 2005, Part 8: Responsibility and Accountability, p. 6. See also Sian Powell, "UN Verdict on East Timor," *The Australian,* Jan. 19, 2006. The full report is at: www.cavr-timorleste.org
193. On Nov. 12, 1979, Indonesia's Foreign Minister Mochtar Kusumaatmadja gave a figure of 120,000 Timorese dead from 1975 to Nov. 1979 (Taylor, *East Timor: The Price of Freedom,* London, 1999, 203).

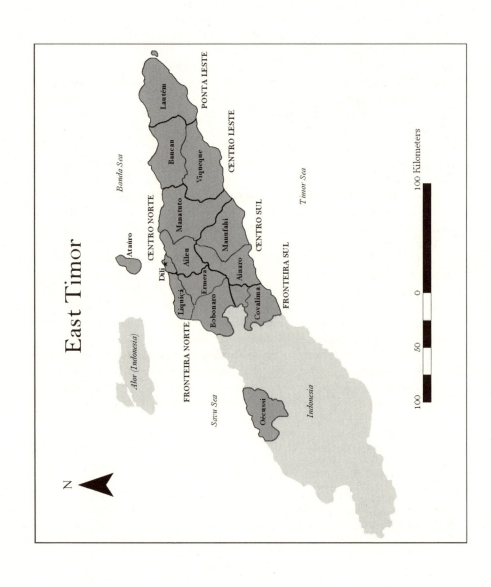

East Timor

N

Alor (Indonesia)

Banda Sea

Savu Sea

FRONTEIRA NORTE

CENTRO NORTE

Atauro

Dili

Liquiçá

Ermera

Bobonaro

Covalima

Oecussi

Aileu

Ainaro

Manufahi

Manatuto

Baucau

Lautém

Viqueque

CENTRO SUL

FRONTEIRA SUL

CENTRO LESTE

PONTA LESTE

Timor Sea

Indonesia

100   50   0   100 Kilometers

4

The Resistance in East Timor: The UN-Sponsored Truth Commission Analysis

The Resistance: Structure and Strategy

Introduction

1. The resistance against Indonesian occupation in Timor-Leste went through a complex development. This part provides an overview of the Resistance movement including its emergence during the period of Fretilin administration following the coup [attempt by the UDT party in the capital, Dili, in August 1975]; the effect of destruction of the Fretilin bases in 1978-79 by the Indonesian military including the loss of a number of Fretilin/Falintil leaders and the end of the protracted people's war strategy; the regeneration of Falintil, the armed front of the Resistance, after 1987 and its structure and strategies until the referendum in 1999; and the structure and strategies of the clandestine front over the course of the occupation. The third front in the Resistance movement, the diplomatic front, is discussed in chapter 7.1: The Right to Self-Determination, and so is not considered in detail here. The Commission notes that this chapter is only a first step in understanding the complex history of this aspect of Timorese history and that there is considerable scope for further research in the future.

2. The Resistance had its origins in the armed conflict triggered by the armed movement of 11 August 1975. The UDT movement aimed to eradicate the so-called "communist" elements within Fretilin, who UDT considered dangerous to the national interest of Timor-Leste. The Revolutionary Front for an Independent East Timor (Frente Revolucionaria de Timor Leste Independente, Fretilin), which succeeded in securing the support from most East Timorese in the Portuguese colonial armed forces, won the conflict in fewer than twenty days. With its

"The Resistance: Structure and Strategy," Part 5 of *Chega! The Report of the Commission for Reception, Truth and Reconciliation in Timor-Leste* (CAVR), October 2005. Reprinted with the permission of the Post-CAVR Secretariat, PO Box 144, Dili, Timor-Leste. The full report may be found online at: www.cavr-timorleste.org.

victory over UDT, and the departure of the Portuguese colonial government, Fretilin found itself having to act as the de facto government of Timor-Leste. Its leadership, which previously believed they could secure independence without armed conflict, suddenly faced a new situation that forced them to reorganize.

3. The invasion of the powerful Indonesian military on 7 December 1975 forced Fretilin and its armed wing, the Armed Forces for the Liberation of Timor-Leste (Forças Armadas de Libertação Nacional de Timor Leste, Falintil) to flee to the mountains to reorganise into an armed resistance force. Fretilin were confronted with many problems during the process of reorganisation. Differences of opinion on the structure and even more so the strategy to be used by Fretilin/Falintil arose. The changes in structure and strategy over time reflected not only the changes in the nature of the conflict, but were also a result of conflicts within the Resistance movement itself.

4. The fact that the majority of people fled to the forest also became a problem. A number of Resistance leaders believed that the war they were fighting was not only about the expulsion of foreign aggressors, but also a revolution to erase the old social order that oppressed people, known as "exploitation of man by man" ("exploração do homem pelo homem") and to build in its place a new social structure without oppression. For them the war was a revolutionary war. In the aftermath of the Indonesian invasion, a majority of Fretilin leaders held this view. In the forest civilians were organised to support the armed resistance logistically or politically. People were organised through social and political programmes to create the new social structures.

5. Other leaders, especially those with a military background, tended to see the war only from its military aspect, and regarded the people as a burden to the Resistance because of the military resources required to protect civilian lives. With the Indonesian military's relentless offensive against Fretilin resistance bases, the conflicts within the Resistance increased. Unable to endure the attacks, some leaders allowed or even advised people to surrender.

6. Other leaders tried to negotiate with the enemy, but these actions were strongly opposed and sometimes became a source of armed conflict within the Resistance itself.

7. The destruction of the "liberated zones" ("zonas libertadas") brought about an entirely new situation. Civilians, some Fretilin civilian leaders and some Falintil troops were captured or surrendered because they could not withstand the Indonesian military assaults. Other Falintil units and a few Fretilin leaders managed to escape the "encirclement and annihilation" operations and survived in the forest by constantly moving from one place to another. The separation of civilians from the armed resistance prompted the Resistance movement to enter a new phase, in which Falintil in the forest were supported by civilians in the settled, Indonesian-controlled areas. Previously, by contrast, civilians had been organised by Fretilin cadres in the Resistance support bases (*bases de apoio*), and Falintil had been responsible only for security.

8. Falintil troops regrouped into small independent units without a fixed base, and made guerrilla attacks on the Indonesian military. Logistical support, which was once provided from civilians in the Resistance bases de apoio, now had to be obtained from civilians in the occupied territory. As such, the armed resistance movement in the forest had to develop new ways to organise civilians as their main source of support.

9. Underground activities (*clandestina*) supporting the armed struggle in the forest and the diplomatic struggle overseas became increasingly important. These activities were first carried out by Fretilin cadres in the city who had not fled to the interior at the time of the Indonesian invasion on 7 December 1975. After the destruction of the zonas libertadas, the Fretilin political cadres as well as ex-Falintil commanders and soldiers also began to undertake clandestine activities to support the struggle. Their role was crucial to providing logistics and information to Falintil, for communication between Falintil forces who were separated from each other, and for communication between leaders of the armed resistance in the forest and leaders of the diplomatic resistance overseas.

10. In 1981 the Revolutionary Council of National Resistance (Conselho Revolucionário de Resistência Nacional, CRRN) was established and formally took over the leadership of the Resistance. In practice Falintil led the Resistance as it represented the only functioning Resistance leadership. Although the commander of Falintil was the National Political Commissar (Comissário Política Nacional), Falintil's real power came from its position as the most active branch of the Resistance. Indeed, political activities among the civilian population at this time were limited to assisting Falintil logistically.

11. The National Council of Maubere Resistance (Concelho Nacional da Resistência Maubere, CNRM) was founded in 1987 to replace the CRRN. This changed Fretilin's role in the leadership of the Resistance to a purely symbolic one. The Resistance leadership accepted that independence could never be achieved through war because of the enemy's military dominance, and instead focused on achieving independence through a peaceful resolution with primary attention to the international arena. The diplomatic struggle, which had been launched before the Indonesian invasion in 1975, was given greater emphasis. International support was sought not only from non-aligned nations and socialist nations, but also from liberal democratic nations that had previously paid little attention to the plight of Timor-Leste.

12. Some Resistance leaders felt the need to establish a new forum to accommodate all political parties and movements that supported independence, particularly those outside Fretilin. The CNRM aimed to be a movement of national unity, struggling against occupation on three fronts: the armed front in the forest and interior, the clandestine front in the villages and towns in Timor-Leste and Indonesia, and the diplomatic front in the international arena (for more information on the diplomatic front see chapter 7.1: The Right to Self-Determination). At this time, Falintil went through a "breaking of party ties" (*despartidarização*)

with Fretilin, and became the national armed forces under the leadership of the CNRM. This arrangement continued after the establishment of the National Council of Timorese Resistance (Concelho Nacional da Resistência Timorense, CNRT) in place of the CNRM in April 1998 in Peniche, Portugal, which led the Resistance until the end of Indonesian occupation in 1999.

Fretilin and the Bases de Apoio

13. The Indonesian invasion caused major displacement of civilians to the forests and mountains with Fretilin. This is considered in detail in chapter 7.3: Forced Displacement and Famine.

14. Providing the large number of refugees with shelter, food and other basic necessities was a huge problem for Fretilin. Fretilin, having written a social and political programme as early as November 1974, appeared well prepared to organise the people. Cadres immediately arranged administration from the sub-village (aldeia), to the village (suco) up to the district (região) level using their existing organisational structures. Administrators at the aldeia level reorganized people from their own aldeia, village administrators reorganized people from their village, and so on, until there was a Fretilin administration in the mountains. It appears that this reorganisation was an initiative from the rank and file cadre. Eduardo de Jesus Barreto, a cadre from the Ermera Zone stated:

"Up until early 1976 there was no strong formal structure at the ground level, but Fretilin militants in the bases managed to organise people although not formally.... People also performed farming activities like growing corn, tubers, and other edible plants individually or in groups."[1]

15. This spontaneous restructuring lasted from the beginning of the war until mid-1976. At that time, the Indonesian army had managed to take control of only the towns, the north coastal road from west to east and the central corridor running from north to south. Xanana Gusmão testified to the Commission:

The enemy came into Dili, Baucau and Lospalos, and people fled. There was still major confusion. After that it began to stabilize....When the enemy managed to take over the main roads, the north road and from north to south, it began to feel stable. Because of this situation the Central Committee came up with the idea to establish six sectors in May 1976...based on the division of the political administration from aldeia, suco, zona, região, and sector.[2]

Organization of civilians

16. The organisation of civilians (and the military) was discussed at the Fretilin Central Committee's second plenary session held in Soibada (Manatuto) in May 1976 (the Soibada Conference).[1*] At this conference, it was decided to form national civilian and military structures. The zonas libertadas were divided

---

* The plenary session was held from 15 May to 2 June 1976. The session decided "three guiding principles of the Maubere Revolution": people's war, protracted war, and self-reliance [Fretilin, Relatório da Delegação do Comité Central da Fretilin em Missão de Serviço no Exterior do Pais, p. 3].

into six sectors.[2+] These sectors defined both military zones under military command and political and administrative units under Fretilin administration. In accordance with the principle that politics commands the gun (*política comanda fuzil*), the military commanders deferred to the civilian political administrators.[3++] However, some of the highest military positions, such as chief of staff and the minister and two deputy ministers of defence, were also members of the Fretilin Central Committee.

17. The position of political commissar (*comissário política*), the supreme leader in each sector with responsibility for both political and military matters, was also created in Soibada. All political commissars were members of the Fretilin Central Committee.[4§] The sectors, the districts they covered and the political commissar in each sector are set out below:

Table 4.1
Fretilin Regional Structure from May 1976

Sector	Districts included	Political Commissar
Ponta Leste (Eastern End)	Lautém	Juvenal Inácio (Sera Key)**
Centro Leste (Central E.)	Baucau and Viqueque	Vicente dos Reis (Sa'he)++
Centro Norte (Central N.)	Manatuto, Aileu, and Dili	João Bosco Soares
Centro Sul (Central S.)	Manufahi, Ainaro	Hamis Bassarewan (Hata)
Fronteira Norte (Northern Frontier)	Ermera, Liquiça, parts of Bobonaro	Hélio Pina (Maukruma)
Fronteira Sul (Southern Frontier)	Covalima, parts of Bobonaro	César Correia (César Mau Laka)

+ There were supposed to be seven sectors, with the Oecusse enclave as the seventh, but circumstances did not allow for the establishment of the Oecusse sector [CAVR Interviews with Jacinto Alves, Dili, 11 May 2004 and Francisco Gonçalves, Dili, 14 June 2003].

++ This principle had already been in effect since the establishment of Falintil in August 1975 after the 11 August movement by UDT. From that time, Falintil was under the command of the Fretilin Central Committee [see, for example, CAVR Interviews with Lucas da Costa, Dili, 21 June 2004, with Taur Matan Ruak, Dili, 9 June 2004 and Xanana Gusmão, Dili, 7 July 2004].

§ According to Xanana Gusmão, who at the time was a member of the Fretilin Central Committee, departments of the RDTL government were no longer functioning at this time [CAVR Interview with Xanana Gusmão, Dili, 7 July 2004]. In the Fretilin Central Committee there was a Permanent Committee, in charge of making decisions if a Central Committee plenary session was not possible [CAVR Interview with Jacinto Alves, Dili, 11 May 2004].

** In the RDTL Board of Ministers, Sera Key was the Minister of Finance. After the Aikurus (Remexio, Aileu) meeting, some parts of Baucau and Viqueque, east of the road connecting Baucau to Viqueque, were included in the Ponta Leste Sector. This change was due to the fact that Indonesian military control of that road made it difficult for the two territories in that sector to communicate [CAVR Interview with Francisco Gonçalves, Dili, 14 June 2003; Xanana Gusmão, Sarah Niner (ed.), *To Resist is to Win! The autobiography of Xanana Gusmão*, Victoria: Aurora Books, 2000, p. 49].

++ In the RDTL Board of Ministers he occupied the position of the Minister of Labour and Welfare.

18. Political commissars worked with assistant commissars (*assistente comissáriado*).[7+] Assistant commissars were each responsible for organising specific tasks such as health, agriculture, education, the women's organizations and political propaganda. The secretariat of the Fretilin administrators was called the Comissáriado. Sectors were divided into smaller administrative units:[8§§]

19. This structure was a continuation of the government system established by Fretilin when it took control of Timor-Leste after the defeat of the 11 August movement of UDT. For instance at the zona level, some informants told the

Table 4.2
Fretilin Administrative Structure

Administrative unit	Area	Leadership
Region (região)	Similar to the area covered by a conselho in the Portuguese colonial administration system, today referred to as district.	A secretary (secretário) and a regional vice secretary (vice secretário regional)
Zone (zona)	Similar to the territory that, in the Portuguese administrative system, was called a posto, today referred to as sub-district.	Zone Committee (Comite de Zona) led by a secretário and vice secretário de zona. In the Comite da Zona there was a Health Commission (Comissão de Saude), Agriculture Commission (Comissão da Agricultura) and Education Commission (Comissão da Educação).3 Attached to each was an activista, whose task was to implement the programmes. There was also an activista responsible for political education.
Village (suco)	Same as a village today. Still generally referred to as a suco.	Secretário de suco, assisted by a vice secretário. They were in charge of suco-level bodies called sections (secções), such as the health section (secção de saude), agriculture section (secção da agricultura), education section (secção da educação) and political propaganda section (secção da propaganda política).
Sub-village (aldeia)	Same as a sub-village today. Still generally referred to as an aldeia.	Responsável da aldeia.

+ In the Ponta Leste sector, the delegado komisariado was better known as "DK" (pronounced "de kapa") [CAVR Interview with Egas da Costa Freitas, 19 May 2004].
§§ Some mentioned the existence of barracas (barracks) units, but they were not part of the formal administrative structure.

Commission that the government was run by a directorate (*direcção*), which consisted of a secretary and vice secretary, assistants, and the local leaders of OPMT and the youth organisation, the Popular Organization of Timorese Youth (Organização Popular de Jovens Timorenses, OPJT).[4] This followed the structural model Fretilin employed at the district level after 11 August 1975 (see part 3: The History of the Conflict).

20. This structure changed little until the destruction of the zona libertadas. In 1977, as the zona libertadas came under growing pressure from Indonesian military attacks, the Fretilin leadership abolished the região level of administration, and the zona was placed immediately under the administration of the sectors. A new position of adjunct (*adjunto*) was created. The adjunto, who like political commissars were members of the Fretilin Central Committee, assisted the zona administrators in the implementation of Fretilin social-political programmes.[5] There were two to three adjunto in each sector. In 1978, the title of activista was changed to assistant (*assistente*).[6]

Military Organization

21. There was also confusion within the military organisation after the invasion of December 1975. Falintil troops assigned to the border areas and towns, which fell immediately after the invasion, retreated to their places of origin. In the zonas, Falintil regrouped into units called companies (*companhias*),[9*] led by a zona commander (*comandante de zona*). Most comandantes de zona were sergeants in the Portuguese colonial armed forces.[10*] There were between one and four companies in each zona, depending on the availability of trained men and weapons.[7] Each company consisted of three or four platoons (*pelotões*).[8]

22. These companies were theoretically under the control of the Falintil General Staff (Estado Maior das Falintil). After the unilateral declaration of

---

* These companies consisted of former East Timorese soldiers of the Portuguese colonial armed forces and civilians who had joined the militia formed by Fretilin after the 11 August movement of UDT and received some military training. Some militia members joined Falintil units that were assigned to face the Indonesian army in the border area following attacks in October 1975 [CAVR Interviews with Xanana Gusmão, Dili, 7 July 2004; Adriano João, Dili, 23 April 2003; Filomeno Paixão de Jesus, Dili, 17 June 2004; Lucas da Costa, Dili, 21 June 2004; Agostinho Carvaleira Soares, Cailaco, Bobonaro, 14 June 2003; Sebastião da Silva, June 2003, and Cornelio Gama (aka Nahak Leki, L-7), Baucau, 9 April 2003; see also Lere Anan Timor, Archives of the Tuba Rai Metin Oral History Project, Submission to CAVR, CD No. 18].
* For instance, the zona commander of Quelicai (Baucau), Aquilis Freitas, had been a colonial soldier with the rank of first sergeant (sargento). He was a cavalry troop company commander in Atabae (Bobonaro) [CAVR Interview with Adriano João, Dili, 10 June 2003]. The zona commander of Cailaco (Bobonaro), José Maria, was a second sergeant (furiel) in the Portuguese army in Timor-Leste [CAVR Interview with Agostino Carvaleira Soares, 13 August 2003].

independence on 28 November 1975, Falintil came under the Department of National Defense, which was led by a minister and two deputy ministers. Rogério Lobato was the minister of defense, as well as the commander of Falintil. The deputy ministers were Hermenegildo Alves and Guido Soares. When Rogério Lobato left Timor-Leste days after the 28 November to seek international support, the two deputy ministers took over the ministry. The department of defense oversaw the Falintil General Staff, which was under the command of the chief of staff, Guido Soares, whose deputy chief was José da Silva.[11+]

23. After the invasion this structure proved ineffective. Companies were under the control of the zona commanders, who operated relatively independently of the central command and focused mainly on defending their own zona. This created problems when it came to conducting military operations. Filomeno Paixão, who was a company commander in Liquiça, told the Commission:

> In one zona…there was one zona commander. The zona commander had between one and three companies under his command. In Liquiça, for example, there were three companies with one zona commander. But each [company] only took the initiative in their own subdistricts…. Some sub-districts had plenty of weapons, while others didn't have any weapons at all.[9]

24. This problem was resolved by a decision made at the Soibada Conference (Manatuto) to reorganise the military. With the establishment of sectors, regions, and zones for all zona libertadas, sector commands (*comandos de sector*), regional commands (*comandos de região*), and zone commands (*comando de zona*) were created and a commander was appointed for each sector, region and zone.[10] In addition to battle companies, the Self-Defense Forces (Força Auto Defesa, Fade) were established in settlements. A Fade unit comprised people from the local area with basic military training. The strength of the Fade varied between local areas; one zone could have up to one company.[11] Some were armed with traditional weapons like spears and arrows, others with automatic rifles. Because most did not have firearms, Fade units were also known as the "white forces" (armed with traditional weapons only) (*armas brancas*). The Fade's main task was to defend settlements, although some were also sent to assist Falintil units on the frontline.[12]

25. The zona commanders continued to oversee the troop companies, but they operated under the authority of the região commander, while the região commander himself was under the command of the sector commander.[12++]

[+] José da Silva was replaced by Domingos Ribeiro in the second half of 1976. José da Silva was replaced because he challenged the decision at the Soibada Conference to reorganise the troops, which brought him into conflict with the political commissar of the Fronteira Norte, Maukruma, who was responsible for implementing the new structure [CAVR Interview with Filomeno Paixão de Jesus, Dili, 17 June 2004].

[++] Up to that point, the biggest army unit was a company (companhia); there were no larger units such as battalions (batalhão).

With this reorganisation, the Falintil General Staff oversaw all the territorial commands. The reorganisation at Soibada increased Falintil's capacity to face the Indonesian army. Falintil's operational territory became larger because they could now operate in areas larger than a zona. Troops and weapons could also be moved from one zona to another according to military need.[13]

26. Further changes in the military structure were decided at the Laline Conference (Lacluta, Viqueque), held between March and May 1977.[13*] The Laline Conference agreed that the concentration of military units in zonas was another weakness. Filomeno Paixão, who attended the conference, recalled:

> We thought that the strategy was not so good, because [the Ermera] região would say "we are Ermera so we belong only to Ermera", and Liquiça would say it belonged only to Liquiça. It was hard to supply weapons and ammunition to other regiões. That was why, after the Laline Conference, sector companies were formed to provide people with security, and intervention companies were formed that no longer could act from behind or outside.... So while previously the war was fought within a região, now it was fought across all the whole sector.[14]

27. Thus every company in a sector was placed directly under the command of the sector commander.

28. Further change took place in mid-1977, related to the Fretilin internal conflict. The Fretilin Central Committee, meeting in Aikurus (Remexio, Aileu), abolished the National Department of Defense, including the deputy minister positions, after an evaluation found it was not effective. Leadership of Falintil fell to the Falintil General Staff. Both deputy defence ministers were demoted to the positions of sector commanders. Hermenegildo Alves became the commander of the Centro Leste Sector and Guido Soares became the commander of Centro Sul. Domingos Ribeiro, who was previously deputy chief of staff, became the chief of staff. The deputy chief of staff position was abolished. In the Falintil General Staff, there were eight staff positions called the colaborador do estado maior, responsible for areas under the General Staff's authority such as operations, codes, information, logistics and training.[15]

29. In accordance with the principle of civilian control of the military, the President of Timor-Leste, also the president of Fretilin, Nicolau Lobato, directed

---

* This was the session of the Highest Resistance Council and the Political Committee of the Fretilin Central Committee, held from 8 March to 20 May 1977 [Fretilin, *Relatório da Delegação do Comité Central da Fretilin em Missão de Serviço no Exterior do Pais*, p. 4]. It is possible that the Highest Resistance Council referred to in this document was the Highest Struggle Council (Concelho Superior da Luta), which consisted of the RDTL President (who also was the president of Fretilin), RDTL Vice President (deputy chairman of Fretilin), Deputy Minister of Defence, Minister of Information and National Security, and Comissário Política Nacional [CAVR Interviews with Jacinto Alves, Dili, 11 May 2004 and Egas da Costa Freitas, 19 May 2004]. If this was its composition, it is clear that the Council was a hybrid between party (Fretilin) and government (RDTL).

the Falintil General Staff. At the same time, Nicolau Lobato also held the position of political commissar for the Falintil General Staff, with the function of providing political orientation to the army.[14+]

30. At this time, a new unit called the Shock Troops (*Brigada Choque*, usually abbreviated as Brichoq) was formed.[15++] This brigade was formed by the chief of staff and was directly under his command. It operated throughout Timor-Leste.[16] Guido Soares, who was previously the chief of the Falintil General Staff, became the commander of the Brichoq.[17] With the establishment of this brigade, there were Brichoq, sector and zona companies, and the Fade.

Fretilin's Socio-Political Program

31. The organization of civilians in the zonas libertadas was the responsibility of the Fretilin civil administration. After the invasion, Fretilin's main focus was launching and supporting the Resistance. Xanana Gusmão, then a member of the Fretilin Central
Committee, told the Commission:

> We had just begun the war and the people were with us [in the interior]. [We established] bases de apoio, with the idea they would function as a base to provide logistical and political support, which we could describe as revolution.... In May 1976 the Fretilin Central Committee put the bases de apoio into effect. So six sectors were established...with that the base de apoio...structure was formed. Bases de apoio were implemented as a mechanism to organize people so they could continue to fight in the war.[18]

32. Settlements, which at first were strategic territories called "retreat zones" (zona retaguarda), changed to become the bases de apoio. The people were organised to run programmes in agriculture, health, education, culture and women's liberation.[19]

Agricultural Production

33. To increase production, agricultural work was performed by people organised into teams.[20] Agricultural land was divided into three types of ownership: private, cooperative and state ownership.[16*] Families owned private land

---

+ While the political commissar for sectors were under the Comissário Política Nacional (CPN, National Political Commissioner), that was not the case with Falintil General Staff's Political Commissar according to Jacinto Alves Nicolau Lobato, who was also the President of RDTL at that time, and who worked daily at the Falintil General Staff [CAVR Interview with Jacinto Alves, Dili, 11 May 2004].

++ This Brigade was also known as the "Brigada Intervenção" ("Intervention Brigade"), "Força de Intervenção" ("Intervention Forces") or "Companhia de Intervenção" ("Intervention Company").

* Meaning the Democratic Republic of Timor-Leste.

and, while all members of a given work group farmed this land, the produce belonged to each family. Cooperative land was owned and worked on by all members of a work group and the produce was distributed equally among its members.[17+] Everybody worked on state property and the produce was used by the state to feed Falintil, the civilian administration, the elderly and disabled, and kept for seed reserves.[21] As well as food crops such as corn, tubers, sweet potatoes and bananas, cotton was also planted.[22]

34. Women also worked in agricultural production performing activities such as pounding sago palm into flour and making plaited items like baskets.[23] If a woman had small children, they were cared for in a crèche, and some people were assigned to a team to maintain the crèche.[24]

35. Initially agricultural production proceeded smoothly. The situation worsened once the major military offensive began in September 1978. Planted land could not be harvested as the population had to move constantly because of attacks by the Indonesian army. These attacks also prevented planting new crops.[25]

Health

36. The Fretilin cadres responsible for health, including traditional doctors, produced medicine from plants including quinine pills and treatments for gunshot wounds.[26] They also cared for the wounded and performed minor operations. Research was conducted to find plants with healing qualities. Lucas da Costa, who was the head of the hospital in Same (Manufahi) during the Portuguese colonial era, recalled his experiences in the Uaimori area (Viqueque):

> I did research on plant therapy and medication using traditional medicines around the middle of 1976.…We built a hospital. We conducted studies on traditional medicines. We gathered together some people who knew about traditional medicines and conducted a number of experiments. We built a pharmacy to make tablets and [methods for] injecting medicine. Our injections didn't work, but our tablets for malaria were a success. We also successfully made tablets for headaches, and, although it was very basic, it was quite effective.[27]

37. Former students provided public education on healthy living and the construction and use of public toilets. Virgílio da Silva Guterres from the Venilale zona (Baucau) described his experiences:

> [Boys] who were in the third grade of primary school were…given training on literacy, health and politics. After the training the participants were divided into groups called Brigada Dinamisadora [Dynamisation Brigades], each consisting of five people. The groups' task was to teach literacy and health and assist people to make toilets to maintain health standards.[28]

+ The Fretilin administrators also had to work in work groups but they only did a small amount of farm work because their time was mostly taken up with politics [CAVR Interview with Virgílio Guterres Silva, Dili, 25 May 2004].

Education and Culture

38. Fretilin provided education in two main areas: literacy and politics. Literacy programs appear to have been conducted in a piecemeal fashion because of the lack of people trained in this field at the time. In certain places OPMT activists ran the programmes and focused particularly on women.[29] In some zones school activities were conducted for children.[30]

39. The most common educational activity was political education. Fretilin gave much attention to providing political training for Fretilin cadres to increase their capacity to organize people and their political and ideological knowledge. The commissariat in each sector established a Centre for Political Training (Centro da Formação Política, Ceforpol). These centres were run by the região and zona committees, or by village and aldeia administrators. Topics covered included the history of Timor-Leste from the arrival of the Portuguese, theories of social development, the philosophy of dialectical materialism, building people-power, the organisational principles of "the mass line" (linha de massa) and democratic centralism, women's emancipation and collective food production. Military strategy and national liberation were also discussed, as well as wars of national liberation in other countries such as Guinea Bissau, China, and Vietnam. The instructors in the Ceforpols were members of the Fretilin Central Committee and Falintil commanders.[31] Overall, the Ceforpols were under the supervision of the Department of Political and Ideological Orientation (Departemento da Orientação Política e Ideológica, DOPI), which was a department of the Fretilin Central Committee.[32]

40. The goal of political education for the general public was to encourage the spirit of nationalism and support the national liberation struggle.[33] Zone administrators conducted "enlightenment" (*esclarecimento*) programs. In certain places brigada dinamisadoras carried out the esclarecimento, travelling to settlements to explain the Fretilin Political Program Manual (*Manual e Programa Políticos, Fretilin*) and the need to work and support the Falintil armed forces fighting to restore independence in Timor-Leste.[34] Where there was no brigada dinamisadora, the assistente de zona carried out the programme. OPMT activists also provided political education.[35] Usually, popular political education was conducted together with cultural activities. A member of a brigada dinamisadora told the Commission:

> Every brigada was sent to an aldeia to teach during the day. At night there were activities like traditional dancing, reading traditional poems and singing folk songs…. The verses in the poems were about the poor people and their suffering because of the invasion, and tributes to the people who had died fighting for the fatherland. Hearing such words aroused people's sympathy for the poor and their determination to fight for the independence of the fatherland.[36]

41. Fretilin cultural activities aimed to develop a sense of nationhood, based on the idea that the nation could progress only if the people fought to free them-

selves from the negative mentality sown by colonialism. The theme of the poor needing to fight for their liberation had been developed before the Indonesian invasion. Fretilin took traditional songs from many regions and politicised the lyrics to further this cause. Songs were sung to traditional dances such as the tebe and dahur.

42. Cultural activities were guided by the Fretilin concept of the equality of all human beings. Fretilin saw colonialism as a form of inequality by which a minority exploited and oppressed the majority. Oppression and exploitation occurred not only between the colonial power and the people of Timor-Leste, but also among the East Timorese population itself between the traditional kings (*liurai*) and the people. This was clear in such practices as mandatory tributes that people were required to pay to the liurai, and the use of forced labour. Inequality was also apparent in the form of discrimination and violence against women as a result of their low status in traditional society.[37] Fretilin introduced the concept of "comaraderie" ("camarada") which viewed each person as a friend and an equal. The need to eradicate inequality caused by exploitation and oppression and replace it with equality became a theme in both songs and verse which were sung at cultural events and in literacy programs.

Women's Emancipation

43. The emancipation of women was also part of Fretilin's socio-political programme. Women were encouraged to get involved in education, health, agricultural production and the production of items to be used by the military such as baskets (lafatik, luhu) and bags. Crèches were built in order to make it possible for women to carry out these activities. Men and women took turns in looking after the children in the crèches. The crèches also served as a place to teach children to become revolutionary nationalists through songs of struggle, poetry and theatre.[38]

44. In some areas, courses were run to prepare women for marriage. For example, OPMT ran a course in Zona Modok in the Centro Norte Sector. The aim was to create nationalist families with respect for men's and women's rights. The future brides were taught the concept of women's emancipation. The tradition of barlaque, which required an exchange of goods between the families of the bride and groom and had previously been considered degrading to women, was reaffirmed as a symbol honouring women's dignity. Through these courses future brides also learned to challenge colonial and feudal attitudes and preconceptions about women, and to defend the dignity of both women and men.[39]

Justice System

45. Fretilin created a justice system to deal with people who committed crimes. People were tried according to the type of crime they committed. For

what were considered relatively minor offences, such as swearing, harassing women and stealing, a process called self-criticism was administered. In this process, the perpetrator pleaded guilty in front of a small public audience, expressed their remorse and promised not to reoffend. The perpetrators would be forgiven once they had received a light punishment, such as gathering firewood or fetching water for the public kitchen for two days. This kind of punishment was called "corrective justice" ("*justo correctivo*").

46. For serious crimes, the process was called popular justice (*justiça popular*). Serious offences included having contact with the enemy, cooperating with the enemy, spying, betraying civilians to the enemy and treason. The accused was considered to have opposed Fretilin policies and were put on trial in public, often in front of a large crowd. The military commander who had captured the person laid the charges, the crowd decided on guilt or innocence, while the political commissar, sometimes with the assistance of the sector commander, handed down the sentence.[40] Punishments ranged from death to rehabilitation in an institution called the National Rehabilitation (Rehabilitação Nacional, Renal). A Renal was "a place to rehabilitate reactionaries to become revolutionaries,"[41] and were under the authority of the sector commissariat. The number of Renals varied from sector to sector (see chapter 7.4: Detention, Torture and Ill-Treatment).[18]**

47. Rehabilitation was the punishment for people who, despite the seriousness of their crimes, were considered to be able to realise their mistakes and change their ways.[42] In the Renals, detainees were required to work during the day, including agricultural production such as planting and working in rice fields, and other tasks like collecting firewood and fetching water. Food produced was used to feed them and to meet Falintil's needs.[43] At night they were required to attend classes in political education. In one Renal, literacy classes were provided.[44]

48. There were at least two kinds of detention facilities in the Renals. The first type was a hole in the ground covered with wooden bars or by a wooden panel with a large rock on top of it. These holes varied in size: some were only eighty centimetres in height, forcing people held in there to sit on the floor, while others, such as the one in Nundamar (Remexio, Aileu), were as much as three metres deep.[45] The second type was an enclosure above ground, which was surrounded by walls of stones two to three metres in height.[46]

49. There were cases where people were deprived of food or water for days in Renals. Sometimes family members were allowed to give them food or water, but on other occasions it was prohibited. Alexandrino de Jesus, a Falintil soldier

---

* Renals were under the direct responsibility of an adjunto. The Renal in Nundamar, Remexio, for example, was under the responsibility of Adjunto Sebastião Montalbão ("Lais") [CAVR Interviews with António Amado de Deus Guterres, 11 December 2003 and Egas da Costa Freitas, Dili, 19 May 2004. See generally Chapter 7.4: Detention, Torture and Ill-Treatment].

captured and accused of trying to surrender to the Indonesian army, told the Commission of his experiences in a Renal:

> We were taken to the Renal in Sau-kata in the village of Ura Hou [Hatulia, Ermera]. We were ordered to work although we were very physically weak and we were not provided with farming tools. They ordered us to pull up and tidy one-and-a-half hectares of grass to plant corn. While we worked there, we were never fed. We split our group into two. One group worked to clear the grass, while the other group of four people, including me, searched for cassava. Luckily there was plenty of cassava around the area. [While we worked] eight Falintil members guarded us.... We slept at the place where we worked, and each week we were required to report to Fatubessi [Ermera]. None of us died. After we had been working for one-and-a-half months at the Renal and the corn was planted the commander of Fronteira Norte Sector, Filomeno Paixão, summoned us. When we arrived at [the sector command centre in Fatubessi Ermera] we were treated well. We were told to line up to receive food rations. Then we were reinstated as Falintil members.[47]

50. People who were held for investigation and the process of justiça popular were also detained in Renals. Interrogation was the main form of investigation and some detainees were tortured during interrogation to extract confessions.[48] Eduardo de Jesus Barreto from the Fronteira Norte Sector, told the Commission:

> I saw the regional commander Martinho [Soares] being buried up to his waist in a standing position, without clothes and with his hands tied. Then they burned a car tyre, allowing the melting rubber to burn his body. I couldn't stand to watch, so I walked away.[49]

51. Not all serious cases were investigated. There were cases where people suspected of having planned to surrender or of being spies for the Indonesian military were simply accused by the local commander, and a decision was made on the spot. A former political assistant told the Commission:

> The guilty person would be brought in front of the public. There, many people would say that he was guilty. Nobody challenged it even if they were innocent. No judge defended them. I witnessed around three cases. One person was suspected and captured in the war zone, and the commander accused him of being a spy. The commander said: "This man was captured in the guerrilla zona. He is a spy." Then people said: "If he is a spy, he must die." A Falintil commander usually handled cases like these and people just went along with whatever he said.[50]

52. As a result, people were punished for crimes they did not commit. A cadre described one such case:

> Some people had gone down to the town...[and] their families came under suspicion. [The commanders] were prepared to do anything to them. Torture them for instance. I opposed that. I said: "Don't do it. Because if someone goes down to the town, it

means [that only] they no longer care about our struggle. Why do we have to harass their families?" I always opposed it. They accused me of having contacts with them, of betraying the struggle. I was eventually imprisoned for no reason. I wasn't tortured but I spent a few months below ground.[51]

Strategy

53. The resistance strategy adopted by Fretilin derived from the idea that it was engaged in a revolutionary war for independence. The concept of revolution was linked to independence, but Fretilin's idea of independence involved more than simply the departure of Portuguese colonial rulers and their replacement by an East Timorese government. For Fretilin, independence without a change in the social structure would mean only replacing one master with another. Fretilin saw independence as the creation of equality among people by "ending the inequality of the colonial situation, which was based on exploitation of the majority by a minority. The colonial minority and the wealthy exploited the majority."[52] The process through which Fretilin wanted to eliminate the colonial social structure was revolution.[19]*

54. The Fretilin Political Program and Manual published around September 1975 stated:

> [Fretilin] is called revolutionary because in order for the Timorese people to live prosperously, for true liberation, people have to change, transform, and REVOLU-TIONISE all structures, which have been in place for five hundred years. We have to make a major transformation by creating new structures to serve the Timorese people. If we do not erase the oppressive structures and replace them with new structures, the Timorese people will never live prosperously, the Timorese people will never gain Independence; only a small number of people will live prosperously, just as has been happening up to this day. Many people would still live in misery.[53]

55. Fretilin considered that traditional East Timorese society was also oppressive. In the traditional social structure the liurai held power over the people by forcing them to work for them and to pay tithes. Colonial rulers also used the liurai traditional status to mobilise people to work on plantations producing goods for export.[20]+ Fretilin saw the liurai authority as feudalism and aimed to eliminate it.

56. Colonialism and tradition were also considered oppressive towards women. Fretilin saw that Timorese women experienced twofold oppression;

---

* Article 2 of the RDTL Constitution stated: "The Democratic Republic of Timor-Leste is led based on FRETILIN's political orientation, which is aimed to erase colonial structures for the creation of a new society free from all kinds of occupation and exploitation." Fretilin also considered that colonialism could take a new form after the nation gained its independence, when foreign capital controlled Timor-Leste's economy. This situation would create an economic dependence called "neocolonialism" that Fretilin wanted to prevent [Fretilin, Manual e Programa Políticos Fretilin, point 5].

+ This forced labour was called "auxiliar" ("helper"), which the Timorese pronounced "assuliar."

the general colonial oppression that all Timorese experienced, and the more specific oppression they suffered as a result of traditional and colonialist attitudes towards women.[54] While general colonial oppression took the form of such practices as forced labour, inadequate wages and racism, women's oppression was manifested in the way women were treated as an object of pleasure for colonialist employers and as commodities traded in barlaque practices and polygamy. Fretilin aimed to eliminate this oppression. Fretilin's revolutionary programme included "the liberation of women as social creatures."[55]

57. To create a new social structure free of oppression, Fretilin conducted socio-political programmes from September 1975. The most important programmes, according to Fretilin, were those in the fields of agriculture, health, education and culture.[56] Fretilin saw that in the agriculture sector, colonialism had made the people of Timor-Leste poorer by focusing on export crops. People starved because of food shortages and a limited variety of food.[57] Fretilin sought to develop an agriculture sector that served the interests of the people and enabled "everyone to get proper food for good health, so everyone can live in prosperity."[58] A system of cooperative ownership and organisation was deemed the most appropriate to achieve this goal.[21]*[*] Fretilin planned to build production, distribution and consumption cooperatives all over the country. When Timor-Leste was still under Portuguese rule, Fretilin put this idea into practice in a number of places, among them Bazartete (Liquiça) and Bucoli (Baucau), the home villages of leaders Nicolau Lobato and Sahe respectively, who had pioneered these projects.[59]

58. In education, Fretilin carried out literacy programmes inspired by the methods developed by the Brazilian educator, Paulo Freire.[22]+[+] Education was considered important because, for Fretilin, true independence would only happen if people actively participated in government, and people could only participate actively if they knew what they wanted and why. If people lived in ignorance, they would always be exploited. From Fretilin's perspective, the education system under the Portuguese colonial administration was the opposite of what was needed.[60] Freire's method of conscientização was preferable because people not only learned to read and write, but also went through a process of gaining awareness of colonial oppression and how to overcome it. The literacy programme, which had been prepared in May 1974, was first implemented in January 1975.[61]

59. Health was viewed as being closely connected to education. Fretilin believed that poor public health was caused by people's lack of knowledge about

---

* Fretilin also developed a land reform programme, planning to confiscate big plantations and give them to people's cooperatives [Fretilin, Manual e Programa Políticos Fretilin, Program Políticos part, point 2.B.1].

+ Fretilin played an important role influencing Portuguese government policy on education when the colonial administration under Governor Mário Lemos Pires formed an Education Committee to oversee reform during the decolonisation period [Helen Hill, *Stirrings of Nationalism in East Timor*, p. 122].

health and nutrition, which was in turn caused by colonialism. That was why, for Fretilin, health education was the only solution to the problem.[62]

60. Fretilin's ideas about culture were closely linked to the need to develop a new national awareness among the people of Timor-Leste. During colonial times people generally understood that they were members of a particular village community, a particular kingdom, or a particular ethno-linguistic group. For instance, people considered themselves as Turiscai (Manufahi) people, as members of the Mambai ethno-linguistic group, rather than as an East Timorese person, and they viewed outsiders, even people from Dili, as foreigners (*malae*).[63] Fretilin tried to develop national awareness through programmes of cultural exchange between regions, and giving all East Timorese people a sense of ownership of these forms. For instance the tebe dance from one place was introduced in literacy programmes in other places. Similarly, songs, such as Kolele Mai which originated in a village in Baucau, were introduced throughout the nation. Fretilin also used Tetum, which was the lingua franca throughout the territory, in their meetings and literacy programmes.

61. Fretilin believed that the revolution could be peaceful for two reasons.[23*] First, it was becoming clearer that the Portuguese policy of decolonisation was more likely to lead to independence at the time Fretilin wrote its programme in November 1974. This assured Fretilin that colonialism was bankrupt politically and administratively.[64] Second, Fretilin was becoming increasingly popular because of its socio-political programmes.[65] For example, in the local election of village chiefs in May 1975 in a number of villages in Lospalos (Lautém), a clear majority of the elected village chiefs were Fretilin supporters.[66] According to Francisco Xavier do Amaral this increased popularity made the leaders of Fretilin confident that the majority of people wanted independence and that they would easily defeat UDT's idea of federation with Portugal and Apodeti's idea of integration with Indonesia, without an armed struggle.[67] For Fretilin, the way to launching the revolution was to mobilise people to accelerate the agricultural, education, health and cultural programmes.[24+]

---

[*]   Francisco Xavier do Amaral stated that Fretilin hoped Portugal "would be willing to give [Timor-Leste independence] peacefully" and therefore there was no plan within Fretilin to organise for armed struggle. According to him, armed activities were conducted only after the armed action of movement of 11 August by UDT [CAVR Interview with Francisco Xavier do Amaral, Dili, 18 June 2004]. Terra Maubulak also mentioned the establishment of an Exercito de Libertaçao Maubere among the Timorese serving in the Portuguese colonial army by a number of Fretilin Central Committee members around May 1975 [Terra Maubulak, Archives of the Tuba Rai Metin Oral History Project, Submission to CAVR, CD No. 18]. But this was denied by Mari Alkatiri (who was a national political commissar) and Francisco Xavier do Amaral (who was the President of Fretilin) [CAVR Interviews with Mari Alkatiri, Dili, 25 June 2004 and Francisco Xavier do Amaral, Dili, 18 June 2004].

[+]   Helen Hill mentioned that Fretilin searched for "a peaceful alternative to the guerilla war, which was to draw on people's power to fight the colonial structures" [Hill, *Stirrings of Nationalism in East Timor*, p. 159].

62. The socio-political program implemented after the Indonesian invasion was a continuation of the programs implemented before 11 August 1975. The difference after the invasion was that the programs were implemented in the bases de apoio to support the war. During the course of the war, Fretilin itself was radicalised, giving greater emphasis to the elimination of classes in society and declaring Marxism to be its ideology.[25++]

Protracted People's War

63. Initially, as noted above, the war was fought as a spontaneous and decentralized reaction to attacks by the Indonesian military, without a clear overall strategy. At the Fretilin Central Committee's second plenary session in Soibada (Manatuto), held between 15 May and 2 June 1976, Fretilin adopted the strategy of a protracted people's war.[26§] Fretilin conceded that the war could not be won easily and quickly, because of Indonesia's much greater economic and military strength.[68] If Timor-Leste wanted independence, the war would have to be long and hard. Based on its analysis of the international political situation, Fretilin believed that Timor-Leste could not depend on foreign assistance for victory.[27**]

64. The three main principles adopted at the Soibada Conference were: that the war would be fought by and for the people, that it would be protracted, and that Timor-Leste would have to depend on its own strength. According to this strategy, war was not simply a military conflict between two armed forces, but was also viewed as a war of the people. From a purely military perspective, the deciding factors would be military and economic. But Fretilin believed that the

---

[++] According to Xanana Gusmão, Marxism officially became Fretilin's ideology at the Laline (Lacluta, Viqueque) Conference in 1977. Fretilin President Xavier do Amaral did not attend this conference. Another source said that Marxism was not confirmed as the official ideology at the conference because of Xavier do Amaral's absence [CAVR Interviews with Xanana Gusmão, Dili, 7 July 2004 and Jacinto Alves, Dili, 11 May 2004]. Fretilin cadres who participated in Ceforpol's political education remembered that they studied Marxism in Ceforpol classes [see for example, CAVR Interview with Egas da Costa Freitas, 19 May 2004; Lere Anan Timor, Archives of the Tuba Rai Metin Oral History Project, Submission to CAVR].

[§] This strategy was formulated by Mao Zedong based on China's experience of war against Japanese imperialism [Mao Zedong, "On Protracted War", 1938, in Selected Works of Mao Tse-tung, Foreign Languages Press, Peking, 1965]. It seemed that some Fretilin leaders learned this strategy from materials from the African national liberation movements in Portuguese colonies.

[**] The idea to ask for Western countries' assistance was rejected because those countries were "imperialists", and were opponents to countries who wanted "true liberation". Indonesia, which launched the military aggression, was viewed as a lackey of the United States, which was seen as the leader of imperialist powers in the world. The idea to seek assistance from socialist bloc countries was also rejected, on the basis that the assistance would bind the country in the future [CAVR Interview with Egas da Costa Freitas, Dili, 19 May 2004].

strength and will of the people would be the deciding factor, and that they could be continuously strengthened through education and mobilization.

65. In the protracted people's war strategy, the bases de apoio played a central role. They provided logistical support for the armed forces, and also built people-power through education and mobilisation.[69] Egas da Costa, an assistente de zona in the propaganda section in one of the zonas in the Centro Leste Sector, said: "Because this war was a protracted war, people were educated, trained in bases, so they could develop a new view on life."[70]

66. Fretilin saw Indonesian military assaults as attacks against the people of Timor-Leste, who were attempting to liberate themselves from the oppression of man by man. In carrying out these assaults, Indonesia was considered an accomplice of the world imperialist powers. A document from DOPI, which was ratified at the Laline Conference in 1977, stated:

> [T]he experiences of other countries in the struggle against colonial powers, and our own experience, show that this kind of movement is met by total violence from the imperialist power, and that the only way for a true nationalist move-ment to protect people from genocide or mass slaughter is to organise, mobilise and educate people to work for the full and complete eviction of the enemy and to beat imperialism.[71]

67. The war was considered a war of all the people against the enemy pow-ers who were promoting their imperialist interests. Mobilising and educating people would create a popular force that was invincible in the face of imperialist aggression. The relationship between the people and the soldiers was likened to that of water and fish, meaning the people were the water that allowed the soldiers to live.[72]

68. In more practical terms people supplied food to Falintil soldiers and were thus the source of power for the armed forces. In turn Falintil was considered to be the protector of the people, allowing them to live a life without oppres-sion and exploitation in the liberated zones.[73] Falintil was under the command of Fretilin, which was the guide (*matadalan*) of the liberation struggle. The principle that regulated this relationship was "politics commands the gun" ("*a política comanda fuzil*"). According to Taur Matan Ruak, "Falintil was like the knife, used by political leaders to cut."[74]

Internal Conflict

69. During the period of the zonas libertadas, conflicts began to surface among the Fretilin leaders. These conflicts have been represented previously as occurring between ideological factions within Fretilin. This view holds that there were nationalist, social democrat, and Marxist, even Maoist groups, in Fretilin, and that the conflict between them was won by the Marxist or radical group.[75] Accounts received by the Commission describe a different ideological

divide centered on military strategy.[28]* This divide manifested through issues such as how the principle of civilian control of the military was to be put into practice, the idea of "ideological suicide" (*"suicido ideológico"*) and the presence of civilians in Fretilin-controlled territories.

Civilian Control of the Military

70. The first conflict arose around the implementation of the principle that "politics commands the gun." According to Lucas da Costa's testimony to the Commission, opposition to this principle had already surfaced soon after Fretilin launched its "counter-coup" in August 1975, and it reached a crisis point in October 1975.[76] At that time, not long after Fretilin took control of the whole territory of Timor-Leste, the military commanders, who were mostly former Portuguese soldiers, had stronger de facto authority than the political leaders.[29]+ Adoption of the "politics commands the gun" principle had reduced their authority. Their dissatisfaction was compounded by the fact that many of the political leaders had less military knowledge and experience than them. Lucas da Costa (Rama Metan) testified to the Commission:

> When Fretilin took control of the territory, frictions were felt between the Fretilin armed forces and several commanders, especially here in Dili. It reached its peak in October.
>
> In Fretilin there was a principle, "A política comanda fuzil" meaning that politics controls the armed forces. [That principle] had been effective since we took control, it was established by the Fretilin Central Committee. Because of that principle, some

---

* Egas da Costa Freitas gave a different categorisation, which were socialist, social democrat, and "a rather fascist right". It seems that the first persons to mention the existence of "groups" within Fretilin were Carmel Budiardjo and Liem Soei Liong, *The War Against East Timor* (Zed Books Ltd., London, 1984). According to them, there were four "groups" inside Fretilin: the underground anti-colonial group, the Casa dos Timorense group, the "group around Xavier do Amaral", and the "group around Alarico Fernandes" (pp. 53-54). John G Taylor, *Indonesia's Forgotten War: The Hidden History of East Timor* (Zed Books, London, 1991) described a different grouping: "social-democrat groups" (represented by José Ramos-Horta, Justino Mota, Alarico Fernandes, and Francisco Xavier do Amaral), the group "that combined the tough anticolonial nationalism with economic independence and political advancement" (Nicolau Lobato with the support of former sergeants of the Portuguese army) and the "nationalist-Marxist" group around Mau Lear and Sahe [in the revised version of East Timor: *The Price of Freedom* (Zed Books, London and New York, 1999), pp. 46-48].

+ According to Jill Jolliffe, at the time the military police placed road-blocks around Dili and sent a delegate to the Fretilin leaders to demand the arrest of a number of Fretilin militants considered to be communists. This incident was resolved through a four-hour discussion on 4 November, which managed to convince the soldiers that their accusations were wrong [Jill Jolliffe, *East Timor: Nationalism and Colonialism*, pp. 185-186].

company commanders felt that their authority had been compromised, because they had to obey the politicians when it was them who actually oversaw the armed forces, the soldiers. They felt uncomfortable about interacting with CCF members who were young or inexperienced.[77]

71. This problem continued in the forest after the invasion, culminating in incidents such as the death of Falintil's deputy chief of staff, José da Silva. José da Silva had been a sergeant in the Portuguese colonial armed forces, and was commander of Falintil's first company in August 1975. He was also deputy chief of staff. After the invasion he fought in Ermera, which became part of the Centro Norte Sector. Conflicts among Fretilin leaders occurred over some of the decisions reached at the Soibada Conference. Hélio Pina (Maukruma), who was elected political commissar with Antonio Carvalho (Fera Lafaek) as his assistant, was given the task of restructuring the civilian and military relationship as decided at the conference. José da Silva refused to accept the restructuring and so he captured Maukruma and several of his commanders. A fire-fight ensued and José da Silva was captured and imprisoned. He was executed by Fretilin in the middle of 1977.[78]

72. It appears that conflicts about the principle of civilian control of military affairs were also factors in the executions of Agostinho Espírito Santo (a commander in the FronteiraNorte Sector), Aquiles Freitas (a commander in the Centro Leste sector) and Martinho Soares.[30*]

Suicido Ideológico

73. Fretilin's ideas about the revolution also caused conflict. As the goal of the revolution was to create a classless society, those from the upper classes, such as liurai, were required to abandon their special status in society and commit suicido ideológico. As Xanana Gusmão stated:

> Revolution was communism. No class, no wealthy people, no poor people, no exploitation, everyone was equal. The revolution followed communist ideology.... So that there would be no classes and all of us would be equal, the upper classes had to commit suicide, those from the top must sit alongside the people.[79]

74. In the zonas libertadas, opposition to Fretilin ideology was denounced as "reactionary" and considered a serious crime.[80] According to Xanana Gusmão, someone who continually committed reactionary actions would be considered a traitor.[81]

75. The execution of Aquiles Freitas is a case in point. Aquiles Freitas was a commander in Atabae (Bobonaro) when Indonesia launched borders raids

---

*   According to Lucas da Costa, Comandante Agostinho Espírito Santo often had disagreements with the political commissar César Maulaka [CAVR Interview with Lucas da Costa, Dili, 21 June 2004].

in October and November 1975. His last rank in the Portuguese military was staff sergeant (primeiro-sargento). After the 7 December 1975 invasion of Dili by Indonesian forces he became a zona commander in Quelicai (Baucau), his home. He was then promoted to the position of second commander of the Baucau Region, under first commander Reinaldo Correia (Kilik Wae Gae). Aquiles Freitas was not happy about being put under Kilik Wae Gae, who had been a private in the Portuguese army, a lower rank than he had been.[82] A former Fretilin administrator in the Uatu-Carbau Zona (Viqueque) told the Commission that Aquiles Freitas could not disguise his contempt for Fretilin and Falintil:

> One day he visited our zona office in Zona Furak Kaun. I was there. I was already the vice-secretary. It was strange because this man contacted only certain people; he never had business with the zona. From his words, "What's Falintil?" he seemed to be derisive of Falintil. So we finally concluded that he was indeed anti-revolutionary. And while I was the vice-secretary, he never came to the office. We were derided as being officials. That is why I dare to say that he was anti-revolutionary. [Aquiles] came to Uatu-Carbau [Viqueque] in 1976, if I'm not mistaken, around 1976 or 1977…I was still the assistant at Uatu-Carbau…I met him there, I knew for certain that he never respected the presence of the secretary, vice secretary, administrators, assistants. He never did. I heard that he said: "Ahh, what is Falintil anyway?"[83]

76. The execution of Francisco Hornay is another example of this conflict. Problems began at the time of the restructuring of Ponta Leste Sector by Political Commissar Sera Key after the Soibada Conference. Francisco Hornay rejected the appointment of Tomás Pinto as the Iliomar (Lautém) Zona secretary because he thought that the position should be held by a liurai. Tito da Costa (Lere Anan Timor, Lere), who was the vice-secretary in Iliomar Zona at the time, told the Commission that:

> They didn't want Tomás Pinto [Lesamau] to be the zona secretary, because they wanted a "blue-blood." He [Francisco Hornay] wanted me to be the zona secretary, because I was a "blue-blood." We opposed him because of the struggle, because we opposed exploitation.…

> Tomás Pinto and I made a report to the Regional Committee and Sera Key, the political commissar of Ponta Leste. On the basis of that report they [denounced] Hornay's action as reactionary and part of the national reaction led by [Francisco] Xavier [do Amaral]. They held a meeting. Noone was allowed to carry arms. [Hornay] stuck to his opinion, and said that Tomás could not be the secretary. In the debate [they] blamed Hornay. They took a unanimous decision.…The political commissar, who had a platoon, ordered the troops to strip them of their weapons.

> The reaction was that almost an entire company was stripped of its weapons. [The commisar's troops] captured around five or six people and took them to Belta Tres [Irara, Lospalos, Lautém] where the comissáriat was, and detained them for between one and seven months. After the political commissar thought they had changed, they were released. But after their release they didn't change, they still continued being reactionary. They were required to report to the zona, but they never did. They went straight to Aquiles in Quelicai [Baucau].[84]

77. According to Lere, Aquiles Freitas gave them weapons.[85] Francisco Hornay and two others were then captured again in Baguia (Baucau) and killed in Iliomar (Lautém).[86]

Military Strategy

78. The most serious internal conflict within Fretilin appears to have been about which military strategy to use against Indonesia. Some political leaders, who came to be in the majority, thought that the East Timorese must depend on their own strengths and not expect outside assistance. Other military commanders and civilian leaders disagreed, believing that foreign assistance was necessary because of Indonesia's superior strength. In the first Central Committee plenary session held in April 1976 in Barique (Manatuto), there was a debate on this question. Requesting assistance from the United States and its allies was rejected because these nations were considered to be imperialist. Requesting assistance from the Soviet Union was also rejected because it was considered to be socialist imperialist.[87] According to Xanana Gusmão, in that meeting Francisco Xavier do Amaral said that it did not matter where the assistance came from as long as it came soon. Many military commanders agreed and showed their dislike of the political leadership.[88]

> Youth were brought in to become mid-level cadres. Many youths were involved because in Fretilin's view youth were easier to educate compared to older people, who were already familiar with colonialist traditions. These youth became the link between the people and the Fretilin Central Committee.[89]

79. Another conflict related to the role of civilian population. Civilians had a very important role in the strategy of a protracted people's war adopted at the Soibada Conference of May-June 1976. At that time further disagreements surfaced between a number of civilian leaders and military commanders, backed by Francisco Xavier do Amaral. For Francisco Xavier do Amaral, the presence of civilians could cause problems for Falintil, as the soldiers would be burdened with the task of guaranteeing their safety. He thought that it would be better for civilians, especially children and the elderly, to surrender to the enemy, while those who were physically strong would remain in the interior to fight with Falintil.[90] This idea won support from military commanders.[91]

80. This difference of opinion was sharpened by the tensions between the military commanders and civilian leaders about the reduced authority of military commanders, which dated from before the exodus to the interior. The tensions were compounded further by the animosity felt by some of the former Portuguese army sergeants towards military commanders who had previously been political leaders. Lucas da Costa (Rama Metan) told the Commission:

> [Falintil soldiers who had served in the Portuguese army] felt uncomfortable interacting with some CCF members, who were young or inexperienced....There were

some [CCF members], especially the young ones who, just because they had been brave enough to take up weapons, declared themselves commanders. Meno Paixão, for example, managed to confiscate a gun then made himself a commander.[92]

81. The former sergeants, who viewed the war from a purely military perspective, believed that the protracted people's war strategy was inappropriate for Timor-Leste.[31]** They believed that foreign assistance was necessary, and that civilians should surrender so that they would not become a burden for Falintil. According to them, Falintil's ammunition was limited, because of the lack of foreign assistance, and would quickly run out if they had to protect civilians. As the war would continue for a long time, it would be better to use ammunition attacking the enemy rather than protecting the civilian population.[93]

82. The supporters of the protracted people's war strategy considered the idea that civilians should surrender to be treachery. They thought that only with the people could they win the war. Strategically, people were considered a source of power, while ideologically the war was seen as a revolutionary war. The CCF was also concerned about the people's support for independence.[32]** Lucas da Costa told the Commission:

> Some people, especially those [who had returned] from Portugal, wanted to keep people in the forest to be educated and become revolutionary. They thought that if the people were to surrender without adequate knowledge of revolution, they would reclaim their previous social status and it would grow back, preventing the success of the proletarian revolution.[94]

83. For those who viewed the war militarily, the problem was how to drive Indonesia out of Timor-Leste. For those who viewed the war as a revolution, war could erase classes in society, and war had to be made with the people. As such, telling the civilian population to surrender was a betrayal of the national liberation struggle.

84. Many commanders who suggested or allowed people to surrender were captured or even killed. Examples include the capture of Sebastião Sarmento and his removal from the position of commander of Fronteira Norte Sector,[95] the capture of Francisco Xavier do Amaral and his removal from the positions of President of Fretilin and President of the Democratic Republic of Timor-Leste,[96]

---

* Xanana Gusmão remembered that a former sergeant, who served in an African country occupied by the Portuguese, opposed the protracted people's war strategy by saying that the strategy had worked in Africa because the guerrilla forces had bases outside the borders of their country, and in those bases they were trained and received foreign assistance. These circumstances did not prevail in Timor-Leste [CAVR Interview with Xanana Gusmão, Dili, 7 July 2004].

* Francisco Xavier do Amaral also mentioned another possible reason, that if people surrendered the world would think that it was only Fretilin that wanted independence, and that they did not have the people's support [CAVR Interview with Francisco Xavier do Amaral, part III, Dili, 18 June 2004].

and the killing of Agostinho Espírito Santo (commander of Fronteira Sul Sector)[33+] and Martinho Soares (a commander in Fronteira Norte Sector).[97]

85. The conflict regarding civilians was not merely ideological, but also related to military developments. With the increase in attacks by the Indonesian military many parts of the zonas libertadas could no longer be defended. There were ad hoc efforts from military commanders and civilian leaders to negotiate surrender with the enemy.[98] Adriano Soares Lemos told the Commission:

> The Fretilin leaders Ali Alkatiri, Meno Paixão and Pedro Gonçalves from the Fronteira Norte Sector agreed to bring people down to surrender to [ABRI], because the people's condition was critical at the time.... If they continued to stay in the forest, everyone would die either from starvation or illness....So Ali Alkatiri and Filomeno Paixão had contacts with [the Indonesian Armed Forces, ABRI] in Fatubessi [Ermera], to inform them that the people would surrender. [ABRI] agreed to it, so on 6 February 1979, we began to come down from Fatubessi to the area of Caisoru [Liquiça]. [We] surrendered to [ABRI] Battalion 512 on 7 February 1979.[99]

86. Such actions aggravated the conflicts between political leaders and military commanders. When Meno Paixão and a large group of political leaders and civilians surrendered in February 1979, the political commissar of Fronteira Norte Sector, Maukruma, refused to join them. He continued resisting until he was killed with his wife in March 1979.

87. These conflicts were never resolved within the Resistance itself. They ended when the Indonesian military offensive of 1978-79 led to the destruction of the zonas libertadas.

The End of Bases de Apoio

88. The period of the bases de apoio ended with the major Indonesian offensive of 1978-79. The offensive, which Fretilin called "encirclement and annihilation" ("*cerco e aniquilamento*"),[34**] began in mid-1978 with heavy assaults on the western territories (Fronteira Sul Sector and Fronteira Norte Sector). The offensive was then directed eastwards with assaults on bases around Mount Matebian and the Natarbora (Manatuto) Plain, and later the base in Manatuto. The attacks resumed in the west and centre in the early months of 1979, aimed at destroying the remaining forces in those regions. This offensive involved strafing and bombings and artillery fire from navy ships, as well as

---

[+] According to Maria de Jesus, Commander Agostinho Espírito Santo had a conflict with Political Commissar César Maulaka on the strategies of war [CAVR Interviews with Maria de Fátima Vaz de Jesus, 23 September 2004 and Lucas da Costa, Dili, 21 June 2004].

[*] It seemed that this term copied the term "encirclement and suppression" used by Mao Zedong in "Problems on War and Strategy", 1938, in *Selected Works of Mao Tse-tung*, Vol. 2 (Foreign Languages Press, Peking, 1967). That term showed on p. 222 of this edition.

attacks by ground troops (see part 3.11: The History of the Conflict: Military Intensification).

89. Falintil could not withstand these new attacks. Its response was static positional defence.[35+] Unlike the Chinese during the war against Japan, Fretilin was unable to retreat to a remote base, unreachable by the Indonesian army, which was one of the basic principles of a protracted people's war strategy. Falintil's bases, such as those around Mount Matebian, Mount Kablaki, and Cailaco (Bobonaro), were reachable by Indonesian soldiers by land, air and/or sea. A Fretilin cadre described the destruction of the base in Manatuto to the Commission:

> In May 1978 the situation became worse. The enemy began to surround us. In July the [Indonesian] military started "encirclement and annihilation" from the Centro Norte Sector. Forces from Manatuto began to advance, then [they] came from Aileu and from Laclubar [Manatuto].
>
> We were forced to leave Hatuconan [Laclo, Manatuto] for Remexio [Aileu]. Then we circled from Aileu back to Hatuconan. Many people died there – because of leg injuries, people couldn't walk, and newborn babies starved. We just covered the dead with mats and then left them because we didn't have time to bury them with the enemy still chasing us.
>
> At night we moved on foot, in the morning we had to hide because the OV-10 fighter planes kept following and shooting at us...and dropping bombs killing many people...[36++]There were also some killed by landmines.
>
> When the OV-10 planes shot, people were not in bushes or the forest. Thousands of them were in open fields. So many died....

[+] Chamberlain, The Struggle in Iliomar , p.18. One Fretilin document , Relatório da Delegação do Comité Central da Fretilin em Missão de Serviço no Exterior do Pais, mentioned that the "encirclement and annihiliation" offensive launched toward the Fatubesi Base on 1 January 1978 was contained by Falintil, but the battles escalated in Fatululik, Dili, Remexio (Aileu), Baucau, Baguia (Baucau) and Bazartete (Liquiça). Further battles took place in Fatululik (Covalima), Fatubesi (Ermera), Fatumean, Suai (Covalima) and Atsabe (Bobonaro) on the second week of March 1978 and many Falintil soldiers died. Then "encirclement and annihilation" was launched toward the Centro Norte, Centro Sul, and Centro Leste Sectors, and at the end of June, Remexio (located 15 km from Dili) fell to the Indonesian army [Fretilin, Relatório da Delegação do Comité Central da Fretilin em Missão de Serviço no Exterior do Pais, p. 5].

[++] In the aerial assaults, as well as testimony about the use of the OV-10 Bronco airplane, the Commission also received reports of Skyhawk bomber airplanes [CAVR Interviews with Adriano João, Dili, 21 September 2004 and Jacinto Alves, Dili, 5 August 2004.] Note however that the British government denied that Skyhawk airplanes were used for combat purposes in East Timor during this period [see written submission of Pat Walsh to the CAVR, based on his testimony as an expert witness to the CAVR National Public Hearing on Forced Displacement and Famine, 28-29 July 2003].

In the encirclement and annihilation [campaign] in July 1978, nobody surrendered. We hid in Ilimanu [Laclo, Manatuto]. The next morning the Indonesian military bombed us in Ilimanu, until we couldn't escape.[100]

90. Maria José da Costa, who at the time was in the Centro Sul Sector base in Alas (Manufahi), gave a similar account:

In 1978, the enemy began the strategic siege in Dolok [Alas, Manufahi]. Many died of starvation. Everyone's food was burned, and some had to abandon their families. The siege was like this: warships fired from the sea, warplanes attacked from the air and burned the dry, tall grass, then the troops attacked on the ground.

It was the dry season [in August]. The army set the tall grass alight and the fire quickly burned the whole area as if it was soaked with gasoline. Those of us who were surrounded didn't have the chance to escape because the fire was so huge. Because of this desperate situation, many people couldn't save themselves. [The Indonesian's] strategy prevented many people from escaping.

People managed to escape the encirclement when the Indonesian soldiers returned to their camps to rest in the middle of the night. When we left we were still showered with bullets from the warships at sea. I witnessed many people being burned to death.... After we managed to escape the encirclement the enemy surrounded us in a semi-circle. With support from the sea, they drove us to a plain. This made us run in all directions and the enemy was able to capture us.[101]

91. The eastern region base on Mount Matebian fell on 22 November 1978.[102] Falintil troops were divided into groups: some headed to the Centro Leste Sector to join the national forces, and some headed east to become guerrilla fighters. Xanana Gusmão, who was an adjunto in Ponta Leste Sector, told the Commission:

[O]n 22 November we split up on Matebian. Even though we were surrounded, we always tried to maintain contacts with the Central Committee in Centro [Leste]. We informed them that we could no longer hold out and they told people to surrender and form a guerrilla company in the Ponta Leste Sector....

We had contact with a nearby Racal [radio operator]. That was how we knew the situation throughout the country. We thought the other sectors were totally destroyed. Some people surrendered, some were captured.[103]

92. The last base destroyed was in Fatubessi (Ermera) in February 1979. Adriano João, a mid-level cadre in Fronteira Sul Sector, told the Commission:

The base de apoio [in Fatubessi] was destroyed on 16 February 1979. People surrendered en masse because they were surrounded by Indonesian military warplanes, which were destroying the defence base around the Cailaco [Bobonaro] mountains. As a result of the Indonesian military campaign, nearly all people came down to the town on the orders of the adjunto, Rui Fernandes, and the commander of Sector Fronteira Norte, Meno Paixão, who wrote to us at that time.[104]

93. Xanana Gusmão states that before the zonas libertadas were destroyed, the Fretilin Central Committee decided that civilians should surrender and that Falintil troops should continue the war of resistance. The news of this decision was spread to all sectors. Jacinto Alves recalled:

> When "encirclement and annihilation" happened, the Central Committee realised that it was better if people surrendered.... It was announced to the people the elderly, aged over 56 years, and those aged below 18 years could surrender, and the rest could stay [in the forest].[105]

94. Surrender, which before the major Indonesian offensive had been condemned as treason, was forced on the Fretilin Central Committee.[37]* The decision did not mean that the continuing struggle was to be carried out only by Falintil soldiers. The Fretilin Central Committee reminded people to keep helping Falintil and keep fighting for the independence of Timor-Leste, although they did not specifically describe how the struggle was to be continued.[106] Benvinda Lopes, an OPMT administrator in the Uatu-Lari area (Viqueque), described her experience:

> On 23 December 1978 a letter came from Baucau informing Commander Calisae and Moiseskin: "Now people must surrender because this war still has a long way to go." On that same day my brother Moiseskin came and explained to us: "Now you can leave, you don't have to stay here. You'll die because there is no more food and medicine. We are telling all of you that you can surrender to Indonesia, but you must never forget one thing. Your hands may work for Indonesia but you must remember us always. You can go there but you must find a way to look for us, continue to contact us, you must not be scared." That night on 23 December 1978 we came down from Kilobuti [Uatu-Lari, Viqueque] to Matebian. Then we surrendered to the Indonesian army.[107]

95. Fretilin suffered many losses in this Indonesian military offensive. Francisco Xavier do Amaral, the former President of Fretilin and of Timor-Leste, was captured by the Indonesian army near the Dilor River (Lacluta, Viqueque) in August 1978.[108] Alarico Fernandes, the Fretilin minister of information and internal security, surrendered with a number of other Central Committee members.[38]** Perhaps the biggest loss was the death of Nicolau Lobato, President

---

* Taur Matan Ruak compared two actions in different circumstances: "In 1976 when people voluntarily surrendered it was a big problem...[A] big problem! Now...1979, this surrender, we didn't voluntarily come down. Because we were forced...and that was why the leaders accepted this. They were forced to accept." [CAVR Interview with Taur Matan Ruak, Part II, Dili, 14 June 2004].

** It is still not clear why Alarico Fernandes surrendered to the Indonesian army. Fretilin's official source said that it was a "treason" caused by his disbelief in their own strength and that he kept hoping for foreign assistance, that Alarico Fernandes tried to compromise with Indonesia and he separated himself from the Fretilin Central Committee and betrayed them [Fretilin, Relatório da Delegação do Comité Central da Fretilin em Missão de Serviço no Exterior do Pais, p. 6]. He was said to be involved in what was called the "Skylight" operation by the Indonesian military, which had

of Fretilin and the RDTL, in battle on 31 December 1978.[109] Other important leaders such as Mau Lear (the vice-president of Fretilin and the RDTL) and Vicente dos Reis (Sahe, the national political commissar) were killed in February 1979.[110] Mau Kruma, the political commissar in Fronteira Norte, was killed in battle around March 1979.[111] After the offensive ended, only three members of the Fretilin Central Committee were left to continue the struggle from the forest after March 1979; all the others died in battle, were captured, or surrendered to the Indonesian military.[39+] Many of those who were captured or surrendered were subsequently executed or disappeared.

96. With the fall of the bases de apoio in 1978-79, the zonas libertadas and the protracted people's war strategy were finished. Any hopes of pursuing a strategy of defending particular areas containing the people was over.[40++] The project of creating a new society without oppression and exploitation was also abandoned. People surrendered to the Indonesian army and then lived life under the occupying power. A number of Fretilin civilian leaders, Falintil commanders and soldiers who managed to escape formed small units and continued the guerrilla war.

---

the objective of capturing or persuading the surrender of Fretilin's highest leaders [CAVR Interview with Xanana Gusmão, Dili, 7 July 2004; "Six Years of Heroic Armed Resistance," East Timor News, Winter 1982, pp. 10-12]. Mari Alkatiri mentioned the possibility that Alarico Fernandes was disappointed because, after the removal of Francisco Xavier do Amaral as the President of Fretilin and the RDTL, it was Mau Lear who was appointed to replace Nicolau Lobato as vice-president of Fretilin and prime minister of the RDTL, not him [CAVR Interview with Mari Alkatiri, Dili, 25 June 2003]. Mari Alkatiri also stated that Alarico Fernandes "didn't have an ideology": he captured Xavier hoping that he would be appointed as Vice-President of Fretilin and Prime Minister of the RDTL, and when that didn't happen, he accused Nicolau Lobato as "the hat that covered communists" and launched anti-communist propaganda [CAVR Interview with Mari Alkatiri, Dili, 25 June 2004]. While Xanana Gusmão called Alarico Fernandes a person who "joga sala, joga ba joga mai" ("played around badly, played back and forth"), he suddenly proclaimed himself Marxist-Leninist in the 1976 Soibada Conference, captured and tortured Xavier do Amaral in 1977, and then surrendered and showed up in the "Skylight" operation. Xanana Gusmão described Skylight as "Alarico's movement", and that Resistance leaders in the Matebian area heard of this movement after Alarico Fernandes surrendered in September and just as Indonesia was preparing to launch incessant offensives at the end of 1978 [CAVR Interview with Xanana Gusmão, Dili, 7 July 2004; see also Part 3: History of the Conflict].

+   The three members of the Fretilin Central Committee were: Xanana Gusmão, Fernando Txay and António Manuel Gomes da Costa (Mau Hunu).

++ According to Ernest Chamberlain, when the base at Matebian fell, Falintil was converting its defence strategy from "positional-bases" to "moving", which involved reorganising troops into mobile troops together with the strength of 11,000 people [Chamberlain, *The Struggle in Iliomar*, p. 19; Indonesian translation version, Perjuangan di Iliomar, p. 20]. It is still not clear why this strategy was implemented only at the end of 1978, when the decision to launch the protracted people's war was taken in May 1976, a decision that meant that positional war would be launched with moving and guerrilla troops.

Restructuring the Resistance: 1981-87

97. For the first two years after the fall of the bases de apoio in the zonas libertadas, the remaining Fretilin leaders in the Ponta Leste Sector searched for Fretilin Central Committee members and Falintil troops in other places. They tried to make contact with Fretilin activists and Falintil commanders who had been captured and were living in areas occupied by the Indonesian army. They sought out those they could trust to resume the struggle in a new form. They also tried to gather intelligence on the conditions under which the population in the occupied areas were living and on the strategy and deployment of ABRI units. Their ability to carry out these activities was limited by continued harassment by Indonesian forces, which culminated with Operasi Keamanan (Operation Security) in mid-1981 and which compelled them constantly to take evasive action to avoid direct combat (see part 3: The History of the Conflict).

98. After the fall of the bases de apoio in the zonas libertadas, Falintil forces divided into small units of three to four people. Previously the smallest unit had been the secção, comprising seven people. If they entered villages in occupied areas to establish contact with civilians, Falintil troop units would not carry their weapons or wear uniforms. Sometimes Falintil was able to form larger units for specific purposes. Xanana Gusmão recalled that in May 1980 he took a company (of about sixty people) as far west as Mount Kablaki in search of Resistance forces still holding out in the mountains.[41]* The military commander, Kilik Wae Gae, attempted to build a fixed base that could support a full battalion.[42]+ One informant told the Commission that in early 1979 Xanana Gusmão and Kilik Wae Gae succeeded in forming a "brigade" consisting of four companies.[43]++

Reorganizing the Resistance for the New Situation

99. At a gathering of surviving military commanders and political cadres in March 1981 a new organisational structure for the Resistance began to emerge. The first "Reorganisation of the Nation Conference" after the fall of the zonas libertadas was held in the area of Maubai on Mount Aitana in the sub-district of Lacluta (Viqueque) from 1 to 8 March 1981. The conference was organised by the two members of the Fretilin Central Committee still actively engaged in the struggle

---

* Xanana Gusmão said that he conducted a search for Central Committee members all the way to Dili with a company of troops [Xanana Gusmão, in Niner (ed.) *To Resist is To Win!*, p. 64].

+ Lere Anan Timor, who at the time was a mid-ranking cadre in Ponta Leste, said that Kilik Wae Gae, a sector commander before the fall of the zonas libertadas, led this effort [Lere Anan Timor, Archives of the Tuba Rai Metin Oral History Project, Submission to CAVR, CD No.18].

++ A source related that "after Nicolau Lobato was shot dead", Xanana Gusmão and Kilik Wae Gae formed a "brigade" consisting of four companies: Lospalos, Laga (and Quelicai), Sul and western Ponta Leste [CAVR Interview with Sebastião da Silva, Viqueque, June 2003].

in the interior, Xanana Gusmão and Mau Hunu Bulerek Karataianu. The first item on the agenda was the inauguration of nine new members of the Central Committee: José da Costa (Mau Hodu Ran Kadalak), Bere Malae Laka, Reinaldo Correia (Kilik Wae Gae), Dinis Carvalho (Nelo Kadomi Timor), Sakin Nere Ulas Timor Lemo Rai, Holy Natxa, Tito da Costa (Lere Anan Timor), Hari Nere and Paulino Gama (Mauk Moruk Teki Timor Ran Nakali Lemo Rai).[112] Together with the two other Central Committee members, Xanana Gusmão and Mau Hunu Bolerek Karataianu, they became the leaders of the internal struggle. The members of the Central Committee living abroad retained their positions: Abílio Abrantes Araújo, Mari Alkatiri, Roque Rodrigues, José Luís Guterres, Guilhermina Araújo, José Ramos-Horta and Rogério Lobato. Abílio Araújo was also appointed Secretary General, while Xanana Gusmão was appointed as the National Political Commissar (Comissário Político Nacional).[113] They became the official Resistance leaders.

100. At the conference, the members of the Central Committee decided to establish the Fretilin Marxist-Leninist Party (Partido Marxista-Leninista Fretilin, PMLF), the Revolutionary Council of National Resistance (Concelho Revolucionário de Resistência Nacional, CRRN), and to form new structures for Falintil.[114] The reason for the change of name from Fretilin to PMLF is not clear.[44§] Xanana Gusmão said that what they did was only to "ratify" the decision taken by the "pioneers" at the Laline Conference in 1977 when, following the lead of the Central Committee's Department of Political Orientation and Ideology (Departemento de Orientação Politica e Ideologica, DOPI) Marxism-Leninism was officially declared the party's ideology.[115] The Commission was unable to gather any information on party structures under the Central Committee. It is possible that the PMLF consisted only of the Central Committee, which had no subordinate organs operating below it.

101. The CRRN was intended to be the organisational vehicle for everyone who wanted to join the struggle to end the Indonesian occupation of Timor-Leste. The CRRN was in effect the PMLF's invitation to all East Timorese regardless of party or other affiliation to join the resistance to the Indonesian occupation. Clear information on CRRN's structures is also not available.[45*] One source testified that the CRRN leadership at the national level consisted of Fretilin's political activists, Falintil military commanders, and "representatives of the

---

§   Several testimonies stated that the reason for that name-change was tactical , to seek assistance from the Socialist Bloc countries. José da Conceição told the Commission that after attending the National Reorganisation Conference, Fretilin Central Committee member Mau Hunu explained to him that the change was needed to gain political and diplomatic support from socialist bloc countries in their struggle for national liberation. Justo Talenta gave a similar explanation [CAVR Interviews with José da Conceição, Dili, 20 October 2004 and Justo Talenta, Dili, 3 November 2002].

*   António Tomás Amaral da Costa (Aitahan Matak) said that the CRRN consisted of: Xanana Gusmão, Mau Hodu Ran Kadalak (José da Costa), Mau Hunu Bulerek Karataianu, Bere Malae Laka, Kilik Wae Gae, Nelo Kadomi Timur (Dinis Carvalho), Mauk Moruk Teki Timor Ran Nakali Lemo Rai, Ologari Asuwain, Lere Anan Timor, Konis Santana, Venancio Ferraz, Merak, Okan and Taur Matan Ruak [CAVR Interview with

people [living] in Indonesian-occupied territories."[116] The Committees for Regional Resistance (Comissões Regionais de Resistência) were to operate as the arm of the CRRN in the districts and below them at the sub-district level would be National Resistance Centres (Centros de Resistência Nacional, Cernac) and at the village-level, Nuclei of the People's Resistance (Núcleos de Resistência Popular, Nureps).[117] These structures operated unevenly throughout the country. An underground activist at the time testified to the Commission:

> The CRRN structure at the time was operating only at top level or in the forest, while there was no structure or base in the towns. It was just a kind of tactic to signal that an armed front [of the] Resistance, which wanted to continue the struggle, still existed. The structure only existed at the level of the Falintil command. The highest official was Xanana Gusmão. Only the members of Falintil knew the structure. We ourselves did not know exactly what the structure was.[118]

102. The CRRN had its headquarters in the forest. Some of the district and sub-district level organs also operated from the forest. Others operated clandestinely in Indonesian-controlled territory in the towns, villages and the new settlements (pemukiman baru).

103. Falintil's highest military authorities were the Commander in Chief (Comandante-em-Chefe) and the Chief of Staff (Chefe do Estado Maior) positions held by Xanana Gusmão and Reinaldo Correia (Kilik Wae Gae) respectively. They were in charge of four Falintil companies placed in each region where guerrillas were operating. Unlike the period of the zonas libertadas, these companies did not have a fixed base but were highly mobile guerrilla units. After the "Reorganization of the Nation Conference", a Red Brigade (Brigada Vermelha), led by Mauk Moruk as the First Commander (Primeiro Comandante) and Ologari Assuwain as the Deputy Commander (Segundo Comandante) was created. It is not clear whether the Brigada Vermelha was one of the units of Falintil or whether all Falintil troops were reorganised under the Brigada Vermelha.[46+]

António Tomás Amaral da Costa (Aitahan Matak), Dili, 18 December 2003]. Six of those people, who were not members of PMLF Central Committee, were Venancio Ferraz, Ologari Asuwain, Konis Santana, Merak, Okan and Taur Matan Ruak, but they were Fretilin's middle ranking cadres or Falintil commanders.

+ It seems that the Brigada Vermelha served the same function as had been performed by the Brigada de Choque before the destruction of the zonas libertadas. Their troops were not stationed in one place but were mobile and would launch surprise attacks on the Indonesian army. Jacinto Alves, a former colaborador (staff) in the Falintil General Staff (1977-78), said that in 1977 the Falintil General Staff devised a strategy of mobile warfare concentrating on a central line running from the extreme east to the western border. At the time the Resistance had evacuated the northern coastal area, and large numbers of people had moved to the fertile lands of the south. The central line stretching from east to west therefore became a shifting battleground for Falintil's Brigada de Choque troops. Several Brigada de Choque companies were formed and trained under the guidance of the former commander of the Fronteira Norte Sector, Sebastião Sarmento. Ernest Chamberlain said that before the fall of the Matebian Base there was a plan to form mobile war units totaling 11,000 people [CAVR Interview with Jacinto Alves, Dili, 16 May 2004; Chamberlain, *The Struggle in Iliomar*, p.19].

104. The CRRN leaders were people who before the fall of the zonas libertadas had been high or mid-level Fretilin cadres (quadros superiores and quadros medios) and Falintil commanders, an indication that the CRRN was dominated by Fretilin.[47*]

105. The military division of the territory changed completely. Previously the country had been divided into six sectors; at the National Reorganization Conference, it was divided into three regions (*regiões*):

Region	Districts covered	Commander
Far Eastern Region (Região Ponta Leste, also known as Funu Sei Nafatin)	Lospalos, Viqueque, Baucau and Manatuto	Kroasu and Lemorai
Central Region (Região Centro, also known as Nakroman)	Dili, Aileu, Same, Ermera and Liquiça	Fera Lafaek
The Border Region (Região Fronteira, also known as Haksolok)	Suai, Ainaro and Maliana	Venancio Ferraz [119]

106. District-level zonas were also established and led by three adjunto - one of them became the main official (responsável principal). Each zona's adjunto oversaw several cells (celula), consisting of assistente (assistants) and activista (activists).[120]

107. These territorial divisions differed completely from those of the period of the zonas libertadas. Then, the territory had been divided into political and administrative units as well as military units. At every level of that structure political activists managed agricultural production, health education and cultural programmes. After the fall of the zonas libertadas, the regions were exclusively military in character and were based on guerrilla operations. There were no large groups of civilians left in the three regiões, making both civilian administrative units and their associated support activities redundant. The main work of the political cadres—the adjunto, the assistente and the activista—was to form underground cells in Indonesian-army occupied villages, to create and disseminate propaganda to sustain the people's commitment to independence, and to provide logistical support and intelligence for the guerrillas in the forest. For these purposes a system of caixas (literally, boxes) was organised in every zona and operated by a liason officer (responsável de caixa) and couriers (ligações).[48+]

---

* Xanana Gusmão and Mau Hunu were members of the Central Committee, which meant they were high ranking cadres. Bere Malae Laka, Lere Anan Timor, Mau Hodu and Konis Santana were cadres responsible for regiões and zonas; they were the mid-level cadres. Kilik Wae Gae and Nelo Kadomi Timor were former Falintil commanders responsible for região, while Taur Matan Ruak was a company commander. There is no information on the non-Fretilin membership of the CRRN.

+ Ligação was then replaced by the term vias de canais and from 1986 the role became better known by the term of estafeta [CAVR Interview with Vasco da Gama, Dili, 18 May 2004]. They functioned as couriers carrying mail, intelligence and goods from one connecting hub (caixa) to another, based on Falintil's needs.

108. Without a civilian population in their midst, the internal Resistance focused on armed struggle. The political cadres maintained contact with the people, not in order to organize them in "building new structures to serve the people," but to assist Falintil guerrilla units with intelligence and logistical support.[121] Their role changed to that of the link between the guerrillas in the forest and the people in the villages and towns under Indonesian occupation.

109. Given that the armed resistance was based in the forest, operationally the core of the Resistance was Falintil, not Fretilin or the CRRN. Fretilin, as the "guide" ("*matadalan*" in Tetum) of the struggle, still formally set the political line, but as the struggle was now primarily an armed one the politics was chiefly that of the armed struggle. In the earlier period the Fretilin Central Committee, either in plenary sessions or, if the Central Committee was unable to convene, through its Permanent Committee, made decisions on the broad issues of policy. Decisions on military strategy had been subordinate. After the fall of the zonas libertadas the decisions that had to be made were chiefly about the armed struggle, and as such fell within the purview of the Falintil commander, sometimes, though not always, acting in concert with the Chief of Staff.[49*] This was inferred in Xanana Gusmão's interview with the Commission in connection with the 1984 restructuring, which was not accepted by several of the reassigned commanders:

> I said as Commander in Chief that in the military there is no democracy. Either we make war or we don't make war. I made a restructuring....
>
> But when it came to the problem of restructuring the military, I gave new instructions on my own initiative.... If it is a political problem, we can have an intelligent discussion. If the problem is a military one, in war the commander gives the orders. [122]

110. The Resistance had become a fully armed struggle, with Falintil playing the main role. Fretilin's civilian structure was subordinate to Falintil's. The Fretilin adjuntos evolved into logistics and intelligence officers for the Falintil company commanders. As a revolutionary party, the PMLF seems to have existed only on paper. There was no longer mass mobilisation to "build new structures to serve the people" or for the "total elimination of all forms of exploitation." The PMLF activists took up arms to fight as guerrillas or to become couriers between the guerrillas and the people, to obtain food supplies, medicine, clothes, and information on the enemy's movements.

---

*   In 1982 the Comissário Política Nacional's function was eliminated in structural readjustment (Rejustamento Estrutural). This meant that Xanana Gusmão relinquished the highest internal political position in Fretilin and from then on acted only as Falintil Commander [Xanana Gusmão, *Timor Leste-Um Povo, Uma Patria*, p. 98; Budiardjo and Liem, pp xii and pp. 67-70].

Strategy

111. The new reality brought about by the fall of the zonas libertadas required new thinking from the Resistance. A protracted people's war strategy was no longer sustainable. The Indonesian army's relentless attacks had forced Falintil to split into small units.[50+] After seriously reconsidering the military strategy, the remaining commanders and political activists determined that the war of resistance against Indonesia was to take the form of guerrilla warfare. Attacks were launched by highly mobile small units around the country. They had no fixed base. Intelligence was obtained from civilians who were organised in clandestine cells in the occupied territories.

112. Falintil's guerrilla attacks had as their tactical objective the destruction of targeted Indonesian troops, though at the same time Falintil recognised that it could never defeat the Indonesians militarily. The war of resistance shifted from its initial objective of expelling the Indonesian aggressors to demonstrating to the international community that Falintil was still capable of fighting against the Indonesian occupation and that the East Timorese people wanted independence.[51++]

113. This military strategy was in line with their changed view regarding negotiations. During the period of the zonas libertadas, Fretilin categorically refused to negotiate with Indonesia. One of the slogans at the time was Negociação – Não e Nunca (Negotiation – No and Never). With the failure of the protracted people's war the leaders slowly began to see negotiation as a means to end the Indonesian occupation. The meetings between Resistance leaders and the Indonesian army leadership were initiated in Timor-Leste in March-April 1983. They were known as the "Kontak Dame" (or "Kontak Damai," "Peace Contacts"). Taur Matan Ruak remembers:

> We sought opportunities for peace. That was why in 1983 Xanana accepted the offer of contacts with Indonesia....Their overriding objective was to use the opportunity to strike at us....On the other hand we were thinking of how it could be used to reach a peaceful resolution of the conflict.[123]

+   Xanana Gusmão and Taur Matan Ruak stated that initially they split troops into small units in response to the situation created by the Indonesian army; it was not a strategy adopted by the Resistance out of choice. [CAVR Interviews with Xanana Gusmão, part II, Dili, 10 August 2004 and Taur Matan Ruak, part II, Dili, 14 June 2004].

++ In 1983 the Indonesian army wrote a summary of the strategy of the Resistance as they saw it, namely that the objectives of the protracted war launched by Fretilin were: (a) to stay alive by avoiding decisive combat, so as to have the time to restore their forces while at the same time cultivating a high spirit of motivation and strong discipline; (b) to preserve and develop support networks in resettlement areas and in the towns; (c) to show their presence or existence, particularly in the months before the UN General Assembly; (d) to create conditions which would make ABRI feel unsafe anywhere in the territory; (e) to establish mobile bases in many regions, particularly in formerly fertile villages now abandoned by their inhabitants [Attachment Document 3 in Budiardjo and Liem, The War Against East Timor, p. 197].

114. During the various Kontak Dame Falintil proposed a plan for resolving the conflict through negotiations between the armed resistance and Indonesia under the supervision of the United Nations. Some of the proposals of the Resistance, such as the unconditional withdrawal of Indonesian troops, were still in the uncompromising tradition of the Fretilin of the zonas libertadas. Others included the establishment of a UN peacekeeping force in Timor-Leste to supervise the withdrawal of the Indonesian army providing security for the transitional government, and retaining Falintil troops "to protect people from pressure." The Resistance also proposed a referendum to decide Timor-Leste's political future.[124] This was clearly a softening of the position that had been taken in 1975. Then Fretilin had asserted that the East Timorese people had the right to independence and that the people had stated their desire for this through the Fretilin Central Committee's Proclamation of Independence on 28 November 1975. By proposing a referendum as a way to end the Indonesian occupation of Timor-Leste, Fretilin was in fact endorsing the position that had been taken much earlier by the diplomatic front: that since Fretilin's Proclamation of Independence stood no chance of gaining recognition from more than a handful of states, the only course open to the independence movement was to seek to gain international backing for the right of the people of Timor-Leste to self-determination (see chapter 7.1: The Right to Self-Determination). If in the past diplomatic efforts had been aimed primarily at winning the support of the Socialist bloc and the non-aligned states, now, the Western bloc countries became important, not least because of their influence at the UN including on the UN Security Council (see section on the Clandestine Front). The idea of the primacy of the struggle on the diplomatic front gained weight in Resistance thinking, until by late 1984 it was the dominant view among Resistance leaders. José da Costa (Mau Hodu Ran Kadalak), a prominent member of the PMLF Central Committee, said that the Resistance leadership now centred its strategy on dialogue and shifted its focus to the diplomatic front, in preference to the armed struggle, although armed operations were to continue whenever possible and necessary.[125]

115. At the same time another shift in thinking was underway. For several years the dominant view within the Resistance had been that Fretilin was the only true champion of independence, and the only true patriots were to be found within Fretilin ranks. After 1982 the idea that other parties and social groupings could also take part in the national liberation struggle began to gain ground. An important milestone in this process was the meeting between the Falintil Commander and National Political Commissar, Xanana Gusmão and the Apostolic Administrator, Monsignor Martinho da Costa Lopes, in the village of Mehara, Tutuala, Lautém District. At that meeting Dom Martinho said that national unity between Fretilin and UDT was needed if the independence struggle was going to succeed. At first Xanana Gusmão rejected the idea,[52*] but slowly it became more acceptable until in 1983

the PMLF Central Committee affirmed National Unity (Unidade Nacional) as its official policy.[126]

116. The politics of National Unity and the idea of a negotiated, UN-sponsored end to the Indonesian occupation of Timor-Leste amounted to a radical shift in the ideology of the Resistance, and it also had organisational implications. Hopes of gaining the cooperation of parties such as UDT, especially its leadership abroad, who rejected Timor-Leste's integration with Indonesia could easily founder on their abhorrence of Fretilin's revolutionary politics. Another party whose cooperation was crucial was the Catholic Church. Several priests, including Monsignor Martinho da Costa Lopes, had shown their sympathy for the predicament of the Resistance, though not for its ideology. The Church often protected people on the run from the Indonesian army and sent information outside the country. Relations between Fretilin and the Catholic Church had been strained in the past, as the conservative Church could not come to terms with several aspects of Fretilin's ideology.[127] To gain the explicit support of UDT and the Catholic Church, the PMLF needed to abandon its revolutionary politics. Monsignor Martinho Costa Lopes addressed this matter at his secret meeting with Xanana Gusmão in Mehara in 1982.[128]

117. The dissolution of the PMLF occurred during a Central Committee meeting held in April 1984.[129] From this time Marxism-Leninism ceased to be Fretilin's ideology, revolutionary politics were abandoned, the principle of "Negotiation – No and Never" adopted in the 1977 Laline Conference was dropped, and the PMLF became simply Fretilin again.[130]

118. With those changes the politics of National Unity and negotiation as a means of defeating Indonesia became central to the struggle. This led to the CRRN becoming increasingly more visible than Fretilin. Although Fretilin, while still the PMLF, formulated the policies of National Unity, their implementation was a matter for the CRRN. This gave the CRRN a more important role. The reality was that the struggle was the armed guerrilla struggle, led by Falintil. For this reason Falintil's role became more prominent, as did Xanana Gusmão's position as a military leader. One indication of this was the decision to abolish the position of the National Political Commissar in 1982.[131]

119. Nonetheless, these changes did not go unchallenged. Several members of the Central Committee, including the Falintil Chief of Staff, Kilik Wae Gae, and the Red Brigade Commander, Mauk Moruk, opposed the decision to disband the PMLF. They also opposed the policy of National Unity adopted the previous year.[132] This conflict caused a crisis in the Resistance leadership. Kilik Wae Gae and friends attempted a coup against Xanana Gusmão, the struggle's highest leader.[133]

---

* José da Conceição, an adjunto at the time, said that in the beginning Xanana Gusmão did not agree with the concept and believed that unification of Fretilin and UDT was like "marrying a frog and a crocodile" [CAVR Interview with José da Conceição, Dili, 20 October 2004].

120. Xanana Gusmão said that the dispute was not really about politics or ideology, but about his decision to change the military structure. Several units under the leadership of Kilik Wae Gae, Mauk Moruk, and Ologari in the Central Sector were not taking the offensive against the Indonesian army, while Falintil troops in the eastern sector were facing repeated Indonesian attacks. Xanana Gusmão reshuffled several command positions, demoting the recalcitrant commanders to operational level. Kilik Wae Gae was demoted from chief of staff to Red Brigade commander. Mauk Moruk was demoted from Red Brigade commander to company commander as was Mauk Moruk's deputy Ologari Assuwain. In an interview with the Commission, Xanana Gusmão said:

> I carried out a reshuffle. Mauk Moruk didn't have real plans to lead the company [into action]. He just sat up there in the mountains. The troops around him [kept him] secure. I said: "If you want to lead a company, then you will." Ologari, who was the Deputy Commander, just sat around doing nothing. I said: "You will also be a company commander." Because of this [change] they called me a traitor, that I was no longer a Marxist. They held on to the ideology, making it into a problem. But the [real] problem was the military reshuffle. I gave new instructions, gave new directions to the companies, ordering them: "Now find the enemy and kill them."[134]

121. Other witnesses agreed that the reshuffle caused problems.[135] Cornelio Gama (Leki Nahak Foho Rai Boot), a company commander at the time, told the Commission:

> [There were] differences over [the dissolution of the] PMLF. There was also an issue about senior commanders not getting positions. In fact most of them were demoted. Like Mauk Moruk, who previously had been the Red Brigade Commander [sic] and Ologari Assuwain, who previously was the Brigade Deputy Commander [sic], and Kilik Wae Gae, who previously was the Chief of General Staff. Kilik became the Red Brigade Commander [sic], while Mauk Moruk and Ologari both became Region Commanders.[136]

122. Taur Matan Ruak, who at the time was a member of the Falintil General Staff, suggested that the attitude of Kilik and his allies was "strange." Taur Matan Ruak reflected:

> Whenever President [Xanana Gusmão] mentioned the Marxist-Leninist Party, they would say: "the Marxist-Leninist Party is the wrong politics; social democratic politics are better." Then when it changed to social democratic politics, they said: "This is not good, the Marxist-Leninist Party is better." Nothing was ever right, what did they want ?...
>
> Basically when a man defends an ideology, a theory or a view, he should have the capacity to defend it, to be ready intellectually to defend his views. But he didn't defend them and he jumped around. That was our situation. We didn't know what we should call [the party], how to name it...I saw that there was something strange going on.[137]

123. Mauk Moruk said that the reason for the opposition from Kilik and his allies was Xanana Gusmão's proposal to separate Falintil from Fretilin.[138] Whatever the cause of the conflict, several of the commanders and political leaders who were at odds with Xanana Gusmão died or surrendered with their troops to the Indonesian military. The dissident group broke away from main body of the resistance group. Kilik Wae Gae and Okan were killed fighting the Indonesian army. Mauk Moruk[53]** and Ologari Assuwain surrendered to the Indonesian army.[139]

124. The deaths and surrender of the opponents of the policy of National Unity strengthened the position of Xanana Gusmão as leader of the Resistance. The Central Committee expelled Kilik and Mauk Moruk. The Falintil commander in chief assumed the position of chief of staff left vacant by the expulsion of Kilik.[140] The demise of the opponents of National Unity did not immediately result in the CRRN becoming an effective vehicle for national unity. UDT, in particular, continued to refuse to cooperate with the CRRN. Taur Matan Ruak reflected:

> There were different interpretations of the CRRN…. For instance UDT said [that the name] "C o n s e l h o Revolucionário"…[the term] "Revolucionário" came from those who were Marxist-Leninist…. So they had their own definition. The important field of strategy, the strategy for resolving the conflict…required a consensus…. Consensus only existed in the armed resistance. But at the political level those who were abroad, those who were closely affiliated, such as the Fretilin [External] Delegation they accepted it, but UDT and the others didn't accept it.[141]

125. This was probably the reason why the CRRN leadership continued to be drawn from Fretilin. A representative of the Resistance in Australia said that CRRN was not effective because of the internal conflicts within the Resistance leadership "and the lack of resources to resist and to fend off Indonesia's attacks."[142] Even so, there was some progress towards National Unity in March 1986 when an agreement was reached in Lisbon between Fretilin and UDT leaders to unite in the diplomatic struggle for the independence of Timor-Leste. This became known as the Nationalist Convergence (Convergência Nacionalista).[143] This agreement proved to be fragile because of the persistent mutual suspicion and the sectarian attitudes among those who were representing Fretilin and UDT abroad. Reflecting on that period, Xanana Gusmão later observed:

> In 1986, the Nationalist Convergence was formed in an attempt to dispel the climate of suspicion that existed between the political parties but, once again, good intentions were not enough to create harmony between our separate objectives.[144]

---

* Aleixo Ximenes told the Commission that before Mauk Moruk surrendered he sent a letter to him saying that Xanana Gusmão would kill him if he found out that Mauk Moruk wrote a letter of surrender. When he met Aleixo Ximenes, Mauk Moruk reportedly told him that after breaking with the Falintil leadership, Kilik faced the possibility of death at the hands of Xanana Gusmão or ABRI, should either find him [CAVR Interview with Aleixo Ximenes, Dili, 2 February 2004.]

Falintil after 1987

126. In 1987, the Falintil commander in chief, Xanana Gusmão, took the important step of establishing Falintil as a non-partisan movement, removing the military wing from the Fretilin structure. This decision, known as the "Structural Readjustment of the Resistance" (*Reajustamento Estrutural da Resistência*), was taken at a meeting in Aitana (Lacluta, Viqueque). It was also decided that the Resistance leadership must remain inside the country and that Xanana Gusmão, as Falintil commander, resign from Fretilin.[145] Detaching Falintil from its political party roots was intended to make the armed front a genuine national force and consolidate its leadership role in the Resistance. Previously, the struggle against the Indonesian occupation had been led officially by the CRRN, with Fretilin at the forefront. With the national unity policy of the Resistance leaders coming increasingly to the fore, the CRRN became associated with the broader national interest. Fretilin, in contrast, was perceived to be more narrow and partisan. As the only real resistance against Indonesian occupation existed in the form of armed struggle, Falintil became the dominant force in the CRRN, with the Falintil commanders leading the struggle. As a consequence, Falintil was seen to be the only organisation truly fighting for the national interest.

127. Falintil's exit from Fretilin was typical of Xanana Gusmão's new approach of the politics of national unity. The previous approach had been to try to unify the political parties of Fretilin and UDT under the CRRN. This had proved unsuccessful because of fundamental differences both within and between the two parties. The perceived "radicalism" of the Fretilin Delegation for the Exterior (Delegação da Fretilin em Serviço no Exterior, DFSE) was one sticking point.[146] The new approach's emphasis on Falintil as a truly non-partisan organisation fighting the Indonesian occupation of Timor-Leste met with some initial resistance. Lere, a Falintil commander at the time, reflected:

> Falintil left Fretilin with a message from Commander Xanana on 7 December 1987.... At the time I was with Mau Hodu...Mau Hodu asked: "Has Commander Xanana spoken about it...about leaving the party...about the dissolution of the Marxist-Leninist Party? What do we think? How do we explain it?" I said: "You explain it. You have to explain it [because] you're the political commissar. I don't know how to explain it." This was a big problem....

> We retreated to a place near Vemasse [Baucau] and at night we held a meeting. [Mau Hodu] called me [but] I refused to [go]. The meeting was being held nearby [so I could hear it]. They started a discussion. Many commanders didn't want to accept it. [They said]: "Many people died, we suffered, we lost families.... Why did he say that? Now the leader is playing games!"

> They didn't want Falintil to separate from Fretilin, didn't want the Marxist-Leninist Part abolished. But slowly, as the situation developed, they [finally] accepted the reasons.[147]

128. The next step in the campaign for national unity was the establishment of the National Council of Maubere[54*] Resistance (Conselho Nacional de Resistência Maubere, CNRM) in December 1988 to replace the CRRN. The CNRM consisted of ten members: three Falintil commanders, five from the clandestine resistance front and two Fretilin members.[148] The Falintil commander in chief, Xanana Gusmão, became the highest leader of the CNRM with the title Responsável Principal. The power of this post was extensive, encompassing "full authority over all matters connected with the struggle in Timor-Leste, including the international diplomatic struggle."[149]

129. In keeping with the decision to keep the Resistance leadership in the country, the Resistance Delegation for External Work (Delegação da Resistência em Serviço no Exterior, DRSE) was formed to carry out resistance activities abroad. Abílio de Araújo (Fretilin's secretary-general), Moisés Amaral, and the outspoken former Apostolic Administrator of Dili, Dom Martinho Costa Lopes, were appointed the caretakers of the DRSE. The new structure replaced the DFSE.[150] The change was intended to reinforce the new non-partisan approach and combat the perceived ineffectiveness of the DFSE, which was attributed to internal conflicts within its leadership. The DFSE resisted the change. Its response was to turn itself into the Fretilin External Delegation (Delegação Externa da Fretilin, DEF).[151]

130. The document Reajustamento Estrutural da Resistência e Proposta da Paz (Structural Readjustment of the Resistance and a Proposal for Peace) set out CNRM's structure, including the new relationship between the DRSE and Falintil. Falintil was named responsible for running the CNRM internally, while the DRSE was to function internationally through diplomatic representations, dissemination of information, cultural activities and aid contributions to East Timorese refugees abroad.[152]

131. In 1989 Xanana Gusmão appointed José Ramos-Horta as CNRM's special representative and his personal representative abroad.[153] José Ramos-Horta subsequently resigned from his position in the DEF to concentrate on representing the CNRM at the UN and elsewhere.[55**] From this time the Resistance struggle at the international level was conducted by the CNRM alone, and Fretilin's role in the struggle at the international level virtually ceased. The consolidation of the CNRM leadership at the international level was strengthened further by the appointment of non-political party representatives to key positions in a number of countries.[56+]

---

* "Maubere" is a common Timorese male name and was first used by José Ramos-Horta to refer to the East Timorese common man. It was subsequently taken up by Fretilin [see Part 3: History of the Conflict].
* One source states that the reason for Ramos-Horta's resignation from Fretilin was that "not all [Fretilin] Foreign Delegation members were active in the struggle." ["Fretilin: Roots of Friction", in Fitun (London) No. 11, September 1993].
+ For example, in the 1990s CNRM's representative for Australia and New Zealand was Abel Guterres, for the United States Constâncio Pinto, for Canada Abe Barreto, for Europe José Amorim Dias, and for Portugal Luis Cardoso ["East Timorese in the Diaspora," http://www.uc.pt/timor/diaspora.htm].

132. The appointment of José Ramos-Horta as the CNRM special representative abroad, and the subsequent consolidation of CNRM's leadership at the international level, resulted in progress being made in the diplomatic struggle. Through the efforts of CNRM representatives abroad, a degree of unity was forged between Fretilin and UDT, who successfully collaborated in carrying out joint diplomatic initiatives. For example, in March 1995, in preparation for the All-Inclusive intra East Timorese Dialogue (AIETD), the leaders of the CNRM, Fretilin and UDT held an official meeting to formulate a joint strategy.[154] In September 1996 a joint delegation from the three organisations visited South Africa and met with the African National Congress (ANC), labour unions and parliamentarians to gain support for Timor-Leste's independence struggle.[57++] In recognition of these efforts, Xanana Gusmão stated in a 1994 message that Fretilin and UDT were "partners" of the CNRM.[155]

133. Despite efforts to turn the CNRM into a broad non-partisan national front, political resistance to CNRM as the leader of the struggle lingered. Xanana Gusmão noted:

> We made a pledge to our people to staunchly uphold the principle of "Unite to be able to resist better!" Side by side with our people, who easily understood the objectives of the CNRM, we were ready to cope with all the consequences. But there were distortions in the way the CNRM was perceived. It was seen as a party and incorrectly regarded as yet another player on the scene. It would have been better had this not been so.[156]

134. Although Xanana Gusmão did not directly name those whom he believed held "distorted perceptions" of the CNRM, he was clearly referring to UDT. At this time UDT still considered CNRM to be just Fretilin in disguise, and was not ready to accept Xanana Gusmão as the ultimate leader of the Resistance. Francisco Guterres (Lu 'Olo), who at the time was the Fretilin vice-secretary, remembers:[157]

> For over ten years the CNRM continued to promote national unity, but national unity still did not exist. Those of us who died remained in the forest, the enemy killed us every day, but what exactly did the people in the towns want? Until finally you understood that [the word] "Maubere" was worse than Marxist-Leninist. That was why it was changed to CNRT in Peniche. [158]

135. The progress in achieving unity was only confirmed at the Timor National Convention at Peniche, Portugal, in April 1998. At this meeting a number of key political achievements were made. Firstly, the CNRT (Conselho Nacional de Resistência Timorense, National Council of Timorese Resistance) was estab-

---

++ The delegation consisted of José Ramos-Horta (CNRM Special Representative), João Carrascalão (Chairman of UDT), and Roque Rodrigues (Timor-Leste Ambassador in Luanda) [African National Congress, "East Timorese Visit," in the African National Congress homepage, http://www.anc.org.za/ancdocs/pr/1996/pr0910b.html].

lished, comprising not only of Fretilin and UDT, but also other political parties such as KOTA and Apodeti (Pro-Referendum), and nonpolitical organisations such as the Church. Secondly, Xanana Gusmão was chosen as the lider maximo (highest leader) and was subsequently appointed President of the CNRT. Two vice presidents were appointed, José Ramos-Horta, and a "silent" (secret) vice president inside Timor-Leste, Mário Carrascalão. Finally, the word "Maubere" in title of the CNRM, which was considered by UDT as being synonymous with Fretilin and containing revolutionary nuances, was replaced by the word "Timorense" ("Timorese").

136. The newly established CNRT consisted of three organs, the National Political Commission, the Executive Commission and the Judiciary Commission. Xanana Gusmão was appointed the leader of the National Political Commission, while José Ramos-Horta became the chairman of the Executive Commission. The membership of the National Political Commission consisted of party representatives, members of non-party organisations and a priest, the Executive Commission was made up of representatives from both the political parties and non-political groups, and the Judiciary Commission technical experts.[159] There were twenty-two representatives selected in Peniche to make up these three bodies, all of whom were outside of Timor-Leste. In September 1998, twelve further members of the CNRT National Political Commission were selected from inside Timor-Leste by the president of the CNRT, pursuant to the authority granted to him at the Peniche Conference in Portugal to establish the structure of CNRT within Timor-Leste.[58*]

137. The detachment of Falintil from Fretilin and the establishment of the CNRM confirmed Falintil as the political and military leader of the struggle. This was reinforced in the document Reajustamento Estrutural da Resistência e Proposta da Paz which set out the Falintil High Command's key responsibilities as:

---

* The members of the National Political Commission selected in Peniche were Xanana Gusmão, José Ramos-Horta, João Carrascalão, Padre Francisco Fernandes, Mari Alkatiri, Ana Pessoa, Alberto Araújo and Domingos Oliveira and four alternate members: Estanislau da Silva, Agio Pereira, Vicente Guterres and Zacarias Costa. The 12 members of the National Political Commission from inside Timor-Leste were: Abel da Costa Belo, David Dias Ximenes, Domingos FJ Sousa, Leandro Isaac, João Baptista Fernandes Alves, Leão P dos Reis Amaral, Lú-Olo, Manuel Viegas Carrascalão, Paulo Freitas da Silva, Taur Matan Ruak, Francisco Lopes Carvalho and Lucas da Costa (based in Indonesia). The members of the Executive Commission were José Ramos-Horta, José Luis Guterres (head of the Foreign Relations Department), Manuel Tilman (head of the Administration and Resources Department), Roque Rodrigues (Central Services), Emilia Pires (Regional Services), Pascoela Barreto (Finance and Resources) and Lucas da Costa (Rama Metan, Youth Department). The members of the Judiciary Commission were Carlos Alberto Barbosa, Jerónimo Henriques, Alfredo Borges Ferreira and Filomeno Andrade [CNRT – National Council of Timorese Resistance, http://www.labyrinth.net.au/~ftimor/cnrt.html].

- Deciding general strategy
- Providing the general political orientation
- Taking necessary action.[160]

138. Endowed with this authority, the Falintil High Command began to take charge of the political and military aspects of the struggle, with the development of the general strategy for the political direction of diplomatic efforts abroad, and the launch of continued armed resistance by Falintil against the Indonesian occupation army. Falintil's role in the overall struggle was described by Taur Matan Ruak: "There were three fronts: the Diplomatic Front and the Clandestine Front took their orders from the Armed Front."[59]* In a speech in Uaimori (Viqueque) on Falintil's anniversary in August 2003 Xanana Gusmão confirmed Falintil's leading role after 1987: "It was decided in 1987 to change Falintil into a nonpartisan body to become the fundamental base to strengthen the whole resistance movement, which could then lead our struggle to final victory."[161]

Falintil's Structures, 1987 to 1999

The Falintil High Command was under the leadership of Xanana Gusmão, as the commander in chief (*comandante-em-chefe*). He was also the chief of staff (*chefe do estado maior*), overseeing the deputy general chief of staff (*sub-chefe do estado maior*) Taur Matan Ruak, political advisor (*conselheiro político*) Mau Hodu, and military advisor (*conselheiro militar*) Mau Hunu Bolerek Karataianu.[162] The guerrilla fighters operated under them in small units of four to eight people. During the CNRM period, the territorial structure of the armed resistance was the same as during the CRRN period. It was divided into three regions, Ponta Leste, Centro and Fronteira. Several guerrilla units operated in each region under the command of a regional commander.*

Between the late 1980s and early 1990s was a difficult period for Falintil. Commander in Chief Xanana Gusmão later stated that Falintil numbers were reduced to fewer than 100 troops.[163] According to Indonesian army reports around this time, there were sixty-seven guerrillas in Ponta Leste, with forty-five rifles operating in units of six people.[164] But in the wake of the Santa Cruz Massacre on 12 November 1991, Falintil's strength grew from 143 guerrillas with 100 rifles to 245 guerrillas with 130 rifles.[165]

---

* CAVR Interview with Taur Matan Ruak, Part II, 14 June 2004. José da Conceição (formerly an adjunto, and also after the fall of the zonas libertadas) said, "After the separation the military was dominant. Civilian activists' role was to support the military, although they shared the same goal, which was independence" [CAVR Interview with José da Conceição, Dili, 20 October 2004].
* Ponta Leste Region Commander was David Alex, Centro Region was Lere Anan Timor, Fronteira Region was Ernesto (Dudu).

During the 1990s there were a number of changes in the leadership of the Falintil High Command as a result of the captures of several of its members by the Indonesian army. Mau Hodu, the political advisor to the chief of staff, was captured in January 1992. After the capture of Xanana Gusmão in November 1992, the CNRM's military advisor, Mau Hunu, took over command of Falintil for a brief period, until he too was captured by the Indonesian army on 3 April 1993. Konis Santana (secretary of Comissão Directiva da Fretilin, the highest Fretilin organ inside Timor-Leste) then took over command of Falintil until his death in March 1998. Despite these changes, formally, the position of Falintil commander in chief and president of the CNRM still belonged to Xanana Gusmão even though he was incarcerated in Jakarta.

In 1998 the territorial structure was overhauled. The country was divided into four regions; Região 1 covering Lautém and most of Baucau districts; Região 2 covering parts of Baucau, Viqueque and parts of Manatuto; Região 3 covering Dili, Aileu, Ainaro and parts of Manatuto; and Região 4 covering Ermera, Liquiça, Bobonaro and Covalima.[+]

Falintil's force of only 300 guerrillas in early 1998 had increased to some 1,500 by late August 1999.[166] From mid-1998, the number of guerrillas increased rapidly for a number of reasons as former guerrillas returned to their units, young clandestine activists ran to the forest to avoid capture by the Indonesian army and the violence of the anti-independence militia, and East Timorese troops in the Indonesian army deserted.

139. Although the Frente Armada (Armed Front) was responsible for leading the Resistance, Falintil's strategy for winning the struggle was not primarily a military one. Falintil commanders and political leaders realised that they did not have the military capacity to defeat the Indonesian army, which was far more advanced in terms of weaponry and personnel. For Falinitil leadership the key to winning the struggle was international diplomacy. Indonesia's invasion and occupation of Timor-Leste violated international law and therefore the integration of Timor-Leste into Indonesia was not internationally recognized.

140. In 1989 the CNRM proposed a peace plan, which envisaged a process sponsored by the United Nations which would eventually lead to the holding of a referendum though which the people of Timor-Leste would exercise their right to self-determination. The process envisaged the following steps:

- The withdrawal of Indonesian troops
- The simultaneous disarmament of Indonesian-armed paramilitary groups and Falintil guerrillas
- The establishment of a transitional government which would set a date for a vote on the political status of Timor-Leste

---

[+] Comandante Região 1 was Lere Anan Timor, Comandante Região 2 Sabica Besi Kulit, Comandante Região 3 Falur Rate Laek (Domingos Raul) and Comandante Região 4 Ular Reik (Virgílio dos Anjos).

- A cooperation agreement between the transitional government and Indonesia, with Australia, the European Union and other countries ensuring the rapid and peaceful development of Timor-Leste
- The establishment of a government of National Unity for a period of 5-15 years at the end of which a referendum would be held and, depending on the outcome, sovereignty transferred.[167]

141. The CNRM believed that through dialogue all parties to the conflict would be persuaded of the need to hold a referendum on self-determination. The struggle for international support came to be seen as more important than victories on the battlefield.* Armed resistance would continue although its purpose was no longer to win the war, but to add weight to the demands of the wider resistance. Agio Pereira described the role of the armed struggle as follows: "Inside East Timor, the Armed Front would mobilise the people to continue for as long as necessary, to at least maintain a quagmire on the battleground so that the diplomatic front could press ahead with a solution which meets the aspirations of the Timorese people and is internationally acceptable."[168]

142. The former Fretilin vice-secretary of Falintil, Francisco Guterrres "Lú-Olo," told the Commission about its strategy:

This defined the concrete strategy of resolving the conflict through negotiations.... Resolution through negotiations did not mean that we didn't bring in the military to win the war...the military alone wouldn't [win]. It was the troops' task to defend [the existence] of the army. As far as the

Indonesian army was concerned, you could say that we were ready to attack by being defensive. But, we couldn't compare our army [with the enemy's] in operating on a military basis. We went on with the guerrilla war and created an objective situation, and a politico-military reality which would achieve the goal of liberating our land.[169]

143. Falintil guerrilla attacks on Indonesian targets were launched mostly for tactical reasons, to obtain weapons and other equipment needed to keep Falintil in existence. Another goal was to exhaust the Indonesian army psychologically. But strategically, the principal goals of the Falintil guerrillas were not military but political. The last Falintil chief of staff, Taur Matan Ruak, told the Commission:

We evaluated the situation daily...on the international scene, we especially evaluated important events, parliamentary elections in [Indonesia], the presidential election

---

* One of the premises of the establishment of the CNRM was that the resolution of the question of Timor-Leste relied on taking the struggle into the international arena, rather than the armed arena [Agio Pereira, "The National Council of Maubere Resistance (CNRM), Overview of the History of the Struggle of East Timor", paper presented at a solidarity meeting, Sydney, August 1994].

[Indonesia], the 20th of May [the anniversary of the founding of the ASDT political party], troop withdrawals. On those occasions we undertook small actions which would have a large impact. That was why we normally made our evaluation based on such events. So, people would not have the impression that the situation was calm, that was why we had to create disturbances, why we always had to do something, however insignificant.

This could be considered a counter-campaign to their campaign to convince people that the situation was stable. The aim was more to destabilise the situation. That was why the operations normally had a specific purpose. It might be an economic purpose, taking food, money, paper, clothes for our use.... It might be diplomatic, if it had international repercussions. It always had repercussions of some kind. The repercussions might be more of a military kind if we took arms and materials. And then there were times when the impact was strictly diplomatic, when we created a security situation which gave people the impression that the war would go on forever.[170]

144. Falintil launched attacks with precision with a view to their impact on the diplomatic struggle, to impress on the world that in Timor-Leste there was still fighting and that the international community must take action to resolve it. From the time of the ceasefire in 1983, the CRRN and then subsequently the CNRM said that it would disarm if a peaceful solution, involving a referendum on self-determination, could be found. When the diplomatic solution bore fruit and President Habibie proposed a referendum to determine the future status of Timor-Leste, Falintil attacks virtually ceased, the Resistance turned its attention to preparing peacefully for referendum, and in July 1999 Falintil unilaterally decided to canton forces, as outlined under the 5 May 1999 Agreements on the implementation of the referendum.[63*]

The Clandestine Liberation Movement

145. The history of the clandestine movement during the Indonesian occupation is highly complex and, because of the nature of the movement, there has been very little written on the structures and strategies of the movement. The following overview has been compiled from interviews with former members of the Resistance, but the Commission notes that there is much scope for further research into this fascinating aspect of Timorese history.

---

* The voluntary cantonment of Falintil troops was completed by 12 August, prior to the Popular Consultation on 30 August. Cantonment for Região 1 were in Atelari (Laga, Baucau District), for Região 2 and Região 3 in Uaimori (Manatuto District), for Região 4 in Poetete (Ermera District) and Odelgomo (Aiassa village, Bobonaro District). According to Falintil's information to UNAMET, 187 guerrillas were placed in Aiassa, 153 in Poetete, 260 in Uaimori, and 70 in Atelari, making a total of 670 people [D Greenlees and R Garran, *Deliverance: The Inside Story of East Timor's Fight for Freedom*, Allen & Unwin, Crows Nest, 2002, p. 182; Ian Martin, Self-Determination for East Timor, 2001, pp. 72-73; see also Part 3: The History of

146. The Commission has heard that clandestine activities began in the first years after the Indonesian invasion. Fretilin activists and their families in Dili and other parts of the country were organised into small groups and helped the guerrilla fighters by providing food, medicines, clothing and information on the situation in the towns. These small groups evolved spontaneously without a common strategy, worked independently and made their own contacts with the Falintil commanders in the interior.[171]

147. These clandestine groups became increasingly important after the obliteration of the zonas libertadas. Two-way radio communication between guerrilla units, which broke down at this time, was replaced by communication through couriers.[64*] The guerrilla leaders in the interior established clandestine networks by forming organisations such as the Democratic Revolutionary Committee (Comité Democrático Revolucionário, CDR) and the Popular Militia for National Liberation (Milicia Popular de Libertação Nacional, Miplin).[172] Their main objective was to establish new support bases for the armed struggle because Falintil had to fight without logistical support in the forest. The network expanded over the years following the destruction of the zonas libertadas and was able to support Falintil's armed struggle, eliminating the need for a permanent base in the interior. The leaders of the Resistance were therefore able to claim that their support base had shifted to urban and rural settlements controlled by the Indonesian military.[173]

148. The Falintil Resistance leadership in the mountains tried to direct the clandestine struggle by forming Miplin. Unlike most clandestine groups, Miplin had a military-type structure. Recruits were organised in unarmed teams and platoons. Taur Matan Ruak, an assistant to the chief of staff in 1981 in the Central region, then operations commander in the eastern region between 1982 and 1984, explained Miplin's role to the Commission:

> The mission of those known as militia was usually to relay information about spies in their midst to prevent [the spies] from doing any harm, and about Indonesian army movements. Normally that is what we called a militia. But it wasn't necessary for them to carry weapons because there were no arms [to give them]....
>
> Miplin is a concept we created and it is difficult to compare it to the classic understanding of the term [militia]. Sometimes foreigners were surprised because they compared it with their classic concept... [laughter].... Their classic militias are armed and trained in the use of arms. We did not have arms...we used [the militias] to motivate the population to remain alert. [174]

149. Despite the early efforts of the leadership to formalise the clandestine structure, groups still operated independently. Groups were established by

---

*   Those who at the beginning were called ligação (liaison), vias de canais (channels) and since the mid-1980s became known as estafeta (couriers) [CAVR Interview with Vasco da Gama (Criado), Dili, 18 May 2004.]

former political activists or guerrillas. At first they only exchanged information on the situation. Later, they started to have contact with Falintil guerrillas and to collect food, medicines and clothes to take to the guerrillas. These groups operated in cells of three to five individuals, known as a núcleos. People in these groups liaised between guerrillas and sometimes with other núcleos. Some groups were organised into networks which were controlled by individuals that the Resistance leadership in the forest appointed. Other clandestine groups were independent but had direct links to Falintil commanders.[175]

150. In 1986, when the CRRN increased the effectiveness of the clandestine network by placing it under the coordination of the Inter-regional Coordination Organisation (Organização Coordinadora Inter-Regional, OCR).[65+] The OCR was the regional arm of CRRN and operated through the civilian population. It remained effective until around 1988. Although its leaders worked hard in all regions to establish networks, not all groups could be placed under the OCR because the number of clandestine groups kept increasing and because the blanket presence of the Indonesian military and its intelligence network restricted their ability to operate.

151. An important development in the clandestine movement was the formation of urban student cells in high schools. These cells successfully infiltrated and controlled legal organisations such as the Catholic Scouts (Escuteiros) and the Intra-School Students Organization (Organisasi Siswa Intra-Sekolah, OSIS), the student bodies in each high school created by the Indonesian government. For example, the members of a clandestine cell called 007 in Dili, Constâncio Pinto and José Manuel Fernandes, were scout leaders.[176] Ricardo Ribeiro, a Sagrada Familia activist who in 1988 became the liaison between the clandestine and Falintil in the eastern zone, also became an OSIS organiser and eventually the chairman of the association in his high school in Dili, Hati Kudus.[177]

152. With the establishment of the University of East Timor (Universitas Timor Timur, Untim) by the Indonesian government in 1986, university students became targets for clandestine organisational activity. In early 1991 the members of several clandestine cells, including those formerly and secretly based at the Externato de São José school, established the Association of Anti-integration Youth and Students (Himpunan Pemuda, Pelajar, dan Mahasiswa Anti-Integrasi, HPPMAI).[66*]

153. A parallel development took place outside Timor-Leste in the early 1980s, when the government of Indonesia started to send East Timorese students

---

[+] According to Vasco da Gama, Aitahan Matak and Paulo Assis Belo were active in this body [CAVR Interview with Vasco da Gama, Dili, 18 May 2004].

[*] The Chairman of this organisation was Agusto Gama (who came from a clandestine cell at the Externato and at the time was a member of the Comité Executivo) with Vasco da Gama as vice-chairman. Formerly Vasco da Gama had been active in the Raculima clandestine cell [CAVR Interview with Vasco da Gama, Dili, 18 May 2004].

to study in universities in Java, Bali and other parts of Indonesia. Among them were people who had been Fretilin activitists during the period of the zonas libertadas. In Indonesia they continued their activism in a student organization called the Organization of East Timorese Students and Youth (Ikatan Mahasiswa, Pemuda, dan Pelajar Timor Timur, IMPPETTU), which had been established by the Indonesian military and government in an attempt to control them. Active students were able to use the organisation to serve the needs of the continuing struggle in Timor-Leste.[67+] In 1988 the National Resistance of East Timorese Students (Resistência Nacional dos Estudantes de Timor-Leste, Renetil) was established in Bali, and in the following two years was established in Java and other islands. At about the same time the Secret Commission of the Timorese Students Resistance (Comissão Secreto da Resistência Nacional dos Estudantes Timorenses, CSRNET) was formed. Among the students who continued their education in Bali and Java there were also activists from the East Timorese Catholic Youth Organization (Organização de Juventude e Estudante Católica de Timor-Leste, OJECTIL), while others organized clandestine groups such as the Clandestine Front of East Timorese Students (Frente Estudantil Clandestina de Timor Leste, FECLETIL) in their own places of study.[178]

154. During this period in Timor-Leste demonstrations and acts of civil disobedience were increasing in number and intensity, along with other political actions in opposition to the Indonesian occupation. These included flying the national flag of the Democratic Republic of Timor-Leste, secretly writing messages on walls that condemned the Indonesian occupation and supported independence, and posting and distributing leaflets with the same messages. In Indonesia, in addition to demonstrations, students jumped the fence into foreign embassies to seek political asylum and to attract international attention.

155. With the proliferation of organisations and political activities, and the need to prepare for the expected visit of the Portuguese parliamentary delegation in 1991, the Resistance leadership tried to coordinate all clandestine groups operating in the territory. In June 1990 the political advisor to the CNRM, José da Costa (Mau Hodu Ran Kadalak), called a meeting in Baucau with leaders of the clandestine movements. As a result of this meeting, several clandestine leaders formed the CNRM Executive Committee of the Clandestine Front (Comité Executivo da CNRM na Frente Clandestina, the Executive Committee)

+ ˙ For example, João Freitas da Câmara, a political assistant in Bobonaro, after his arrest by the Indonesian military was employed by the sub-district administration of Same and then obtained a scholarship to study at the Atmajaya University, Jakarta in 1981. He became active in support of the clandestine resistance inside Indonesia until his arrest and imprisonment for organising the first demonstration held in Jakarta on 19 November 1991 to protest the Santa Cruz Massacre a week earlier [CAVR Interview with João Freitas da Câmara, Dili, 5 June 2004].

in Dili. This became the official organ of the CNRM for the coordination of all clandestine groups.[68*] Constâncio Pinto, who at the time was working as a teacher and was active in the clandestine group Orgão 8, was elected secretary of the Executive Committee, with Donaciano Gomes and José Manuel Fernandes as his deputies.[179] António Tomás Amaral da Costa (Aitahan Matak) was later added to the executive.[69+]

156. The decision to form the Executive Committee was also related to a new strategy adopted by CNRM.[180] This strategy, which aimed to obtain independence through diplomatic channels rather than armed struggle, required that the Resistance gain international visibility. When political actions such as the entry of students into foreign embassies attracted international attention, Resistance leaders began to see that the combination of clandestine activity and civil disobedience could achieve this goal. Avelino Coelho, one of the clandestine activists at the time, told the Commission:

> After we sought asylum [and] after the demonstration in Tacitolu [Dili], actions started being coordinated. Students sought asylum in the embassies of the Vatican and Japan [and] then [Pope] John [Paul II] visited [Timor-Leste] and there was a demonstration on 12...October [1989] in Tacitolu. Xanana also changed his strategy...[having realized] the great power of the youth movement. So there was still a guerrilla movement but [it was] not active in a military sense. It was more active in a political sense, as a source of inspiration for the struggle, not using Falintil as a military movement because of lack of ammunition and for other reasons and also to protect the movement itself. So in 1989 the strategy of the struggle started to shift towards seeking asylum and [holding] demonstrations. In this period...the students' initiatives started to change Xanana's thinking, to change how he led the movement.[181]

157. The Executive Committee was placed directly under Xanana Gusmão, the President of the CNRM and the commander in chief of Falintil. The role of the Executive Committee was to monitor, direct and coordinate all clandestine movements.[182] It comprised several sections including ones for Youth and Mass Mobilisation, Agitation and Propaganda, Study and Analysis, Information and Security, and Finance. Although the Executive Committee was formally under the CNRM leadership, this did not mean that all clandestine organisations and groups were under its authority. Some of the organizations active in Indonesia

---

* Constâncio Pinto said that the Committee was under the CNRM because with the increasing number of UDT and Apodeti members and their children joining the clandestine struggle there was concern that putting the Committee under Fretilin would cause a schism [Constâncio Pinto and Matthew Jardine, *East Timor's Unfinished Struggle*, South End Press, Boston, 1997, p. 123].
+ Avelino Coelho Silva, one of the founders of OJECTIL, said that Aitahan Matak was included in the Executive Committee leadership by Mau Hodu, after a protest [CAVR Interview with Avelino Coelho Silva, Dili, 17 July 2004; see also CAVR Interview with Vasco da Gama, Dili, 18 May 2004].

worked with the Committee but continued to operate independently. Similarly, in Timor-Leste many clandestine groups maintained their individual relationships with Falintil commanders in the forest.[70*] Gregório Saldanha, who was responsible for the Youth and Mass Mobilisation section, related an incident to the Commission to illustrate the problem:

> Sometimes there was stubbornness. For example, Constâncio Pinto brought a letter to Motael for Julião Mausiri about the visit of the Portuguese parliamentarians. Constâncio said: "This is a letter with instructions from Xanana."

> At that time [Mausiri] said: "I want all orders to come directly from Xanana and not through intermediaries." He asked Constâncio: "Where is the letter of instructions?" So, formally he was refusing because he did not want to acknowledge the Executive Committee, but independently he asked his courier to ask for that information.[183]

158. António Tomás Amaral da Costa (Aitahan Matak), a vice-secretary of the Executive Committee at the time, remembers: [184]

> Organizations like 3-3, 5-5, 7-7 were all under the CNRM structure but they struggled for independence. Ojetil and Renetil were part of the CNRM structure.

> All organizations under the umbrella of Orgão 8 [joined the CNRM]. Sometimes [there were organisations that] had a network with specific commanders, like David Alex, Konis [Santana], Venancio Ferras, Merak and others. Those were special networks that did not go through Orgão 8.

159. Over time the importance of the clandestine movement in the overall struggle to free Timor-Leste from Indonesian occupation increased. Falintil, which did not receive any logistical support or weapons from overseas, relied on the clandestine activists to obtain food, ammunition, intelligence and the support of the local population. Falintil's very survival depended on the clandestine movement. The Falintil leadership also relied on the underground movement to send information out of the country to activists playing their role in the Diplomatic Front who, without information from inside, would have found it very difficult to convince the international community to continue to take an interest in the Timor-Leste issue.

160. Despite its importance, there was no mention of the clandestine movement in the CNRM structure. The document Structural Readjustment of the Resistance and a Proposal for Peace from the CNRM leadership only mentioned

---

* For example, the Fitun youth organisation established after the formation of the Executive Committee operated independently and maintained direct relations with the Chairman of CNRM/Commander in Chief of Falintil, Xanana Gusmão [CAVR Interview with a Fitun founder, Armando José Dourado da Silva, Dili, 10 June 2004]. Gregório Saldanha admitted that the CE "could not control" all clandestine groups because there were too many and that some "did not admit to being involved in the struggle" [CAVR Interview with Gregório Saldanha, Dili, 5 June 2004].

the existence of two organs under the CNRM: the Falintil command and the DRSE. This indicated that the movement was considered to be under the command of Falintil as a channel of communication between Falintil on the one hand and the domestic support base and the Diplomatic Front on the other, in support of the armed resistance.

161. The Executive Committee experienced great difficulties when some leaders had to go into hiding to escape the security forces, which were hunting them after the incident at the Paulus VI High School in October 1990. One of the leaders fled to the forest to join Falintil.[185] This difficulty was overcome by including people with past experience in clandestine work. One of those who joined the Executive Committee remembered:

> When they began looking for us after the Paulus school incident, we managed to get away…I hid and then I surfaced again. Some of my friends went into hiding and only came out after Indonesia left Timor-Leste. Some even left the country. Others hid and when the situation improved came back to continue their activities. At that time Constâncio Pinto continued to work. José Manuel Fernandes ran into the forest and Donanciano [Gomes] left the country. So the Executive Committee's programmes stopped. I hid in Balibar [Dili] and after conditions improved I returned and got in touch with Constâncio Pinto and other friends such as Juvencio Martins, Jacinto Alves, Francisco Branco and Filomeno da Silva. Then we revived and reactivated the Executive and the climax came when we were arrested again on 12 November 1991 [after Santa Cruz].[186]

162. The Executive Committee was hit badly by the crackdown that followed the Santa Cruz Massacre of 12 November 1991. Some Executive Committee officials including Filomeno da Silva, Francisco Branco, Jacinto Alves, Juvencio Martins, and Gregório Saldanha were arrested, tried and sentenced to long terms of imprisonment. The Executive Committee secretary, Constâncio Pinto, managed to escape overseas. The next blow was the arrest in Dili in November 1992 of the president of the CNRM and commander in chief of Falintil, Xanana Gusmão.[187]

163. To restore its links with the clandestine movement in 1993 and to resume control of its activities, the CNRM, at the time under the leadership of Konis Santana, established the Executive Committee of Struggle/Clandestine Front (Comité Executivo da Luta/Frente Clandestina, CEL/FC). The CEL/FC was formed as a wing of the CNRM with the specific task of coordinating the clandestine movement. The Executive Committee of Struggle/Armed Front (Comité Executivo da Luta/Frete Armada, CEL/FA) was established at the same time to conduct the armed struggle from the interior.[188] With the formation of the CEL/FC the position of the clandestine resistance within the CNRM structure continued to gain in strength. Probably at this time three forms of struggle – the armed struggle from the forest, the clandestine struggle of civilians in the villages and the towns, and the diplomatic struggle in the international arena – were "made official" under the names of Armed Front, Clandestine Front,

and Diplomatic Front although the Falintil leadership continued to be highly visible. Regarding the role of Falintil, the last leader of the Clandestine Front, Francisco Guterres "Lú-Olo" told the Commission:

> All groups, so that they could control the work of the Clandestine Front, were in contact with the Armed Front. But the Armed Front also established its own clandestine people. The practical structure of the Clandestine Front functioned in Dili but it was mostly the Armed Front that coordinated the clandestine people. Hence the Clandestine Front here in Dili had to coordinate with us [the Armed Front] so that the activities of the clandestine people could be developed with various commanders.[189]

164. After the Indonesian military captured Xanana Gusmão it was suggested that the leadership be replaced by a "troika" comprising the leader of the armed struggle, the leader of the clandestine resistance and the leader of the diplomatic resistance. Konis Santana, CNRM's chief of staff, and Xanana Gusmão rejected the idea. Xanana Gusmão retained his position as Falintil commander in chief and chairman of the CNRM while in Jakarta serving a twenty-year sentence. However, according to Agio Pereira, the day to day operations were in the hands of Taur Matan Ruak, Konis Santana and José Ramos-Horta, who were responsible forthe armed front, the clandestine front and the diplomatic front respectively.[190]

165. The CEL/FC was led by Keri Laran Sabalae (Pedro Nunes) as secretary and David Dias Ximenes as vice secretary. They were helped by three adjuntos, Paulo Alves (Tubir Loke Dalan), Paulo Assis (Funo Matak), and Virgílio Simith (Kranek).[191] The adjuntos were given the task of organising the clandestine movement throughout the country. The CEL/FC formed Regional Directive Organ (Orgão Directiva Regional, ODIR), which had responsibility for organising the clandestine movement in the districts. There were three ODIRs covering the whole of Timor-Leste: the eastern region (Paulo Assis), the central region (Paulo Alves) and the western region (Aquilino Fraga Guterres, Ete Uco). In theory the ODIRs presided over a structure consisting of the Zone Executive Committee (Comité Executivo de Zona, Cezo), operating at sub-district level, Nucleus of Popular Resistance (Núcleo de Resistência Popular, Nureps) at the village level and Community Cells (Celula de Comunidade, Celcoms) at the aldeia level. In practice this structure did not function at all levels throughout the country.[192]

166. With the disappearance of Sabalae on 1 June 1995, Konis Santana, who was heading the CNRM in the country at the time, took over the leadership of the Clandestine Front.[193] With the formation of the CNRT to replace the CNRM in April 1998, the CEL/FC was replaced by the Internal Political Front (Frente Politica Internal, FPI).[194] Konis Santana remained the leader of the clandestine movement until his death on 11 March 1998 due to illness. Francisco Guterres (Lu'Olo), who until Konis Santana's death had been the vice

secretary of the Comissão Directiva da Fretilin (the highest Fretilin organ in the country) became the secretary of the FPI with David Dias Ximenes still in the position of vice secretary.[195]

167. The formation of the CNRT was followed by extensive organisational changes in the clandestine movement. The movement was restructured to bring it into line with the four regions structure of Falintil, with the addition of an extra region, Região Autonómica Dili, covering the capital and its district. The CNRT executive in the regions were drawn from the Clandestine Front and the Armed Front. According to clandestine activists, the CNRT executive unified the Clandestine Front and Armed Front structures.[196]

168. The top officials in each region were those of secretary and vice secretary.[71*] The secretary of Região 1 was Renan Selac, the secretary of Região 2 was Sabika Bessi Kulit (who was Falintil commander for that region) with Marito Reis as vice secretary. The secretary of Região 3 was Falur Rate Laek (who was also Falintil commander in the region) with Virgílio Simith (Kranek) as his vice secretary. The secretary of Região 4 was Riak Leman with Aquilino Fraga Guterres (Ete Uco) as his vice secretary. The secretary of the Região Autonóma Dili was José da Silva (Fo Laran).[197]

169. The existing clandestine organs from sub-district to aldeia became organs of the CNRT, but retained their old names (Cezo, Nurep and Celcom). A layer was created to operate at district (sub-região) level.

170. Not long after the formation of the CNRT, President Soeharto fell and Indonesia began to undergo a process of democratisation. This gave more room for clandestine activists to manoeuvre. The new Indonesian President, B J Habibie, created even more space for the movement to operate in when in June 1998 he offered "broad autonomy" to Timor-Leste. In 1999 the president went further with his offer of two options: broad autonomy or independence. Although in 1998 TNI/ABRI-backed militias began to form to spread terror among independence activists, this did not shake the resolve of those in the clandestine network. The clandestine organs from aldeia to regional level stepped up their activities and the population was emboldened in its demands for independence. With the arrival of UNAMET to conduct the Popular Consultation, the focus of the CNRT's work became the task of preparing the population to vote for independence in the ballot of 30 August 1999. Having achieved independence through the vote, the main task of the clandestine movement was over.

---

* Marito Reis, vice secretary of Região 2, said that when establishing the structure of CNRT it was decided that the secretary had to be a military commander, while the vice secretary should be "a political activist living in the city" [CAVR Interview with Nicolau Marito Reis, Baucau, 17 November 2002].

Notes

1. CAVR Interview with Eduardo de Deus Barreto, Gleno (Ermera), 12 August 2003.
2. CAVR Interview with Xanana Gusmão, Dili, 7 July 2004.
3. CAVR Interviews with Adriano João, Dili, 23 April 2004; Egas da Costa Freitas, Dili, 19 May 2004; and Jacinto Alves, Dili, 11 May 2004.
4. CAVR Interviews with Egas da Costa Freitas, Dili, 19 May 2004 and Adriano João, Dili, 23 April 2004.
5. CAVR Interviews with Jacinto Alves, Dili, 11 May 2004; Adriano João, Dili, 23 April 2004; Egas da Costa Freitas, Dili, 19 May 2004. See also CAVR Interview with Francisco Gonçalves, Dili, 14 June 2003.
6. CAVR Interview with Adriano João, Dili, 23 April 2004.
7. CAVR Interviews with Julio Maria de Jesus (Unetim activist in Ponta Leste), 29 May 2004; Filomeno Paixão de Jesus, Dili, 17 June 2004; Tomás Araújo, 14 October 2003; and Agostino Carvaleira Soares, Cailaco (Bobonaro), 14 June 2003. See also Lere Anan Timor, Archives of the Tuba Rai Metin Oral History Project, Submission to CAVR, CD No. 18.
8. CAVR Interview with Agostinho Carvaleira Soares (former company commander in Fronteira Norte), Cailaco (Bobonaro), 14 June 2003.
9. CAVR Interview with Filomeno Paixão de Jesus, Dili, 17 June 2004.
10. CAVR Interview with Jacinto Alves (who after 1977 became a staff member of the chief of staff of Falintil), Dili, 11 May 2004. See also CAVR interviews with Filomeno Paixão de Jesus, Dili, 17 June 2004; Xanana Gusmão, Dili, 7 July 2004; and Taur Matan Ruak, Dili, 9 June 2004.
11. CAVR Interview with Lucas da Costa, Dili, 21 June 2004.
12. CAVR Interviews with Sebastião da Silva ("Mendeo"), June 2003; Agostinho Carvaleira Soares, Cailaco (Bobonaro), 14 June 2003; and Eduardo de Deus Barreto, Gleno (Ermera), 12 August 2003.
13. CAVR Interview with Filomeno Paixão de Jesus, Dili, 17 June 2004.
14. Ibid.
15. CAVR Interview, Jacinto Alves, Dili, 11 May 2004.
16. Ibid.
17. CAVR Interview with Lucas da Costa, Dili, 21 June 2004.
18. CAVR Interview with Xanana Gusmão, Dili, 7 July 2004.
19. CAVR Interviews with Lucas da Costa, Dili, 21 June 2004; Xanana Gusmão, Dili, 7 July 2004; and Filomeno Paixão de Jesus, Dili, 17 June 2004.
20. CAVR Interview with Lucas da Costa, Dili, 21 June 2004.
21. CAVR Interviews with Jacinto Alves, Dili, 11 May 2004 (from researcher's notes); Egas da Costa Freitas, Dili, 19 May 2004; António da Silva, Dili, 10 June 2003; José Francisco Silva, Dili, 12 January 2004; Fausto do Carmo Mendonça, Dili, 16 October 2003; and Fernando Amaral, Dili, 28 May 2003.
22. CAVR Interview with Eduardo de Deus Barreto, Gleno (Ermera), 12 August 2003.
23. CAVR Interview with Umbelina Pires, Manumera (Turiscai, Manufahi), (undated).
24. CAVR Interviews with Jacinto Alves, Dili, 11 May 2004 and António Amado de Deus Ramos Guterres, Manatuto, 11 December 2003; Office for Promotion of Equality, Office of the Prime Minister of the Democratic Republic of Timor-Leste, *Written with Blood*, Dili, 2004, pp. 18-19.
25. CAVR Interview with Virgílio da Silva Guterres, Dili, 25 May 2004.

26. CAVR Interviews with Eduardo de Deus Barreto, Gleno (Ermera), 12 August 2003 and Fausto do Carmo Mendonça, Dili, 16 October 2003.
27. CAVR Interview with Lucas da Costa, Dili, 21 June 2004.
28. CAVR Interview with Virgílio da Silva Guterres, Dili, 25 May 2004.
29. Office for Promotion of Equality, *Written with Blood*, p. 19.
30. Ibid., p. 23 mentioned this activity in Modok Zona, Centro Norte Sector.
31. CAVR Interviews with Lucas da Costa, Dili, 21 June 2004 and Egas da Costa Freitas, Dili, 19 May 2004. See also Office for Promotion of Equality, *Written with Blood*, p. 20.
32. CAVR Interview with Lucas da Costa, Dili, 21 June 2004.
33. CAVR Interview with Taur Matan Ruak, Dili, 9 June 2004.
34. CAVR Interview with Virgílio da Silva Guterres, Dili, 25 May 2004.
35. Office for Promotion of Equality, *Written with Blood*, p. 23.
36. CAVR Interview with Virgílio da Silva Guterres, Dili, 25 May 2004.
37. "Timorese Women 'Are Fighting on All Fronts'", *East Timor News*, Australia, No. 14, 25 August 1977. This was written by the first OPMT Secretary, Rosa Bonaparte "Muki" and was translated and a little shortened by the East Timor News editor.
38. CAVR Interview with Jacinto Alves, Dili, 11 May 2004. See also Office for Promotion of Equality, *Written with Blood*, pp. 18-19.
39. Office for Promotion of Equality, *Written with Blood*, p. 21.
40. CAVR Interview with Egas da Costa Freitas, Dili, 19 May 2004.
41. CAVR Interview with Jacinto Alves, Dili, 5 August 2004.
42. CAVR Interview with Gaspar Seixas, Iliomar, Lautém, 29 May 2003.
43. CAVR Interview with Eduardo Jesus Barreto, Gleno (Ermera), 12 August 2003.
44. CAVR Interview with Xanana Gusmão, Dili, 7 July 2004.
45. CAVR Interview with António Amado de Jesus Ramos Guterres, Manatuto, 11 December 2003.
46. CAVR Interviews with António da Silva and Raquel da Silva, Dili, 10 June 2003 and Bernardo Quintão, Dili, 4 June 2003.
47. CAVR Interview with Alexandrino de Jesus, Hatulia (Ermera), 20 October 2003.
48. CAVR Interview with Jacinto Alves, Dili, 5 August 2004. Incidence of torture was also reported in CAVR Interviews with Francisco Gonçalves, Dili, 14 June 2003; António da Silva and Raquel da Silva, Dili, 10 June 2003; Domingos Maria Alves, Aileu, 15 October 2003; Filomeno Paixão de Jesus, Dili, 17 June 2004; António Amado de Deus Ramos Guterres, Manatuto, 11 December 2003; and Xanana Gusmão, Dili, 7 July 2004.
49. CAVR Interview with Eduardo de Deus Barreto, Gleno (Ermera), 12 August 2003.
50. CAVR Interview with Egas da Costa Freitas, Dili, 19 May 2004.
51. CAVR Interview with António da Silva, Dili, 11 August 2004.
52. Departamento da Orientação Política e Ideológica (DOPI), Fretilin Central Committee document titled "The National Liberation Movement, Imperialism and the Puppet Parties," approved at the Highest Resistance Board session, Laline (Lacluta, Viqueque), 20 May 1977. This document was published again in ETNA with the title "National Independence is not only a flag and an Anthem", *East Timor News*, No. 36, June 29, 1978.
53. Fretilin, Manual e Programa Políticos Fretilin, Fretilin Manual and Political Programme, 1974, point 3.
54. "Timorese Women 'Are Fighting on All Fronts'", *East Timor News*, No. 14, 25 August 1977.

55. Ibid.
56. Fretilin, Manual e Programa Políticos Fretilin, point 6.
57. Ibid., point 9.
58. Ibid., point 10.
59. Helen Hill, *Stirrings of Nationalism in East Timor: Fretilin 1974-1978: the origins, ideologies and strategies of a nationalist movement*, Otford Press, 2002, pp. 104 and 107.
60. Manual e Programa Políticos Fretilin, Fretilin Manual and Political Programme, points 11 and 12.
61. Hill, *Stirrings of Nationalism in East Timor*, pp. 131-132, 138.
62. Manual e Programa Políticos Fretilin, Fretilin Manual and Political Programme, point 13.
63. Hill, *Stirrings of Nationalism in East Timor*, p. 95.
64. Mari Alkatiri, testimony to the CAVR National Public Hearing on The Internal Political Conflict 1974-76, 15-18 December 2003; CAVR Interview with Mari Alkatiri, Dili, 25 June 2004.
65. Jill Joliffe, *East Timor: Nationalism and Colonialism* , University of Queensland Press, St. Lucia, Queensland, 1978, p. 90; CAVR Interviews with Mari Alkatiri, Dili, 25 June 2004 and Francisco Xavier do Amaral, Dili, 18 June 2004.
66. See testimonies of Mário Carrascãlao, João Carrascãlao and Francisco Xavier Amaral at the CAVR National Public Hearing on The Internal Political Conflict 1974-76, 15-18 December. See also Hill, *Stirrings of Nationalism in East Timor*, p. 126.
67. CAVR Interview with Francisco Xavier do Amaral, Dili, 18 June 2004.
68. CAVR Interviews with Egas da Costa Freitas, Dili, 19 May 2004; Taur Matan Ruak, Dili, 9 June 2004; and Xanana Gusmão, Dili, 7 July 2004.
69. CAVR Interviews with Xanana Gusmão, Dili, 7 July 2004; Egas da Costa Freitas, Dili, 19 May 2004; Filomeno Paixão de Jesus, Dili, 17 June 2004; Taur Matan Ruak, Dili, 9 June 2004; and Lucas da Costa, Dili, 21 June 2004.
70. CAVR Interview with Egas da Costa Freitas, Dili, 19 May 2004.
71. "National Independence is not only a Flag and an Anthem", East Timor News , No. 36, 29 June 1978, p. 2.
72. CAVR Interview with Marito Reis, Dili, 19 June 2003.
73. CAVR Interviews with Egas da Costa Freitas, Dili, 19 May 2004; Jacinto Alves, Dili, 11 May 2004; and Albino da Costa, Soibada (Manatuto), June 2003.
74. CAVR Interview with Taur Matan Ruak, Dili, 9 June 2004.
75. CAVR Interviews with Xanana Gusmão, Dili, 7 July 2004 and Francisco Xavier do Amaral, Dili, 18 June 2004.
76. CAVR Interview with Lucas da Costa, Dili, 21 June 2004.
77. Ibid.
78. CAVR Interviews with Filomeno Paixão de Jesus, Dili, 17 June 2004 and Jeronimo Albino, Dili, 10 September 2003.
79. CAVR, Interview with Xanana Gusmão, Dili, 7 July 2004.
80. CAVR Interview with António da Silva, Jakarta, 11 August 2004.
81. CAVR Interview with Xanana Gusmão, Dili, 7 July 2004.
82. CAVR Interview with Egas da Costa Freitas, Dili, 19 May 2004.
83. CAVR Interview with António da Silva, Jakarta, 11 August 2004.
84. Lere Anan Timor, Tuba Rai Metin Oral History Project, Submission to CAVR, CD No. 18.
85. Ibid.
86. Xanana Gusmão, "Autobiography", in Sarah Niner (ed.), *To Resist is To Win! The autobiography of Xanana Gusmão with selected letters and speeches*, Aurora

Books, Victoria, 2000, p. 50; Ernest Chamberlain, *The Struggle in Iliomar: Resistance in Rural East Timor*, Point Lonsdale, 2003, p. 16.

87. Xanana Gusmão, "Autobiography", in To Resist is To Win!, p. 32. See also CAVR Interview with Xanana Gusmão, Dili, 7 July 2004.
88. Ibid.
89. CAVR Interview with Jacinto Alves, Dili, 16 May 2005.
90. CAVR Interview with Francisco Xavier do Amaral (part III), Dili, 18 June 2004.
91. CAVR Interviews with Lucas da Costa, Dili, 21 June 2004 and Xanana Gusmão, Dili, 7 July 2004.
92. CAVR Interview with Lucas da Costa, Dili, 21 June 2004.
93. CAVR Interviews with Jacinto Alves, Dili, 11 May 2004 and Xanana Gusmão, Dili, 7 July 2004.
94. CAVR Interview with Lucas da Costa, Dili, 21 June 2004.
95. CAVR Interview with Filomeno Paixão de Jesus, Dili, 17 June 2004.
96. CAVR Interviews with Francisco Xavier do Amaral, 18 June 2004; Lucas da Costa, Dili, 21 June 2004; and Xanana Gusmão, Dili, 7 July 2004.
97. CAVR Interviews with Alexandrino de Jesus, Hatulia (Ermera), 20 October 2003; Eduardo de Deus Barreto, Gleno (Ermera), 12 August 2003; and Adriano João, Dili, 10 June 2003.
98. CAVR Interview with Adriano João, Dili, 10 June 2003.
99. CAVR Interview with Adriano Soares Lemos, Hatulia (Ermera), 12 August 2003.
100. CAVR Interview with Manuel Carceres da Costa, Dili, July 2003.
101. CAVR Interview with Maria José da Costa, Manufahi, February 2003.
102. CAVR Interview with Xanana Gusmão, Dili, 7 July 2004.
103. Ibid.
104. CAVR Interview with Adriano João, Dili, 10 June 2003.
105. CAVR Interview with Jacinto Alves, Dili, 5 August 2004.
106. CAVR Interviews with Celestino de Carvalho Alves, Dili, 6 October 2003; José da Silva Amaral, Dili, 18 September 2003; José da Silva, Dili, 18 March 2003; Francisco Gonçalves, Dili, 14 June 2003; and Taur Matan Ruak, Dili, 14 June 2004.
107. CAVR Interview with Benvinda G D Lopes, Dili, 16 September 2003.
108. CAVR Interview with Francisco Xavier do Amaral, Dili, 18 June 2004.
109. "Memoria Comandante Falintil Ida Kona Ba Nicolau Lobato," Nacroman, No. 2/VIII/2002, p. 3 ("Remembering a Falintil Commander, about Nicolau Lobato", *Nacroman*, No. 2/VII/2002, p. 3).
110. Chamberlain, *The Struggle in Iliomar*, p. 20.
111. CAVR Interview with Eduardo de Deus Barreto, Gleno (Ermera), 12 August 2003.
112. Lere Anan Timor, Tuba Rai Metin Oral History Project, Submission to CAVR, CD No. 18.
113. "Reajustamento Estrutural da Resistência Nacional e Proposta da Paz," in Xanana Gusmão, *Timor Leste: Um Povo, Uma Pátria*, Editora Colibri, Lisbon, 1994, p. 96. ("The Strucutural Readjustment of the National Resistance and the Peace Proposal", in Xanana Gusmão, *Timor Leste: A People, A Fatherland*, Edition Colibri, Lisbon, 1994, p. 96)
114. CAVR Interview with Xanana Gusmão, part II, Dili, 10 August 2004.
115. Xanana Gusmão, "Ideological Turnaround", in Niner (ed.) *To Resist is To Win!*, p. 133; Xanana Gusmão, "Reajustamento Estrutural da Resistência e Proposta de Paz," in Xanana Gusmão, *Timor Leste: Um Povo, Uma Patria*, p. 96; CAVR Interview with Xanana Gusmão, part II, Dili, 10 August 2004.

116. Carmel Budiardjo and Liem Soei Liong, *The War Against East Timor*, Zed Books, London, 1984, p. 71.
117. Ibid., p. 71.
118. CAVR Interview with Eduardo de Jesus Barreto, Gleno (Ermera), 12 August 2003.
119. CAVR Interview with Francisco Guterres "Lú-Olo", Dili, 26 March 2003.
120. CAVR Interview with José da Conceição, Dili, 20 October 2004.
121. Ibid.
122. CAVR Interview with Xanana Gusmão, part II, Dili, 10 August 2004.
123. CAVR Interview with Taur Matan Ruak, Dili, 14 June 2004
124. Carmel Budiardjo and Liem Soei Liong, *The War Against East Timor*, pp. 72-73; Jill Jolliffe, "Timor, Terra Sangrenta", O Jornal, Lisboa, 1989, p. 137 (Jill Jolliffe, "Timor, Bloody Land", O Jornal, Lisbon, 1989, p. 137).
125. Agio Pereira, "The National Council of Maubere Resistance (CNRM), Overview of the History of the Struggle of East Timor", paper presented at a solidarity meeting in Sydney, August 1994.
126. Ibid.
127. Hill, *Stirrings of Nationalism in East Timor*, pp. 161-162.
128. CAVR Interviews with Xanana Gusmão, 10 August 2004; José da Conceição, Dili, 20 October 2004; and Lere Anan Timor, Tuba Rai Metin Oral History Project, Submission to CAVR, CD No. 18. See also Part 3: The History of the Conflict.
129. CAVR Interview with Cornelio Gama, Baucau, 9 April 2003; Lere Anan Timor, Tuba Rai Metin Oral History Project, Submission to CAVR, CD No.18.
130. Agio Pereira, "The National Council of Maubere Resistance (CNRM)", 1994.
131. "Reajustamento Estrutural da Resistência e Proposta de Paz," in Xanana Gusmão, *Timor Leste: Um Povo, Uma Pátria*, p. 96.
132. CAVR Interviews with Francisco Guterres "Lú-Olo", Dili, 26 March 2003 and Cornelio Gama (L-7), Baucau, 9 April 2003; Lere Anan Timor, Archives of the Tuba Rai Metin Oral History Project, Submission to CAVR, CD No. 18.
133. Lere Anan Timor, Tuba Rai Metin Oral History Project , Submission to CAVR, CD No. 18; Xanana Gusmão, "Message to the Nation of HE The President of the Republic Kay Rala Xanana Gusmao on the Occasion of Falintil Day Commemoration", Uaimori (Viqueque), 20 August 2003 (English translation available at www.etan.org/et2003/august/17-23/20fal.htm).
134. CAVR Interview with Xanana Gusmão, part II, Dili, 10 August 2004.
135. CAVR Interviews with Francisco Guterres "Lú-Olo", Dili, 26 March 2003 and Cornelio Gama, 9/4/2004; Lere Anan Timor, Tuba Rai Metin Oral History Project, Submission to CAVR, CD No. 18.
136. CAVR Interview with Cornelio Gama, Baucau, 9 April 2003.
137. CAVR Interview with Taur Matan Ruak, Dili, 14 June 2004.
138. CAVR Interview with Aleixo Ximenes, Dili, 2 February 2004.
139. CAVR Interviews with Cornelio Gama, Baucau, 9 April 2003; Taur Matan Ruak, Dili 14 June 2004; and Francisco Guterres "Lú-Olo", Dili, 26 March 2003; Lere Anan Timor, Tuba Rai Metin Oral History Project, Submission to CAVR, CD No.18.
140. "Reajustamento Estrutural da Resistência e Proposta de Paz," in Xanana Gusmão, *Timor Leste: Um Povo, Uma Pátria*, p. 98.
141. CAVR Interview with Taur Matan Ruak, Dili, 14 June 2004.
142. Agio Pereira, "The National Council of Maubere Resistance (CNRM)", 1994.
143. Xanana Gusmao, "Message to the Nation", Uaimori (Viqueque), 20 August 2003.

144. Xanana Gusmão, "Message to the National Timorese Convention", in Sarah Niner (ed.), *To Resist is To Win!*, p. 214

145. Adelino Gomes, interview with Xanana Gusmão, Timor-Leste, 2-3 June 1991, published in O Publico, 6 September 1991, in Sarah Niner (ed.), *To Resist is to Win!*, p. 149.

146. "Reajustamento Estrutural da Resistência Nacional e Proposta da Paz," in Xanana Gusmão , *Timor Leste: Um Povo, Uma Pátria*, Editora Colibri, Lisbon, 1994, p. 99.

147. Lere Anan Timor, Archives of the Tuba Rai Metin Oral History Project, Submission to CAVR, CD No. 18.

148. Agio Pereira, "The National Council of Maubere Resistance (CNRM)", 1994; Chamberlain, *The Struggle in Iliomar*, p. 34.

149. Ibid.

150. Ibid.

151. Ibid.; "Readjustamento Estrutural da Resistência," in Xanana Gusmão, *Timor Leste: Um Povo, Uma Patria*, p. 102, footnote no. 14.

152. "Reajustamento Estrutural da Resistência", in Xanana Gusmão, *Timor Leste: Um Povo, Uma Patria*, pp. 102-103.

153. Agio Pereira, "The National Council of Maubere Resistance (CNRM)", 1994.

154. Carla Baptista, "Timorese Summit Meeting", *Diario de Noticias*, 16 March 1995 republished in http://www.hamline.edu/apakabar/basisdata/1995/03/29/0009.html.

155. Xanana Gusmão, "Message to the East Timor Talks Campaign", in Sarah Niner (ed.), *To Resist is to Win*, p. 197.

156. Xanana Gusmão, "Message to the Timorese National Convention," in ibid., p. 214.

157. CAVR Interview with Francisco Guterres "Lú-Olo", 26 March 2003.

158. CAVR Interview with Francisco Guterres "Lú-Olo", 26 March 2003.

159. CNRT – National Council of Timorese Resistance, www.labyrinth.net.au/~ftimor/cnrt.html.

160. Fretilin, "Reajustamento Estrutural da Resistência e Proposta de Paz", in Xanana Gusmão, *Timor Leste: Um Povo, Uma Pátria*, p. 103.

161. Xanana Gusmão, "Message to the Nation", Uaimori (Viqueque), 20 August 2003.

162. "Reajustamento Estrutural da Resistência e Proposta de Paz", in Xanana Gusmão, *Timor Leste: Um Povo, Uma Patria*, p. 102. See "Fretilin: Roots of Friction," first published in *Fitun* (London) No. 11, September 1993, then posted in reg.easttimor www.hamline.edu/apakabar/basisdata/1993/10/13/0006.html.

163. Xanana Gusmão's address to the Falintil transition to FDTL ceremony, Aileu, 1 February 2001 (English version, "Address to the Transition Ceremony of Falintil to the New East Timor Defence Force" available at www.pcug.org.au/~wildwood/febxanana.htm).

164. Quoted in Chamberlain, *The Struggle in Iliomar*, p. 35.

165. Chamberlain, *The Struggle in Iliomar*, p. 36.

166. Chamberlain, *The Struggle in Iliomar*, p. 46; Xanana Gusmão, "Address to the Transition Ceremony of Falintil", 1 February 2001.

167. "Reajustamento Estrutural da Resistência e Proposta da Paz," in Xanana Gusmão, *Timor Leste: Um Povo, Uma Patria*, pp. 106-107.

168. Agio Pereira, "The National Council of Maubere Resistance", 1994.

169. CAVR Interview with Francisco Guterres "Lú-Olo", Dili, 26 March 2003.

170. CAVR Interview with Taur Matan Ruak, Dili, 14 June 2004.

171. CAVR Interview with Cornelio Gama ("L-7"), former commander of Região 3, Dili, 9 April 2003.
172. CAVR Interviews with António Tomás Amaral da Costa (Aitahan Matak), Dili, 28 April 2004; Henrique Belmiro da Costa, Dili, 25 May 2004; and Vasco da Gama, Dili, 18 May 2004.
173. CAVR Interview with Egas da Costa Freitas, Dili, 19 May 2004.
174. CAVR Interview with Taur Matan Ruak, Dili, 14 June 2004.
175. CAVR Interviews with António Tomás Amaral da Costa (Aitahan Matak), Dili, 28 April 2004 and Francisco Guterres "Lú-Olo", Dili, 26 March 2003; Constâncio Pinto and Matthew Jardine, *East Timor's Unfinished Struggle: Inside The Timorese Resistance*, South End Press, Boston, 1997, pp. 96-97.
176. Pinto and Jardine, *East Timor's Unfinished Struggle*, p. 3; Constâncio Pinto, "The Student Movement and The Independence Struggle in East Timor: An Interview", in Richard Tanter, Mark Selden & Stephen R Shalom (eds.), *Bitter Flowers, Sweet Flowers, East Timor, Indonesia and The World Community*, Rowman & Littlefield, London, p. 34.
177. CAVR Interview with Ricardo Ribeiro, Dili, 14 May 2004.
178. CAVR Interview with Avelino Coelho da Silva, Dili, 17 July 2004.
179. Pinto and Jardine, East Timor's Unfinished Struggle, p. 124
180. CAVR Interview with Avelino Coelho Silva, Dili, 17 July 2004.
181. CAVR Interview with Avelino Coelho Silva, Dili, 17 July 2004.
182. Pinto and Jardine, *East Timor's Unfinished Struggle*, p. 123.
183. CAVR Interview with Gregório Saldanha, Dili, 5 June 2004.
184. CAVR Interview with António Tomás Amaral da Costa (Aitahan Matak), Dili, 8 December 2003.
185. CAVR Interviews with Gregório Saldanha, Dili, 5 June 2004 and José Manuel Fernandes, Dili, 31 October 2002.
186. CAVR, Interview with Gregório Saldanha, Dili, 5 June 2004.
187. CAVR Interview with Francisco Guterres "Lú-Olo", Dili, 26 March 2003.
188. CAVR Interview with Vasco da Gama, Dili, 18 May 2004.
189. CAVR Interview with Francisco Guterres "Lú-Olo", Dili, 26 March 2003.
190. Agio Pereira, "Obituary for Konis Santana", *Timor Link*, No. 43, June 1998.
191. CAVR Interviews with Vasco da Gama, Dili, 18 May 2004 and António Tomás Amaral da Costa (Aitahan Matak), Dili, 11 February 2004.
192. CAVR Interviews with Eduardo de Deus Barreto, Gleno, Ermera, 12 August 2003; António Tomás Amaral da Costa (Aitahan Matak), Dili, 11 February 2004; and José da Silva Amaral, Ossu, 27 February 2003.
193. CAVR Interview with Francisco Guterres "Lú-Olo", Dili, 26 March 2003.
194. CAVR Interview with Vasco da Gama, Dili, 18 May 2004.
195. CAVR Interview with António Tomás Amaral da Costa (Aitahan Matak), Dili, 11 February 2004.
196. CAVR Interviews with Vasco da Gama, Dili, 18 May 2004 and Marito Reis, Baucau, 17 November 2002.
197. Ibid.

Part 2

Description, Documentation, Denial, and Justice

5

Grappling with Genocide, 1978-79

Introductory Note

My historical research on the Khmer Rouge movement started in 1974, when I was an undergraduate at Monash University in Melbourne, Australia. I wrote an empirical study of the 1967-70 Khmer Rouge insurgency against the Sihanouk regime and soon published several shorter articles. At first I was relatively sympathetic to their purported reforms and nationalism, but when I commenced my Ph.D. research in 1978, I acknowledged my error and began what became a quarter-century project of documenting the crimes of the Khmer Rouge regime.

"Why's Kampuchea Gone to Pot?" was my first newspaper article, the work of a twenty-five-year-old, first-year postgraduate student in Southeast Asian colonial history. It was a modest beginning, an attempt at contemporary international-relations analysis, and the start of a journey of historical documentation. In this 1978 article, reproduced here, I sought to explain the escalating catastrophe in Cambodia, a closed country from which refugees provided the primary source of information, partly in terms of international Communist rivalries and China's foreign policy factionalism, as well as Khmer Rouge "nationalist revivalism" and racism. Three years of secretive CPK rule, dozens of interviews with Cambodian refugees in Australia and Thailand, and numerous press accounts had eventually impressed on me the apparent scale of the tragedy inside the country. It was also clear that the Khmer Rouge regime had taken a sharp turn for the worse the previous year.

However I still knew little of the regime's persecution of Cambodia's ethnic minorities, and did not yet comprehend the Khmer Rouge violence as genocide. Nor did I use that term in a public acknowledgement of my previous error, nor in an interpretive piece, "Kampuchea: Why the Slaughter?," both written in 1979 (also reprinted in this chapter). But in France that same year, I wrote what I believe was the first report on the 1978 Eastern Zone massacres, based on interviews with newly arrived Cambodian refugees. I subtitled my report, "A Final Solution ?," and in early 1980 I co-authored the first analysis of Pol Pot's secret prison known as Tuol Sleng or "S-21," published that May as "Bureaucracy of Death," in the London weekly *New Statesman*. The next month the Dutch journal *Vietnam Bulletin* published my 1979 report under the title "Genocide in the Eastern Zone." A week later, I arrived in Phnom Penh for four months' research in rural Cambodia. Only there did I learn, from the international lawyer Gregory H. Stanton, the legal definition and applicability of the term "genocide" to the Khmer Rouge crimes against Cambodia's religious groups and ethnic minorities, such as the ethnic Chams and Vietnamese, more than to crimes against political or geographic groups such as the Khmer of the Eastern Zone. By November 1980, I had interviewed several hundred Cambodian survivors and estimated the Khmer Rouge death toll at approximately 1.5 million. I began working with Stanton to help bring the Khmer Rouge leaders before the International Court of Justice, known as the World Court, in The Hague, or to another international tribunal, the subject of chapters 6 and 7.

The first and third articles reproduced in this chapter appeared, like my 1979 reporting from the Thai-Cambodian border reprinted in chapter 10, in the Australian independent weekly *Nation Review*, which became a monthly in 1980. The second article here appeared in 1979 in the *Bulletin of Concerned Asian Scholars*, since renamed *Critical Asian Studies*.

"Why's Kampuchea Gone to Pot?"
Nation Review (Melbourne), 17 November 1978

The power struggle in China has influenced relations between Kampuchea and Vietnam, especially since early 1976. Whereas the Chinese radicals (and their supporters in Kampuchea) had significant differences with Vietnam, this was within a framework of solidarity. Their defeat by the Teng Hsiao-ping line, however, directly contributed to the serious escalation of Kampuchea's genuine historical and territorial grievances and ideological differences with Vietnam into full-scale fighting. In Kampuchea during this period, supporters of China's radicals and of Vietnam were crushed.

The argument is supported by a look at the stand taken by Albania, formerly China's closest ally, which claims China has now "abandoned Marxism-Leninism," and by analysis of China's "Three Worlds Theory."

After the public break between Vietnam and Kampuchea in January [1978], Albania reportedly urged Peking not to pour oil on the flames. Soon after, Albania supported Vietnam's cause against China, who then withdrew aid from Albania. Albania accused China of "big-country chauvinism" and "warmongering" and implicated China, the USSR and the U.S. in the creation of "a difficult atmosphere around Vietnam."

China's radicals shared this perspective. Their zenith in Peking, April to October 1976, saw the best ("comradely," not "warm") relations between leaders of Kampuchea and Vietnam from 1975 to the present. Differences exist between communists of Kampuchea and Vietnam, and clashes have occurred, but their escalation into war since early 1977 (and the reluctance of Kampuchea and China to negotiate with Vietnam) is qualitatively different and related to the foreign policy of China's new leaders.

China's Three Worlds Theory calls for a united front of Third World with Second World (advanced capitalist countries) against the super powers. Although Teng launched it in 1974, under the radicals *Peking Review* approved it, but not as a "theory." The enemy was seen as both super-powers equally, in articles like, "USSR and the USA Arraigned in the Same Dock." This contrasts with the theory in 1977-78, since the radicals' downfall. In January, *China Reconstructs* spoke of the need "to isolate the two super-powers, Soviet Social-Imperialism in particular" (Teng's 1974 formulation) and said, ignoring the U.S. here, that the theory is "a blow to the heart of Soviet Social Imperialism." China's foreign policy thrust since the radicals has changed to an anti-Soviet united front, including possibly the U.S., certainly the U.S.'s allies. *Peking Review* talks of "the revolutionary policy of forming the broadest united front, whatever the content, to strike at the main enemy."

In January 1977, Albania parted company with China over this, having warned in 1971 against "relying on one imperialism to oppose the other." The Three Worlds Theory was (to my knowledge) first publicly attributed to Mao not long before this, on October 5, 1976, after his death and within days of the arrest of the radicals.

China's relations with another of its former closest allies, Vietnam, have also drastically changed in 1977-78, with the new interpretation and emphasis on the Three Worlds Theory. For instance, under the radicals *Peking Review* discussed the Non-Aligned Nations without mentioning the Theory, and approvingly quoted Egypt's Sadat: "....[T]he initial definition of a non-aligned country as one not adhering to either power bloc should be changed into one with a free will, free from big power pressure." Within this framework, Vietnam's independence, despite its adherence to the Soviet bloc, would make it China's ally as a non-aligned, not to say socialist. Only in the framework of a united front everywhere aimed at the Soviet Union is Vietnam's China's enemy.

Kampuchea and not China, however is fighting fiercely with Vietnam, and one would have to find other reasons for that continuing conflict if Phnom Penh did not subscribe to China's changed foreign policy. It is widely assumed, incorrectly I think, that Prime Minister Pol Pot's group are disciples of China's radicals; an influential group in the Communist Party of Kampuchea (CPK) that did fit this description have disappeared, especially since late 1976.

During 1975 and early 1976, Kampuchean leaders were deeply divided. Phnom Penh now says "attempted coups" took place before April and in September, 1975. The national radio stopped for two days on September 16. The outcome is unknown, but it seems no group held complete sway. Some changes in 1976 were reversed in 1977, and Pol Pot and Ieng Sary emerged supreme. Sary described these events on March 17 as four more illegitimate coup attempts in 1976-77. Although what happened on these occasions is unclear, serious divisions are evident and the dates Sary gives mark a series of turning points.

Neither Pot nor Sary have ever publicly indicated support for the Chinese radical line. Other Kampuchean revolutionaries have. They include Phouk Chhay, secretary of the Kampuchean-China Friendship Association in Phnom Penh which was banned by Prince Sihanouk during the Cultural Revolution. Influential in the CPK during the war, Chhay has not been officially mentioned since 1975.

Hu Nim, vice-president of the Friendship Association during the same period, and revolutionary Information Minister from 1970, was perhaps concerned in December 1976 when he publicly expressed confidence that China "would not allow revisionism and the capitalist classes to rear their heads" after the radicals' downfall. He was last mentioned publicly the next month. (Nim was not publicly replaced until December 1977, and not for foreign consumption until February 1978. His downfall seems significant). Pol Pot has since moved from strength to strength by large scale purges throughout 1977, pursuing the conflict with Vietnam to galvanize internal support.

Before this, the last Vietnam-Kampuchea clash took place in January 1976. That March, an anti-Teng campaign developed in Peking; on April 7 he was sacked and the radicals rose to their zenith. In Phnom Penh, Sary mentions an April 1976 "coup attempt by Vietnamese and KGB agents." Was he referring to Sihanouk's resignation (April 4), related to the death of the Prince's friend Chou En-lai and the impending demise of Chou's protégé Teng? More likely he meant the rise to vice-presidency of So Phim, a Kampuchean revolutionary with pre-1970 Vietnamese connections.

On April 14, Phnom Penh Radio introduced six new leaders, including Phim, whose political paths have since diverged. This "coup attempt" probably marks the end of a period on the outer for Phim, who in early 1975 was in the (secret) five-person inner leadership. The appointments thus appear as a new compromise between supporters of Pol Pot, supporters of Vietnam, and supporters of China's radicals who differed with Vietnam within a framework of solidarity.

The Central Committees of the Communist Parties of Kampuchea and Vietnam agreed in April to sign a border treaty in June. A preparatory meeting was held on May 4-18. Lack of agreement postponed the June talks. But, "following the meeting," according to Vietnam, "border incidents decreased in number." Neither side, even Vietnam's detailed history of clashes, mentions *any* border fighting for the rest of 1976. Also following the meeting, Phan Hien and Vietnamese media visited much of Kampuchea, reporting favorably. Women's delegations exchanged visits, and agreement was reached over air links, Kampuchea resumed foreign trade and departed from a policy of strict self-reliance by contacting U.S. firms and UNICEF about anti-malarial purchases and aid.

The situation in Phnom Penh developed: on September 27, 1976, Pol Pot was sacked. "For health reasons," he was replaced as prime minister by Nuon Chea, whom sources close to Vietnam call "correct line." Pot was really ousted: in 1978, Sary revealed another "coup attempt" in September 1976. Also in 1978 the Kampuchean cadre in Vietnam reported a fierce struggle in the CPK in September 1976.

Four days after Pot's removal, Kampuchea unprecedentedly attacked Teng Hsiao-ping. Leadership was now in the hands of a group favorable to Vietnam, in coalition with supporters of China's radicals.

But by October 10, the radicals were arrested in Peking, clearing the stage for Teng and changes in China's internal and foreign policy. It is difficult to believe that Kampuchea was not affected: *within a fortnight*, Pol Pot was back as Prime Minister. Then Phnom Penh publicly denounced China's radicals, using terms stronger than those of any ruling communists.

Pot's return was thus a major setback for one group opposed to him (but not yet for the other). Kampuchea formerly congratulated Vietnam's Fourth Party Congress the following December [1976]. But by then the Vietnamese had read the writing on the wall. At that Congress, leaders associated with China were dropped from Vietnam's Central Committee. This no doubt reflected Soviet influence also; but leadership divisions in Vietnam, minimal compared to Kampuchea's, do not provide outside powers with comparable internal leverage.

After a year of peace, fighting resumed between Kampuchea and Vietnam in January 1977, when Kampuchea began to withdraw from all border liaison committees. Albania first disputed China's Three Worlds Theory that same month, Kampuchean diplomats withdrew from Albania, and in January, Phnom Penh last mentioned Hu Nim (at an Albanian Embassy reception) and another Minister, Touch Phoeun. An associate of Phoeun, 1970–75 revolutionary Interior Minister Hou Yuon, made a radio speech in early 1976 but there is no news of him since early 1977. Nor any, since 1975, of the two People's Party resistance leaders, or two veteran revolutionaries of the 1946–54 period, publicly mentioned in 1975 and 1976.

Of the ten revolutionary ministers and vice-ministers during 1970–75, two hold public office in 1978. One is Khieu Samphan, not described even as a member of the CPK central committee since its proclamation in September 1977. Nearly all public positions are now held by the Pol Pot-Ieng Sary group, their wives, or people unknown to outsiders or using aliases.

January 1977 was a turning point, but the struggle in Kampuchea was not over. Refugees report widespread purges at the time of the downfall of Hu Nim, described by Bangkok as a February "coup" in which Pot gained ground at the immediate expense of Nuon Chea. Refugees report the execution of senior revolutionary Koy Thuon, just prior to what Sary calls a "coup attempt" in April and border clashes which Vietnam calls "most serious." Still domestic opposition was apparently too strong for Kampuchea to publicly congratulate China's

Eleventh Party Congress, in which radicals (a third of the Central Committee) were sacked.

More wide ranging purges from late August left Pol Pot supreme (but not unchallenged by another "coup attempt" in September). In mid-September, Vietnam claims Kampuchea mounted "particularly serious" border attacks; on September 17 Phnom Penh Radio clearly described Vietnam as the enemy. Pol Pot's trip to Peking on the 29th and public emergence as CPK Secretary-General elicited full Chinese support. From November 1977, Phnom Penh named about thirty new leading cadres.

The wide ranging purges indicate Pol Pot is after unchallenged authority as much as the implementation of any program. Still today's austere but egalitarian emphasis on collective labor was recognized in a nineteenth-century rural rebellion. Significantly, this and some aspects of Asian communism have been harnessed to a chauvinism that demands big continuing sacrifices from the people to build a powerful state. Class issues have been involved: the revolution received widespread support from peasants and may well retain some, although since 1976 many peasants and peasant cadres have been repressed.

Nationalist revivalism sweeps away all in its path. In April, Kampuchean leaders first talked publicly of "defending the race of Kampuchea" to make it "everlasting."

China is today less enthusiastic about Kampuchea's internal situation than in 1976 when both countries followed other courses, but gives Kampuchea economic and military aid. Exactly how this affects Kampuchea is unknown, but it is clear that it does and that in the interest of their foreign policy, China's leaders have favored the return and subsequent supremacy of Pol Pot's regime. But a deeper explanation of the nature of that regime, lies in the U.S. attack on Kampuchea by massive military force. Fanon described this process in another colonial context, the French in Algeria:

"The violence of the colonial regime and the counter-violence of the native balance each other and respond to each other in an extraordinary reciprocal homogeneity. This reign of violence will be more terrible in proportion to the violence exercised by the threatened colonial regime."

Statement in the *Bulletin of Concerned Asian Scholars* 11:4, Oct-Dec. 1979

I have been asked by the editors to explain why I have "changed my mind" about Kampuchea. As can be seen from a comparison with what is now known about recent Kampuchean history and my article "Social Cohesion in Revolutionary Cambodia" (*Australian Outlook*, Dec. 1976), I was late in realizing the extent of the tragedy in Kampuchea after 1975 and Pol Pot's responsibility for it. It is quite clear that I was wrong about an important aspect of Kampuchean communism: the brutal authoritarian trend within the revolutionary movement after 1973 was not simply a grassroots reaction, an expression of popular outrage at the killing and destruction of the countryside by U.S. bombs, although that helped it along decisively. There can be no doubting that the evidence also points clearly to a systematic use of violence against the population by that chauvinist section of the revolutionary movement that was led by Pol Pot. In my opinion this violence was employed in the service of a nationalist revivalism that had little concern for the living conditions of the Khmer people, or with the humanitarian socialist ideals that had inspired the broader Kampuchean revolutionary movement.

One notable error I made was to regard Kampuchean ultra-nationalist sentiment as somehow progressive, simply because it was understandable in the light of the damage done to the country by foreigners. I quoted a junior official of the Lon Nol government who had said that he would be prepared to accept a communist government in Kampuchea provided it was "really independent" and that "domination by the Vietnamese, whether communist or not, could only bring us misery." This statement has been invalidated by history: "really independent" (although propped up by Chinese military aid) the Pol Pot group sowed unprecedented misery in Kampuchea, leading to the death of a huge section of the population and forcing the rest to submit to enormous sacrifices in the name of building a powerful nation. And, subsequently, what the official would no doubt have called "Vietnamese domination" since January 1979 has been generally welcomed by the Kampuchean people. And now the defeated remnants of the Pol Pot group are massacring large numbers of Kampuchean villagers who don't want to support the racist crusade against the Vietnamese instituted by Pol Pot (who in Paris in 1952 had signed his handwritten contributions to a Khmer student magazine as the "Original Khmer" [*khmae daem*, see *Khemara Niset*, no. 14, August 1952]). Clearly, the "nationalism" expressed by the official I quoted is not the force most aligned with the interests of the people in this tragic equation.

Further, I was too willing to believe that information from the most important sources about post-1975 Kampuchea, the refugees and the government radio, could be reconciled. I was unprepared for the vastness of the gulf that came to separate them, and for the propaganda emanating from Phnom Penh during those years, the cynicism of which was eventually exposed by discussions I had with many working class Kampucheans who had lived under that government and had no reason to invent stories.

Also, the many proven falsehoods spread in the Western Press led to preoccupation with the correction of specific lies or distortions (fake atrocity photographs, fake interview, etc. (See, for example, Torben Retbøll, "Kampuchea and the Reader's Digest," in the *Bulletin of Concerned Asian Scholars*, 11:3 (July-Sept. 1979), pp. 22-27.) While such correction is important to anyone sorting through the evidence, it does not by itself establish the truth about the actual situation in Kampuchea. As George Orwell pointed out in reference to atrocity stories about the Spanish Civil War, those whose interests are against social change will always spread disinformation about revolutions; but these stories are irrelevant to the truth, neither its identity nor its opposite. It is up to those interested in the truth to establish it positively.

The most reliable source about the plight of the vast, predominantly peasant, working class in Kampuchea in 1975-76 was working class refugees, carefully questioned in a democratic atmosphere. But relatively few of these people fled their country in 1975-76, and they mostly came from one specific region. Further, Thai officials allowed only pro-Western researchers to interview refugees systematically and without the constraining presence of authorities, and these people paid little or no attention to gathering evidence from peasants or workers. So it was difficult for a non-specialist, or even a specialist lacking resources and suitable political connections, to track the real direction of the Kampuchean revolution as far as the vast majority of the country's people were concerned.

Finally, in 1975-76 the direction to be taken by the Kampuchean revolution had not yet, in my opinion, been fully resolved in Kampuchea itself. Chanthou Boua and I have in 1979 interviewed a significant number of Kampuchean refugees, many of whom state that, in 1975 or 1976 or both years, the peasants in the villages they lived in gave support to the revolution. Many others say the opposite; here we have evidence of divisions in the revolution which have hitherto been greatly ignored. But all the refugees point out that in late 1976 or early 1977 (following Pol Pot's return to power after being briefly out manoeuvred in Phnom Penh), where this peasant support had existed it changed to bitter hatred as food rations were cut, executions of recalcitrants increased, children were separated from their parents, and daily life became more rigorously regimented. In villages where the peasants had in 1975-76 been motivated by fear of the revolutionaries as much as, or more than, by support for them, life also became noticeably harsher. The political situation in Kampuchea clearly changed from late 1976, and very much for the worse. I personally didn't pick this up before early 1978.

Also in early 1978, a number of disturbing facts about recent Kampuchean foreign policy became known: premeditated, systematic Kampuchean clashes with Vietnam, Thailand and Laos. After a brief but hopeless attempt to see the situation Kampuchea was in as a product of a Soviet desire for world hegemony, I decided that Kampuchea's external relations could not be divorced from its disastrous internal plight. It was quite clear that Pol Pot was manufacturing foreign aggression to try to distract the attention of his people and his opponents inside the country from the horrific problems they faced, for which Pol Pot and his team were largely responsible.

Support for the Pol Pot regime may or may not be deemed logical from deductive argument concerning its "struggle for independence." But what might give such argument credibility, a detailed convincing analysis showing the regime's internal policy to have served the interests of the Kampuchean workers and peasants, is still lacking. And having talked at length with workers and peasants who lived in many provinces of Kampuchea under Pol Pot through 1977-78, I am certain it will never be produced.

"Kampuchea: Why the Slaughter?"
Nation Review (Melbourne), January 1980.

Why was the Pol Pot regime so murderous? I interviewed more than fifty Kampuchean refugees at length this year in Thailand and France. And over and over came the reply, "I don't understand."

The new Heng Samrin government in Phnom Penh estimated that three million Kampucheans, out of a population barely over seven million, died between April 1975 and January 1979, when Vietnamese troops helped put an end to Pol Pot's rule. Informed Western sources such as French priest François Ponchaud put the toll at around two million. At first skeptical, I now believe such astronomical figures may be correct.

One aspect of the violence not generally appreciated is that it accelerated as time passed, assuming very widespread proportions from early 1977. With Chinese support, Pol Pot and close associates such as Ieng Sary gained full control of the communist government. At the same time, Kampuchea began fighting with all three of its neighbors: Vietnam, Laos and Thailand.

Then in 1978 perhaps half a million Kampucheans from the east were shipped west, away from the Vietnamese border. For years these people had been living under a pro-Vietnamese local administration, which was then purged by Pol Pot. Heng Samrin's government claims many of the deportees were systematically slaughtered in the western province of Pursat. Three refugees I talked with recently, from different villages in Pursat, all report the arrival of many thousands of frightened easterners in their village in 1978, and their subsequent selective starvation and execution.

Why such a slaughter? The answers are rooted in both the current and the recent historical aspects of Kampuchean society: the destruction of the rural economy by the American air war, widespread social dislocation and repressive political tradition inherited both from the Kampuchean monarchy and Stalinist communist parties.

In just seven months, from January to August 1973, the US military dropped a quarter of a million tons of explosives on Kampuchea alone, fifty per cent more than the total tonnage dropped on Japan throughout World War II. Target maps, obtained by author William Shawcross under the Freedom of Information Act, show that these bombs were concentrated with astonishing intensity on the most densely populated areas of the country. By 1975, the US war machine had effectively destroyed Kampuchea's economy, inevitably bringing large-scale famine for at least one or two years.

The widespread bitterness resulting from the bombing was such that revolutionary soldiers who entered the city of Battambang in April 1975 headed straight for the town's airport. With their bare hands, they ripped to pieces two

212 Genocide and Resistance in Southeast Asia

bombing aircraft that they found there. "They would have eaten them if they could," one refugee says.

However, the undercurrent of violence and of poverty in Kampuchean society predates the US bombing. Soldiers massacred rebellious peasants in Battambang province in the early 1950s. A well informed source reports the discovery in 1965 of four to five hundred bodies in a cave in Kompong Speu; they were peasants who had tried to resist attempts by military officers to drive them off their land. This affair was kept quiet in Phnom Penh, but in 1967-68 more army massacres took place, and were reported, in Battambang and in Rattanakiri.

This is not to say that Kampucheans are by nature savage killers – the vast majority undoubtedly are not – but it does show that life in Kampuchea before the war began in 1970 was not all smiles.

Kampuchea's very poor had been getting even poorer (for instance by being thrown off their land) at an alarming rate as the 1960s wore on. And so there developed a rootless rural class which had very little at all to lose from any kind of social revolution.

Undoubtedly, the massive U.S. bombardment of populated rural areas drove thousands of now outraged and dislocated peasants into the ranks of the Pol Pot forces. It was a decisive year in Kampuchean history.

But what motivated the educated people like Ieng Sary – and Pol Pot himself – at the leadership level? One must allow for the war's brutalization of them, too, and for its increasing militarization of their politics; but in my view Pol Pot had, from the outset, harnessed communist ideals to a chauvinist program to build a powerful state.

Marxist terminology was often used to express chauvinist goals, such as making Kampuchea "the world's first real communist state," one with "great strength for national defense." In July 1975, Pol Pot told his troops that the American enemy had been defeated "in record time. Never before had there been such an event in the annals of the world's revolutionary wars," he added. And because victory had been won so rapidly, Pol Pot pointed out, "we must thus build up the country rapidly as well."

One great irony is that in order to make the Khmer race "great and power-ful," huge numbers of Khmers who were judged unfit for the warrior state had to die as well. Another irony is that to build "the first real communist society," the Communist Party of Kampuchea had to be overturned. A Pol Pot document, left behind in Phnom Penh and released by the new government at this year's genocide trial of Pol Pot and Ieng Sary, lists more than 250 Kampuchean com-munist and socialist leaders arrested for execution between 1976 and April 1978 alone. Officials of the post-1975 communist government who disappeared or were arrested and killed by Pol Pot include the Ministers of the Interior, Public Works, Information, Agriculture, Industry, Communications, Health, and Rubber Plantations, as well as the Deputy Prime Minister and Minister of the Economy and the first and second vice-president of the State.

After all of this bloodshed, the now-exiled government of Democratic Kampuchea is left with six leaders: Son Sen, Ieng Sary, Pol Pot and Yun Yat, Khieu Thirith and Khieu Ponnary. The first three, who fled to the jungle together in 1963, are married to the second three, and the last two are sisters.

6

Advocating Accountability, 1980-90

"Genocide must be punished"
Illawarra Advertiser, **September 23, 1987**

It was November 2, 1978, and they had less than two months to live. In Pol Pot's notorious Tuol Sleng prison, the two Australians were tortured and forced to write confessions' that they were spies. They were then murdered.

A million or more Kampucheans were also victims of Pol Pot's genocide from 1975 to 1979. But genocide is not a punishable offence. Pol Pot can still get medical attention in Bangkok hospitals after a grueling rainy season campaign in his war to retake power in Kampuchea.

To destroy a race of people or cultural group was one of Hitler's political aims on World War II. But at the time no international law prohibited such extermination. So the Nuremberg trials could find Nazis like Rudolf Hess, guilty of "war crimes" or "crimes against humanity," but not of genocide.

In 1950, a World Genocide Convention was agreed to, and it entered the International Law Books. But it has never been enforced. Genocide has since been committed, but never punished. An example is the extermination campaign against people of the Baha'i religion in Iran. Nothing much has been done about that.

Something can be done about genocide closer to home. Pol Pot's regime murdered or starved to death over a million Kampucheans in 1975-79. Although his regime was ousted by a Vietnamese invasion, and the Heng Samrin government has been ruling the country for nine years, Pol Pot still holds Kampuchea's seat in the United Nations. Led by the U.S. and China, most countries have voted for that result. No Western country has ever voted against Pol Pot's "Democratic Kampuchea" holding the UN seat.

Now this is an international scandal, a political dance on a million graves. But it does have one advantage. Australia can file a case against Pol Pot's regime in the International Court of Justice, alleging genocide, note the vast evidence, and ask for a verdict. The case would go ahead, and there is little doubt about the result.

Pol Pot's state of Democratic Kampuchea would become a pariah regime in UN eyes, and he and his associates would become international outlaws. Countries like Thailand which regularly support them would be susceptible to the charge of flouting international law.

So what? Justice for Kampuchean victims of genocide might not be worth the trouble, some say. But there is more to the case than that. If the Genocide Convention is not enforced this time, it may never be, and if it never is, future genocides are all the more likely. That prospect is worth the trouble. Hitler is reputed to have said while his regime murdered Jews, "Who ever heard of the Armenians?" A million Armenians were murdered by Turks during World War I.

Australia has two good reasons to take the action to the World Court. Firstly, Australians were murdered by Pol Pot's forces. Secondly, Australia has an interest in peace in our region. The Pol Pot army, campaigning to return to power in Kampuchea, is the main obstacle to peace. Vietnam has offered to withdraw its forces from Kampuchea if the Pol Pot threat is removed. (If Hanoi is bluffing, the bluff should be called.)

Australia's foreign minister Bill Hayden has already called for some kind of "tribunal" to try the Pol Pot regime. Indonesia now favors the idea, but Thailand is opposed. Last April in the USA, 200 Kampuchean survivors of the Pol Pot regime called for its prosecution in the International Court of Justice for the crime of genocide.

They were supported by the current Nobel Peace Prize winner, Elie Wiesel, a survivor of Auschwitz, and by representatives of the Armenian and Baha'i victims of genocide, as well as by Dith Pran, whose story is the basis of the film *The Killing Fields*, and the Academy Award-winning actor who played Pran's part, Dr. Hang S Ngor.

The 200 Khmers also wrote to Prime Minister Bob Hawke, praising Bill Hayden's stand on the issue and calling on Australia to proceed with steps to have Pol Pot leadership brought to justice. They said of the Kampuchea issue: Any solution is very difficult to foresee without the punishment or at least the removal from their present positions, and exile, of those most responsible for the genocide. So far the Australian government has yet to reply to this appeal.

It only takes one country to file the case in the World Court. Three thousand Australians have already shown their concern by signing a petition calling on the Federal Government to do so. More petition forms can obtained from *The Kampuchea Genocide Project*, PO Box 150, Enmore, NSW 2042.

"Cambodian Genocide"
Far Eastern Economic Review, 1 March 1990

The Pol Pot regime can still be held accountable for its crimes in the World Court.

In Cambodia, it is common to hear expressed the view that "Pol Pot was worse than Hitler." This is because "the Nazis killed Jews but not Germans," whereas "Pol Pot massacred his own Khmer people." The first claim is incorrect, of course, but the second is true: more than 1 million Cambodians died or were killed by Pol Pot's communist Khmer Rouge during their rule from 1975-79. The word "auto-genocide" has since been coined to describe extermination of members of one's own race.

A little-known fact is that the 1948 UN Convention on Genocide does cover auto-genocide. The crime of genocide consists of acts such as "killing members of the group" or other acts "committed with intent to destroy, in whole or in part, a national, ethnical, racial or religious group, as such." There is no clause requiring genocidists and their victims to be of different races.

In fact the convention applies to the Khmer Rouge regime's persecution and slaughter of three categories of their Cambodian victims. These are: "religious groups," such as Cambodia's Buddhist monks; "ethnical or racial groups," such as the country's Cham and Vietnamese minorities, and at least one "part" of the majority Khmer "national" group – the eastern Khmer population from the provinces near Vietnam (and possibly the Khmer urban population too). All were targeted for destruction "as such," and are therefore cases of attempted genocide by the Khmer Rouge.

As early as March 1976, a Pol Pot regime memorandum divided up what it called "the authority to smash people inside and outside the ranks." Some political killings were held to be the prerogative of the "Centre," others were delegated to the regime's regions. Thus, the Pol Pot group formally legitimized the murder of perceived opponents. Who were these opponents?

Pol Pot's government definitely implemented a policy of eradicating Buddhism. Eye-witness testimony abounds about the Khmer Rouge massacre of monks and the forcible disrobing and mistreatment of survivors. For example, of a total of 2,680 Buddhist monks from eight of Cambodia's 3,000 monasteries, only seventy monks were found to have survived in 1979. In a study of the subject, specialist Chanthou Boua pointed that "Buddhism was eradicated from the face of the country in just one year."

The largest ethnic minority groups in Cambodia before 1970 were the Vietnamese, the Chinese and the Muslim Cham. Unlike most other communist governments, the Pol Pot regime's view of these and the country's twenty other national minorities, who had long made up more than 15 percent of the Cambodian population, was virtually to deny their existence. The regime officially proclaimed that they totaled only 1 percent of the population. Statistically, they were written off.

Their physical fate was much worse. The Vietnamese community, for example, was entirely eradicated. About half of the 400,000-strong community had been expelled by the U.S.-backed Lon Nol regime in 1970 and several thousand were killed in pogroms. More than 100,000 others were driven out by the Pol Pot regime in the first year after its victory in 1975. The rest were simply murdered.

In more than a year's research in Cambodia since 1979, I could not find a Vietnamese resident who survived the Pol Pot years. However, plenty of witnesses from other ethnic groups, including Khmers who were married to Vietnamese, testify to the terrible fates of their Vietnamese spouses and neighbors. This was a campaign of systematic racial extermination.

The Chinese under Pol Pot's regime suffered the worst disaster ever to befall any ethnic Chinese community in Southeast Asia. Of the 1975 population of 425,000, only 200,000 Chinese survived the next four years. Ethnic Chinese were nearly all urban. They were seen by the Khmer Rouge as archetypal city dwellers and, therefore, as prisoners of war. In this case, they were not targeted for execution because of their race per se but, like other evacuated city dwellers, were made to work harder and under much more deplorable conditions than rural dwellers. The penalty for breaking minor regulations was often death. This was systematic discrimination based on geographic or social origin.

The Chinese succumbed in particularly large numbers to hunger and to diseases like malaria. The 50 percent of them who perished is a higher proportion even than that estimated for Cambodia's city dwellers in general, about a third.

Further, the Chinese language, like all foreign and minority languages, was banned and any culturally and ethnically distinguishable Chinese community was not tolerated. That was to be destroyed "as such."

The Muslim Chams numbered at least 250,000 in 1975. Their distinct religion, language and culture, large villages and autonomous networks threatened the atomized, closely supervised society that the Pol Pot leadership had planned. An early 1974 Pol Pot document records the decision to "break up" the Cham people: "Do not allow too many of them to concentrate in one area." Cham women were forced to cut their hair short in the Khmer style, not wear it long as was their custom. Then the traditional Cham sarong was banned, as peasants were forced to wear only black pajamas. In addition, restrictions were placed upon the Chams' religious activities.

In 1975, the new Pol Pot government turned its attention to the Chams with a vengeance. Fierce rebellions broke out. In one case, the authorities attempted to collect all copies of the Koran in a village, whose inhabitants staged a protest demonstration. Khmer Rouge troops fired into the crowd and the Chams then took up swords and knives and slaughtered half a dozen troops. The retaliating armed forces massacred many Chams and pillaged their homes.

Soon the Pol Pot army forcibly emptied all 113 Cham villages in the country. About 100,000 Chams were massacred, and the survivors were dispersed in small groups of several families. Islamic schools and religion, as well as the Cham language, were banned. Thousands of Muslims were physically forced to eat pork. Many were murdered for refusing. Of 113 Cham *hakkem*, or community leaders, only 20 survived in 1979. Only 25 of their 226 deputies survived. All but thirty-eight of about 300 religious teachers at Cambodia's Koranic schools perished. Of more than 1,000 who had made the pilgrimage to Mecca, only about thirty survived.

The toll goes on. The Thai minority, of 20,000 was reportedly reduced to about 8,000. Only 800 families survived of the 1,800 families of the Lao ethnic minority. Of the 2,000 members of the Kola minority, "no trace…has been found."

Finally, of the majority Khmers, 15 percent of the rural population perished and 33 percent of urban dwellers. The most horrific slaughter was in the last six months of the regime, in the politically suspect Eastern Zone bordering Vietnam. A total 1978 murder toll of more than 100,000 (more than a sixth of the eastern population) can be regarded as a minimum estimate. The real figure is probably much higher. But even a conservative reading of the evidence suggests that this massacre also falls well within the UN's definition of genocide.

Further, the perpetrator of all these massacres, the State of Democratic Kampuchea, remains a member of the UN, represented there by Pol Pot's hand-picked ambassador. Since 1979, all Western and ASEAN countries have refused every opportunity to challenge the Pol Pot regime's right to speak for its victims, though the European Community has announced their support will end.

But ironically, one last chance derives from this. While still a member state of the UN, the Pol Pot regime can be held accountable for its crimes in the World Court. And its overthrow has meant that the evidence could be gathered against it. The chance is unique in the annals of mass murder. Failure to seize it will undoubtedly encourage future genocidists in the knowledge that the UN convention will never be applied. The long delay has already buoyed Pol Pot's forces, now pursuing a war to retake power.

Only fellow members of the UN, who have signed the convention without reservations, can take the case to the World Court. Australia and Brunei can and should do so. It is in everyone's interest, not only to prevent another genocide but also to help end this war in the region.

The Pol Pot forces are the major obstacle to peace in Cambodia. Negotiations have consistently broken down over their role because of Chinese and U.S. demands for the ouster of their only opponent, the Hun Sen regime. A World Court case for genocide would threaten international support for Pol Pot, and conviction would make his regime international outlaws. This would relax their grip on Cambodia's UN seat, clearing the major sticking point in the search for a UN-administered peace settlement.

7

Bringing the Khmer Rouge to Justice

In the late 1970s, I interviewed hundreds of Cambodian survivors of the Khmer Rouge regime, and begun to publish their accounts.[1] In Australia during the 1980s, I translated most of these interviews and a number of confidential Khmer Rouge documents, and published detailed accounts of specific aspects of the genocide and historical analyses of the Khmer Rouge rise to power.[2] At Yale University in 1994, I established the Cambodian Genocide Program (CGP) to continue this work with a $500,000 grant from the U.S. Department

---

1. Ben Kiernan, "Kampuchea: A Refugee's Account," *Journal of Contemporary Asia* 9:3 (1979), 369-74; "Die Erfahrungen der Frau Hong Var in Kampuchea der Jahre 1975-1979," *Kursbuch* 57 (Oct. 1979), 122-129 (with C. Boua); "Motsattningarna inom den kommunistiska rorelsen i Kampuchea," *Kommentar* 8 (1979), 4-25; "Pol Pots uppgång och fall," *Kommentar* 11 (1979), 16-34; "Flyktingintervjuer om mat, arbete, halsa samre 1977-78?" *Vietnam Nu* 4 (1979), 10-11 (with C. Boua); "Het Verhal Van Hok Sarun: Het level van een arme boer onder Pol Pot," *Vietnam Bulletin* 8 (Nov. 15, 1979), 22-24 (with C. Boua); "Background to a Tragedy," *New Straits Times*, Dec. 20, 1979; "Bureaucracy of Death: Documents from Inside Pol Pot's Torture Machine," *New Statesman*, May 2, 1980, 669-676 (with C. Boua and A. Barnett); "Students Killed in Kampuchea," Sydney *Tribune*, May 14, 1980; and articles reprinted here in chs. 5, 10.
2. Ben Kiernan, "Genocide in de Oostelijke Zone," *Vietnam Bulletin* 16 (June 25, 1980), 20-22; "Conflict in the Kampuchean Communist Movement," *Journal of Contemporary Asia* 10:1-2 (1980), 7-74; *Peasants and Politics in Kampuchea, 1942-1981* (London, 1982) (with C. Boua); *How Pol Pot Came To Power: A History of Communism in Kampuchea, 1930-1975* (London, 1985); "Wild Chickens, Farm Chickens, and Cormorants: Kampuchea's Eastern Zone under Pol Pot" (reprinted here as ch. 1); "Kampuchea and Stalinism," in *Marxism in Asia*, ed. C. Mackerras et al. (London, 1985), 232-250; *Cambodia: The Eastern Zone Massacres* (Columbia University, Center for the Study of Human Rights, 1986); "Kampuchea's Ethnic Chinese Under Pol Pot," *Journal of Contemporary Asia* 16:1 (1986), 18-29; "Orphans of Genocide: The Cham Muslims of Kampuchea under Pol Pot," *Bulletin of Concerned Asian Scholars* 20:4 (1988), 2-33; D.P. Chandler, B. Kiernan, and C. Boua, eds., *Pol Pot Plans the Future: Confidential Leadership Documents from Democratic Kampuchea, 1976-77* (New Haven, 1988); "The Genocide in Cambodia, 1975-1979," *Bulletin of Concerned Asian Scholars* 22:2 (1990), 35-40.

of State. In January 1995, we opened the Documentation Center of Cambodia in Phnom Penh. Four years later, the United Nations Group of Experts completed its report to UN Secretary-General Kofi Annan on the legal ramifications of the Cambodian genocide. In March 1999, this report was published by the secretary-general. It stated:

> Over the last 20 years, various attempts have been made to gather evidence of Khmer Rouge atrocities to build a historical record of these acts. For nearly 20 years, scholars have been accumulating such evidence by talking with survivors and participants in the terror and reviewing documents, photographs, and gravesites. The most impressive and organized effort in this regard is the Documentation Center of Cambodia, located in Phnom Penh. Originally set up by Yale University through a grant from the Government of the United States of America, the Center now functions as an independent research institute with funding from several governments and foundations. It has conducted a documentation project to collect, catalogue and store documents of Democratic Kampuchea, as well as a mapping project to locate sites of execution centres and mass graves.[3]

The report went on to recommend the creation of an international tribunal to judge the crimes of the Khmer Rouge leadership. Since then, Cambodia and the United Nations have jointly established a "mixed" national and international tribunal to try the surviving senior leaders of the Khmer Rouge regime. These successes for the CGP and its mission were achieved under fire, not only from the Khmer Rouge, but also a sustained barrage from the West's most powerful newspaper.

The Cambodian Genocide Program, 1994–2006

"The only research operation in the world that focuses on Khmer Rouge atrocities, apart from Yale's genocide program." This is how the Editor-at-Large of the *Asian Wall Street Journal* described the Documentation Center of Cambodia in 1997.[4] Despite this, the U.S. *Wall Street Journal* led a campaign against Yale's Cambodian Genocide Program (CGP) throughout the two-year period in which the CGP created the Documentation Center.[5]

April 17, 1995, marked the twentieth anniversary of the seizure of power by the genocidal Khmer Rouge regime. The *Wall Street Journal* chose the occasion for a long editorial-page article appealing to the U.S. State Department and Congress to revoke the Department's inaugurating grant to the CGP,

---

3.   United Nations, AS, General Assembly, Security Council, A/53/850, S/1999/231, March 16, 1999, Annex, Report of the Group of Experts for Cambodia established pursuant to General Assembly resolution 52/135, 16.
4.   Barry Wain, "Pol Pot's Paper Trail," *Asian Wall Street Journal*, May 9-10, 1997.
5.   I refer specifically to the *Wall Street Journal* editorial page, with its tradition of ham-fisted ideological campaigning. See "The Big Lie Theory of the Country's Biggest Newspaper," in *Extra!*, the journal of Fairness and Accuracy in Reporting (FAIR), 8:5 (Sept./Oct. 1995), 13-24.

labeling its Director (me) a "communist" with Khmer Rouge sympathies. The appeal failed after the *Journal* published responses, but the paper followed with further *ad hominem* barrages, again directed at the CGP's source of funds. Fortunately, this provoked an encouraging display of support, including letters from twenty-nine leading international Cambodia specialists and various other scholars in my defense.[6] The Khmer Rouge, meanwhile, "indicted" me as an "arch-war criminal" and an "accessory executioner of the U.S. imperialists."[7] Despite attacks from two sides, we pursued our mandate to establish a comprehensive, publicly accessible archive and documentation database on the Khmer Rouge genocide, and to train Cambodian scholars and archivists to manage and enhance it.

The next year, the *Asian Wall Street Journal* fired another volley at the CGP, this time chastising us for not giving priority to the search for U.S. servicemen missing in action from the 1970-75 Cambodian war—before the Khmer Rouge takeover.[8] To discourage further funding for the CGP, the article described me as "the grant world's equivalent of box office poison." The *Wall Street Journal* republished this piece and even proclaimed to readers in an accompanying editorial that the CGP was closing down its operations the next month.[9] None of this was true—though the Journal now declined to print responses or corrections.[10] In that three-month period, the CGP in fact raised another $1.5 million, quadrupling its original grant. The CGP and the Documentation Center of Cambodia were now assured of funding for the next five years, a prospect beyond our wildest hopes in 1995. The Documentation Center, with the massive archive of Khmer Rouge internal documents we assembled in 1995-96, has now become Cambodia's first independent research institute on the history of Pol Pot's Khmer Rouge regime, Democratic Kampuchea (DK), which presided over the deaths of 1.7 million people.

Why did the *Wall Street Journal* launch such a campaign in 1995? Why the attempt to scuttle the world's only research operation on the Cambodian geno-

---

6. Stephen J. Morris, "The Wrong Man to Investigate Cambodia," *Wall Street Journal*, April 17, 1995; "Scholars Speak Out on Cambodian Holocaust," *Wall Street Journal*, July 13, 1995. Other attacks and responses appeared on April 28, May 15 and 30, June 15, and July 13, 1995. For a description and correction of my views on the Khmer Rouge before 1978, see "Vietnam and the Governments and People of Kampuchea," *Bulletin of Concerned Asian Scholars* 11:4 (1979), 19-25; 12:2 (1980), 72 (in ch. 5, above).
7. Khmer Rouge radio broadcast, August 14, 1995. U.S. CIA, Foreign Broadcast Information Service, EAS-95-157, August 15, 1995, 67. The Khmer Rouge also described me as "a protégé of the United States."
8. "America's Cambodian Coda," *Asian Wall Street Journal*, October 29, 1996.
9. "Will Yale Deliver?" *Wall Street Journal*, December 19, 1996. For a different view of the CGP, see "Cambodia's Blinding Genocide: A Website Exhumes the Faces of the Dead," *New York Times* Editorial Notebook, April 21, 1997.
10. Unpublished letters to the *Wall Street Journal* in response to its December 19, 1996, article and editorial on the CGP were posted on the web at www.yale.edu/cgp

cide? Why did the *Journal* choose the same target as the Khmer Rouge did? Why did it fail? What is the nexus between denial of genocide and attempts to foreclose its investigation? In this case, as we shall see, there is a complex relationship between assertion and suppression.[11]

I will discuss two forms of denial of the Cambodian genocide and one of suppression. First, the outright attempt to deny that anything serious occurred. In 1984, Bunroeun Thach, then of the University of Syracuse's political science department, took this position. He praised "Democratic Kampuchea political leaders" for having successfully "buried the past," attacked what he called Hanoi's campaign "to discredit the Communist Party of Kampuchea," and argued for including the Khmer Rouge in Cambodia's future.[12] Thach won few scholarly converts, but another Cambodian with similar views was Sorpong Peou, who opposed legal accountability for the Khmer Rouge genocide. As late as March 1997, Peou proclaimed: "Punishing Pol Pot will not solve the problem." He added: "Prosecution in a condition of anarchy is wishful thinking and may hinder national reconciliation." The journalist who interviewed him reported that Peou "says he is willing to forgive for the sake of breaking the cycle of deception and pre-emptive violence." The reporter also wrote: "Sorpong supports reconciliation with the Khmer Rouge rather than punishment for past crimes [and] supports the pragmatic strategy of incorporating Khmer Rouge defectors into the government structure in the hope that the movement will die a natural death."[13]

Sorpong Peou's apologetics for the Khmer Rouge was more influential than Bunroeun Thach's. The journal *Holocaust and Genocide Studies* published his review of my 1996 book *The Pol Pot Regime*. In his review, Poeu called the Khmer Rouge leaders "so-called 'genocidists.'" He linked what he called "the pre-emptive nature of the violence" to "Pol Pot's egalitarianism," his "prudence," "insecurity," and "vulnerability," and "the fickleness of popular support."[14] Extraordinarily, Peou claimed, "From 1970 to 1975, the Cham Muslims were not persecuted at all." When he did acknowledge massacres of Chams, he denied

---

11. On academic suppression, see for instance Brian Martin et al., eds., *Intellectual Suppression: Australian Case Histories, Analysis, and Responses* (Sydney: Angus and Robertson, 1986).

12. Bunroeun Thach, letter to the editor, *Far Eastern Economic Review* (FEER), July 5, 1984. Thach later moved to the University of Hawaii; see his "Two Eggs in the Same Baskets," *Khmer Conscience* (Winter 1991), my reply, "Bunroeun Thach's Basket Case," and the subsequent exchange (Spring-Summer 1991), 19-23. Thach later became Acting Director of the Preah Sihanouk Raj Academy in Phnom Penh, but his incompetence and racism created internal strife and controversy. In 1995 King Sihanouk withdrew his endorsement for the Academy. Thach was dismissed and left Cambodia, and the Academy re-formed as the Center for Advanced Study.

13. Steve Sharp, "Sites of Genocide," *Good Weekend* (Sydney), March 29, 1997, 33-34, 37.

14. *Holocaust and Genocide Studies* (Winter 1997), 413-425. The quotations appear on pp. 414, 416, 420, 423, respectively.

they were premeditated, despite overwhelming evidence. He then claimed that "the Pol Pot group made several—unsuccessful—attempts to limit the killing."[15] It was extraordinary to read these assertions in the journal of the U.S. Holocaust Memorial Museum. Few authors have shown such boldness in defending the Khmer Rouge genocidists.

In 1991 a colleague of Peou's, former intelligence officer Stephen R. Heder, described most of the top-level Khmer Rouge leaders as "dissidents" who were "suspect in the eyes of Pol Pot." These alleged "dissidents" even included Son Sen, deputy prime minister and CPK security chief, Chhit Choeun alias Ta Mok, the Khmer Rouge military commander, Ke Pauk, the deputy military commander, and Deuch, the chief of the notorious Tuol Sleng prison. Heder wrote that "such surviving dissidents as Son Sen and Kae Pok and perhaps even Ta Mok and Deuch have been wrongly depicted as 'Pol Pot loyalists.'"[16]

Heder went on to assert that "there were only two prominent Kampuchean communists who were not suspect in the eyes of Pol Pot and Nuon Chea. They were Ieng Sary...and Khiev Samphan.... Both Ieng Sary and Khiev Samphan were apparently considered completely loyal and lacking the domestic political strength with which to challenge Pol Pot and Nuon Chea in any way."[17] However, when Ieng Sary and Khieu Samphan came within reach of legal action, Heder backpedalled. In 1996, Ieng Sary defected to the Cambodian government. Heder now described Ieng Sary as having shown signs of "dissent and deviation" from Pol Pot's policies. In Ieng Sary's zone in the 1980s, "it was possible for peasants to accumulate small amounts of wealth," Heder said, adding that "China would have seen Ieng Sary as more reasonable" than Pol Pot. Moreover, Heder reportedly went on, "those differences may have existed" under the Pol Pot regime from 1975 to 1979, "with Ieng Sary advocating a more tolerant attitude toward intellectuals and being accused in the Communist inner circle of wanting to coddle the bourgeois elite." Heder added, "There's no evidence to suggest that Ieng Sary was ever No. 2, or that he had the kind of power base to allow him to enforce his will."[18] (Sary was in fact No. 3 to Pol Pot. Hypocritically, Heder branded the Cambodian Genocide Program as soft on Sary!)[19] A Khmer Rouge aide to Ieng Sary even quoted Heder's statements on Radio France-Internationale that, "according to the documents I have referred to, Mr. Ieng Sary is the only one, among Khmer Rouge leaders, about whom

---

15. For contrary evidence that Sorpong Peou deliberately ignored in his review, see *The Pol Pot Regime*, 67-68, 258-267, and 93, respectively; and my response in *Holocaust and Genocide Studies* (Summer 1998).

16. Stephen Heder, "Khmer Rouge Opposition to Pol Pot," in *Reflections on Cambodian Political History*, Australian National University, Strategic and Defence Studies Center, Working Paper no. 239, 1991, 5.

17. Heder, "Khmer Rouge Opposition to Pol Pot," 5.

18. Keith Richburg, "Timing of Khmer Rouge Defections Suggests Possible Role by China," *Washington Post*, August 24, 1996, A18.

19. *Phnom Penh Post*, October 18 and November 1, 1996.

I have so far been unable to gather tangible evidence showing that he initiated or applied purges against intellectuals."[20]

Khieu Samphan was certainly not in that category. In another 1991 paper, Heder had concluded: "Khieu Samphan's political star rose literally on heaps of corpses. He continued to rise in importance as he helped Pol Pot purge other communists...." Samphan, according to Heder, was "one of the key accomplices in the political execution machine that Pol Pot created" and "one of Pol Pot's chief servitors, second perhaps only to Nuon Chea."[21]

But again, in 1999, after Khieu Samphan surrendered with Nuon Chea, Heder suddenly began to state that the case against Samphan was inadequate: "There are cases to be answered by Khieu Samphan and Ieng Sary, but on the available documentary evidence you have to be less confident they would ever be convicted.... There is other evidence against Khieu Samphan that implicates him in the purge process but little or no documentary evidence that would stand up in court. But that's not to say we won't suddenly dig up such a document tomorrow."

Indeed, Heder has dug up evidence to convict those he had described in 1991 as anti-Pol Pot "dissidents." Mok and Ke Pauk, as well as Nuon Chea, could be indicted on the basis of transcripts of messages between these central leaders and zone commanders relating to arrests and killings. But in an interview with a reporter, "Heder said the weakness of the cases against Khieu Samphan and Ieng Sary related to 'indirect command responsibility,' a contentious issue under international law."[22]

This is false. War crimes cases do require proof of "command responsibility," but in cases of crimes against humanity and genocide, what is needed is proof of a conspiracy. International lawyer Dr. Gregory Stanton writes:

> Heder is wrong about Khieu Samphan and Ieng Sary's culpability for crimes against humanity and genocide. All one needs to show for those crimes is participation in a conspiracy. To prove their attendance at meetings of the Central Committee where decisions were made to eradicate Chams or to uproot everybody in the Eastern Zone would be enough. Ieng Sary's diary evidently shows that he was well aware of the plans to exterminate the enemies of the party. Khieu Samphan can probably be shown to have been equally aware of the party's policies.[23]

He was. We have complete copies of the minutes of fifteen meetings of the most powerful body in Democratic Kampuchea—the Standing Committee of

---

20. Former Khmer Rouge official Suong Sikoeun, *Phnom Penh Post*, November 15-28, 1996, quoting Stephen Heder on Radio France-Internationale, August 22 and October 10, 1996.

21. Stephen R. Heder, *Pol Pot and Khieu Samphan*, Monash University, Centre of Southeast Asian Studies, Working Paper no. 70, 22-23.

22. "Evidence Against K. Rouge Leaders Varies—Researcher," News America Digital Publishing, Phnom Penh, January 5, 1999, wire report distributed on Camnews, January 5, 1999.

23. Gregory Stanton, personal communication.

the Central Committee of the ruling Communist Party of Kampuchea. These crucial Standing Committee meetings were held between October 9, 1975 and May 30, 1976. Khieu Samphan is recorded in the minutes (under his revolutionary name Hem) as having attended twelve of these fifteen meetings. The minutes of two of the meetings do not record who was present, but it is likely that Samphan was there as well, totaling fourteen out of the fifteen meetings for which we have evidence. At the meeting of October 9, 1975, the Standing Committee put Samphan "in charge of the Front and the Royal Government; [and of] the accountancy and pricing aspects of commerce." Samphan was also made President of the State Presidium (i.e., Head of State of Democratic Kampuchea) by a decision of the Central Committee on March 30, 1976.[24] In 1977-78, he also headed the powerful Office of the CPK Central Committee ("Office 870"). In April 1977, soon after he assumed this post, Samphan declared publicly, "We must wipe out the enemy [and] suppress all stripes of enemy at all times."[25] The diary of an aide to Ieng Sary reveals the following view: "In our country, one percent to five percent are traitors, boring in.... [T]he enemies are on our body, among the military, the workers, in the cooperatives and even in our ranks.... These enemies must be progressively wiped out."[26]

More common than Heder's mental gymnastics is a consistent view that what occurred under the Khmer Rouge, though murderous, was not genocide. Two historians of Cambodia, Michael Vickery of the University Sains Malaysia and Monash University's David P. Chandler, both take this position. They oppose the Khmer Rouge, but they have categorized the regime's crimes as other than genocidal.[27]

Vickery, who considers the Khmer Rouge guilty of "intolerable violence" and "mass murder," argues that in Cambodia, unlike China and Vietnam, "nationalism, populism and peasantism really won out over communism."[28] "The violence of DK was first of all because it was such a complete peasant revolution, with the victorious peasant revolutionaries doing what peasant

---

24. *Pol Pot Plans the Future*, 7.
25. Khieu Samphan, speech broadcast on Phnom Penh Radio, April 15, 1977, extract in *New Statesman*, May 2, 1980, 675.
26. See *Ieng Sary's Regime: A Diary of the Khmer Rouge Foreign Ministry, 1976-79*, full translation by Phat Kosal and Ben Kiernan, available on the Cambodian Genocide Program website at www.yale.edu/cgp/iengsary.htm
27. See Michael Vickery, *Cambodia 1975-1982* (Boston: South End Press, 1984); David P. Chandler, *The Tragedy of Cambodian History* (New Haven, CT: Yale University Press, 1991), 3; David Chandler, *Brother Number One* (Boulder, CO: Westview, 1992), 4-5, and *Journal of Asian Studies* 55:4 (November 1996): 1063-1064.
28. Michael Vickery, "Violence in Democratic Kampuchea," paper distributed at a conference on State-Organized Terror, Michigan State University, November 1988: 14; and Vickery, *Cambodia 1975-1982*, 289-90. He correctly adds: "DK theory had multiple origins, one of which was 'Thanhism' and another of which was Marxism. It is not easy to say which became of greater importance in the synthesis" (p. 256).

rebels have always wanted to do to their urban enemies."[29] Vickery believes an orthodox Marxist regime would have been preferable. Chandler, by contrast, holds Marxism responsible for the violence, downplaying other factors like racist or genocidal policies. He argues, "Under the regime of Democratic Kampuchea (DK), a million Cambodians, or one in eight, died from warfare, starvation, overwork, misdiagnosed diseases, and executions. Most of these deaths, however, were never intended by DK. Instead, one Cambodian in eight fell victim to the government's utopian program of total and rapid social transformation, which its leaders had expected would succeed at far less cost."[30]

This technical denial of genocide, though in my view incorrect, is quite legitimate.[31] Vickery and Chandler do not fit into the category of Holocaust revisionists like Serge Thion, who deny the very concept and the plausibility of genocide. Thion indefensibly prefers the term "deportation" for the fate of Jews in Nazi-occupied Europe, and casts doubt on the evidence for the gas chambers.[32] (In the Cambodian case, Thion argued that the Khmer Rouge's crimes should be tried in a Cambodian court, rather than an international one.)[33] By contrast, arguments that the Cambodian people suffered not genocide but "a peasantist revolution of the purest sort" (Vickery) or "the purest and most thoroughgoing Marxist-Leninist revolution" (Chandler),[34] have a defensible intellectual basis.

The analyses of Vickery and Chandler are also more honest than a third position which consists, in the style of the *Wall Street Journal* editorial page, in noting that genocide occurred, while attempting to block investigation of it. I shall now examine various attempts to suppress the CGP's historical accounting of the Cambodian genocide, in the hope of uncovering a lesson for

---

29. Vickery, "Violence in Democratic Kampuchea," 17.
30. Chandler, *The Tragedy of Cambodian History*, 1. He correctly adds: "This does nothing to alleviate the horror or their responsibility for it."
31. For my critique of Vickery's and Chandler's views, see Kiernan, *The Pol Pot Regime: Race, Power, and Genocide in Cambodia under the Khmer Rouge, 1975-1979*, (New Haven, CT: Yale University Press, 1996), and my review in the *Journal of Asian Studies* 52:4 (November 1993), 1076-78.
32. See Serge Thion, *Vérité historique ou vérité politique: affaire Faurisson* (Paris: La Vieille Taupe, 1980).
33. For instance, Serge Thion, "Genocide as a Political Commodity," in *Genocide and Democracy in Cambodia: The Khmer Rouge, the United Nations, and the International Community*, ed. Ben Kiernan (New Haven, CT: Yale Council on Southeast Asia Studies, 1993), esp. 187: "We should first clean our own house.... Who are we to give moral lessons to others?" Thion's premise is that all Westerners are responsible for U.S. or French government war crimes, an immobilizing notion of Caucasian collective guilt. A harsher view is that he also had no expectations of his appeal for a Cambodian domestic tribunal. (For my critique of Thion's view of the Cambodian genocide itself, see p. 17.)
34. Vickery, *Cambodia 1975-1982*, 287 ; Chandler, *Brother Number One*, 3.

future chroniclers of crimes against humanity. In conclusion, I shall weigh the arguments of those who reject use of the term "genocide" in the Cambodian case, against the actions of those who have tried either to turn public inquiry to other issues, or simply to suppress the facts of the case.

The first attempt to derail the CGP came from a man describing himself as "a poor Chilean, a citizen of the Third World."[35] Julio A. Jeldres had left Chile before the 1973 military coup, and subsequently moved to Australia and then Cambodia. In the 1970s, Jeldres not only was a supporter of the Pinochet military dictatorship in Chile, but was also a member of a Khmer Rouge international front organization.[36] Within weeks of our launching the Cambodian Genocide Program, in 1995 Jeldres published an article entitled "Genocide Investigation Off on the Wrong Foot."[37]

In reply, I noted Jeldres' support for the Pinochet regime.[38] Jeldres quickly denied "doing work for the regime" of General Pinochet, claiming he was "a member of the Chilean Folk Dance Group, a non-political, cultural association."[39] But a statement Jeldres published in Australia in 1975, which he signed as "President of the Chilean Club," made no mention of folk dance. In it, Jeldres expressed his sympathies with Pinochet's Chile, which he called a victim of "the Australian government's attitude to my country." He praised Pinochet's 1973 coup for ensuring merely that "marxism was ousted." Instead of protesting the destruction of Chilean democracy, Jeldres denounced the international outcry over it. Like Pinochet, he equated democracy with communism, and complained that the Chilean dictatorship was "the 'target' of a communist international campaign against us."[40]

---

35. Julio A. Jeldres, "A Response to Michael Vickery," distributed by Hann So, Cam-news Internet discussion list, June 17, 1996.
36. See *Private Eye* (London), May 7 and July 16, 1993; *Phnom Penh Post*, November 30, 1996; and below.
37. Julio A. Jeldres, "Genocide Investigation off on the Wrong Foot," *Cambodia Daily*, January 27, 1995.
38. Ben Kiernan, "Jeldres Wrong to Point Finger at Alleged 'Pol Pot Apologists,'" *Cambodia Daily*, February 1, 1995. I added that in less than a year (in 1977-78) Jeldres had received three invitations to visit the Chilean consulate in Sydney, Australia. I was aware of this because Jeldres had written to me at the time (on March 14, 1978), revealing also that "the programmes were rather heavy and I did not have a minute to spare." These three invitations followed Jeldres' earlier visit to the Chilean consulate in May 1977.
39. "Jeldres vs. Kiernan," *Cambodia Daily*, February 10, 1995, and Rosanna Barbero, "Jeldres Falls into His Own Trap," *Cambodia Daily*, February 14, 1995.
40. Australia, Jeldres went on, "has now joined the communist countries and the so-called non-aligned ones in their attacks against Chile. We are getting sanctions because we did not want a communist government. The change of government in Chile is our problem and not Australia's." Julio A. Jeldres, "Insult to Chile," Melbourne *Age*, January 21, 1975. For the *Wall Street Journal* editorial page's defense of Pinochet, see *Extra!* 8:5 (September/October 1995), 15, 19; and of mass murder in El Salvador, 14-18.

So it was not surprising to find Jeldres later attempting to block action against another murderous regime, this time in Cambodia—especially because for at least five years, he had been an "Honorary Member" of the Khmer Rouge front organization known as FUNK. In 1976, he had privately boasted of this continued "honorary" status.[41] In 1978, at the height of the genocide, Jeldres sided with the Khmer Rouge against their Vietnamese opponents, and even claimed that the Pol Pot regime told him all he needed to know. As he then put it, "I am kept fully informed by the Cambodian Embassy in Peking."[42] In 1995, campaigning against the CGP's investigation of the Khmer Rouge period, Jeldres continued to claim that in 1978, Pol Pot's embassy "was the only source of information on what was going on in Cambodia."[43] He was alone in excluding consideration of information from refugees and victims of the genocide.

In the 1980s, Jeldres was associated with another Khmer Rouge front, the exiled Coalition Government of Democratic Kampuchea.[44] In the early 1990s, he joined the magazine Khmer Conscience, which published the writings of Bunroeun Thach (see note 12 above).[45] In Cambodia's English-language press in 1995 and 1996, Jeldres continued to denounce the CGP's investigation of the Khmer Rouge regime.[46]

Attempts by such people to suppress the only research program to document Khmer Rouge crimes comprise a new variation on the politics of genocide "denial." Longtime allies and even members of Khmer Rouge organizations have portrayed themselves as opponents of the genocide, thus seeking credibility for their demand that its investigation be cut short. This political chicanery should not, however, be confused with differing definitions of genocide, or with other scholarly debate about the nature of the tragedy.

The *Wall Street Journal* attack on the CGP was begun by Stephen J. Morris, who had met Julio Jeldres in Bangkok a decade earlier.[47] Throughout the 1980s,

---

41. In a letter to the author dated July 1, 1976, Jeldres revealed that, "In 1971, I was made Honorary Member of FUNK"; copy in my possession. FUNK was the Front Uni National du Kampuchéa, a coalition of Sihanoukists and Khmer Rouge dominated by the latter.
42. Jeldres, letter to the author dated March 14, 1978; copy in my possession.
43. *Cambodia Daily*, February 10, 1995.
44. *Far Eastern Economic Review*, May 31, 1984. See my reply to Jeldres of June 21, 1984.
45. William Shawcross denied Jeldres' association with *Khmer Conscience* (see *Private Eye*, July 2 and 16, 1993), but its editor Hann So continued to distribute Jeldres' writings. See Jeldres, "A Response to Michael Vickery," distributed by Hann So, Camnews discussion list, June 17, 1996, copy in my possession.
46. See, for instance, Jeldres' articles in *Cambodia Daily*, February 28, 1995, and *Phnom Penh Post*, July 28, 1995 and September 20, 1996; also Jeldres' statements on Radio Australia, September 13, 1995.
47. In 1996 Jeldres revealed: "I met Stephen Morris twice in Bangkok in 1985/86....I have since spoken to him three times on the phone" (Jeldres, "Response to Michael Vickery," distributed by Hann So, Camnews discussion list, June 17, 1996).

Morris, like Jeldres and Bunroeun Thach, devoted himself to political activism in support of Cambodian factions who were allied to the communist Khmer Rouge, but whom Morris praised as "anti-communist." In 1989, Morris complained that the democratic government of Thailand was selling out the Khmer Rouge. "It has now gone so far that Thai commanders have provided Phnom Penh's artillery commanders with precise intelligence on the location of Khmer Rouge units."[48] In the winter of 1990, Morris addressed a meeting of Cambodians in Brighton, Massachusetts. According to witnesses, Morris "took the floor and in an impassioned speech warned Cambodians in the room that they should not do anything that would appear to support the Vietnamese-backed government of Cambodia, including bringing attention to Khmer Rouge atrocities. He did not support a trial of the Khmer Rouge and attributed his inside information about the Cambodian situation to having dined with Khmer Rouge leaders."[49] Morris wrote, "The real Khmer Rouge military aim...is to force Phnom Penh to accept a comprehensive political settlement such as the UN peace plan."[50] His attack on the CGP's investigation of the Khmer Rouge was predictable. So was Morris' praise for Stephen Heder, whose "pro-Khmer Rouge views" Morris had once noted.[51]

---

48. "Thailand's Separate Peace in Indochina," *Asian Wall Street Journal*, September 4, 1989.
49. Mary Scully, R.N.C.S., and Theanvy Kuoch, unpublished letter to the *Wall Street Journal*, May 19, 1995.
50. Morris argued further that the Khmer Rouge were not the problem: "The danger lies in the Vietnamese Communists' determination to subvert such an agreement." Stephen J. Morris, "Skeletons in the Closet," *New Republic*, June 4, 1990. Morris labeled critics of the UN plan, and of its inclusion of the Khmer Rouge, as proponents of "an immoral, lost cause" beholden to Hanoi. The UN plan, he asserted, "is morally right, and offers real hope of success." It gave the Khmer Rouge, Morris wrongly predicted, an "incentive to lay down its arms," which "will end the war." Morris, "US Choice in Cambodia," *Boston Globe*, August 7, 1990.
51. Morris had once described Cornell University's Southeast Asia Program (America's most distinguished such institution) as "a comfortable milieu for those fond of totalitarian dictatorship." Morris attacked Heder, a former Cornell student, for his "pro-Khmer Rouge views" and for "propounding the moral virtue" of communism (Stephen J. Morris, "Ho Chi Minh, Pol Pot, and Cornell," *National Interest* (Summer 1989), 60). But in 1995, Morris shamelessly recommended Heder as one of a team he suggested should have been awarded the State Department grant that I received to document the crimes of the Khmer Rouge (*Asian Wall Street Journal*, April 17, 1995). In one of his own attacks on my work, Heder cited an unpublished draft by Morris (*Southeast Asia Research* 5:2 (July 1997): 128, n. 57). Though François Ponchaud also described Heder as "un Américain pro-Khmers Rouges" (*Le Point*, April 25, 1998), Henri Locard has cited Heder's work to attack mine. Locard asserted inter alia that the Khmer Rouge were "sincere idealistic leaders" and had not massacred Cambodia's Vietnamese minority, but had expelled and "spared" them (*Le Monde*, April 28, 1998). See my response (*Le Monde*, May 14, 1998), and my article, "Le communisme racial des Khmer rouges," *Esprit* 252 (May 1999): 93-127.

More surprising was the *Wall Street Journal*'s readiness to give space to a writer who had embarrassed it once before. In 1990 Morris attacked Lesley Cockburn, an American Broadcasting Company producer, for her feature on Cambodia.[52] Objecting to the feature's accurate portrayal of the United States' diplomatic support for the Khmer Rouge in the 1980s, Morris also pilloried what he called "Ms. Cockburn's 1987 PBS Documentary, 'Murder on the Rio San Juan.'" Cockburn had had nothing to do with that program, and the Journal's Editor conceded that Morris had made "an error."[53]

The *Journal*'s assault on the CGP attracted the attention of the *Reader's Digest*, which investigated reprinting it. A *Digest* research editor called me on May 22, 1995, to ask, among other things, if I had ever used Marxist terms. He then called the head of my department at Yale and asked if I was a communist. More confidently, he questioned another senior member of the department, "Did you know Kiernan was a communist?" But when my reply to Morris' second attack appeared in the *Wall Street Journal* on May 30, the *Digest* decided not to republish his article.

The *Journal* gave Morris a third opportunity to repeat his allegations. The last word came when twenty-nine international Cambodia scholars wrote that "Kiernan has been an outspoken and untiring opponent of the Khmer Rouge for 17 years," while "Morris supported a coalition government-in-exile which was dominated by the Khmer Rouge." These scholars, who included Vickery and Chandler, despite their differences with the CGP on the issue of genocide, added: "We have full confidence in Professor Kiernan's integrity, professional scholarship, and ability to carry out the important work of the Cambodian Genocide Program."[54]

Thus, a phase of the campaign ended. Having lost the debate in the academic world and the media, Morris moved to the realm of raw power. Ron Marks, a CIA officer seconded as Special Assistant to then Senator Bob Dole, drafted a letter

---

52. Morris, "ABC Flacks for Hanoi," *Wall Street Journal*, April 26, 1990.

53. *Wall Street Journal*, June 6, 1990. Morris has a history of McCarthyist witch-hunting. Once affiliated with Harvard's Russian Research Center, Morris fell out with its Associate Director, Professor Marshall Goldman, whom Morris calls an "ally" of "the pro-Hanoi left" (*Washington Times*, September 29, 1993). Neil Sheehan, author of the Pulitzer Prize-winning work, *A Bright Shining Lie: John Paul Vann and the Americans in Vietnam*, is dismissed by Morris as someone who "holds a benign view of the Vietnamese Communist Party" (*Washington Times*, September 29, 1993). John McAuliff and Eileen Blumenthal, organizers of a 1990 Cambodian dancers' tour of the United States, were attacked by Morris for possible "criminal" activity (Boston *Globe*, October 14, 1990) and for holding 39 dancers as "prisoners." Morris's charges were investigated and proved to be totally unfounded by both the State Department and the Immigration and Naturalization Service. McAuliff's and Blumenthal's alleged victims, in both Cambodia and the U.S., remain their colleagues and friends (letter to the *Wall Street Journal*, April 28, 1995).

54. "Scholars Speak Out on Cambodia Holocaust," *Wall Street Journal*, July 13, 1995. See also *Washington Post*, July 8, 1995.

repeating Morris' charges against me. Six senior Republican Senators—Dole, Senate Majority Leader Trent Lott, Senate Foreign Relations Committee head Jesse Helms, and three others—sent the letter to the U.S. Secretary of State Madeleine Albright on August 7, 1995. Two of the signatories, Trent Lott and Jesse Helms, were associated with the Council of Conservative Citizens, which claims, among other things, that interracial marriage "amounts to white genocide," that Jews have "turned spite into welfare billions for themselves," and that African Americans and Latinos suffer from "high crime and low intelligence." In 1992, Senator Trent Lott had given the keynote speech to a national board meeting of the Council. "The people in this room stand for the right principles and the right philosophy," he said. Six years later Lott falsely claimed that he had "no firsthand knowledge" of the Council's views.[55]

As the letter went off to Albright, a Morris backer from the conservative Heritage Foundation approached Alphonse LaPorta, head of the State Department's Office of Cambodian Genocide Investigations, and said, "If you don't get rid of Kiernan, we'll go after you."[56] LaPorta concluded that if I did not step down, the Senate would revoke the grant to the CGP, ending our investigation of the Khmer Rouge regime. I held my ground, with strong support from Yale University. On October 2, new support arrived. An editorial in the conservative *Washington Times* praised the CGP's achievements and described the Morris and Dole campaign against me as "lunacy."[57] The issue blew over with the CGP's Congressional backing enhanced.[58]

On September 17, 1996, Nancy deWolf Smith of the *Asian Wall Street Journal* called me from Hong Kong. She said something "is becoming an issue." This was that the previous month the Pentagon had not gained immediate access to the archives of the Khmer Rouge secret police (*Santebal*), which CGP staff from the Documentation Center had discovered in Phnom Penh in March 1996. Smith had the impression, which we could not confirm, that these 1975-79 documents contained information on the fate of Americans missing in Cambodia from the 1970-75 war. I explained that the Pentagon had not consulted me before sending its contract researchers directly to Cambodia the previous month. They had arrived at the Documentation Center saying, "It's all settled." They wanted to start work then and there, before the files had been catalogued.

---

55. See John Kifner, "Lott, and Shadow of a Pro-White Group," *New York Times*, January 14, 1999, A9; Frank Rich, "Scandals Sans Bimbos Need Not Apply," *New York Times*, December 26, 1998, A27; People For the American Way, *PFAW News* (Winter 1999), 5.
56. Alphonse La Porta, personal communication, August 22, 1995.
57. "The Academic Killing Fields," *Washington Times*, October 2, 1995.
58. See for instance, Eyal Press, "Unforgiven," *Lingua Franca* (April/May 1997): 72. A letter to the Secretary of State from Rep. Martin Hoke of Ohio, backing Morris' charges and circulated to the 435 members of Congress, drew only one signatory, that of Robert K. Dornan of California (June 19, 1995).

On September 12, I invited them to return in January, after we had completed our documentation of the Khmer Rouge genocide for the State Department. The Documentation Center, with CGP funding, would then be free to serve the Pentagon's different needs. On October 23, James W. Wold of the Pentagon's MIA office accepted my offer. I responded on October 25, reconfirming to General Wold that his researcher David Chandler was welcome to work in the Documentation Center's archives in January-February 1997.[59] Wold's office called that afternoon to thank me. The State Department followed suit, as did Chandler.[60]

Three days later, on October 29, in the *Asian Wall Street Journal*, Smith falsely accused me of withholding cooperation from Pentagon researchers.[61] I replied by fax on November 4, but Smith's newspaper held back my reply, passing it on to the *Wall Street Journal* in New York. On December 5, Mr. George Melloan, the *Journal*'s Deputy Editor (International), requested a copy of "the letter you received from General Wold."[62] I faxed it to Melloan immediately. This letter confirms my September 12 offer to the Pentagon. However, on December 19, the *Journal* republished Smith's October piece, alongside an editorial stating: "Mr. Kiernan refused the Pentagon researchers access to the documents. He continues to do so to this day, and will continue to do so until his project closes."[63] Two weeks earlier, Melloan had received irrefutable evidence that we had scheduled the Pentagon's visit for the following month. This dishonest editorial appeared simultaneously in the *Asian Wall Street Journal*.[64] Both newspapers also finally printed my short letter of November 4, but refused to publish corrections to their new editorial. Mr. Terrill E. Lautz, Vice-President of the Henry Luce Foundation, wrote that I had received a $250,000 grant from his foundation—in October 1996, just as Smith was describing me as "the grant world's equivalent of box office poison." The *Journal* declined to print this letter, Yale's own reply, or even a letter from the Pentagon. The paper left readers, potential funders, and the Khmer Rouge with the false impression that the CGP was to "close" in January 1997.[65]

On the contrary, in January 1997 the CGP launched a new World Wide Web site, including four large databases documenting the crimes of the Khmer Rouge

---

59. Copies of Wold's and my letters were posted at the CGP's World Wide Web site (*www.yale.edu/cgp*), under More Findings: "CGP Assistance to the Search for US MIA's."

60. Chandler e-mailed me on November 19, 1996: "Thanks for your supportive response to the MIA people, with whom I'll be working in Phnom Penh in Jan.-Feb."

61. Nancy DeWolf Smith, "America's Cambodian Coda," *Asian Wall Street Journal*, October 29, 1996.

62. For evidence of Melloan's McCarthyist false charges against journalist Raymond Bonner on El Salvador, see *Extra!* 8:5 (September-October 1995), 15.

63. "Will Yale Deliver?" *Wall Street Journal*, December 19, 1996.

64. "Will Yale Deliver?" *Asian Wall Street Journal*, December 20, 1996.

65. For the facts, see the unpublished letters posted on the CGP's website at www.yale.edu/cgp.

regime.[66] Chandler worked in the Documentation Center's archives in February 1997 as arranged, and returned in May. Though neither he nor his Pentagon employers announced whether he found any information on American MIAs, Chandler again thanked us for our cooperation. We saw no such acknowledgement from the *Wall Street Journal*. But the Editor-at-Large of the *Asian Wall Street Journal* reported our continued existence as "the only research operation in the world that focuses on Khmer Rouge atrocities." In a turnaround paralleling that in the U.S. Senate, the *Readers' Digest* praised the CGP and the Documentation Center: "Even today, project workers are uncovering masses of files that point to Pol Pot's 'bureaucracy of death.' Moreover, Yale won a commitment from the Cambodian government to endorse initiatives that would bring the evidence—and Khmer Rouge leaders—to a criminal trial."[67]

Meanwhile, the Khmer Rouge split, with one faction led by Ieng Sary launching its own "Research and Documentation Center" to defend itself.[68] In June 1997, the two Cambodian prime ministers appealed to the United Nations to establish a tribunal to judge the crimes of the Khmer Rouge period. In early 1998, the UN assembled a group of distinguished legal experts to report on this issue. They visited the Documentation Center of Cambodia in November 1998 and examined the evidence in detail. Their report, delivered to the UN secretary-general in February 1999, recommended the establishment of an Ad Hoc International Criminal Tribunal to pass judgment on the Khmer Rouge leaders, and a truth commission to be held in Cambodia to allow the surviving victims to air their grievances more fully.

Pol Pot died in his sleep in April 1998, less than a year after murdering his former Security chief, Son Sen, whom he suspected of attempting to follow Ieng Sary's defection to the Cambodian government side. But the 1998 mutiny and defection of former Khmer Rouge deputy commander Ke Pauk and the surrender of Khieu Samphan and Nuon Chea meant that at least three of the last Khmer Rouge leaders at large were now capable of being apprehended and indicted. The lone, one-legged military commander Chhit Choeun, alias Mok, did not last long in the jungle. He was captured in March 1999 and sent before a Cambodian military court. (He died in prison in 2006; Ke Pauk died in 2002.) Meanwhile, four of the five Permanent Members of the UN Security Council made strong statements in support of the establishment of an international tribunal.

In this period, new attempts were made to stymie the work of the Cambodian Genocide Program. In May 1998, Congressman Tom Campbell (R-California) wrote another letter to the U.S. Secretary of State, supported by Vietnam veteran and former Reagan and current George W. Bush appointee John Parsons

66. The Cambodian Genocide Data Base and other materials on the Khmer Rouge can be found at www.yale.edu/cgp.
67. Peter Michelmore, "Legacy of the Killing Fields," *Reader's Digest* (May 1997), 66. See also A. Barnett, C. Boua and B. Kiernan, "Bureaucracy of Death: Documents from Inside Pol Pot's Torture Machine," *New Statesman*, May 2, 1980.

Wheeler III, drawing upon false allegations by Craig Etcheson. This time the allegation was mismanagement of the CGP's State Department grant. After a six-month inquiry, the Office of Investigations of the U.S. Inspector-General found "no evidence of wrongdoing" and closed its investigation.[69] Meanwhile Campbell's colleague, Congressman Dana Rohrabacher (R-California) and Senator Jesse Helms of North Carolina proposed a resolution (H.Res. 533) that would try Cambodian Prime Minister Hun Sen as a "war criminal"—rather than pursue what Rohrabacher called the "obsession with a handful of geriatric Khmer Rouge leaders."[70]

When two of the geriatric genocidists, Nuon Chea and Khieu Samphan, surrendered to the Cambodian government and the U.S. government called for them to be sent before an international tribunal, Stephen Morris made a final attempt to prevent a genocide trial. He wrote a short piece for *Commentary* criticizing the "useless Genocide Warning Center" which the Clinton administration had established the previous month. Morris now pronounced that "genocide is extremely rare" and that "the only unambiguous example of genocide to have occurred since the Nazi Holocaust" was the 1994 Rwandan case. In Morris's view, Cambodians did not suffer a genocide, because "the persecution of ethnic minorities was only a relatively minor aspect of policy" in the Khmer Rouge period.[71] Morris's colleague, Adam Garfinkle, writing in the *Los Angeles Times*, took up the case against an international tribunal for Cambodia. Firstly, he agreed that "the atrocities of Cambodia represented a nearly pure political and ideological madness, not an ethnic or religious one. For this reason, the application of the term genocide to what happened in Cambodia between 1974 and 1979 is improper." Secondly, Garfinkle added, "What business is the fate of two aged and defeated killers—Khieu Samphan and Nuon Chea—to the U.S. Government? Did any American perish at the hands of these deranged thugs?" And thirdly, he concluded, a tribunal "is liable to dredge up no little amount of embarrassment about the American role in recent Cambodian history.... [W]e were indeed there at the creation of Cambodia's troubles. For purely prudential reasons, then, a U.S. initiative aimed at exhuming our own policy ancestor, so to speak, seems very ill-advised."[72]

68. See *Cambodia Daily*, September 10-11, 1996.
69. Letter to the author from the Inspector-General, Jacquelyn L. Williams-Bridgers, dated November 5, 1998.
70. Statement by Rep. Dana Rohrabacher (R-Ca) on the House floor, October 10, 1998, quoted in *Indochina Interchange* 9:1 (Winter 1999), 14.
71. Stephen J. Morris, "Clinton's Genocide Confusion," *Commentary*, January 12, 1999. four years later, Morris urged that "the US and its allies must first quicklydisarm, if necessary by overthrowing Saddam Hussein.... To back away now without Hussein handing over his weapons of mass destruction will deprive the US of any credibility in future crises." Stephen Morris, Retreat no longer an option, *Australian*, February 10, 2003.
72. Adam Garfinkle, "Be Careful Which Graves We Exhume," *Los Angeles Times*, January 24, 1999.

This close look at the failed efforts to impede the task of the CGP enables us to see firsthand how denial and suppression of information about genocide work. Both the creation of historical memory and its erasure depend upon contemporary politics as much as history itself. Bunroeun Thach, Julio Jeldres, Stephen Morris, Congressional Republicans, and the *Wall Street Journal* editorial page all considered their own political agenda more important than documenting the crimes of the Khmer Rouge and bringing the criminals to trial for genocide. This agenda reflected the anti-Soviet alliance between the United States and China during the later stages of the Cold War, an alliance which often brought together conservative anti-communists and Maoist radicals. We see such a combination in this case. Priorities for members of this coalition usually included disguising their own past support for the Khmer Rouge, burying the history of the Vietnam War, and yet refighting it by both covering for the Khmer Rouge and fanning the flames of the MIA issue.[73] Justice for the victims of the Khmer Rouge was not among their priorities. Those who sought it were often attacked from two sides. Neither Congressional Republicans nor the *Wall Street Journal* denied that the Cambodian genocide occurred. Rather, they took extraordinary measures to prevent or divert investigation of that genocide. A determined campaign by some of the United States' most powerful politicians and one of the world's most powerful newspapers failed. But it posed a larger obstacle to a historical accounting for the genocide than did scholars preferring to use their own concepts, or explanations beyond the wording of the Genocide Convention. Most scholars reflexively welcome further research and documentation. By contrast, political pressure is the greatest threat to honest inquiry. And the best defense is a deeper exchange of ideas, further scholarship, and more determination.

Pol Pot died in 1998, and the Khmer Rouge army collapsed in division and defeat. All surviving Khmer Rouge leaders have surrendered, defected, or been captured. A mixed Cambodian/United Nations tribunal is preparing indictments against them. The first trial, perhaps that of the Khmer Rouge Security Chief, Kang Khek Iev (alias Deuch), may begin in Phnom Penh in 2007, followed by further charges against Nuon Chea, Khieu Samphan and others. In spite of all of the politics involved in the documentation of events in Cambodia, it appears that getting history right has proceeded hand in hand with the quest for justice.

---

73. H. Bruce Franklin, *M.I.A. or Mythmaking in America* (New York, Lawrence Hill, 1992). Stephen Morris' claimed 1993 "find" of an alleged Russian document on U.S. POWs in Vietnam was quickly shown to be full of errors (Nayan Chanda, "Research and Destroy," *Far Eastern Economic Review*, May 6, 1993), and was reported to be a CIA fake (Susan Katz Keating, *Prisoners of Hope*, 1994).

8

Cover-Up and Denial of Genocide: Australia, East Timor, and the Aborigines

"As the crowd were walking up the hill, we could hear a car speeding towards us. EVERYBODY DOWN, Denis yelled, and we all dropped to the ground, hidden by the tall spear grass.... Except Topsy Secretary, an Aboriginal elder of the Larrakia people who along with Fred Fogarty had come along in support. Without hesitation Denis applied a classic flying tackle and brought her to the ground. The driver would have been watching the road and wouldn't have gazed up to his left on the sweeping curve. He followed the empty bus..."[1]

This late 1970s Australian outback scene, sketched by Darwin trade unionist Brian Manning, was one incident in a five-year campaign to maintain radio contact with the beleaguered people of East Timor. After invading the territory in 1975, killing the six Australian journalists there, and imposing a news blackout, Indonesian forces were closing in on the Timorese resistance.[2] Almost the only news from East Timor was broadcast by the resistance from a radio mounted on the back of a donkey in the rugged highlands. The weak signal barely crossed the Arafura Sea to the Top End of the Northern Territory. There the Australian government, in appeasement of Jakarta, attempted to block the transmissions and prevent their contents being passed on to the outside world. It was fear of official surveillance that brought Topsy Secretary to the ground in the outback that day.

In 1974, Denis Freney of the Communist Party of Australia (CPA) had come through Darwin en route to Timor, before returning to Sydney to establish the Campaign for an Independent East Timor (CIET). Freney met Brian Manning,

---

1. Brian Manning, "Charlie India Echo Tango Calling Timor Leste," paper read at the 7th Biennial Labour History Conference, Australian National University, Canberra, 2001.
2. See "The Roger East Story," *New Journalist* 32 (May 1979): 9-14; Rodney Tiffen, *Diplomatic Deceits: Government, Media, and East Timor* (Sydney: UNSW Press, 2001): 22, 25-26, 38; Desmond Ball and Hamish McDonald, *Death in Balibo, Lies in Canberra* (Sydney: Allen and Unwin, 2000); Paul Monk, "Balibo: Murdani and the Memory Hole," *Quadrant*, November 2000, 50-58; Jill Jolliffe, *Cover-Up: The Inside Story of the Balibo Five* (Melbourne: Scribe, 2001).

who was also a CPA member,* and found him "able to see the importance of the independence struggle in Timor more than anyone else I had met."[3] Manning and Lai Con Liong, a Timorese-born Darwin wharf laborer, traveled to East Timor for a week in May 1975. Leftist Fretilin leaders passing through Darwin stayed in Manning's caravan.[4] CIET shipped six radio transceivers to Fretilin in Dili a few weeks before the December 1975 invasion. Manning kept a seventh transceiver in Darwin and was able to receive details of the first killings after the Indonesian landing. But the next month, the Australian Security Intelligence Organization seized the transceiver operated by a Timorese in Darwin.[5]

Manning moved his radio operation into the outback. It was another three years before Indonesian forces tracked down and killed the Timorese resistance leader, and finally silenced the radio broadcasts. During that time, with the help of other wharf laborers, CPA activists, local Timorese Toni Belo and Estanislau da Silva, and Queensland-born Aborigine Fred Fogarty, Manning kept open the radio link to the closed territory.[6] Australian federal police, in years of wild emu chases through the outback, pursued this unique team who were playing an undiplomatic role – informing the world of an unfolding tragedy. Perhaps 150,000 of East Timor's approximately 650,000 people perished in crimes against humanity that a UN-sponsored Truth Commission described in 2005 as "extermination," and that also fit most scholarly definitions of genocide, and arguably, the United Nations legal definition of genocide of a "national group."*

---

* Manning joined the CPA in 1959 in his Queensland home town, on the advice of "an ex-Party member who had been expelled during the early fifties in some Stalinist purges." This dissident communist "encouraged me to join and advised that I continued to retain a capacity to think for myself" (personal communication, 9 June 2001). Manning was founding Secretary of Darwin's Trades and Labor Council (1971-74) and Secretary of the Darwin branch of the Waterside Workers' Federation (1968-74, 1978-82, 1996-2000).

3. Denis Freney, *A Map of Days* (Melbourne: Heinemann, 1991): 340, 343.
4. Brian Manning, "Charlie India Echo Tango."
5. Freney, *A Map of Days*, 354.
6. Manning, "Charlie India Echo Tango"; Ball and McDonald, *Death in Balibo*, 178-80; Freney, 357-64, 369-73; Tiffen, *Diplomatic Deceits*, 27.
* Leo Kuper, *Genocide* (New Haven: Yale University Press, 1981), 174-75, 186, 241; Frank Chalk and Kurt Jonassohn, *The History and Sociology of Genocide* (New Haven: Yale University Press, 1990), 408-11; *The Encyclopedia of Genocide*, Israel W. Charny, ed. (Oxford: ABC-Clio/Institute on the Holocaust and Genocide, 1999), 191-94; Arnold Kohen and John Taylor, *An Act of Genocide: Indonesia's Invasion of East Timor* (London: Tapol, 1979); Roger Clark, "Does the Genocide Convention Go Far Enough? Some Thoughts on the Nature of Criminal Genocide in the Context of Indonesia's Invasion of East Timor," 8 *Ohio Northern L.J.* 321 (1981); A. Barbedo de Magalhaes, *East Timor: Indonesian Occupation and Genocide* (Porto: Oporto University, 1992); James Dunn, "East Timor: A Case of Cultural Genocide?", in George Andreopoulos, ed., *Genocide: Conceptual and Historical Dimensions* (Philadelphia: University of Pennsylvania Press, 1994), 171-190; Matthew Jardine, *East Timor: Genocide in Paradise* (Tucson: Odonian Press, 1995); Ben Saul, "Was the Conflict in East Timor 'Genocide' and Why Does it Matter?," *Melbourne Journal of International Law* 2 (2001): 477-522; Ben Kiernan, "East Timor: Indonesia's actions 'genocide'" (abc.net.au/ra/asiapac/programs/s354635.htm), Radio Australia, 3 October 2001.

Article II of the United Nations
Convention on the Prevention and Punishment of the Crime of Genocide, 1948
In the present Convention, genocide means any of the following acts committed with intent to destroy, in whole or in part, a national, ethnical, racial, or religious group, as such:
a)   Killing members of the group;
b)   Causing serious bodily or mental harm to members of the group;
c)   Deliberately inflicting on the group conditions of life calculated to bring about its physical destruction in whole or in part;
d)   Imposing measures intended to prevent births within the group;
e)   Forcibly transferring children of the group to another group.

Two decades later, in the run-up to the 2000 Olympic Games in Sydney, the international spotlight focused on Australia's Aborigines. Prime Minister John Howard had served as treasurer in the 1975-83 government that enforced the crackdown on radio contact with East Timor. He now refused to make an official apology to the Aboriginal people for the dispossession and genocide which Australia's High Court and Human Rights Commission ruled they had suffered under previous governments.[*] Howard offered a personal expression of regret, but public pressure mounted for an official apology. At this time, the U.S. Bureau of Indian Affairs accepted "moral responsibility" for the "sorrowful truths" that "the United States enforced its ambition against the Indian nations," waged "war on Indian people" by "threat, deceit and force," and committed "acts so terrible that they infect, diminish and destroy the lives of Indian people decades later, generations later." Now, a U.S. official said, "the legacy of these misdeeds haunts us…. These wrongs must be acknowledged."[7] But Australian domestic defenses withstood this foreign example. As the Olympics opened, Howard made no apology to Aborigines. Instead,

---

7.   Kevin Gover, Assistant Secretary, Indian Affairs, U.S. Department of Interior, September 8, 2000; see www.naswdc.org/nasw/diversity/gover.htm
*   Human Rights and Equal Opportunity Commission, *Bringing Them Home: Report of the National Inquiry into the Separation of Aboriginal and Torres Strait Islander Children from their Families*, April 1997; Colin Tatz, *Genocide in Australia* (Canberra: Australian Institute of Aboriginal and Torres Strait Islander Studies [AIATSIS], Research Discussion Paper 8, 1999); Ian Clark, *Scars in the Landscape: A Register of Massacre Sites in Western Victoria, 1803-1859* (Canberra: AIATSIS, 1995); P.D. Gardner, *Gippsland Massacres: The Destruction of the Kurnai Tribes, 1800-1860* (Ensay, Vic.: Ngarak Press, 1993); Jan Critchett, *A Distant Field of Murder: Western District Frontiers, 1834-1848* (Melbourne: Melbourne University Press, 1990); A. Dirk Moses, "An Antipodean Genocide? The Origins of the Genocidal Moment in the Colonization of Australia," *Journal of Genocide Research*, 2, 1 (March 2000): 89-106; Alison Palmer, *Colonial Genocide* (Adelaide: Crawford House, 2000); Ben Kiernan, "Australia's Aboriginal Genocide," *Yale Journal of Human Rights*, 1, 1, Spring 2001, 49-56; Ray Evans and Bill Thorpe, 'Indigenocide and the Massacre of Australian History," *Overland* 163 (July 2001): 21-39; Henry Reynolds, *An Indelible Stain? The Question of Genocide in Australia's History* (Ringwood: Viking, 2001).

conservative Australian columnists and publishers backing his refusal launched a media campaign to deny that Aborigines had suffered genocide.

The Australian attempts to cover-up mass murder in East Timor and deny the Aboriginal genocide both involved groups associated with the conservative journals *News Weekly* and *Quadrant* – though neither exclusively nor unanimously. Domestic politics and foreign diplomacy often intersect. A view current in official circles was, "If we criticize Indonesia for its takeover of East Timor, they could have a lot to say about our treatment of the Aborigines."[8] One result was, in Beverley Smith's words, "a conspiracy of silence between two established orders."[9]

Denying or downplaying genocide is the exclusive province of neither the right nor the left. Communists had denied the evidence of Stalin's mass murders in the USSR. In the case of Cambodia, leftists welcomed the 1975 Khmer Rouge victory and rightists resisted their 1979 defeat.[10] In Australia, international anti-communism fostered denial of two genocides committed by non-communists close to home. Yet critics of these genocides included other members of the Australian right, as well as independents and leftists. Support for the Timorese and the Aborigines, as for the victims of Stalin and Pol Pot, came from many viewpoints, including religious groups. A small but diverse team kept open the radio link to Timor. For a quarter century, however, influential Australian anti-communists helped cover-up or deny the mass murder there. Why? The tragedy ended only in 1999 when Howard, bowing at last to public opinion, sent troops to Timor's rescue. What were the motives of his influential backers who meanwhile denied the genocide of the Aborigines? How were the two causes linked?

The Timor Tragedy

The weak radio signal between East Timor and northern Australia was not the first connection between the two countries. Australians had fought in Timor

---

8.   Beverley Smith cited a statement by Dr. Peter McCawley of the Australian National University, on the ABC Radio program, "The World Today," 20 June 1984. (Smith, "White Nomad: Burchett's Approach to Asia in the Australian Context," in Ben Kiernan, ed., *Burchett: Reporting the Other Side of the World, 1939-1983*, Quartet, London, 1986, 126.) Patrick Walsh adds: "Indonesia has sometimes used Australia's treatment of Aborigines to hit back in response to criticism of Indonesian behaviour in East Timor" ("Australia and East Timor," *Arena* 34 [April-May 1998]: 25).
9.   Beverley Smith, "White Nomad," 126.
10.   On my initial misjudgment, see "Vietnam and the Governments and People of Kampuchea," *Bulletin of Concerned Asian Scholars*, 11, 4 (1979): 19-25; 12, 2 (1980): 72 (in ch. 5, above). On anti-communist support for the Khmer Rouge: Ben Kiernan, ed., *Genocide and Democracy in Cambodia: The Khmer Rouge, the United Nations, and the International Community* (New Haven: Yale Council on Southeast Asia Studies, 1993), ch. 6, and "Bringing the Khmer Rouge to Justice," *Human Rights Review*, 1:3 (April-June 2000): 92-108 (ch. 7, above).

during the Second World War, when possibly 50,000 East Timorese had perished under Japanese occupation. The victims comprised ten percent of the population of the small Portuguese colony. Australia's consul in the territory in 1962-64, James Dunn, called this "one of the great catastrophes of World War II in terms of relative loss of life."[11] Australian troops who battled Japanese forces there in 1942-43 have always been grateful to the Timorese who supported them, especially in light of the deadly Japanese retribution against Timorese after the Australian withdrawal.[12] "In areas where the Australians had been active, villages were razed to the ground and whole families wiped out," Dunn wrote.

Years later, the commander of the 2/2nd Independent Company, Colonel Bernard Callinan, still remembered the debt his men owed the Timorese. He named his Australian home "Belulic" after his former headquarters in Timor.[13] And after the 1974 coup in Portugal raised hopes of Timorese independence, Callinan wrote that Australian veterans "would feel betrayed by an Australian government that made a facile decision on the future of these friendly, loyal and courageous people." He urged, "Our Government should ensure that at least ample time and facilities are given them in their time of uncertainty to determine and express freely their desires for the future."[14]

Sadly, self-determination for East Timor was a quarter century away. In mid-1975 the leftist independence movement, Fretilin, won 55 percent of the vote in village-level elections.[15] But Australian governments quickly supported Indonesia's brutal invasion of December 1975, which caused the deaths of perhaps 120,000 Timorese by 1979.[16] As in World War Two, the Timorese had to fight on alone.

11. James Dunn, *Timor: A People Betrayed* (Milton, Queensland: Jacaranda Press, 1983): 26.
12. See Bernard Callinan, *Independent Company* (London: Heinemann, 1953); Tom Uren, *Straight Left* (Sydney: Vintage, 1995): 17-26, 300-3, 475-82; Cliff Morris, "Australian WWII Commando Remembers," *Retrieval* (Melbourne) 36 (April/May 1977): 12-18. Australian units involved in East Timor were the 2/2nd Independent Company (Callinan) and the 2/4th (Morris); in West Timor, the 2/21 and the 2/40 Infantry Battalion, and the 2/1 Heavy Battery (Uren).
13. Callinan, *Independent Company*, 204, and map, 213 (1984 edition). I am grateful to John Waddingham for this information; Patrick Walsh, "Australia's Support for Indonesia's Takeover of East Timor," testimony before the Permanent People's Tribunal, Lisbon, 19-22 June, 1981, 19.
14. Sir Bernard Callinan, letter to the *Australian*, 18 September 1974, quoted in Bill Nicol, *Timor: The Stillborn Nation* (Melbourne: Visa, 1978): 277-78.
15. Dunn, *Timor: A People Betrayed*, 100.
16. East Timor's population fell from 689,000 in 1974 (635,000 according to Jolliffe, *Cover-Up*, 46) to 522,000 in mid-1979. See John G. Taylor, *Indonesia's Forgotten War: The Hidden History of East Timor* (London: Pluto, 1991), expanded edition, *East Timor: The Price of Freedom* (London: Zed, 1999): 89-90, 98. Indonesia's Foreign Minister Mochtar Kusumaatmadja gave a figure of 120,000 Timorese dead from 1975 to November 1979 (Taylor, *East Timor*, 203).

And unfortunately for them, Colonel Callinan had also changed his mind about their right to self-determination. In April 1975, along with Australia's Joint Intelligence Organisation, Callinan is said to have advised Fretilin's then coalition partner, the UDT party, to quit the coalition for an "anti-communist" alliance with a tiny pro-Indonesian grouping, Apodeti.[17] In a reversal of his initial call for self-determination, Callinan wrote in 1977: "Having lived with, and closely with, these people, I am convinced that East Timor is not a viable independent nation. To talk of these people exercising a "free choice" is to be quite unrealistic..."[18] By 1981, according to Patrick Walsh, Callinan was "the only ex-commando who was in Timor in World War II to publically support East Timor's integration into Indonesia."[19] Why did he abandon the people he once saw as friends? The answer lies not in East Timor, but in Australian anti-communism, including its specific domestic features, coupled with U.S. policy towards Indonesia.

Australian Anti-Communism and Asia

Colonel Callinan was an important figure in the secretive, right-wing National Civic Council (NCC).[20] Unlike Callinan, the Council's President, B.A. (Bob) Santamaria (1915-1998), had been exempted from military service in World War II, at the instigation of the Catholic Archbishop of Melbourne.[21] During the 1930s, he had been a vocal supporter of Fascism, with what has been called an "even-handed" and a "generous view of the rise of Nazism."[22] He opposed Hitler's repression of Catholics, but on 28 May 1939 he denied Germany was "sufficiently criminal in its mentality to desire war,"[23] and he opposed aerial

17. Denis Freney, "East Timor: The Modest Revolution," *Australian Left Review* 48 (September 1975): 3-10, details, 8. See also *Tribune*, 6 May and 1 September 1975.
18. Bernard Callinan, letter, Melbourne *Age*, 19 August 1977, quoted in Walsh, "Australia's Support", 19.
19. Walsh, "Australia's Support," 19.
20. Val Noone, *Disturbing the War: Melbourne Catholics and Vietnam* (Melbourne: Spectrum, 1993): 246. On the the NCC's predecessor, the Movement, see Bruce Duncan, *Crusade or Conspiracy?: Catholics and the Anti-Communist Struggle in Australia* (Sydney: UNSW Press, 2001). On the Movement's secrecy, see 64, 103, 159, 192, 211, 229-30, 252, 259, 265, 268, 271, 285, 289, 297, and esp. 325-27, 333-34; also Edmund Campion, *Rockchoppers: Growing Up Catholic in Australia* (Ringwood: Penguin, 1982): 108-9.
21. Paul Ormonde, ed., *Santamaria: The Politics of Fear* (Melbourne: Spectrum, 2000): 103.
22. Ormonde, 98, and documentation in C. Thornton-Smith, "The Young Santamaria and His Mentors," in Ormonde, 55-96, esp. 68-71; Duncan, *Crusade or Conspiracy?*, 15-17, 21, 27, 93. See also John D. Legge, *Australian Outlook: A History of the Australian Institute of International Affairs* (Sydney: Allen & Unwin, 1999): 65-66.
23. James Griffin, "A Towering Intellectual," in Ormonde, ed., *Santamaria*, 27. For his response to Hitler's Jewish policy, see Thornton-Smith, 77-80, Duncan, 20.

bombardment.[24] Following Hitler's invasion of Poland, Santamaria spent the war years quietly organizing Australian Catholic anti-communist groups, including the Movement, forerunner of the NCC. He "made no public contribution to debate on the issues involved" in World War Two.[25] After 1945, no longer opposed to aerial bombing, Santamaria made vociferous public statements favoring all of Australia's other wars during his lifetime.[26]

Working mostly behind the scenes, Santamaria was an enduring and influential public figure. The Movement, which he led in the 1940s and 1950s, fought communist-led trade unions and sought control of the Australian Labor Party (ALP).[*] Like the Communist Party, the Movement used scare-mongering, ballot-rigging, hounding of dissidents, and *ad hominem* attacks on public opponents.[27] The ALP split in 1955. Santamaria sponsored the minority Democratic Labor Party (DLP), which controlled the balance of power in Australian parliaments for two decades. Santamaria's NCC and the DLP both supported the conservative government headed by the Liberal party and successfully kept the ALP out of office until the election of the Whitlam Labor government in 1972.

Santamaria and the NCC advanced a mix of principles and policies to lead a mostly working-class Irish Catholic minority away from its traditional Labor allegiance and towards conservative anti-communism. Along with the left, Santamaria opposed the discriminatory "White Australia" immigration policy, but by contrast he also opposed Indonesian independence from Dutch colonial rule in 1949.[28] He hoped Australia "could be a major force in the conversion of Asia to Christianity," making "the great sacrifice which will be needed to preserve Australia as a nation of primarily European

24. In a speech to a peace rally on 28 May 1939, Santamaria described aerial bombardment as "the new creation…as hideous as any invented by the perverted genius of fallen man" (quoted in Ormonde, 98).
25. Ormonde, ed., *Santamaria: The Politics of Fear*, 99.
26. Paul Ormonde, "An Authoritarian Man," in *Santamaria: The Politics of Fear*, 99-100.
*   Bruce Duncan, *Crusade or Conspiracy?*, quotes a Movement resolution "to secure the control of the [ALP] Federal Executive and Conference…by July 1952 at the latest" (Sydney: UNSW Press, 2001, 177).
27. For documentation of Movement attempts to control labor organizations, see Duncan, *Crusade or Conspiracy?*, 64, 99, 128, 155-57, 159, 177, 183-84, 189, 191, 209, 219, 278, 289, 314-15; of scare-mongering, 89, 157-59, 164, 185, 214, 235, 280, 292; ballot-stuffing, 181, 209, 219; victimization of dissidents, 139, 252, 265; *ad hominem* attacks, 167-68, 182, 208, 231, 247, 321-24.
28. Stuart Macintyre, *The Reds: The Communist Party of Australia from Origins to Illegality* (Sydney: Allen & Unwin, 1999): 126-28, 131-32; Duncan, *Crusade or Conspiracy?*, 65, 124, quoting *News Weekly*: the "so-called Indonesian Republic had next to no support from the Indonesian people" (12 January 1949, 1, 5, 4); R. Lockwood, *Black Armada: Australia and the Struggle for Indonesian Independence, 1942-49* (Sydney: Hale & Iremonger, 1982): 230; Paul Ormonde, *A Foolish Passionate Man: A Biography of Jim Cairns* (Ringwood: Penguin, 1981): 41-42.

texture."[29] Santamaria warned that "Australia will be destroyed as a nation" by communism, Islam, Hinduism or a pagan occupying power, and in 1951 he predicted war "against the Asiatic countries within ten years."[30] Citing the conflict in Korea, the NCC magazine *News Weekly*, which he edited, warned that 1952 "might well be one of the last years in the history of the Australian nation as we know it."[31]

As fighting escalated in Vietnam, Colonel Callinan became an advisor to the Catholic-led Diem regime in Saigon, and Santamaria became an early and prominent advocate of the US and Australian intervention. They worked hard to contest the critique mounted by a growing domestic anti-war movement. *News Weekly* ran editorials stating that there were "no children burned by napalm" in Vietnam (April 1967), with titles like "Napalm? No, Stolen Petrol" (20 September 1967), and "The Great Napalm Lie Exposed" (27 March 1968). Santamaria argued that "the number of victims is minimal, because the Americans have undertaken extraordinary precautions." His preferred explanation for injuries caused by napalm bombing was: "Many children were burned by overturned oil lamps or by the explosion of kerosene lamps into which their parents had poured high-octane petrol taken from fuel dumps."[32] In 1969, Santamaria called the slaughter of civilians at My Lai a "battle." The hundreds of women and children killed were falsely termed surrendered combatants.[33] Santamaria regarded Nixon's 1970 invasion of Cambodia as "long overdue" and urged its expansion.[34] He dismissed the publication of the *Pentagon Papers* the next year, denouncing "North Vietnamese wolves in *New York Times* clothing."[35]

Santamaria appeared regularly in the mainstream media and was also active in right-wing intellectual circles.[36] In 1956 he had successfully recommended a Catholic convert and Movement official, the anti-modernist poet Professor James McAuley, as editor of the new conservative magazine *Quadrant*, launched with

---

29. Ormonde, 27, quoting Santamaria in *The Future of Australia*, 1951.
30. Duncan, *Crusade or Conspiracy?*, 159, 163.
31. Duncan, 185, quoting *News Weekly*, 31 December 1952, 1.
32. Val Noone, "Santamaria, War and Christianity," in Ormonde, *Santamaria*, 131, citing *Age*, 25 and 27 July 1967.
33. Santamaria, "A matter of justice," and Editorial, both in *News Weekly*, 2 November 1969; Santamaria, "The Doves and Song My," *News Weekly*, 15 December 1969. In April 1971, *News Weekly* called for Lieutenant William Calley to be tried.
34. Santamaria, "The Impact of the Nixon Decision," *News Weekly*, 22 April 1970, 3-4, and "The Cambodian Operation," 22 July 1970, 16, cited in Noone, *Disturbing the War*, 244.
35. Santamaria, "New York Times," *News Weekly*, 30 June 1971, 16, cited in Noone, *Disturbing the War*, 254.
36. Legge, *Australian Outlook*, 66-67, 125-26.

CIA funding by the Australian Committee for Cultural Freedom.[37] McAuley, an expert on the Australian colony of New Guinea, urged officials to "Christianise not Westernise," warned that an independent New Guinea would be "a coconut republic which could do little good for itself," and advocated the territory's incorporation with full citizenship rights in a "perpetual union" with Australia.[38] Under his editorship, *Quadrant*'s literary content and aggressive anti-communism expanded its intellectual influence, government patronage, and political discretion. McAuley visited Jakarta several months after Suharto's takeover of Indonesia, at the height of the 1965-66 massacre of 800,000 communists, which the CIA privately described as "one of the worst mass murders of the 20th century."[39] In *Quadrant*, McAuley wrote just this: "The coup and its bloody aftermath had resulted in a strange stalemate at the time of my visit. From such a fluid and ambiguous situation anything can arise, and I shall not speculate upon possibilities..."[40] Its CIA sponsor had already found *Quadrant* "too right wing," and "wanted to distance the magazine from its regular contributors," including Santamaria. *Quadrant* ignored the advice.*

37. Duncan, 235, 290, 300-1, 306-7, 357, 389; Cassandra Pybus, "*Quadrant* Magazine and CIA Largesse," *Overland* 155, 1999 (http://dingo.vu.edu.au/~arts/cals/overland/155pybus.html); Pybus, *The Devil and James McAuley* (St. Lucia: University of Queensland Press, 1999): 122-48, 164; James McAuley, "CIA," *Quadrant* XI: 3 (May-June 1967): 4-6; Christopher Lasch, "The Cultural Cold War," *Nation* (US), 11 September 1967, 198-212; Humphrey McQueen, *Nation Review*, 5-11 May 1977, and *Gallipoli to Petrov* (Sydney, Allen & Unwin, 1984): 180-195; Stuart Macintyre, "Righteousness and the Right," *Overland* 92 (1983): 21-26; Gavan McCormack, "The New Right and Human Rights: "Cultural Freedom" and the Burchett Affair," *Meanjin* 3 (1986): 389-403; Frances Stonor Saunders, *The Cultural Cold War: The CIA and the World of Arts and Letters* (New York: New Press, 1999), misportrays *Quadrant* as a journal of the "Non-Communist Left" (215).
38. James McAuley, "Australia's Future in New Guinea," *Pacific Affairs* 26, 1 (March 1953): 63-64. Urging an end to "social discrimination on grounds of race," McAuley also predicted a "one-way assimilation of native life to Western culture" in which "indigenous traditional cultures... seem bound to be more or less completely effaced" (67, 69). See also Pybus, *The Devil and James McAuley*, 115, 119-22, 183-84.
39. According to former CIA agent John Stockwell, the Agency estimated the death toll in the massacres of Indonesian Communist Party (PKI) members at 800,000 (*Harpers*, September 1984, 42). A CIA report added that "in terms of the numbers killed the anti-PKI massacres in Indonesia rank as one of the worst mass murders of the 20th century, along with the Soviet purges of the 1930s, the Nazi mass murders during the Second World War and the Maoist bloodbaths of the 1950s" (Central Intelligence Agency, Directorate of Intelligence, *Intelligence report: Indonesia-1965, The Coup that Backfired*, Langley, 1968).
40. James McAuley, "Three kinds of trouble," *Quadrant* 40, X: 2 (March-April 1966), 3-15, quoted in R. Tanter, "Witness Denied: the Australian Response to the Indonesian Holocaust, 1965-66," in Peter Van Ness, ed., *Redressing History*, forthcoming.
*   Cassandra Pybus, *The Devil and James McAuley* (St. Lucia: University of Queensland Press, 1999): 193, and "Quadrant Magazine and CIA Largesse," *Overland* 155, 1999, quoting a letter to McAuley from *Quadrant*'s founder Richard Krygier, who added: "I intend to ignore all of this." Krygier to McAuley, 27 October 1963, box 4, AACF (Australian Association for Cultural Freedom) papers, National Library of Australia.

In 1968 Professor Heinz Arndt, a former refugee from Hitler now at the Australian National University and later to become co-editor of *Quadrant*, wrote that "there is still much exercise of arbitrary power by civil and military officials, especially outside Djakarta, acts of oppression, even persecution of actual or suspected enemies of the new regime. But most of this reflects, not the will of the Suharto Government, but its inability or reluctance to assert its will.... The Suharto Government is genuinely and desperately anxious not to be thought undemocratic, militaristic, dictatorial. It wants to educate and persuade, not to ride roughshod over anyone.... Indonesia now has a very much more moderate, more rational, more pragmatic leadership than for many years..."[41]

Kissinger and Timor

As in Vietnam, Australian anti-communists looked to the United States for foreign policy leadership. Washington supported Suharto's destruction of Indonesia's communists, which *Time* hailed as "the West's best news for years in Asia."[42] A decade later, the U.S. was more discreet in backing Jakarta's invasion of East Timor. President Ford and Secretary of State Kissinger paid a visit to Suharto on 6 December 1975, and approved the Indonesian invasion he launched the next day.[43] When Suharto requested "understanding," Ford replied: "We will understand and will not press you on the issue." Kissinger then added: "You appreciate that the use of US-made arms could create problems.... It depends on how we construe it; whether it is in self-defense or is a foreign operation. It is important that whatever you do succeeds quickly. We would be able to influence the reaction in America if whatever happens happens after we return. This way there would be less chance of people talking in an unauthorized way.... If you have made plans, we will do our best to keep everyone quiet until the President returns home."[*]

41. H.W. Arndt, "A Comment", *Australian Outlook* 22, 1 (April 1968): 92-95. Arndt joined *Quadrant*'s editorial board in 1978 and was its co-editor from 1981 to 1983. On his early life and career, see his "Uncle Leo," *Quadrant*, Jan.-Feb. 1981, 29-30, and Peter Drake and Ross Garnaut, "H.W. Arndt: distinguished fellow," *Economic Record*, March 1995, v. 71, n. 212.
42. R. Kerson, "The Embassy's Hit List," *Columbia Journalism Review* 29 (November-December 1990): 9-14; *Time*, 15 July 1966, 26.
43. Taylor, *East Timor: The Price of Freedom*, 64, says the State Department dubbed the visit "the big wink"; C. Pinto, A. Nairn, "Ask Kissinger About East Timor" (www.etan.org/news/kissinger/ask.htm).
*   Text of Ford-Kissinger-Suharto discussion, US Embassy Jakarta Telegram 1579 to Secretary State, 6 December 1975, in *East Timor Revisited: Ford, Kissinger and the Indonesian Invasion, 1975-76*, National Security Archive Electronic Briefing Book No. 62, William Burr and Michael L. Evans, eds., December 6, 2001 (www.gwu.edu/~nsarchiv/NSAEBB/NSAEBB62).

But back in Washington on December 18, Kissinger saw a State Department cable describing Indonesia's use of U.S. arms in East Timor as violating the terms of their supply, requiring an end to deliveries. He scolded his aides: "I thought we had a disciplined group; now we've gone to pieces completely. Take this cable on East Timor.... I would not have approved it. The only consequence is to put yourself on record." He feared the cable might leak. "I had told you to stop it quietly." There was no need to record a token order. "I said do it for a few weeks and then open up again." Assistant Secretary of State Philip Habib was more confident: "The cable will not leak." Kissinger retorted: "Yes it will and it will go to Congress too and then we will have hearings on it." Habib replied: "I was away. I was told by cable that it had come up." This dismayed Kissinger: "That means there are two cables. And that means twenty guys have seen it." He warned: "It will have a devastating impact on Indonesia. There's this masochism in the extreme here. No one has complained that it was aggression... And we can't construe a Communist government in the middle of Indonesia as self-defense?..."** When his legal advisor asked: "What do we say to Congress if we're asked?," Kissinger replied: "We cut it off while we are studying it. We intend to start again in January."[44] There was thus no effective interruption of U.S. arms supplies to Indonesia.

Cover-Up Down Under

Australian diplomats in Indonesia admired Kissinger's approach. A few weeks later, on January 5, 1976, Canberra's ambassador to Jakarta, Richard Woolcott, cabled home recommending "Kissingerian realism."[45] Like Woolcott and former Prime Minister Gough Whitlam, Bernard Callinan and Bob Santamaria now became spokespersons for Indonesia's incorporation of East

---

**   Kissinger feared that the cable "will leak in three months and it will come out that Kissinger overruled his pristine bureaucrats and violated the law.... You have a responsibility to recognize that we are living in a revolutionary situation. Everything on paper will be used against me.... [T]o put it into a cable 30 hours before I return, knowing how cables are handled in this building, guarantees that it will be a national disaster." Kissinger asked: "Am I wrong in assuming that the Indonesians will go up in smoke if they hear about this?... I know what the law is but how can it be in the US national interest for us to... kick the Indonesians in the teeth." Memorandum of Conversation, December 18, 1975, Washington, D.C., "Subject: Departmental Policy."

44.   Memorandum of Conversation, December 18, 1975, Washington, D.C., "Subject: Departmental Policy." Participants: "The Secretary" (Kissinger), Robert Ingersoll, Joseph Sisco, Carlyle Maw, Lawrence Eagleburger, Philip Habib, Monroe Leigh, Jerry Bremer. See www.etan.org/news/kissinger/secret.htm

45.   Wendy Way, ed., *Australia and the Indonesian Incorporation of Portuguese Timor, 1974-1976* (Melbourne: Department of Foreign Affairs and Trade/Melbourne University Press, 2000): 657. This cable was leaked to the *Canberra Times*, 16 January 1976; Tiffen, *Diplomatic Deceits*, 12.

Timor.[46] Callinan gave priority to regional political interests. He said that "to talk of Indonesia withdrawing is not only unreal, it can also only cause unnecessary friction between Australia and its nearest neighbour."[47]

Santamaria, according to Patrick Walsh, "actively and continually maintained a public defence of Jakarta over its East Timor actions."[48] *News Weekly* and *Quadrant* took similar stances. Rather than criticize Indonesia, *News Weekly* assailed its opponents. The Fretilin resistance, the magazine stated, was guilty of "mass executions," including "horrors like the beheading of babies and small children."[49] Santamaria and *News Weekly* falsely alleged that James Dunn, former Australian consul in East Timor, was "a committed supporter of Fretilin," leading a "Campaign against Indonesia," and that Australian Jesuit Fr. Mark Raper belonged to "the vanguard of Marxism."[50] Walsh described Santamaria's approach:

> A report from Indonesian Church sources compiled in late 1976 painted a black picture of 60,000 to 100,000 deaths [in East Timor], widespread opposition to Indonesia and widespread support of Fretilin. Clearly there was a need to keep the source of the document confidential – such information from Church sources in Jakarta was in direct contradiction to everything Jakarta was saying about Timor. Mr. Santamaria's "Point of View" article (9.2.77) claimed that the source of the report "has never been identified" (true) but then falsely claims, "nobody knows who produced" the reports (false). The reason the source had to remain confidential was obvious -- but Santamaria used this to discredit the information.[51]

---

46. Noone, "Santamaria, War and Christianity," 125.
47. Callinan, *Age*, 19 August 1977, quoted in Walsh, "Australia's Support," 19. Walsh describes Callinan as "a prominent businessman, a commissioner for the A.B.C. [Australian Broadcasting Commission] and the Victorian State Electricity Commission and a member of the Vatican's Pontifical Commission for Justice and Peace." Freney adds that Callinan was a director of British Petroleum (Australia) and a "top" official of the Democratic Labor Party ("East Timor: The Modest Revolution," 8).
48. Walsh, "Australia's Support," 14-16, naming also Heinz Arndt and Gough Whitlam.
49. Walsh says these accusations, relating to Fretilin's August 1975 takeover, were "discredited by Australian journalists" ("Australia's Support," 15). On Fretilin atrocities after Indonesia's invasion, see Ball and McDonald, *Death in Balibo*, 175 (cf. Dunn, *Timor: A People Betrayed*, 283); Sarah Niner, "A Long Journey of Resistance," in R. Tanter, M. Selden, and S. R. Shalom, eds., *Bitter Flowers, Sweet Flowers: East Timor, Indonesia, and the World Community* (Lanham, Md: Rowman & Littlefield, 2001), 19.
50. *News Weekly*, 2 March 1977, and 17 December 1975, 13; editorial, 5 November 1975; Santamaria, "Point of View", 9 February 1977, quoted in Walsh, "Australia's Support," 14-15. Fr. Mark Raper became International Director of the Jesuit Refugee Service, Rome, from 1990 to 2000.
51. Walsh, "Australia's Support," 15, quoting Santamaria, "Point of View", 9 February 1977.

Two months later, Indonesian Foreign Minister Adam Malik conceded that "50,000 people or perhaps 80,000 might have been killed during the war in Timor, but we saved 600,000 of them."[52]

Australians followed three imperatives to cover up genocide in East Timor. First, as he had during World War Two, Santamaria devoted his energies to opposing communism. He warned that "a government dominated by the Fretilin would extend the tentacles of Communist subversion to Australia's doorstep." An independent East Timor would be "open to Red Chinese or Russian influence, [and] could easily become a base of subversion."[53] It would sooner or later be "influencing all these repressed and discontented elements" in other parts of Suharto's Indonesia.[54] As in Vietnam, the potential for communist subversion, rather than outright invasion, was the real threat. In this worldview, a critic commented, "even the Catholics of East Timor had to lose their rights,"[55] and Indonesian Church sources had to be ignored. The Indonesian voice Santamaria heeded belonged to what he called "the most influential foreign policy-making body associated with the Indonesian Government": the Centre for Strategic and International Studies headed by Harry Tjan Silalahi and Jusuf Wanandi, who had helped plan the first Indonesian operations against Timor from 1974.[56]

For slightly different reasons than those propounded by former Prime Ministers Gough Whitlam, Malcolm Fraser, Bob Hawke and Paul Keating, Santamaria effectively supported the official view that close relations with anti-communist Indonesia were crucial to Australia's security.[57] Canberra would not risk antagonizing a populous, militarized neighbor, even if its regime was committing mass

52. Melbourne *Age*, 1 April 1977. See Noam Chomsky and Edward Herman, *The Political Economy of Human Rights*, vol. 1, *The Washington Connection and Third World Fascism* (Boston: South End, 1979): 175-76.

53. *News Weekly*, 12 December 1975, 13, and 28 January 1976, 14, quoted in Walsh, "Australia's Support," 16.

54. On West Papua, an example given by *News Weekly*, see Robin Osborne, *Indonesia's Secret War: The Guerrilla Struggle in Irian Jaya* (Sydney: Allen and Unwin, 1985).

55. James Griffin, in Ormonde, *Santamaria*, 28.

56. Santamaria, *Australian*, 9 September 1977, quoted in Walsh, "Australia's Support," 16, citing Hamish McDonald, *Suharto's Indonesia*, ch. 9, on Harry Tjan Silalahi (Harry Tjan Tjoen Hok) and Jusuf Wanandi (Lim Bian Kie); also Paul Monk, "Secret Intelligence and Escape Clauses: Australia and the Indonesian Annexation of East Timor, 1963-76," *Critical Asian Studies* 33, 2 (June 2001): 189-91, 194-97.

57. Walsh, "Australia's Support," 16, quotes Santamaria fearing "a severe rift with our closest neighbour and ally, Indonesia." On government policy, see Way, *Australia and the Indonesian Incorporation of Portuguese Timor*. Monk, "Secret Intelligence," shows that official Australia's preference for Timor's incorporation into Indonesia goes back long before Whitlam's 1972-75 government, to 1963 (pp. 193, 206), when Whitlam, in opposition, had supported East Timorese independence (Walsh, 2, citing *The First Thousand Days of Labor*, vol. 1, 339). On Australian business support for Indonesia's takeover: Walsh, 17, and *Retrieval*, no. 29 (Feb.-March 1976): 6-8. For my views of Australian policy on Timor and Cambodia, "Two Rules on Kampuchea," *Sydney Morning Herald*, 13 August 1985, 13 (chapter 11, below).

murder. Whitlam and Australian officials and diplomats rejected the argument that Australia should not support violations of international law like the invasion of East Timor.[58] If Whitlam was moved by *realpolitik*, for Santamaria the key was anti-communism. The combination was persuasive in upholding the policy, but the *realpolitik* proved illusory: like Indonesian control, Australian policy eventually proved ineffective, and both collapsed in 1999.

A third factor was the view of Santamaria and others that Australia's domestic "left" could not be allowed to go unchallenged, whatever the truth of its case for East Timor. Credible policy criticisms were the most dangerous: silence or acknowledgement of the truth would yield domestic political ground to the left. Given such priorities, the very indefensibility of a policy ensured that it would be defended. Like many international ideologues, Santamaria's priority was not to address problems facing East Timor, but to combat "communist" influence at home. One commentator remarked that conservative motivations in defending Indonesia "are generally more connected with ideological struggles that are going on in Australia, and within particular Australian institutions."[59]

For these purposes, then, the genocide had to be hidden from view, a tactic the U.S. pursued and one that Canberra aimed to follow. As Kissinger left office, other U.S. politicians stepped forward to cover up what was happening in East Timor. The Australian conservative attacks on James Dunn were echoed in the U.S. Congress in 1977. Republican Congressman Herbert Burke lambasted Dunn and asserted that "it is in all our interests to bury the Timor issue quickly and completely."[60] The State Department's 1977 Human Rights Report did not mention East Timor, and that year the *New York Times* gave zero coverage to events there, while tens of thousands perished.[61]

In Australia, it was far more difficult to hide events so close at hand. There, by contrast, press coverage was extensive. Domestic public outrage made Timor policy an embarrassment to the government. Anti-communists struck back with excess, ranging from denunciation to denial. In *Quadrant* in May 1976, Heinz Arndt blamed "the left" as "part of the explanation" for the press and public turning against Indonesia. He wrote: "At no stage has there been any assertion by Indonesia of irredentist claims on East Timor," adding that

58. See for instance, Richard Woolcott, "Myths and Realities in Our Approach to Indonesia," *The Sydney Papers*, Winter 1992, 81-91. Woolcott was Australian ambassador to Indonesia in 1975-76. On Whitlam and Woolcott's positions, see Monk, "Secret Intelligence."
59. Brian Brunton, "Australia's Indonesia Lobby Observed," *Inside Indonesia*, no. 11 (August 1987): 23-24. "The real danger of the struggle within Indonesia, as it was in Vietnam, to conservative Australia, is not the domino effect ... The real danger lies in the possible spillover into Australian politics of nationalist sentiment that would move Australia out of the ANZUS alliance."
60. Letter to the *Far Eastern Economic Review*, 11 November 1977. See Chomsky and Herman, 152.
61. Chomsky and Herman, 200, 151.

"President Suharto's deference to foreign (and not least Australian Government) pressure to abstain from the use of force may have been a mistake."[62] Arndt joined *Quadrant*'s editorial board in 1978. The next year, at the height of the tragedy, he published another article, "Timor: Vendetta Against Indonesia." Decrying the "unrestrained abuse and wild charges" made against Jakarta, Arndt denounced its critics as "radical ideologues, aggrieved journalists, emotional priests and Wilsonian idealists." But events in Timor had already vindicated such diverse critics, especially James Dunn, whom Arndt considered "motivated and grossly inaccurate."[63] Just the previous month, Indonesia's new Foreign Minister Mochtar Kusumaatmadja had estimated that 120,000 Timorese had died since 1975.[*] The admission did not threaten Canberra's support for Jakarta, but *Quadrant*, like *News Weekly*, facilitated the government's defense of its policy against strong public protest.

Still Suharto's forces could not destroy Fretilin, which they termed "gangs of security disruptors" (GPK).[64] Indonesian commanders aimed "to obliterate the classic GPK areas" and "crush the GPK remnants to their roots."[65] News of the continuing death toll in East Timor grew, along with Australian public concern. Anti-communist denial became more strident, and the domestic left was still blamed for publicizing the facts. But it was also more difficult to hold this line, and in 1983-84 a voice of dissent was heard. *Quadrant*'s new foreign policy columnist, former Labor senator John Wheeldon, called Jakarta's takeover of East Timor "an act of patently unjustified aggression" without "anything resembling a *bona fide* act of self-determination."[66] He was responding to a *Quadrant* cover story which had questioned the charge of Indonesian "aggression," and asserted that "there is now no hope that East Timor will become an independent sovereign state." The article's authors called for a negotiated peace, an end to Fretilin resistance, and admission of more refugees into Australia. These authors also chastised critics of Jakarta for "virulence" and "intemperate denunciation," adding: "Those who maintain the pretence that independence for

---

62. H.W. Arndt, "Timor: Expediency or Principle," *Quadrant* 106, XX: 5 (May 1976), 17, 19.
63. H.W. Arndt, "Timor: Vendetta Against Indonesia," *Quadrant*, December 1979, 16-17. Following Santamaria, Arndt denounced dissident "Catholic priests with radical-left leanings," and one "young Jesuit priest with radical leanings" (13, 16-17).
* Taylor, *East Timor*, 203. If Mochtar's November 1979 statement came too late for Arndt's December article, Arndt again omitted it (and Adam Malik's 1977 estimate) in re-publishing much of the same material twenty years later. H.W. Arndt, "Remembering the Past to Secure the Future," *Australian Financial Review*, 23 April 1999, 8-9.
64. Indonesian internal documents, translated in Carmel Budiardjo and Liem Soei Liong, *The War Against East Timor* (London: Zed, 1984): 82.
65. Budiardjo and Liong, *The War Against East Timor*, 182, 215, 222, 227, 194-96, 216, 242, 193.
66. John Wheeldon, "East Timor," *Quadrant*, May 1983, 61-62, and September 1984, 24-25.

East Timor is still a possibility have in the result hampered efforts to assist the East Timorese."[67] When Wheeldon responded, Heinz Arndt asserted: "Evidence of breaches of human rights by the Indonesians in East Timor is confined to highly suspect reports…"[68] *Quadrant*'s media columnist, Anthony McAdam, praising Singapore and Malaysia as "genuine democracies," lauded Suharto's Indonesia as "relatively pluralistic."[69]

Quadrant's continuing support for Jakarta reinforced official policy. John Howard, who became leader of the conservative Opposition in Canberra in 1985, complained that "the preoccupation of the left of Australian politics with East Timor has needlessly soured our relations with Indonesia."[70] Arndt asserted that Indonesia's claim to East Timor was "exactly on a par" with China's claim to Hong Kong, yet Jakarta was receiving a "flood of abuse" motivated by "Left-wing hostility" and "racist arrogance."[71] A *Quadrant* editorial compared leftist critics of Arndt and fellow members of the "Indonesia Lobby" to "fanatical anti-semites."[72] In 1995, the magazine's columnist Peter Ryan rejoined the attack on "these left-wing lunatics": "The Timor claque increasingly resemble the English prigs of the left in the 1930s…. Timor is unfortunate, and when President Suharto shuts down a newspaper it does not make me happy. But it probably makes the ordinary people of Indonesia very happy indeed that he is steadily improving their living standards."[73]

Arndt again excoriated "the fanatical East Timor lobby," for "its perennial campaign of propaganda and disinformation against Indonesia." He asked why have "sections of the Australian Press and public objected so violently to the incorporation of East Timor into Indonesia?" Arndt had posed this same question in 1976, finding leftist influence to be "part of the explanation." By 1995, it had become "the chief explanation."[74] The right-wing response was

---

67. John Traill and Kenneth Rivett, "A Bid for Peace in East Timor," *Quadrant*, April 1983, 9-15. See also Walsh, "Australia's Support," 22-23.

68. Heinz Arndt, "'Finlandising' Australia," *Quadrant*, October 1984, 3.

69. Anthony McAdam, "Innocence abroad is a grave menace," Melbourne *Herald*, 18 November 1983. To McAdam, the Philippines under Marcos was also "relatively pluralistic." Equally pluralistic, McAdam described himself in one journal as a "socialist," in another as a "liberal," and in *Quadrant* as "a self-confessed [*sic*] conservative." *Nation Review* (25 January 1979), *The Age "Green Guide"* (11 June 1981), and *Quadrant*, August 1983.

70. Quoted in Tiffen, *Diplomatic Deceits*, 77.

71. H.W. Arndt, "The Jenkins Affair," *Quadrant*, June 1986, 75.

72. "The Indonesian Lobby," *Quadrant*, March 1987, p. 6. See also Brunton, "Australia's Indonesia Lobby Observed," 23, and Scott Burchill, "The Jakarta Lobby -- Mea Culpa?", *Age*, 4 March 1999.

73. Peter Ryan, "Indonesia and Me," *Quadrant*, July-August 1995, 120.

74. Heinz Arndt, "Portugal's litigation just an excuse for propaganda," *Canberra Times*, February 10, 1995 (www.dfa-deplu.go.id/english/arndt.htm). Arndt had posed this question in *Quadrant* twenty years earlier (May 1976, p. 17). Now, "the chief explanation is that support for an independent East Timor came from the beginning from the left of the political spectrum."

defensive. A *Quadrant* contributor who, like Santamaria, had defended the repressive Diem regime in South Vietnam, went so far as to assert that "even in human rights there is a case for Suharto,* who was merely "a monster of the Left's imagination."[75] After Howard was elected Prime Minister in 1996, his Deputy PM, Tim Fischer, eulogized Suharto as "the man of the second half of the century."[76]

As late as 1995 Arndt claimed that "there is little evidence that the majority of East Timorese want independence…. The majority who have benefited greatly from very large Indonesian expenditure on roads and other infrastructure and on health and education, so long neglected by the Portuguese, are by all disinterested accounts not dissatisfied."[77] Just four years later, however, 79 percent of the Timorese would vote for independence in the August 1999 UN-organized referendum.

As the referendum approached, Indonesian officers and Timorese militia commanders met on 16 February, 1999. Indonesian Lieutenant-Colonel Yahyat Sudrajad called for the killing of pro-independence movement leaders, their children and even their grandchildren. "Not a single member of their families was to be left alive, the colonel told the meeting," after receiving orders from senior Indonesian military commanders.[78] Militia killings commenced the next day. Survivors sought refuge in churches and priests' homes. On March 26, the Indonesian-appointed governor of East Timor, Abilio Soares, gave orders

---

*   Greg Sheridan, *Australian*, 20 May 1998, quoted in Burchill, "The Jakarta Lobby". Sheridan had praised Ngo Dinh Diem as "a man of great personal rectitude" and, with the Philippines' Marcos, "a genuine nationalist." Sheridan mused: "It is one of the most ghostly ifs of history: What if the Americans had supported President Diem?" (*Australian*, 4-5 October 1986). The *Pentagon Papers* term Diem's South Vietnam "essentially the creation of the United States", which according to CIA chief Edward Lansdale helped "to promote a fascist state" there. The US Secretary of Defense accused Diem in 1963 of "large-scale oppressions" but ruled out withdrawal of the 15,000 US troops supporting him. George Kahin, *Intervention* (New York: Knopf, 1986): 96, 170-71.

75.   Greg Sheridan, "No Dili dallying", *Australian Review of Books*, Vol. 5, Issue 11, December 2000; see Scott Burchill, "Australian and Asia: Between arrogance and deference," keynote address at the Asia Link Seminar Series in association with Radio Australia, Melbourne, 14 March 2001.

76.   Tiffen, *Diplomatic Deceits*, 77; Burchill, "The Jakarta Lobby".

77.   H. Arndt, "Portugal's litigation just an excuse for propaganda," *Canberra Times*, 10 February 1995.

78.   Annemarie Evans, "Revealed: the plot to crush Timor," *South China Morning Post*, September 16, 1999, quoting Tomas Goncalves, 54, former head of the PPPI militia. Andrew Fowler later reported that in early 1999, Indonesian military and militia commanders threatened to "liquidate… all the pro-independence people, parents, sons, daughters, and grandchildren." "The Ties that Bind," Australian Broadcasting Corporation, February 14, 2000, quoted in Noam Chomsky, *A New Generation Draws the Line: East Timor, Kosovo, and the Standards of the West* (London: Verso, 2000): 72.

"that the priests and nuns should be killed."[79] In Australia, Heinz Arndt again denounced charges of genocide as anti-Indonesian "propaganda."[80] In Dili, Indonesia's military commander Tono Suratman warned that "if the pro-independents do win... all will be destroyed."[81] In May 1999, an Indonesian army document ordered that "massacres should be carried out from village to village after the announcement of the ballot if the pro-independence supporters win." The East Timorese independence movement "should be eliminated from its leadership down to its roots." The forced deportation of hundreds of thousands was also planned.[82] It was implemented after the vote when Indonesian-sponsored militias went on a rampage, killing over a thousand people and destroying up to 80 percent of the territory's houses.[83] Australian public opinion, which had long favored independence for East Timor, even "if a left-wing group gains control there,"[84] finally forced the abandonment of Canberra's policy.

Western appeasement of Indonesia since 1975, including over $1 billion in military supplies from the U.S., Britain, and Australia, had enabled the initial Timor tragedy to be repeated.[85] Even now Douglas Paal, President of the U.S. Asia Pacific Policy Center, told the *Washington Post* that "Timor is a speed bump on the road to dealing with Jakarta, and we've got to get over it safely."[86] It was not this view, however, that Heinz Arndt decried in criticizing "the one-sidedness of Western opinion, which focused on the hostilities but overlooked the major effort which the Indonesian government was devoting to improving the economic and social infrastructure of the territory."[87] In 2001, the UN organized

79. Evans, "Revealed: the plot to crush Timor," *South China Morning Post*, September 16, 1999, again quoting Tomas Goncalves, a witness to Governor Soares' statement.
80. H.W. Arndt, "Remembering the Past to Secure the Future," *Australian Financial Review*, 23 April 1999, 8-9.
81. Brian Toohey, "Dangers of Timorese Whispers Capital Idea," *Australian Financial Review*, 14 August 1999; John Aglionby, et al., "Revealed: army's plot," *Observer*, 12 September 1999; other sources quoted in Chomsky, *A New Generation Draws the Line*, 72-76, and Tanter, *et al.*, *Bitter Flowers*, 141.
82. Chomsky, *A New Generation*, p. 74.
83. See James Dunn, *Crimes Against Humanity in East Timor, January to October 1999: Their Nature and Causes*, report to the United Nations, 14 February 2001 (www.etan.org/news/2001a/dunn1.htm), 15-16.
84. Walsh, "Australia's Support," 24, poll published in the *Bulletin*, "Portuguese Timor Should be Free," 25 October 1975, 29.
85. See Budiardjo and Liong, *The War Against East Timor*, 8-11; Taylor, *East Timor*, 84, 133-34, 174-75, 203; Ball and McDonald, *Death in Balibo*, 182; Tanter, *Bitter Flowers*, 135-36, 163-72.
86. *Washington Post*, 9 September 1999, quoted in Chomsky, *A New Generation Draws the Line*, 77.
87. H.W. Arndt, "Goa and East Timor: Contrasting Histories," *Quadrant*, July-August 2001, 26-28. Arndt also suggested that a Nobel Peace Prize should have been awarded to Indonesia's Foreign Minister rather than to East Timor's Jose Ramos Horta (*Australian Financial Review*, 23 April 1999, 9).

the territory's first free election. Fretilin won 57 percent of the vote, close to the 55 percent it had received in village-level elections before the invasion. In the interim, 100,000-200,000 Timorese had died.[88]

The Australian Aborigines

The Australian cover-up of the mass murder in East Timor in the service of anti-communism and misguided *realpolitik* echoes in ongoing denial of the genocide of Australian Aborigines. While the latter springs in part from conflict over material resources on Aboriginal land, it shares the common feature of demonization of the domestic "left."

Australian politicians of the two-party conservative coalition were not unanimous in support of Jakarta. Liberal parliamentarians Alan Missen and Michael Hodgman criticized Indonesia's invasion, as did Australia's first Aboriginal Senator, Neville Bonner, also a Liberal, who had visited East Timor.[89] But support for both East Timor and Aboriginal rights was more widespread among independent religious organizations, the ALP, and the unions, especially on the left.

The Aboriginal rights issue emerged slowly against a backdrop of genocide. The Aboriginal population of Australia at the time of British settlement in 1788 is estimated to have been roughly 750,000. It fell to possibly 31,000 by 1911, with up to 600,000 deaths following the initial British arrival,[90] mostly from new diseases like smallpox.[91] Historian Henry Reynolds plausibly estimates that approximately 20,000 more blacks were killed resisting the white occupation of Australia between 1788 and 1901.[92] Then in the twentieth century,

88. See Tanter, *Bitter Flowers*, 260; Tiffen, *Diplomatic Deceits*, 30; Robert Cribb, "How Many Deaths? Problems in the Statistics of Massacre in Indonesia (1965-66) and East Timor (1975-80)," in I. Wessel and G. Wimhofer, eds., *Violence in Indonesia* (Hamburg, Abera Verlag, 2001), 82-98.
89. Dunn, *Timor: A People Betrayed*, 199, 203, 262, 383.
90. The 750,000 figure is that of anthropologist Dr. Peter White and pre-historian Prof. D.J. Mulvaney, quoted in *Sydney Morning Herald*, February 25, 1987. See also Noel Butlin, *Our Original Aggression: Aboriginal Populations of Southeastern Australia, 1788-1850* (Sydney: Allen and Unwin, 1983): xi, 37, 91, 119ff., 143, 175. The 1911 figure is from Colin Tatz, *Genocide in Australia* (Canberra: AIATSIS, 1999): 9. The 1921 census produced a figure of 62,000. C.D. Rowley, *The Destruction of Aboriginal Society* (Ringwood: Penguin, 1972): 382.
91. Butlin, *Our Original Aggression*, 17ff., and Judy Campbell ("Smallpox in Aboriginal Australia," *Historical Studies*, 21, no. 84 [April 1985]: 336-58) differ on whether British introduced the smallpox. See also John Goldsmid, *The Deadly Legacy* (Sydney: University of New South Wales Press, 1988).
92. Henry Reynolds, *The Other Side of the Frontier: Aboriginal Resistance to the European Invasion of Australia* (Ringwood: Penguin, 1982): 122-23, 200, 121 (estimating the white death toll at 2000-2500); also Richard Broome, "The Struggle for Australia: Aboriginal-European Warfare, 1770-1930," in M. McKernan *et al.*, eds., *Australia: Two Centuries of War and Peace* (Sydney: Allen & Unwin, 1998): 116-20.

Australian governments took thousands of "half-caste" children from their mothers, to "breed out the colour."[93] From 1910 to 1970, possibly 10 percent of Aboriginal children were separated from their families.[94] Queensland's chief protector of native affairs from 1913 to 1942 aimed to "preserve the purity of the white race from the grave social dangers that always threaten where there is a degraded race living in loose condition at its back door."[95] The Northern Territory's chief protector from 1927 to 1939 advocated eugenics, arguing that by the sixth generation, "all native characteristics of the Australian Aborigines are eradicated. The problem of our half-castes will quickly be eliminated by the complete disappearance of the black race."[96] At a 1937 Canberra conference of Australian officials responsible for Aboriginal affairs, Western Australia's chief protector, A. O. Neville, explained his view to a reporter, who wrote "that within one hundred years the pure black will be extinct. But the half caste problem was increasing.... Therefore their idea was to keep the pure blacks segregated and absorb the half-castes into the white population.... The pure black was not a quick breeder. On the other hand the half-caste was.... In order to secure the complete segregation of the children...[at age two] they were taken from their mothers and reared in accordance with white ideas."[97] Neville asked the conference: "Are we going to have a population of one million blacks...or are we going to merge them into our white community and eventually forget that there were any Aborigines in Australia?"[98]

As with East Timor, the Aboriginal rights cause attracted early support from the left, and some from the right. From 1931 the Communist Party of Australia denounced the "mass physical extermination" to which Aborigines had been subjected, and called for "absolute prohibition of the kidnapping of Aboriginal children."[99] Leftists supported the Aboriginal Day of Mourning and Protest in 1938, the *Catholic Worker* took up Aboriginal causes in 1942, and a human

---

93. Robert Manne, *In Denial: The Stolen Generations and the Right*, in *The Australian Quarterly Essay*, 1, 1, 2001, 64-65, citing Australian Archives, Canberra, AA ACT A659/1 40/1/408. See also 38-40.
94. Manne, 35, 60.
95. *Bringing Them Home*, 73 (W. Bleakley), quoted in Raimond Gaita, "Genocide and Pedantry," *Quadrant*, 338, v. 41, nos. 7-8, July-August 1997, 43.
96. Cecil Cook, quoted in Raimond Gaita, *A Common Humanity* (Melbourne: Text, 1999): 122-23; Manne, 64-65.
97. *Bringing Them Home*, 30, quoted in Manne, 39.
98. Manne, 40, quoting *Aboriginal Welfare: Initial Conference of Commonwealth and State Aboriginal Authorities* (Canberra, 1937): 11.
99. The CPA's 1931 policy stated: "no struggle of the white workers must be permitted without demands for the aborigines being championed." Macintyre, *The Reds*, 265-67 (also 126, 130, 353). The policy was the first on Aboriginal rights to be adopted by a major Australian political party. The first novel with an Aboriginal woman as the major character was *Coonardoo* (1928), by Australian communist Katherine Susannah Pritchard. See F.S. Stevens, ed., *Racism, The Australian Experience*, vol. 2, *Black Versus White* (Sydney: ANZ Books, 1972), ch. 3.

rights movement emerged in 1946. The next year Santamaria's *News Weekly* decried the mistreatment of Aborigines and suggested they be taught agriculture.[100] Removals of Aboriginal children continued. Aborigines gained the right to vote in Australian federal elections only in 1963.[101]

Santamaria and other conservatives, initially not hostile to Aborigines, hardened their stance after the issue became restitution rather than citizenship. Many outback Aborigines began to fight for land rights to gain economic autonomy and compensation for their dispossession. The cause slowly gathered support. Santamaria began to oppose Aboriginal land rights activists, whether radicals or religious conservatives.[102] As substantial uranium deposits were discovered on Aboriginal lands, pastoral and mining company lobbyists opposed land rights, and *Quadrant* authors joined the fray. While many of the Aboriginal movement's leading figures were politically independent, anti-communists often neglected and increasingly opposed Aboriginal causes, while communists, leftists and many liberals were supportive.

The Land Rights Movement

In 1961 Brian Manning, two Aboriginal brothers, Dexter and David Daniels, and twenty-two other Aborigines founded the Northern Territory Council for Aboriginal Rights. They aimed to prod trade union organizations to improve Aboriginal wages.[103] In 1963, thirteen tribes sent the Australian Parliament a bark petition protesting the "secret" excision from their reserve, for the Nabalco bauxite mining company, of 140 square miles of "hunting and food gathering land for the Yirrkala tribes from time immemorial; we were all born here." They feared "the fate which has overtaken the Larrakeah tribe."[104]

At Daguragu (Wattie Creek), also in the Northern Territory, Aboriginal stockmen received a weekly wage of only A$6.32. In mid-1966 a hundred Gurindji stockmen demanded wage parity and went on strike against the world's largest cattle station, the Wave Hill Pastoral Company, owned by Lord Vestey.[105] With

---

100. Duncan, *Crusade or Conspiracy?*, 48, 89; Don Watson, *Brian Fitzpatrick* (Sydney: Hale & Iremonger, 1979): 202-3.

101. C.D. Rowley and Henry Reynolds, "Aborigines Since 1788," *The Australian Encyclopedia* (Terrey Hills, NSW: Australian Geographic Society, 1988): 284.

102. Val Noone, "Reading Santamaria Backwards," *Arena*, 34 (April-May 1998), 23-25.

103. Manning, personal communication, 4 June and 12 July 2001; Aborigines joined "from all over the place."

104. "Petition of the Yirrkala People," in Sharman Stone, ed., *Aborigines in White Australia* (Melbourne: Heinemann, 1974): 203; C. Jennett, "Aborigines, Land Rights and Mining," in E.L. Wheelwright and Ken Buckley, *Essays in the Political Economy of Australian Capitalism*, vol. 5 (Sydney: ANZ, 1983): 128ff.

105. "Gurindji Tribe," *Australian Encyclopedia*, 1482-83. In 2000 at the Wattie Creek commemoration, Manning said he was "proud to have been a part of the organization of the 1966 walk off." See also Ann McGrath and Kay Saunders, *Aboriginal Workers*, special issue of *Labour History* 69 (November 1995): 45.

Dexter Daniels, by then Aboriginal organizer for the North Australian Workers Union, Manning drove the first truckload of stores to Wattie Creek to support the Gurindji strikers' camp. His 1.5-ton truck, "loaded to the gunnels" with flour, sugar, tea, baking powder, rice, and tobacco, "shook to pieces over the rough roads."[106] The Gurindji re-occupied and claimed their traditional tribal lands. In 1970 the Waterside Workers' Federation imposed a $1 levy on all members, producing a $17,000 donation to enable the Gurindji to fence their land.[107] In 1972, Lord Vestey handed over ninety square kilometers, and soon sold another 3,250 to the government to be given to the Gurindji.[108] When he joined the Campaign for an Independent East Timor in 1974, Manning was working with the Larrakia people and their traditional elder, Bobby Secretary, who were claiming tribal land in Darwin.[109] His actions made connections between domestic and foreign concerns that others worked hard to obscure.[110]

Bob Santamaria and his anti-communist allies, by contrast, believed that Timorese independence, acknowledgement of Jakarta's crimes against humanity, recognition of the genocide of the Aborigines, or redress for their dispossession by granting land rights, would be first steps down a slippery slope of communist appeasement. Just as he denounced leftist and Jesuit supporters of the Timorese, Santamaria now campaigned against the Catholic Commission for Justice and Peace (CCJP) which took up the land rights cause. Among his targets was the Aboriginal priest Pat Dodson, who in 1980-81 headed a joint task force of the CCJP and the Australian Council of Churches on Aboriginal land rights education. Dodson left the priesthood in 1981 and later chaired the Council for Aboriginal Reconciliation.

Like its left-liberal counterpart *Meanjin*,[111] during its first decades *Quadrant* had run some thoughtful pieces on Aboriginal themes, including a critique of "the inability of Australians to come to terms with their genocidal past" in

---

106. For details, see Frank Hardy, *The Unlucky Australians* (Sydney: Pan, 1978, first edition 1968), 114-17, 282-87; Dennis Schulz, "Gurindji fight to do things their way," *Age*, 21 August 2000. Other Aboriginal groups and "white northern sympathisers" like Manning played a "decisive" role in support of the Gurindji (*The Australian Encyclopedia*, 285).
107. C. Jennett, "Australian Aborigines: Modern Politics," in James Jupp, ed., *The Australian People*, Sydney, Angus and Robertson, 1988, 229; Manning provided the donation amount.
108. In 1975, the Australian government purchased from Vestey 3,250 square kilometers, which was awarded to the Muramulla Gurindji Company. "Gurindji Tribe," *The Australian Encyclopedia*, 1482-83.
109. See William Bartlett Day, *Bunji: A Story of the Gwalwa Daraniki Movement* (Canberra: Aboriginal Studies Press, 1994).
110. See e.g. Val Noone, "Reading Santamaria Backwards," *Arena* 34 (April-May 1998): 25.
111. See Lynne Strahan, *Just City and the Mirrors: Meanjin Quarterly and the Intellectual Front, 1940-1965*, (London: Oxford University Press, 1984): 5-6, 76, 111, 121-22, cf. 42, 48-54.

which "settlers systematically destroyed the blacks."[112] But now the rise of the land rights movement met conservative opposition. Western Mining Company executive director Hugh Morgan campaigned against Aboriginal causes, especially after he became president of the Australian Mining Industry Council in 1981.[113] An anonymous *Quadrant* article accused "sections of the affluent middle class" of "a guilt complex about the Aborigines which at times assumes grotesque proportions." The author compared the Aboriginal tragedy "to that of unemployed youth, drug addicts, deserted wives and other groups of victims." Criticizing advocates of "cultural convergence," the author asked: "How does a platypus converge with a sheep dog?" As for land rights, "History, to have been there first, is a weak ethical basis for claims to possession.... Australia is today...what the descendants of white settlers have made it. It is they, not the Aborigines, who have established the more substantial claim to possession." Aborigines merely needed help to "rise from their present state of backwardness and misery."[114] When Bob Hawke's Labor government came to office in 1983 proposing uniform federal land rights legislation, *Quadrant* proclaimed Aboriginal lands "better suited than almost any others in the world for disposal of the nuclear waste materials which the world's ever growing nuclear power industry will generate."[115]

Quadrant contributor Elizabeth Durack (1915-2000) wrote: "Sad as it was for both mother and child, most, if not all Aboriginal women, were resigned to the idea of their half-caste children being taken from them.... Many came forward with them as babies or youngsters and tearfully presented them to the Mission or to the recruiting parties that went through the stations and out-back towns collecting pale-skinned infants and placing them either with white foster-parents or in Church orphanages. Aboriginal women were well aware of all this. That was why they *had* half-caste children. That was what they used, as opportunity arose, their bodies *for*."[116]

On the next page began Roger Scruton's argument against land rights. He described "the *Untergang* of the savage" as the "inevitable" result of "a weak culture confronted with a strong one," adding: "we shouldn't even contemplate undoing the supposedly illegitimate settlement." It "would have happened anywhere" – "when finite, mortal beings, imperfect beings given to evil, settle anywhere – they destroy as much as they build." Scruton asked, "Whom was the

112. Peter Kerr, *Quadrant*, 99, XIX: 7 (October 1975): 65; Les Murray, "The Coming Republic," April 1976, 37-42, and Kerr's rejoinder, July 1976, 4. For thoughtful early pieces, see A.P. Elkin (Spring 1957), R. Berndt (Summer 1960-61), J. Beckett (Spring 1958, July-August 1965), C.D. Rowley (Nov./Dec. 1967).
113. C. Jennett, "Aborigines, Land Rights, and Mining," 140.
114. Anon., "The Aboriginal Complex," *Quadrant* 165, XXV: 5 (May 1981): 66-67.
115. "An Aboriginal Industry for the 21st Century," *Quadrant* 194, XXVII: 10 (October 1983): 8.
116. Elizabeth Durack, "Land Wrongs," *Quadrant* 208, XXIX: 1-2 (January-February 1985): 75.

land taken from?, [and] what makes the Aborigines now alive, the true inheritors of the ones that are dead?... The only thing that the present Aborigines have in common, if anything, with those from whom the original land was taken – if it were taken – is their race." Restoring land to Aborigines "introduces an element of race hatred, at least in the more primitive white Australians."[117]

Quadrant columnist Anthony McAdam attacked John Pilger's 1985 film about Aboriginal suffering, *The Secret Country*. McAdam wrote that "terrible things were done to Aboriginal people...just as I believe terrible things were done to many whites." But he ridiculed "the now fashionable charge of 'genocide,'" and denounced "this exercise in national denigration" as an assault on "the nation's honour." He added: "Pilger's apparent use of the Aboriginal issue to play on 'white guilt' for political purposes other than the one at hand appears to be an increasingly fashionable stratagem."[118]

In a 1992 *Quadrant* article, Robert Murray denounced "inaccurate clichés that seem to be rapidly settling into the national consciousness," including "Myth 1: Aborigines." He posed "the big questions: Did we steal their land? And did our forebears commit "genocide" against them?" To the first question, Murray replied: "Governors and governments nearly always meant well towards the blacks, but at the crunch favoured the development of the country – meaning whites moving into black land.... Was the land stolen? It's a matter of which way you look at it, but we should avoid being glib..." Turning to the second issue, Murray wrote that "settlers in Australia shot many thousands of Aborigines, mainly as grossly overreactive self-defence.... The shooting of 20,000 Aborigines – or even twice that number, as is possible – in a population of half a million to one million over 100 years, is tragic and shameful. It decimated communities. But it hardly amounts to 'genocide'..."[119]

In 1990, *Quadrant* appointed a new editor, Robert Manne, an admirer of Bob Santamaria though no apologist for Jakarta. Meanwhile, with the end of

---

117. Roger Scruton, "Does Australia Belong to the Aborigines?," *Quadrant* 208, XXIX: 1-2 (Jan.-Feb. 1985): 76-78.

118. McAdam offered no examples here of the "terrible things" done to Aborigines; for whites, he cited Port Arthur convict prison. "The Watchman Rides Again," *Quadrant* 216, XXIX: 10 (October 1985): 66-68.

     McAdam later became corporate affairs manager for Philip Morris (*Age*, 11 June 1988). Roger Scruton earned a monthly retainer from Japan Tobacco International ("Advocating Tobacco, On the Payroll of Tobacco," *New York Times*, March 23, 2002: B9). Elizabeth Durack admitted she had "created the persona of Aboriginal painter Eddie Burrup, and exhibited 'his' paintings with explanatory statements in Pidgin," fuelling controversy over ownership of Aboriginal art (Oxford Companion to Australian History [Melbourne: Oxford University Press, 1999]: 200).

119. R. Murray, "Seven Myths About Australia," *Quadrant* 286, XXXVI: 5 (May 1992): 40-41. Four years later Murray surveyed the killings and wrote that their impact "was close to genocidal in limited areas, but it was not genocide." *Quadrant* 331, XL: 11 (November 1996): 19.

the Cold War, Santamaria's own views mellowed in his last years.[120] Rejecting the economic rationalism of the New Right, he revisited some of his early anti-corporate concerns. Manne, too, fell out with *Quadrant*'s board after he began in 1996 to print differing views on Aboriginal issues and on High Court judgments in favor of land rights.[121] Then, in April 1997, the national Human Rights and Equal Opportunity Commission presented its finding that the removal of Aboriginal children had constituted genocide.[122] This provoked a rightwing crisis. In June, *Quadrant* literary editor Les Murray accused Manne of taking "the received leftist line on Aborigines" over the previous year. Manne had lost the support of the *Quadrant* "old guard." He resigned a few months later, and wrote afterwards: "Over the next three years *Quadrant* became devoted to ever wilder and more extreme attacks on every cause and belief of the contemporary Aboriginal political leadership and its support base."[123]

Olympian Denial

Before the 2000 Olympics, Prime Minister Howard was reported to be reading *Quadrant* "religiously," and he attended a conference sponsored by the magazine. In September 2000 the magazine held another conference, on Aboriginal matters.[124] Onetime leftist Keith Windshuttle introduced a paper which *Quadrant* was to publish over its next three monthly issues: "The Myths of Frontier Massacres in Australian History."[125] Windshuttle looked simply at "the evidence of four events that recent historians have described as massacres," and argued that "only one of them deserves this description." Two he considered "legitimate police operations" and a third, contrary to the finding of a Royal Commission, was "pure mythology. Not only was there no massacre but there was no good evidence that any Aborigines were ever killed."* "Most killings

---

120. Former *Quadrant* editor Donald Horne writes that late in life Santamaria regretted his association with James McAuley. *Into the Open: Memoirs, 1958-1999* (Sydney: HarperCollins, 2000): 109.
121. See e.g. Richard H. Bartlett, *The Mabo Decision* (Sydney: Butterworths, 1993).
122. Human Rights and Equal Opportunity Commission, *Bringing Them Home*, 275.
123. Manne, *In Denial*, pp. 57-8. For details of the *Quadrant* attacks on the Aboriginal case, 58-59.
124. *Australian*, 22 July 2000, quoted in Manne, *In Denial*, 113; Manne, "Bitter Olympic Ironies," *Age*, 18 September 2000.
125. Keith Windshuttle, "The Myths of Frontier Massacres in Australian History," *Quadrant*, October-December 2000. For my view, see "Australia's Aboriginal Genocides," *Bangkok Post*, 10 September 2000.
* Windshuttle wrote of another case that diaries of members of Stirling's 1834 expedition say "they killed only a proportion" of 70-80 Aborigines ("The Myths of Frontier Massacres," *Quadrant* 370 [XLIV, 10, October 2000]: 18). Citing Jan Critchett, *A Distant Field of Murder: Western District Frontiers, 1834-1848* (Melbourne University Press, 1990), he also asserted that "only three events… involved mass killings" of Aborigines in Western Victoria in 1834-48, while he labeled the Aboriginal killing

of Aborigines occurred not in large numbers but in ones and twos... there were some massacres, but they were rare and isolated," "unusual events" with "their own specific causes."[126]

Windshuttle asserted: "The notion that the frontier was a place where white men could kill blacks with impunity ignores the powerful cultural and legal prohibitions."[127] But, as Henry Reynolds and Charles Rowley noted, Aborigines were barred from giving court testimony, on grounds that heathens could not be sworn. Only from 1876 were they allowed to testify in New South Wales courts, and from 1884 in Queensland.[128] Ignoring this but citing Rowley as "the most reputable historian in the field,"[129] Windshuttle also omitted Rowley's many descriptions of the "massacres" and "exterminations" of Aborigines.* Accusing a missionary of having in 1838 "invented the notion of ... 'a war of extirpation,'" Windshuttle further ignored an 1836 official report to the British Colonial Secretary recalling a "war of extermination...here."[130] Instead, he accused Aborigines' supporters and historians who publicized their tragedy of

---

of six shepherds a "mass killing of Europeans" (*Quadrant*, November 2000, 21). But Critchett documented *11* events (not 3) meeting Windshuttle's definition of a mass killing. The Aboriginal victims numbered, respectively, 10, '35-40,' 30-51, 8, 7, 9, 9, 8-20, '9 or 10,' 6, and 9 (Appendix 3). Windshuttle claimed Critchett "counts a total of 200 Aborigines killed by whites" (21); her figure was 300-350 (130-31). Ian Clark, *Scars in the Landscape: A Register of Massacre Sites in Western Victoria, 1803-1859* (Canberra: AIATSIS, 1995) details 107 killing sites, including twenty-one where six or more Aborigines were killed.

126. Windshuttle, "Aboriginal Deaths: Why the Guesswork is not Educated," *Age*, 20 September 2000.

127. Windshuttle, *Quadrant*, November 2000, 23, and "When History Falls Victim to Politics," *Age*, 14 July 2001.

128. C.D. Rowley and Henry Reynolds, "Aborigines Since 1788," *The Australian Encyclopedia*, 280.

129. Windshuttle, *Quadrant*, October 2000, p. 21 (stating that Rowley termed the Australian killings "comparatively small-scale homicide"); Windshuttle, "The Fabrication of Aboriginal History," *New Criterion*, 20, 1, September 2001.

  * C.D. Rowley, *The Destruction of Aboriginal Society* (Ringwood: Penguin, 1972), 112, 117 ("extermination"), 18, 36, 42, 113-4, 151-52, 157 ("massacres"), 33, 161 ("indiscriminate slaughter"), 41, 149 ("war waged against" Aborigines, "with all the suspending of morality involved"), 217 ("punitive expeditions"). Windshuttle's honesty may also be judged by his claim that I noted "the 'hundreds of massacres' that took place in the twentieth century" (Windshuttle, "The Fabrication of Aboriginal History," *New Criterion*, 20, 1, September 2001). No, I referred mostly to the nineteenth century, saying: "troopers killed 25 Aborigines at the "Battle of Pinjarra" in 1834. "Hundreds of massacres" followed over the next century." ("Australia's Aboriginal Genocides," *Bankgok Post*, September 10, 2000, p. 6, quoting Colin Tatz, *Genocide in Australia*, 16.)

130. *Quadrant*, December 2000, 7, citing the 1838 claim of a continuing "War of extirpation"; cf. George Mackillop to Col. Sec., 28 July 1836, in *Historical Records of Victoria*, Foundation Series, Volume 2A, *The Aborigines of Port Philip 1835-1839*, Melbourne, Victorian Government Printing Office, 1982, 40.

having "fabricated" and "manufactured" stories to further their own careers.[131] Windshuttle has been answered effectively by Henry Reynolds, *An Indelible Stain?* Ray Evans and Bill Thorpe, "Indigenocide and the Massacre of Australian History," *Overland*, no. 163, July 2001, 21-39, and *Age*, July 2001; Manne, *In Denial*.

Just as Heinz Arndt explained that "sections of the Australian Press...objected so violently to the incorporation of East Timor into Indonesia" because support for its independence came "from the left," now Windshuttle pleaded that his opponents dominated the media too. To him, Robert Manne had become "a member of the Left establishment," while my own work on Aboriginal genocides was supposedly "syndicated to English-language newspapers around the world."[132] The reverse was true. The new campaign to deny the Aboriginal genocide, led by *Quadrant*, was taken up in the Australian mass media by a chorus of right wing columnists with records of antagonism to Aborigines and "leftist" supporters, and easy access to a wide public.[133]

Just as Santamaria targeted "Marxist" Jesuits, Windshuttle denounced the "tradition begun by missionaries in the early nineteenth century and perpetuated by academics in the late twentieth – of the invention of massacre stories." He accused missionaries of lying – not the perpetrator troops, who in one case provided "the only eyewitness accounts."[134] He criticized the land rights movement as a modern secular version of the same Aboriginal "separatism" previously favored by the missionary with "a heady vision of himself as their physical protector." Just as separatism "meant the missionaries would keep their funding and their jobs," so "Massacre stories, then and now, were often invented as ideological supports for the policy of separatism."[135]

---

131. Windshuttle, quoted in Manne, "Bitter Olympic Ironies," *Age*, 18 September 2000. This followed Anthony McAdam's dismissal of "the radical academic Henry Reynolds," *Quadrant*, October 1985, 68. Windshuttle has been answered effectively by Henry Reynolds, An Indelible Stain? Ray Evans and Bill Thorpe, "Indigenocide and the Massacre of Australian History," Overland, no. 163, July 2001, 21-39, and Age, July 2001; Manne, In Denial.
132. Windshuttle, "The Fabrication of Aboriginal History," *New Criterion*, 20, 1, September 2001. I had in fact sent my article to the *Australian* newspaper, which replied: "Space is at a premium given the Olympics" (Features Editor, 7 September 2000). The Melbourne *Age* undertook to print my article, but did not. I successfully placed it in the *Bangkok Post* (September 10, 2000).
133. For details see Colin Tatz, "'It Didn't Happen': Depictions of Denial," paper read to the Association of Genocide Scholars, Minneapolis, 9-12 June 2001, forthcoming as "Why Denialists Deny," in Tatz, *With Intent to Destroy: Aborigines, Armenians, and Jews* (Sydney: Brandl & Schlesinger, 2002); Manne, *In Denial*, 67ff.
134. Windshuttle, "The Myths of Frontier Massacres," *Quadrant*, October 2000, 9, 16-17.
135. Windshuttle, "The Fabrication of Aboriginal History," *New Criterion*, 20, 1, September 2001; *Quadrant*, December 2000, 10, 19.

At bottom, Windshuttle opposes Aboriginal land rights and covers up the history of massacres that strengthens the case for restitution. Rather, he favors assimilation. "Instead of land rights, customary law and traditional culture, most of them want simply to live like the rest of us. The assimilation of the great majority of the Aboriginal population is an accomplished fact."[136] Yet, some Aborigines wish to live on their traditional land and reclaim it. Denial of their land rights favors white claimants such as pastoral and mining corporations. Denial of the genocide, too, undercuts Aboriginal claims based on justice. It also helped a recalcitrant prime minister out of a tight corner at the Olympic Games.

Conclusion

Denial of genocide is often a function of simple political priorities – often ones not directly related to the genocide. In many cases the truth of the matter becomes clear and would not be denied, even if it could plausibly be. But in other cases, the stakes prove too high, or the victims too lowly. Revelation of such genocides might threaten a keystone policy (in these cases: anti-communism, *realpolitik*, refusal to redress injustice), require resource re-allocation (land rights), embarrass a domestic political leader (John Howard) or international ally (Jakarta, Washington), or rehabilitate ideological dissidents (the "left"). In some such cases, genocide can be denied even when intellectually, the facts are undeniable. Raw power, of course, often requires only a fig leaf of legitimacy. Policy plows ahead and almost automatically, action produces its own apologists. Victims of genocide in small foreign territories like East Timor, or domestic groups with reduced surviving populations, like Australian Aborigines, cannot easily contest geopolitical *or* domestic government priorities. Media attention to small countries, even those threatened with genocide, is usually insufficient to threaten domestic policymakers or make them pressure foreign perpetrators, for instance by cutting military supplies, which could have restrained Jakarta but embarrassed a powerful ally, the USA. Public opinion on foreign policy rarely determines national elections. Likewise, remnant survivors of genocides wield minimal electoral clout. In the Aboriginal case, on such a domestic issue their conservative opponents rebuffed the example of the same powerful ally: U.S. recognition of injustices to Native Americans. Even when media monopolies don't consign the facts to obscurity, governments can often ignore both foreign models and domestic protests by victimized minorities – as well as protests against policies on faraway tragedies.

Genocide is the most serious crime against humanity. No politician wants to be accused of facilitating it. No American politician took any blame for the East Timor genocide, even though the United States armed Indonesia for years while the *New York Times* gave East Timor so little attention that as late as 1998

136. Windshuttle, *Quadrant*, December 2000, 20.

it mislabeled the territory a "former Dutch colony."[137] US policymakers could afford to be laconic. But under greater media scrutiny, as in Australia, policies favoring genocidal regimes require fantastic denials and defenses.

In the case of East Timor, for twenty-four years, a few conservatives attempted to cover up the unfolding truth both to defend established Australian and U.S. policy, and to deny "leftists" political points or moral credit. The plight of the Timorese came a poor third to these priorities. But in the end, official policy unraveled as the brutal nature of the Indonesian regime made stability impossible. Timorese resistance again outlasted a foreign occupier. Far from *realpolitik*, Indonesia's adventure contributed to loss of its international standing and the eventual fall of the Suharto regime itself, with new threats to Indonesian unity and possibly to Australia's security. And in a unique series of events, Australian public opinion, informed with the help of a citizen solidarity organization by knowledge of the carnage, swept away a bankrupt policy.

In 1999, Australian troops in UN berets dug in on the Indonesian border of East Timor. Just as John Howard, who sent them there, had once served in the Cabinet that policed the communications blackout on Timor, he now termed the memory of the Aboriginal genocide a "black armband" view of Australian history,[138] recalling Japanese nationalists resentful of "masochistic" views of Japan's war crimes.[139] Conservatives denied the Aboriginal genocide not on the historical facts, but largely because Aborigines had liberal or leftist supporters, corporate opponents threatened by land rights, and an embattled prime minister. Timorese and Aborigines were pawns in much larger games. The stakes of recognizing past injustices remain grounded in the present, in domestic debate, and perennial issues of power.

---

137. *New York Times*, 18 May 1998, A6. Samantha Power, *"A Problem from Hell"*: *America and the Age of Genocide* (New York: Basic, 2002) asserts that "the United States looked away" from East Timor (146-47). For a critique, see Christopher Hitchens, *The Trial of Henry Kissinger*, Verso, London, 2001.
138. See Colin Tatz, "'It Didn't Happen": Depictions of Denial."
139. Kiroku Hanai, "Close the Book on Censorship," *Japan Times*, 2 April 2001; Gavan McCormack, "The Japanese movement to 'correct' history," in Laura Hein and Mark Selden, eds., *Censoring History: Citizenship and Memory in Japan, Germany, and the United States*, London/ New York, M.E. Sharpe, 2000, 53-73. In light of Timor's World War Two suffering, the view of a leading Japanese newspaper seems more enlightened: *Asahi Shimbun* warned against attempts "to sweep Japan's negative wartime behaviour under the rug, such as its victimization of people in other countries, in the guise of 'overcoming a masochistic view of history.' If children are confined to such a normative view, their 'understanding of – and affection for – the land and history of the country,' the supposed object of study, will only have a very frail foundation." 'Even with Changes, Textbooks not Fit for Tomorrow's Leaders," *Asahi Shimbun*, 4 April 2001, published 5 April 2001.

9

The Demography of Genocide in Southeast Asia: The Death Tolls in Cambodia, 1975-79, and East Timor, 1975-80

The scale of the death tolls in these two catastrophes has been the subject of scholarly discussion, but the demographic evidence suggests that they were proportionately comparable. Though many more people died in Cambodia, the toll in each case was 20-25 percent of the country's population.

Cambodia's Population before and after the Khmer Rouge

Cambodia's last census before the Khmer Rouge came to power in April 1975 was held in 1962. It counted the country's population at 5.729 million. The demographer Jacques Migozzi, in the most extensive study of Cambodia's population, considered this an undercount, and came up with an estimate of 7.363 million for 1970. Migozzi anticipated in 1972 that the population would continue to increase at 2.9 percent per annum, despite the ongoing 1970-75 war, and he predicted a 1975 population of 8.5 million.[1] But the war took a substantial toll and also slightly reduced the population growth rate. A mid-1974 United Nations (UN) estimate produced a figure of 7.89 million, representing growth of 2.46 percent p.a. The UN estimate was corroborated at the time by an independent statistician, W.J.Sampson, then working in Cambodia.[2]

Demographers Judith Banister and Paige Johnson estimated the April 1975 population at 7.3 million; Marek Sliwinski estimated 7.566 million.[3] These

---

1. Jacques Migozzi, *Cambodge: faits et problèmes de population*, Paris, PUF, 1973, pp. 204, 226, 213, giving 7.363m. as his preferred precision for 1970, and a round figure of 7.3m. (pp. 20, 212).
2. *Economist*, 26 March 1977.
3. Banister and Johnson, in Ben Kiernan, ed., *Genocide and Democracy in Cambodia: The Khmer Rouge, the United Nations, and the International Community*, New Haven, Yale Council on Southeast Asia Studies, 1993, p. 90; Marek Sliwinski, *Le Génocide Khmer Rouge: une analyse démographique*, Paris, L'Harmattan, 1995, pp. 26, 40.

two figures seem low in the light of Migozzi's estimate for five years earlier, those of 1974, and concurring higher estimates for later years (see below). More recently, the demographer Patrick Heuveline of the University of Chicago calculated a population of 7.562 million for April 1970, and assuming 300,000 excess wartime deaths in 1970-75, postulated a figure of 8.102 million by April 1975.[4]

The mid-1974 estimates suggest a similar April 1975 figure of 8,044,000. After its victory, Pol Pot's new Democratic Kampuchea (DK) regime quickly expelled 150,000 ethnic Vietnamese residents.[5] I have therefore calculated a population of 7.894 million remaining in Cambodia in April 1975; Heuveline's figure would be 7.952 million.[6] A Cambodian statistician working for the DK regime also learned in 1975 that the population was "about 8 million" in that year.[7]

From a base figure of 7.894 million, the harsh living conditions that the DK regime immediately imposed probably restricted Cambodia's 1975-79 natural population growth rate (births minus "normal" deaths) to around 1 percent p.a. This would project an "expected" January 1979 population of 8,214,528 – minus "excess" deaths since April 1975.

Documentary evidence for not only excess deaths but actual population decline after April 1975 includes an official, published DK figure of 7,735,279 in March 1976.[8] Another official DK source gave a confidential estimate of 7,333,000 in August 1976, a statistical loss of over 400,000 in just six months.[9] It is clear not only that the lower estimates for the pre-1975 population are wrong, but also that the post-1975 population was declining.

The Population Size After the Genocide Ended in January 1979

The most detailed post-genocide population figure is a government count of 6,589,954 people at the end of 1980, documented by the Cambodian Department of Statistics in 1992.[10] From this, Banister and Johnson have calculated a

---

4.   Patrick Heuveline, personal communication, 23 April 2003. See his "'Between One and Three Million': Towards the demographic reconstruction of a decade of Cambodian history (1970-79)," *Population Studies*, 52 (1998), pp. 49-65.
5.   Nayan Chanda, *Brother Enemy*, New York, 1986, p. 16.
6.   Patrick Heuveline, personal communication, 30 May 2003.
7.   Author's interview with San, Paris, 29 May 1980.
8.   Phnom Penh Radio, 21 March 1976; BBC, *Summary of World Broadcasts*, FE/5166/B1-3.
9.   *Kumrung pankar buon chhnam khosang sangkumniyum krup phnaek rebos pak, 1977-1980* ("The Party's Four-Year Plan to Build Socialism in All Fields, 1977-1980"), July-August 1976, Table 1.
10. Banister and Johnson, in Kiernan, *Genocide and Democracy in Cambodia*, table 2, p. 84. For slightly lower figures: *AFP*, Hong Kong, 22 January 1980; *Far Eastern Economic Review*, Dec. 19, 1980, p. 37.

population figure of 6.36 million for the end of 1978.[11] This means a statistical loss from the projected early 1979 figure (8,214,528) of around 1,854,528. Alternatively, a figure of 1,671,000 results from calculating and combining the different estimated tolls for Cambodia's various ethnic and geographic communities.[12] Marek Sliwinski calculates the 1975-79 nationwide toll at 1.843-1.871 million.[13] We may safely conclude from known pre- and post-genocide population figures and from professional demographic calculations that the 1975-79 death toll was between 1.671 and 1.871 million people.

Evidence from Mass Graves?

Against this, on the basis of a survey of locations of DK-era mass graves, Craig Etcheson has suggested that the death toll could have been as high as three million. His assertion arises simply from a partial, incomplete mapping (by 1999) of an estimated 20,438 mass grave pits: "According to the Documentation Center of Cambodia, these mass graves contain the remains of 1,110,829 victims of execution." Etcheson adds that with location of all the Khmer Rouge-era mass graves, "it is likely that the estimate of the number of victims in mass graves will rise significantly…. The total could reach as high as 1.5 million."[14] However, the precise figure of "1,110,829 victims of execution" is quite impossible to substantiate without exhumations of all the mass grave pits, a count of all bodies in them, and forensic determination of the causes of each death. Nor does the estimate result even from a sampling. This figure for executions is based on assertion alone: "the twenty thousand mass graves mapped so far are virtually all located at, or near, Khmer Rouge security centers. Eyewitnesses at most of these mass grave sites have testified that the graves contain victims brought there by Khmer Rouge security forces, and that the victims were murdered…. Thus one can conclude that virtually all of the mass graves contain victims whose cause of death was execution by the Khmer Rouge."

Note the wording here. Etcheson is grammatically careful not to state that the mass graves contain *only* victims of execution. Though necessary for his case, that is impossible to demonstrate. But employing that very assumption, Etcheson goes on to suggest accepting the undocumented count of "1,110,829" bodies as a figure for executions alone. To this he adds an additional figure for victims of "other causes of death during the Khmer Rouge regime, such as starvation, disease and overwork". Then, proceeding from a presumption

11. Banister and Johnson, in Kiernan, *Genocide and Democracy in Cambodia*, p. 90.
12. Ben Kiernan, *The Pol Pot Regime: Race, Power and Genocide in Cambodia under the Khmer Rouge, 1975-1979*, New Haven, Yale University Press, 2nd edition, 2002, p. 458.
13. Marek Sliwinski, *Le Génocide Khmer Rouge*, p. 57.
14. Craig Etcheson, "Did the Khmer Rouge Really Kill Three Million Cambodians?" *Phnom Penh Post*, April 30, 2000.

that executions caused only 30-50 percent of total DK deaths, he triples the undocumented figure of 1.11 million executions. He suggests alternatively that it should be merely doubled if the number of bodies in mass graves reaches 1.5m. "It begins to look possible that the original Cambodian estimate of 3.3 million deaths during the Khmer Rouge regime might be very nearly correct." This baseless calculation not only ignores all the Cambodian demographic data surveyed above. It relies totally on two false assumptions: that all bodies in the mass graves have been counted, and that *all* are victims of execution. The misleading language ("all of the mass graves contain victims whose cause of death was execution" – possibly true but still unproven) by no means establishes the cause of death for all "1,110,829" uncounted corpses. Nor can eyewitnesses from "most" of the sites do so, even if they witnessed every single death at many of them. Etcheson carefully makes neither of the claims necessary for his case. Neither is close to being demonstrated. He overlooks the evidence of Pin Yathay that in Pursat in 1976-77, for instance, graves were dug for the victims of hunger and disease, not execution.[15] Such sloppiness is unworthy of the Documentation Center of Cambodia. Exaggerating a horrific death toll, it contributes to the ethnic auctioneering of genocide research.

Cambodia's Cham Muslim Minority

In 1990 the *Bulletin of Concerned Asian Scholars* published an exchange between Michael Vickery and myself on the size of the Cham Muslim population in Cambodia and its demographic losses from 1975 to 1979. Vickery suggested that the 1975 Cham population was around 191,000, and in 1979, approximately 180,000, representing a death toll in the DK years of 11,000 or more.[16] My estimate of the 1975 Cham population was higher -- 250,000. To this I applied the very low 1 percent p.a. population growth rate (births minus "normal" deaths) for 1975-79, calculating a projected 1979 population of 260,000. From this I subtracted my estimate of the number of survivors in 1979 (173,000) to arrive at a figure for "excess" deaths, a loss of over 87,000, more than 36 percent of the 1975 Cham population of Cambodia.[17] This was double the death rate suffered by the country's ethnic Khmer majority, around 18.7 percent.[18]

A recent publication has challenged our assessments by asserting that the Cham population in Cambodia in 1974 "comprised 10 percent of Cambodia's

15. Pin Yathay, *L'Utopie Meurtrière*, Paris, Laffont, 1979, p. 149.
16. Michael Vickery, "Comments on Cham Population Figures," *Bulletin of Concerned Asian Scholars*, 22, 1, Jan.-Mar. 1990, pp. 31-33.
17. Ben Kiernan, "The Genocide in Cambodia, 1975-1979," *Bulletin of Concerned Asian Scholars*, 22, 2, April-June 1990, pp. 35-40. See also p. 36, n. 9.
18. Kiernan, *The Pol Pot Regime*, New Haven, Yale University Press, 2nd edition, 2002, p. 458.

population (roughly 700,000 of the country's 7,000,000 people)." It adds that either 138,607, or possibly, 200,000 Chams survived in 1979, and that the demographic losses were thus approximately 500,000-560,000, or 71-80 percent. These high figures for both the Cham population and the genocide they suffered are advanced by Ysa Osman in *Oukoubah: Justice for the Cham Muslims under the Democratic Kampuchea Regime*.[19] However there is no reliable evidence for the assertion that as many as ten percent of Cambodians were Cham. It more than triples the true proportion.

An 1874 French census counted 25,599 Chams in Cambodia, or 3 percent of the population. A July 1936 official count produced a figure of 73,465 Chams, which the French expert Marcel Ner revised upwards to 88,000. Ner considered the official count a 20 percent underestimation.[20] If the Cambodian population was 3.1 million in 1936,[21] the 88,000 Chams would comprise 2.84 percent (73,465 would be 2.37 percent).

A 1955 official tally of Cambodian adult males counted 29,786 Cham men on Cambodia's electoral roll.[22] This minimum figure suggests a Cham population of at least 59,572 men and women aged twenty-one or older, and from this can be calculated a total Cham population in Cambodia of 152,126 in 1955.[23] The national population in 1955 was around 4.8m, of whom Chams thus comprised 3.16 percent.[24]

Migozzi offers a 1968 figure of "about 150,000."[25] This represents 2.14 percent of the population, far too low to reconcile with the three previous figures representing 3 percent or more. Migozzi seems to have been unaware of the 1955 count of Cham adult males. From the more precise and reliable 1955 figure of 152,126, using Migozzi's estimated national population growth rates for 1955-60 (2.65 percent), 1960-65 (2.83 percent), and 1965-70 (2.95 percent), we may calculate a Cham population of 230,531 in 1970, or 3.16 percent of the

19. Ysa Osman, *Oukoubah: Justice for the Cham Muslims under the Democratic Kampuchea Regime*, Phnom Penh, Documentation Center of Cambodia, 2003, pp. 2, 6, 119.
20. Marcel Ner, "Les Musulmans de l'Indochine française," *Bulletin de l'Ecole Française d'Extrême-Orient*, 41, 2 (1941), pp. 179-80.
21. The 1921 census counted a Cambodian population of 2,402,485. Migozzi considers this an undercount and estimates 2.6m in 1920, and 3.945m in 1945 (pp. 203, 226). A 1950 estimate is 4,073,967 (David J. Steinberg, et al., *Cambodia: its people, its society, its culture*, New Haven, HRAF, 1959, p. 291, table 1).
22. "Les Khmers Islam...," *Angkor*, 30 June 1956, p. 4.
23. See Kiernan, *The Pol Pot Regime*, p. 254n32.
24. "Estimates of total population for 1955 varied from approximately 4,800,000 (by the United States Department of Commerce) to 5,125,000 (a projection by Canada's Department of Mines and Technical Surveys figures, based on a sharp increase since 1946 of approximately 2.5 percent per year). The official Cambodian government figure of 4,740,000 for 1958 is used in this book." David J. Steinberg, et al., *Cambodia: its people, its society, its culture*, p.28.
25. Migozzi 1973, p. 42.

national population, precisely consistent with previous estimates. This would suggest a population in April 1975 of 249,450.

Unfortunately, in the meantime, Cambodia's official records had not only accepted the low 1936 figure of 73,000 rejected by Marcel Ner, but also, inexplicably, continued to cite it as the size of the Cham population as late as 1955, acknowledging no population growth at all in the intervening decades.[26] Migozzi cites no source for his low 1968 figure of 150,000, but it was probably based on the official 1936 figure as restated for 1955.[27] That initial underestimate, and the failure to update it for twenty years, may understandably have provoked countervailing exaggerated claims on the part of Cham leaders, who probably knew that the Cham population had increased significantly from 1936 to 1955. But like the underestimates, the exaggerations were never documented, and could not be.

In 1974, for instance, the Central Islamic Association of the Khmer Republic published a much higher claim: "The Chams or Khmer Muslims...represent more than 10 percent of the Khmer population of the capital of Phnom Penh and the provinces of Kandal, Kampot, Kompong Cham, Pursat, Battambang and Kompong Chhnang. Other small Cham villages are found throughout the rest of the Khmer territory..."[28]

What Cham population size was being claimed here? No figure was given, but rough calculations are possible. In 1968, the populations of Phnom Penh and the six provinces named totaled 4.005 million, or 57.3 percent of Cambodia's total population of 6.995 million. Assuming for the moment that Chams did comprise ten percent of Phnom Penh and the six provinces, they would have numbered 400,500 in 1968, and 452,000 in 1975 (5.73 percent of 7.89 million). If we accept the claim of "*more than* ten percent," and also add inhabitants from the "other small Cham villages" in the remaining thirteen provinces, one might reach a figure of 500,000 for 1975. Were these claims better documented, that would be an absolute maximum. Though high, this 1974 official Cham estimate is careful not to claim a nationwide percentage

---

26. According to Steinberg: "In 1955 the combined estimate of Chams and Malays was about 73,000, or one percent of the total population" (*Cambodia*, p. 45). Apparently derived from this incorrect figure is that of "about 80,000 Chams in Cambodia" in the late 1950s, in F. P. Munson, et al., *Area Handbook for Cambodia*, Washington, D.C., 1968, p. 56.

27. Migozzi thus suggests Chams comprised 2.2 percent of the Cambodian population (p. 42).

28. *The Martyrdom of the Khmers Muslims*, Directorate of Islamic Affairs, Central Islamic Association of the Khmer Republic, Association of Islamic Youth, Phnom Penh [undated, 1974?, after May 19], 74 pp., at p. 36. The book adds: "One hundred and thirty-two mosques with Hakem are situated in all of the large Muslim villages" (p. 39). For a total of 118 Cham villages, see my *The Pol Pot Regime*, p. 255n33. For exaggerated claims of 220 and 242 villages before 1975, see Osman, *Oukoubah*, pp. 2-3.

of 10 percent, for which there is no documentary evidence whatsoever. Thus, a figure of 700,000 is impossible to sustain. It is based entirely on retrospective claims advanced in 1999-2000 by interviewees asserting that in the early 1970s they had "seen statistics" or "heard an announcement," or on the undocumented "memories of Cham elders."[29]

No other document suggests that Chams comprised as much as 10 percent even of the six provinces and the capital, let alone of the whole population. To the contrary, all existing documentary evidence consistently indicates that Chams comprised around 3 percent of the national population in 1975.

In November 1975, secret DK reports mentioned 150,000 Chams in the Eastern Zone (Prey Veng and Svay Rieng provinces, and the eastern part of Kompong Cham). This is not a precise count but seems to be an estimate, comprising round figures of 50,000 and 100,000.[30] We have inadequate pre-1975 Cham population data from those specific provinces to compare fruitfully with this.[31] There is therefore no way to extrapolate from this 150,000 to any nationwide 1975 figure, certainly not to 700,000.

The next figure for the Cham population in Cambodia was reported in December 1982. It was 182,256. Had the Cham population grown at the estimated national rate of over 2.8 percent p.a. for the preceding four post-DK years,[32] the surviving Cham population in January 1979 would have been under 163,200. Adding the 11,700 who fled abroad, we reach a maximum of 174,900 Cham survivors of the genocide. The improbable figure of 138,607 for January 1979 (first published only in 2002) is simply too low to reconcile with the 1982 count of 182,256 only four years later. Conversely, rough estimates of 200,000 survivors in 1979 are clearly too high.[33]

---

29. Osman, *Oukoubah*, 2002, p. 2.
30. See Ben Kiernan, *The Pol Pot Regime*, 2002 edition, p. xiii.
31. Marcel Ner recorded in 1941 that a quarter of Cambodia's 88,000 Chams lived in just two districts of eastern Kompong Cham province: 22,113 in Suong and Krauchhmar (pp. 176-77). In the 1950s, well over 20,000 Chams lived in Krauchhmar alone (J. Delvert, *Le paysan cambodgien*, Paris, 1960, pp. 605, 610-11), when the nationwide Cham population was 152,000. It is quite possible that three-fifths of Cambodia's Chams – 150,000 of 250,000 – lived in the Eastern Zone in 1975.
32. Banister and Johnson write: "The year-end 1980 count of children at ages zero and one is higher than expected... the apparent rise in fertility in 1979 indicates that underlying mortality conditions may have improved somewhat during the latter part of 1978 and in 1979." The 1979 total fertility rate of 5.8 births per woman suggests a population growth rate of 2.8 percent; that of 6.3 births per woman in 1980, around 3.1 percent. The growth rate for 1980-90 was estimated to average 2.8 percent p.a. ("After the Nightmare: The Population of Cambodia," in Kiernan, ed., *Genocide and Democracy in Cambodia*, p. 86. See also J. Huguet, "The Demographic Situation in Cambodia," *Asia-Pacific Population Journal*, 6:4, 1992, pp. 79-91.) Patrick Heuveline estimates 3.2 percent for the early 1980s (personal communication, 30 May 2003). Other sources cite various rates: 1.9 percent for 1980, 4 percent for 1980-81, and for 1981, "4.6-5.2 percent -- one of the highest in the world." If the latter figure is actually the crude birth rate, subtracting the crude

Thus, the statistical loss from the projected 1979 Cham population of 260,000 (assuming only 1 percent natural growth from 1975) was over 85,000, or 34 percent of the 1975 Cham population. To these 85,000 "excess" Cham deaths, I would add another 5,000 or so, representing 28 percent of the 17,750 Chams statistically likely to die naturally in 1975-79 given a crude death rate of 1.73 percent p.a., but who most probably died prematurely within that period due to harsh DK policies that especially impacted those same at-risk groups -- the aged, infirm and infants. This suggests a total of 90,000 Cham deaths from causes attributable to the DK regime, comprising 36 percent of the 1975 Cham population.[34]

East Timor under Indonesian Rule, 1975-1999

The last census in East Timor before the December 1975 Indonesian invasion was carried out by the Portuguese colonial rulers in 1970. This produced a figure of 609,477 people in the territory. In 1974, the Catholic Church provided a count of 688,771, indicating a population growth rate over 3.0 percent p.a., compared to the 1.8 percent which has been postulated for the 1960s and if continued would have produced a population of 654,558 by 1974. However, the Portuguese authorities carried out post-census sampling on a quarterly basis, and in 1974 they produced a population figure of 635,000, representing an increase of only 1 percent p.a. since 1970.[35] We can assume this to be an absolute minimum. An annual growth rate of 2.2 percent in this period was "the lowest increase in Southeast Asia."[36] In 1970 the Cambodian growth rate reached 2.9 percent.[37] There is no reason to assume an East Timorese rate below 2.2 percent, which would produce a 1974 population of 664,906. Robert Cribb has pointed out that "there is prima facie more reason to imagine that the figures provided by the Portuguese administration are actually understated, because Portugal collected an unpopular poll tax which would have given the East Timorese every reason to avoid being counted. The same is true of the church figures. In 1975, fewer than

death rate of 1.76 percent suggests a population growth rate of 2.84-3.44 percent for 1981. In 1982, Cambodia's Ministry of Health estimated the crude birth rate at 45.6 per thousand (a fertility rate of 5.8 births per woman) and the death rate at 17.6: again, a population growth rate of 2.8 percent. Grant Curtis, *Cambodia: A Country Profile*, SIDA, Stockholm, 1989, p. 7; Kimmo Kiljunen, *Kampuchea: Decade of the Genocide*, London, Zed, 1984, pp. 34, 44n17; Banister and Johnson, in *Genocide and Democracy*, p. 93.

33. Osman, *Oukoubah*, p. 2n5.
34. Sliwinski variously cites the Cham toll as 33.7 percent and 40.6 percent (*Le Génocide Khmer Rouge*, pp. 77, 144).
35. Jill Jolliffe, *Cover-Up: The Inside Story of the Balibo Five*, Scribe, Melbourne, 2001, p. 46.
36. Russell R. Ross, ed., *Cambodia: A Country Study*, Washington, D.C., U.S. Government Printing Office, 1990, p. 83.
37. Jacques Migozzi, *Cambodge: faits et problèmes de population*, Paris, CNRS, 1973, p. 212.

50 percent of the East Timorese population was Catholic, and any church estimate of the population must be seen in the light of its incomplete access to society."[38] The 1974 Church estimate included figures of 460,112 animists for only 220,314 Catholics. Portuguese officials considered the census, for its part, to be a 5 percent undercount.[39] There is no reason to believe that the census data overstates either the numbers or the population growth rate from 1970 to 1974. Though the much higher 1974 church count may also be incomplete, for the purpose of calculating a safe conservative estimate, I use it here as a possible maximum.

If we increase the minimum 1974 figure of 635,000 by the low 1960s estimate of 1.8 percent annual growth suggested by both John Taylor and Robert Cribb (citing a demographer), we arrive at a 1975 population figure of 646,430. If we assume the 1974 figure was for mid-year rather than December 1974, and increase it again by 0.9 percent to arrive at a December 1975 figure, we get 652,250. The same calculation for the higher Church figure produces a December 1975 maximum of 707,500. The range of possibilities thus seems to be 652,250-707,500.

From this we must subtract the numbers of those killed in the August-September 1975 civil war (usually estimated at 1,500-2,000); the defeated UDT soldiers and their families who fled to Indonesian West Timor in September-October (3,000); the 140-50 prisoners killed by Fretilin in December 1975 immediately after the Indonesian invasion; and the 4,000 Timorese who fled to Australia and other countries.[40] The total population loss to the territory by December 1975 was thus around 9,000. The minimum figure for the surviving population in East Timor in December 1975 is therefore 643,250, and the real figure possibly as many as 698,500.[41]

Estimates of the East Timorese Population during Indonesian Rule

The first Indonesian estimate of 329,271 in December 1978, naturally "aroused alarm," as Robert Cribb has written, and "was apparently revised up-

38. Robert Cribb, "How Many Deaths? Problems in the Statistics of Massacre in Indonesia (1965-1966) and East Timor (1975-1980)", in *Violence in Indonesia*, edited by Ingrid Wessel and Georgia Wimhofer, Hamburg, Abera, 2001, p. 88. The church estimated that fewer than a third of Timorese were Catholic in 1975. *Pro Mundi Vita*, no. 4/1984, p. 1.
39. John Waddingham, "East Timor: How Many People Missing?", *Timor Information Service* (Melbourne), no. 28, February 1980, pp. 3-14, at pp. 4n13, 7n24.
40. James Dunn, *Timor: A People Betrayed*, Brisbane, Jacaranda, 1983, pp. 321-22, 180, 305, 178, 322; Desmond Ball and Hamish McDonald, *Death in Balibo, Lies in Canberra*, Sydney, Allen and Unwin, 2000, p. 175. Heinz Arndt cited a figure of 40,000 Timorese refugees living abroad or in other parts of Indonesia, but this is considered exaggerated. Waddingham, "East Timor," pp. 5, 10; Dunn, *Timor*, p. 322; Robert Cribb, e-mail, 10 October 2001; John Taylor, personal communication.
41. This supports Waddingham's early 1980 estimate of the range 656-693,000. "East Timor," p. 10.

wards" to attempt to include the large numbers of people still living under Fretilin administration in the hills. This produced a figure of 498,433 for December 1978.[42] That month, Indonesian forces surrounded and killed Fretilin president Nicolau Lobato, completing the decimation of the resistance. Military pressure continued to drive Timorese into Indonesian-controlled areas until April 1979, when the flow "slowed to a trickle." A June 1979 Indonesian count produced a population figure of 523,170.[43] A 1980 Catholic Church count came up with only 425,000 survivors. But the 1980 Indonesian census found a population of 555,350, which Cribb regards as "probably the most reliable figure of all, but it is not clear that it takes into account those Timorese who had managed to evade Indonesian supervision in the interior."[44] Taylor estimates the latter in 1980 at several thousand, including about 1,200 resistance fighters (personal communication, April 2003). This would put the East Timorese population of the territory at around 560,000 in 1980. This seems corroborated by the 1981 Indonesian count of 567,000.[45] Given the low June 1979 tally, the census figure for 1980 may be too high, but does not appear to be an undercount.

But Cribb placed greater reliance on "the Indonesian investigation led by Professor Mubyarto [which] concluded that the population in 1987 was 657,411," in light of which, Cribb argued, "The 1980 census figure of 555,350 becomes all the more implausible." Cribb considered the latter too low, because it "implies a population growth rate of about 2.5 percent -- very high given the difficult circumstances in Timor." The lower 1980 church figure of 425,000 requires even higher subsequent growth rates to conform to Mubyarto's 1987 figure. Cribb rightly ruled it out. The official Indonesian counts of 498,000 for 1978 and 523,000 for 1979 are harder to dismiss.

For the population figure of 657,411, Mubyarto cited the official Indonesian publication, *East Timor in Figures, 1987*. But that total clearly includes Indonesian transmigrants who arrived between 1980 and 1987. Mubyarto's report estimated that 20 percent of the population of East Timor – "Protestants, Muslims, Hindus, and Buddhists" – were "relatively recent immigrants."[46]

---

42. Cribb, "How Many Deaths?" p. 88.

43. Waddingham, "East Timor," pp. 14 and 9-11, citing June 1979 Indonesian figures supplied by a Timorese (esp. table, p. 11), corroborated by P. Rodgers, *Sydney Morning Herald*, 1 November 1979.

44. Cribb, "How Many Deaths?," pp. 88-89.

45. Gabriel Defert, *Timor-Est. Le Génocide oublié, Droit d'un Peuple et Raisons d'Etat* (Paris: L'Harmattan, 1992), p. 148, cites the figure of 567,000 from *Statistik Indonesia* (1983) which apparently refers to December 1981. Defert assesses the annual population growth rate from December 1975 to December 1981 at 1.1 percent, suggesting a toll of 170,000. Thanks to Peter Carey for drawing this to my attention.

46. *East Timor: The Impact of Integration, An Indonesian Socio-Anthropological Study*, by Prof. Dr. Mubyarto et al., Gadja Madha University, Yogyakarta 1990, English translation by Indonesia Resources and Information Program, Northcote, Australia, December 1991, p. 38, table 4.2, p. 30.

Animists were not mentioned; clearly all indigenous East Timorese were now being classified as Catholics, except perhaps the Muslims native to the territory who numbered under a thousand before 1975.[47] If we subtract 20 percent from Mubyarto's total, indigenous East Timorese in the territory in 1987 would have numbered only 526,000. Mubyarto offers a consistent 1990 figure of 540,000 Catholics in East Timor.[48]

Who were the rest? From 1980, 500 Javanese and Balinese families began to arrive in East Timor in an officially sponsored transmigration program.[49] By 1984 about 5,000 Balinese had been settled across the territory.[50] More arrived before 1987 and all would need to be subtracted from Mubyarto's figure of the East Timorese population for the purposes of measuring its natural growth rate since 1980. The most precise figures available are presented by the Indonesian analyst Soewartoyo, in a monograph published by Jakarta's Center for Strategic and International Studies. According to Soewartoyo's figures, a total of 14,142 transmigrants arrived in East Timor in the period 1980-85 alone. Another 15,550 arrived in 1986-88, of whom possibly one-third arrived in 1986, making a total of around 19,000 transmigrants for the period 1980-86, before Mubyarto's population figure was tallied in 1987. After subtracting return and outward migration from the territory, Soewartoyo gives a total of 12,193 "lifetime" transmigrants to East Timor by 1985.[51] Extrapolating for the period 1985-1986, a figure of 15,000 seems reasonable.

We may also need to subtract from the 1987 population figure any unofficial transmigrants included in the tally. While Soewartoyo counts 33,618 "lifetime" transmigrants by 1990, Frédéric Durand estimates total transmigrants in East Timor then at 85,000.[52] The official 1987 population figure of 657,411 must be reduced to around 642,000 by subtracting at least 15,000 "lifetime" transmigrants. Consistent with this, a 1980-87 annual growth rate of only 2.0 percent would have increased the 1980 population of 560,000 to 643,000 in 1987. But the growth rate might have been much lower. Including unofficial arrivals, the

47. Helen M. Hill, *Stirrings of Nationalism in East Timor: Fretilin 1974-1978: The Origins, Ideologies and Strategies of a Nationalist Movement* (Sydney: Otford, 2002), p. 36.
48. Mubyarto, *East Timor*, p. 32.
49. Taylor, *East Timor*, p. 124.
50. Defert, *Timor-Est. Le Génocide oublié*, p. 182.
51. Soewartoyo, *Migrasi internal di Timor Timur: Kajian di daerah tujuan pasca-integrasi*, Analisis CSIS, thn 26, no. 3, May-June 1997, pp. 265-275. Gerry van Klinken and Akihisa Matsuno drew this data to my attention.
52. Frédéric Durand, *Timor Lorosa'e: pays au carrefour de l'Asie*, Bangkok, IRASEC, 2002, p. 87. Soewartoyo's figure for the 1990 population of East Timor is 747,557. A 1995 estimate for transmigrants is 180,000 (Mauro di Nicola, *Uniya*, spring 1995). In March 1997, the Vice-Rector of the University of East Timor, Armindo Maia, indicated to Peter Carey that there were 161,095 non-Timorese inhabitants of East Timor at that time in the 15-60 age group. I am grateful to Carey for forwarding these 1995 and 1997 statistics; personal communication, 19 May 2003.

total 1987 transmigrant population could well have reached 60,000, with possibly fewer than 600,000 indigenous East Timorese.

It may be impossible to determine the exact number of indigenous survivors and their offspring. What is clear is simply that the official 1987 East Timor population figure includes tens of thousands of transmigrants. It is therefore not so high a count of the indigenous population as to rule out the 1980 census figure (along with the 1979 Indonesian counts) as an underestimate.

Even a post-1980 population growth rate of 2.5 percent p.a. (excluding the arriving transmigrants) may be unlikely but is not impossible, especially after a massive loss of life had occurred from 1975-80. There is no reason to dismiss the 1980 census figure on the grounds that annual growth of 2.5 percent is out of the question. We have already seen that the Catholic Church count of the 1974 population implies a 3 percent p.a. increase after 1970. Cribb writes that the demographer suggesting a pre-1975 growth rate of 1.8 percent "as a likely figure in a relatively stable agricultural society", also noted "that rates like 3.5 percent were possible (and were known from the Philippines), but that they should be regarded as exceptional, a consequence of improved disease control (though not necessarily prosperity), social disruption and rural economic opportunities caused by capitalist penetration…, and the availability of major towns and cities as absorbers of population."[53]

To factors favoring rapid population growth we must also add the East Timorese context: the rebuilding of families after large-scale losses in 1976-80. The pre-1970 Cambodian growth rate was 2.6 percent or even 2.95 percent in 1970. And following the proportionately comparable genocide there, growth rates in 1981-88 reached "an extraordinary 4 percent per year," before leveling off to 2.8 percent by 1988.[54]

A 1981-87 annual population growth rate of 2.5 percent from the 1980 census figure would suggest a 1987 population of at least 660,000, higher than the official total. The difference could be explained by the 1981-82 famine and documented mass killings which continued from 1981 to 1987. For instance, in a September 1981 massacre southeast of Dili, Indonesian troops reportedly killed 400 people. In August 1983, sixty men, women and children were tied up and bulldozed to death at Malim Luro near the south coast. On August 21-22, 1983, troops burned alive at least eighty people in the southern village of Kraras, and then made a "clean-sweep" of the neighboring area in which another five hundred died.[55] The 1980 census figure of 555,350 can therefore easily

53. Robert Cribb, personal communication, 10 October 2001.
54. Grant Curtis, *Cambodia: A Country Profile*, SIDA, Stockholm, 1989, pp. 6-7; Jacques Migozzi, *Cambodge: faits et problèmes de population*, p. 209; Kimmo Kiljunen, ed., *Kampuchea: Decade of the Genocide*, London, Zed, 1984, p. 34.
55. John G. Taylor, *East Timor: The Price of Freedom* (London, 1999), pp. 101-3, 142, 206; Paulino Gama, "The War in the Hills, 1975-1985," in *East Timor at the Crossroads,* ed. P. Carey and G. C. Bentley (New York: SSRC, 1995), p. 102.

be reconciled with Mubyarto's 1987 official maximum even without allowing for the tens of thousands of transmigrants and without presuming the possible annual population growth rate of 2.5 percent.

There is every reason to accept the 1980 census figure. So by then, the territory's population must have fallen to 560,000 from the December 1975 minimum of 643,000, to which any births (minus "normal" deaths) from 1976 to 1980 should be added. We may accept that the famine and terror conditions of 1976-80 could have reduced this "normal" population growth from at least 1.8 percent to as low as 1 percent p.a. Starting from the minimum 1975 population of 643,000, if we apply to the five-year period 1976-80 only the very low natural growth rate of 1 percent p.a. (as I have assumed for the DK period in Cambodia), the total population of East Timor should have reached 675,799 in 1980. But the number of survivors was no more than 560,000. The 1975-80 population loss, above the normal death rate, was at least 116,000.

On the other hand, if we accept the 1974 church count instead of the Portuguese census quarterly updates, the 1975 population of 698,000, increasing in 1976-80 by only 1.0 percent p.a., should have reached 733,605 by the end of 1980, suggesting a loss of 174,000. Increasing annually at even 0.5 percent p.a., it should have reached 715,625 by the end of 1980, which means a loss of 155,625. The order of magnitude of the 1975-80 toll is therefore within the range of 116,000 to 174,000. A median estimate would be 145,000. Cribb is correct to specify that for the 1975-80 period "the figure of 200,000 should be dropped," but a toll of 150,000 is likely close to the truth.[56] If we include victims of post-1980 massacres and of the 1981-82 famine, the figure is substantially higher.[57] Gabriel Defert, assuming a 1970-75 growth rate of 2.2 percent and 1.1 percent for 1975-81, calculates a toll of 170,000 deaths by December 1981.[58]

This is all consistent with estimates of the death toll from various Indonesian sources. The president of the pro-Indonesian provisional government of East Timor, Lopes da Cruz, announced on 13 February 1976 that 60,000 people had already been killed "in the six months of civil war in East Timor," suggesting

---

56. My conclusion, reached before reading John Waddingham's 1980 article, "East Timor: How Many People Missing?," confirms his toll range of 133,000-217,000, "at least one-fifth" of the population.

57. On the 1981-82 famine, exacerbated by the Indonesian army's 1981 "fence of legs" operation, see Taylor, *East Timor*, pp. 117-20; "Recent Developments in East Timor," *Hearing before the sub-committee on Asian and Pacific Affairs of the Committee on Foreign Affairs, House of Representatives*, 97th Congress, Second Session, September 14 1982 (Washington, D.C., U.S. Government Printing Office, 1982); Rod Nordland, "Hunger. Under Indonesia Timor Remains a Land of Misery," *Philadelphia Inquirer*, 28 May 1982; International Committee of the Red Cross, "East Timor Situation Report no. 6," 1.7.1981-31.12.81; and no. 7, 1.1.1982-30.6.1982 (Geneva, 1981-82); Arnold S. Kohen, "The Shattered World of East Timor," *Los Angeles Times*, 7 January 1982. I am grateful to Peter Carey for these references.

58. Defert, *Timor-Est. Le Génocide oublié*, p. 149.

a toll of over 55,000 in just the two months since the invasion. A late 1976 report from the Indonesian Catholic Church estimated that 60,000 to 100,000 Timorese had perished. In March 1977, Indonesian Foreign Minister Adam Malik conceded that "50,000 people or perhaps 80,000 might have been killed during the war in Timor." On 12 November 1979, Indonesia's new Foreign Minister Mochtar Kusumaatmadja estimated that 120,000 Timorese had died since 1975.[59]

---

59. Dunn, *Timor*, pp. 302-3, 310; Taylor, *East Timor*, p. 201, 203; Jill Jolliffe, *East Timor: Nationalism and Colonialism*, St. Lucia, Australia, University of Queensland Press, 1978, p. 278; Melbourne *Age*, 1 April 1977. See Noam Chomsky and Edward Herman, *The Political Economy of Human Rights*, vol. 1, *The Washington Connection and Third World Fascism* (Boston: South End, 1979): 175-76. For more recent estimates on the death toll in East Timor, see *Chega ! The Report of the Commission for Reception, Truth and Reconciliation in Timor-Leste* (CAVR), October 2005, online at: www.cavr-timorleste.org

Part 3

War and Recovery: Reporting from Cambodia, 1979-90

10

Reports from the
Thai-Cambodian Border, 1979

Introductory Note

Several weeks after the overthrow of the Pol Pot the regime on January 7, 1979, I left Australia for Thailand to commence the fieldwork for a planned Ph.D. dissertation on early twentieth-century Cambodian colonial history. The next four months in Thailand, spent mostly in a Khmer-speaking village in Surin province near the Cambodian border, improved my Khmer and offered opportunities to visit refugee camps and speak to Cambodians who had recently crossed the border. Within a month of the Vietnamese invasion of Cambodia, China launched its own invasion of northern Vietnam, with chilling implications for many Cambodians living near the Thai border. I wrote several reports from there. By the end of 1979, I had revised my planned dissertation topic. I set about writing a history of the Khmer Rouge and of the Pol Pot regime that had perpetrated mass murder against its own people and their neighbors, and had brought Cambodia to the center of an international storm.

"People Heng in Against Pol Pot"
Nation Review (Melbourne), April 5, 1979

Unless China's leaders are afflicted with a Nixonian desire to "punish" Vietnam for the sake of it, the aim of their invasion was to force Vietnamese troops out of Kampuchea. They must have seen these troops as rapidly demolishing any chances of the return to power of their ally Pol Pot, ousted on 7 January.

But Pol Pot's radio, thought to be based in China, claims its forces have the Vietnamese bogged down in a quagmire. It plays heavily on traditional ethnic barriers between Kampucheans and what Pol Pot on 5 January called their "hereditary enemy," the Vietnamese.

The radio of the new pro-Vietnamese government of Heng Samrin makes few statements about fighting in Kampuchea. It describes the "cruel nature" of the Pol Pot regime and promises an end to the repression of the population.

We must look to other sources for information about Kampuchea today. Western intelligence agencies for the last few months have reported that heavy fighting continued throughout January. They also indicate popular support for the new pro-Vietnamese government.

Intelligence reports quoted in the *Far Eastern Economic Review* in December 1978 considered this support to be "surprising" in view of traditional ethnic prejudices, and reported in January that Kampuchean villagers were assisting the Heng Samrin and Vietnamese troops to round up unpopular Pol Pot cadres. Similar reports come from Thai military sources. Noting that Kampuchean villagers ceased fleeing into Thailand in large numbers after the change of government in Phnom Penh these sources added: "If Pol Pot wins the fight we expect to have a bigger inflow of refugees, because most Kampucheans are now in favour of the new regime led by Heng Samrin."[1]

But since then another 1,800 villagers have crossed the Thai border from northwest Kampuchea. A Christian volunteer who has been doing relief work in Khmer refugee camps here for three and a half years has chatted with quite a few of them. I talked with him on 3 March. He said "most of them speak well of the Vietnamese," who "behaved well" when they entered the Kampuchean villages and left after a time.

Popular feelings about the foreign army were at first based on the fact that the Vietnamese "did nothing," quite unlike the Pol Pot troops who treated them very badly, he said. In two villages from which the Vietnamese withdrew, Pol Pot troops returned, and began a large-scale massacre. He said in one such village only thirteen survived, and escaped to Thailand. Refugees arriving later brought news that the Vietnamese were distributing arms to villagers so they could protect themselves from Pol Pot troops.

American Congresswoman Elizabeth Holzer said some of these refugees said that if the pro-Vietnam forces won the war they would return home "although they would prefer not to."[2]

Journalists have also interviewed recent refugees from Kampuchea in Thailand. According to Bangkok's *Nation Review* of 8 March: "The refugees say that Vietnamese and new government troops came into their villages, treated the people well, and held elections for local leaders, but then pulled out. In some cases the Pol Pot forces returned, and killed those who had co-operated with the new regime, the refugees say." These reports confirm a statement made recently in Washington by U.S. Assistant Secretary of State for Asia, Richard Holbrooke, that "there was evidence that Pol Pot's troops were still employing brutality and terror against the population."

Another part of Kampuchea, the north, has also yielded civilian refugees since the change. Kampucheans in the refugee camp in the Thai province of Surin

---

1. *Far Eastern Economic Review* (Hong Kong), 22 Dec., 1978 and 26 Jan., 1979; *Nation Review* (Bangkok), 16 Feb. 1979.
2. *Nation Review* (Bangkok), 19 February 1979.

have been able to contact them. I talked with several people in the Surin camp on 2, 3 and 6 March. They said the war was all over in the north, adding that the Pol Pot regime was so harsh and cruel that people welcomed the Vietnamese forces. They had heard that summary execution of villagers, confiscation of rice produced, and forced separation of families, had ended.

They reported that the Vietnamese, as well as distributing food, clothes, and cooking utensils, were arming the people (one gun for five civilians, one refugee said): and that where they held out, the Pol Pot troops were "crueller than ever." This confirmed the reports from different sources of events in the northwest.

Thai officials at the border town of Aranyaprathet differed from most in their prediction of the outcome of the war in Kampuchea. They said the Vietnamese would lose, partly because Pol Pot troops were being re-supplied though they claimed they did not know by whom. There is considerable evidence of continuing unofficial trade between Thai merchants and Pol Pot forces. As for the official level, China's Deng Xiaoping, Kampuchea's Norodom Sihanouk, and U.S. intelligence have all stated that Pol Pot troops are obtaining supplies from China via Thailand.

A Kampuchean refugee member of a right wing guerilla movement told me that Thai officials had twice asked him to fight alongside Pol Pot troops against the new government. He steadfastly refused he said, adding that Pol Pot would never regain power anyway "now that the people have guns." It was unusual to hear Kampucheans who described themselves as anti-communist state wistfully, but quite categorically as they did, that the Kampuchean population was pleased with the communist Vietnamese presence. Pol Pot, whose regime in its last two years was – in their own words – "socialists" became so unpopular that deep rooted ethnic and political barriers have broken down.

Such a political climate in Kampuchea spells a very quick doom for Pol Pot *unless*:

1. His troops receive supplies of military equipment on a scale much larger than any successful guerilla movement has enjoyed, and
2. Vietnamese troops are forced to pull back to defend their own country before they can arm and train the many Kampucheans who don't want Pol Pot to return to power.

It appears that China is doing its best to bring about these two conditions, so far with mixed success.

"Thai Neutrality a Farce"
Nation Review (Melbourne), May 24, 1979

From 22 to 26 April [1979] about 100,000 refugees, including at the very least 20,000 soldiers with arms, crossed into Thailand from Kampuchea. Within a few days, they had all returned to another part of their country. Who were these people and what were their motives in crossing into Thailand?

On January 7, the brutal regime of Pol Pot was overthrown in Kampuchea by a pro-Vietnamese group led by Heng Samrin and backed by Vietnamese troops. The new government quickly seized control of all major towns. The flow of refugees into Thailand, which had been going on since 1975, stopped.

Then, on 17 February, China invaded Vietnam. Vietnamese troops were pulled back home in larger numbers, at least from western Kampuchea near the Thai border. Over the next five weeks, 2,800 refugees fled that area into Thailand.

The Thai government immediately classified these people as "illegal immigrants" and distinguished them from those who had fled in the four years to 7 January. Although some had husbands, wives or children among the earlier arrivals, the two groups were kept rigidly apart, in separate camps.

The UN High Commission for Refugees was refused all access to the newcomers. So were virtually all journalists who wished to interview them. One did get in, however, and talked to a number of refugees, including one from a village near Phnom Penh. He reported that the refugees said they had received "good treatment" from the troops of the new pro-Vietnamese Government.[3] But those troops had since withdrawn, they said, and in some villages Pol Pot troops had returned and executed hundreds of people, causing the refugees to flee to Thailand.

Kampucheans residing abroad hoping to talk to the newcomers to seek news of their families were also refused access to them by Thai authorities. These refugees have in fact been put "under military supervision."[4]

Quite by accident we came across one woman refugee as she was undergoing medical treatment. We were able to talk to her for several hours on 2 April, and recorded the conversation. Hong Var and her two daughters fled to Thailand on 12 March, with 204 others. She said every one of the peasants and people from other backgrounds in her village hated the Pol Pot regime bitterly, especially after the year 1978, during which she said half the population in the village died or were executed. The Vietnamese troops were welcomed, and treated the people well. There was a feast; the Vietnamese distributed food and medicine, and re-established freedom of travel. Then they withdrew. Fifty or sixty families of former Phnom Penh residents decided to return home and set out after them. These people were ambushed twice by Pol Pot troops and nearly all of them were killed, Var said. Pol Pot troops returned to the village. Not long after, Var joined the people of a nearby village who fled to Thailand (while Pol Pot forces were attending a meeting), almost down to the last person.

Var's account of the contrasting behavior of the pro-Vietnamese and the Pol Pot troops confirms the accounts of the refugees who fled from other villages two weeks earlier. On March 3, I was able to hear those accounts from a refugee camp worker (see *Nation Review*, 5 April). On 7 April, I talked to him again; he said that another group of sixty-three Kampuchean refugees had crossed into

3.   *Bangkok Post* [BP], 27 March 1979.
4.   BP, 13 April 1979.

Thailand in early April. They also recounted that the Vietnamese had "behaved well" and then withdrawn, and returning Pol Pot forces had committed large scale atrocities.

A missionary who speaks fluent Khmer and works closely with the Kampuchean refugees told me on 3 April that in several villages in Battambang province, returning Pol Pot troops had executed every single adult male in the village. He added, on the other hand, that "the Vietnamese seem OK, so far."

Other sources with access to the new refugees report similarly. Pol Pot forces have recently "massacred a large number of villagers," according to U.S. Assistant Secretary of State for Asia, Richard Holbrooke. He told a congressional hearing that "the Pol Pot forces killed the villagers, because they had accepted pots and pans from the Vietnamese."

According to intelligence sources, "the new regime is gaining popular support from the Cambodian people because of its more liberal policy towards the people – a complete contrast to the harsh treatment and atrocities imposed by the Pol Pot regime."[5]

Nevertheless, Thailand regards these refugees as "Khmer Rouge [read Pol Pot] troops and their families who fled from Poipet and a Vietnamese onslaught all along the border regions."[6] Their officials claim this is the main reason they are kept apart from "old" refugees and under military supervision.

There is increasing resentment in Thailand against the influx of refugees. But, is Thailand in fact also unwilling to allow the news carried by these refugees to become widely known?

This may be a logical step, if Thailand is actively trying to undermine the Vietnamese-backed Heng Samrin regime. It was almost common knowledge along the border in March that this was undoubtedly the case. And an extremely well-placed source, involved with both the Kampuchean refugees and the Thailand authorities, told me in Aranyaprathet on 2 April that Thailand was sending food and medicine and some weapons across the border to Pol Pot forces.

Thailand is not just backing Pol Pot, however. The same source added that members of the Khmer Serei, a right wing guerilla group under Thai influence, have been sent into Kampuchea to try to infiltrate the Heng Samrin administration. Pol Pot forces have been asked by Thailand not to attack such infiltrators passing through their territory along the border, the source said.

In Surin on 2 March, a leading member of the Khmer Serei had told me Thai officials had twice approached him and asked him to support Pol Pot against the new regime. He refused both times. On 3 March, Agence France-Presse reported that the Khmer Serei were opposed to the new regime, but that they admitted the population was "generally approving" of it, because it "has given people back their freedom."

---

5. *Business Times*, Bangkok, 27 March 1979
6. BP, 10 April 1979.

Early in April, the new Kampuchean government began a large scale offensive against the most significant remnants of the Pol Pot army, those along the Thai border. This was not totally a Vietnamese affair.

Within a short time, Thai and Western intelligence agencies reported that the Heng Samrin offensive had made "huge gains."[7] These included the capture of Pol Pot's main base. More importantly, the bulk of the Pol Pot army was driven into a corner on the Thai border as Heng Samrin slowly closed in on them.

By 22 April, probably more than 100,000 Kampucheans were reported waiting to cross into Thailand. These included 300 high-ranking Pol Pot officials and at least two former ministers (BP, 14 and 15 April). One group of 20,000 and another of 25,000 included 8,000 and 10,000 Pol Pot soldiers respectively. But is it correct to label all the rest as "civilians loyal to Pol Pot"?

During February and March, many refugees arriving in Thailand reportedly said that Pol Pot troops had forced people into the forests and hills before the advancing Vietnamese troops arrived in their villages. In March I interviewed two young Kampuchean boys who had been evacuated from their villages with Pol Pot troops and had crossed into Thailand.

When it first became clear that a Heng Samrin offensive was imminent in the area bordering Thailand, the *Bangkok Post* reported on 31 March: "Some 20,000 refugees who have fled from the Khmer Rouge in recent months are hidden in the region." On 5 April, the Heng Samrin news agency SPK claimed that when Pol Pot's main base was captured, "tens of thousands of people force to live there were freed."

Nam Sal Tang, a former Kampuchean journalist, crossed into Thailand on 13 April. He said "that the Pol Pot forces had forced thousands of civilians (including himself) to evacuate with them in the long march to escape the Vietnamese-led offensive. He said that at the start of the march from Phnom Penh about three months ago, there were some 40,000 troops and civilians, and by the time they reached the Thai border only some of 25,000 remained."[8]

Four days later, a group of sixteen civilians fled into Thailand from a Pol Pot-held pocket of territory. They said that "civilians were trying to escape into Thailand because of the intense fighting, fear of Pol Pot soldiers and their cruel methods, and because of shortages of food and medicine."[9]

This was to be the last contact between the new refugees and journalists. In expectation of a large influx, Thai military had several days before begun mining a 50km. stretch of the border, leaving sections open through which people could be guided. Arrangements were obviously being made with certain people on the other side.

---

7.   *Business Times*, 6 April 1979.
8.   BP, 14 April 1979.
9.   BP, 18 April 1979.

As from 15 April, "all newsmen were banned near the border and all villagers were told not to venture close to the border at a risk to their lives from the landmines."[10]

Meanwhile, the 1,800 of the 2,800 refugees who arrived in February and March who had not yet been sent to the detention centers in Trat province, were shipped there from their camp on 12 April. Few, if any, journalists have ever been allowed access to the Trat centers, and no-one expects that anyone will be now. There is in fact speculation among Westerners working in the other camps that these people will be secretly sent back to Kampuchea. At any rate they are being accorded "neither the rights of refugees nor the care of the UN High Commission for the Refugees" and remain under military supervision.[11]

As far as fleeing soldiers were concerned, Thailand's PM Kriangsak had said on 5 April, "Normally we don't allow any foreign troops to enter our country. But if we cannot block them, then we would disarm them and put them into separate detention." It was apparent very early that Thai forces were not adhering to such a policy. On 11 April, eighty-eight Pol Pot soldiers who crossed into Thailand were fed and given medical attention as newsmen watched.

On the same day, civilians fleeing from Kampuchea were already being pushed back against their will. When 500 people crossed the border in panic, "reporters and a UN refugee official were not initially allowed to pass an army roadblock.... When they arrived at the border, one last man was pushed back across.... [As he disappeared] he was heard to say three times in Thai that he would be killed if he went back."[12]

When the tens of thousands of Kampucheans finally crossed the border on 22 April, two things became quite clear:

1. Thailand was giving valuable military assistance to Pol Pot forces, by allowing the large group of over 50,000 soldiers and civilians to trek through Thailand for two days, and recross into Kampuchea at a point behind the Heng Samrin lines. On both border crossings they were presumably guided through the minefields by Thai military forces. Additionally, two other groups of Pol Pot guerillas, each numbering 2,000 soldiers, were allowed into Thailand at different points, "and reentered Cambodia behind their opponents' lines for what appeared to be preparation for a counterattack."[13] The Heng Samrin government accused Thailand on 16 April of firing artillery up to 4km. inside Kmapuchea at several points, overflying Kampuchean airspace and "supporting the Pol Pot army." The specific allegations could not be confirmed, because journalists were barred by Thailand from approaching the border.

10. BP, 16 April 1979.
11. BP, 13 April 1979.
12. BP, 14 April 1979.
13. BP, 26 April 1979.

2. A large number of the civilians involved were unwilling followers of Pol Pot. Despite the blockade, some observers did manage to get to the refugee column. According to *Nation Review*: "Thai villagers told newsmen that four or five civilians with the Pol Pot group had been killed, and others were forced back to Kampuchea against their will, by the Pol Pot soldiers. The villagers said those who resisted were tied to bamboo poles and forced to march along at gunpoint."[14] The next day, the Thai Interior Ministry confirmed the deaths and added that two Thai peasants had been killed by Pol Pot troops as well.

There was no attempt by Thailand to disarm the Pol Pot troops, "most of whom appeared to be only 10 or 12 years old."[15] Two photographs taken at the scene show Pol Pot troops, heavily armed, "escorting" the civilians through Thailand, in the words of the *Bangkok Post*. In fact, the Pol Pot soldiers' supervision of the civilians seems to have benefited from Thai military co-operation. According to the *Post*, "Thai soldiers warned reporters not to talk to the refugees. They said it could create danger for them if seen by Khmer Rouge soldiers who marched alongside the column in groups of three or four."[16]

It appears that Thailand may well have "saved the Khmer Rouge army in the northwest – at least for now,"[17] prolonging the war in Kampuchea and the immense suffering of the people of that country. Thailand evidently sees a continuing war in Kampuchea as being in its best "security" interests. In carrying out this policy, Thailand has also refused a large number of people their rights as refugees, and sent many others to an uncertain fate with the Pol Pot forces.

On the other hand, though, it is clear that the Heng Samrin forces have now dealt a severe blow to Pol Pot. According to Associated Press, this "may have helped avert famine…. Analysts had feared that insecurity in the countryside would prevent the ploughing of the all-important rice fields this month and the laying down of the rice crop…. The level of fighting in central and eastern Kampuchea has dropped off sharply in recent weeks."[18]

It should be pointed out, too that the refugee flow is not all one way. Well-placed sources told me recently that, during February and March, over 500 Kampucheans secretly returned to their country from the Surin refugee camp in Thailand. One came back early in April, and reportedly said that there was sufficient food in Kampuchea now and that villagers were not being harassed. When he returned, 400 more refugees went back to Heng Samrin's Kampuchea with him.

One refugee told us in Aranyaprathet on 2 April of his wish to return home. He added that there were more than one hundred others who wanted to go back now.

---

14. *Nation Review* (Bangkok), 25 April 1979.
15. BP, 24 April 1979.
16. BP, 25 April 1979.
17. BP, 27 April 1979.
18. BP, 27 April 1979.

"Kampuchea: One in Four Doomed"
Nation Review (Melbourne), October 4, 1979

Paris: An official of the French medical aid organization, Médecins Sans Frontières, has concluded after a week's visit to Kampuchea that one-quarter of the population is already doomed to die of starvation. He also points out that massive aid is absolutely necessary to try to save the rest. Basic aid is what is needed, Dr. Jean-Luc Lubrano-Lavadera said. There is not a single cake of soap in Kampuchea today and without elementary hygiene all medical action is ineffective, he said. The doctor also calls for enormous supplies of rice to be sent to Phnom Penh.[19]

The problem blocking Western aid to Kampuchea is the presence of Vietnamese troops there. A French nun, Françoise Vandermeersch, also recently returned from Kampuchea, where she had accompanied the French Committee for Medical and Sanitary Aid to the Cambodian People. In Hanoi on 10 September, she stated that "the actions of the new Khmer authorities [the Heng Samrin government in Phnom Penh] must be supported," "without claiming to set oneself up as a judge and without demanding an immediate balance-sheet." She protested against the "guarantees demanded by the Western countries as far as the destination of the aid sent to Kampuchea is concerned."[20]

So far, aid to Kampuchea in its recovery from the depredations of the Pol Pot regime has come only from UNICEF, the International Committee of the Red Cross, and the British and French Medical Aid Committees for Vietnam and Kampuchea, as well as from Vietnam and the Soviet Union.

But this is not enough. It is clear that only huge contributions from the West, including the United States and Australia, who played their part in the destruction of Kampuchea, can bridge the gap that separates the Kampucheans from their future as a people. Dr. Lubrano-Lavadera brought home the seriousness of the situation when he noted the "almost total" disappearance of children under five years of age, and near general barrenness among the Kampuchean women due to malnutrition or psychological trauma undergone during the Pol Pot period.

Someone who might attract the favors of the Western powers towards Kampuchea is Prince Norodom Sihanouk, who lives in North Korea and pronounces himself in "complete agreement" with American policy in Southeast Asia.[21] But while he refuses any alliance with what he calls the "tyrannical, Hitlerian" Pol Pot remnants, he also declines to lend his support to the Heng Samrin government which is now calling for large scale humanitarian aid. He criticizes Heng Samrin as a "pro-Vietnamese traitor," although he apparently see no contradiction in saying that he himself is "and will remain in spite of everything a faithful friend of China," the country that has strongly backed Pol Pot.

---

19. *Le Monde*, Sept. 16-17, 1979.
20. *Le Monde*, Sept 12, 1979.
21. *Le Monde*, Aug. 30, 1979.

Meanwhile in Kampuchea itself, the Prince's cousin, Princess Lola Sisowath, who lost her husband, three daughters and twenty-four relatives to the Pol Pot regime, takes a different view. She reproaches Sihanouk for not being "grateful to Vietnam," claiming "he will never understand what happened in Kampuchea because he wasn't in the middle of it. Sihanouk was a prisoner of Pol Pot, of course, but in a palace. He doesn't know what the people endured."[22]

And what of the Vietnamese troops who helped put an end to the Pol Pot reign of terror? In a new book, *Chronicles of War...and Hope*, Prince Sihanouk says: "I assume a heavy responsibility before history in stating that the presence of the Vietnamese army in my country today, as unpleasant and as humiliating as it is for we Khmers, constitutes the only protection – although imperfect – that the Khmer people have against being massacred by the partisans of Pol Pot, Ieng Sary and other Khmer Rouge."[23]

This is indisputably true; so is the fact that the Vietnamese army moved into Kampuchea primarily to put an end to border attacks by Pol Pot forces on Vietnamese villages that were almost as murderous as the treatment of Pol Pot meted out to his own people.

So why doesn't the Prince either, as his cousin suggests, "stop meddling in Kampuchean affairs," or lend the tremendous prestige that he enjoys on the world stage to a vast campaign for aid to save his people from starvation? This would seem to be the most logical and useful thing for him to do while waiting for what he calls the "eventual" Vietnamese withdrawal, which he says must await the arrival in Kampuchea of "a powerful international army to prevent the Khmer Rouge from cutting the throats of the innocent Khmer people."[24] When will that be?

Here is Sihanouk's chance to prove himself the "real nationalist" he has always claimed to be. And Australia's chance to win goodwill by ceasing to recognize the Pol Pot regime and immediately dispatching food and medicine to Phnom Penh.

Cambodia in 1979*

In December 1978, the *Far Eastern Economic Review* discussed the prospects of the newly formed United Front for National Salvation (UFNS) in Kampuchea led by Heng Samrin. It quoted Western intelligence sources as saying that in villages where it was established, one of the first moves the UFNS made was to demolish

22. *Le Matin*, Sept. 15, 1979.
23. Norodom Sihanouk, *Chroniques de guerre. . . et d'espoir*, Paris, Hachette-Stock, 1979.
24. *Le Monde*, Sept. 15, 1979.
*   "Vietnam and the Governments and People of Kampuchea," *Bulletin of Concerned Asian Scholars*, 11:4, Oct.-Dec. 1979. The original *Introductory Note* to this article appears in chapter 5.

the communal dining halls built by the Pol Pot forces. The sources commented: "surprisingly, the Front seems to be getting popular support."[25]

After the overthrow of the Pol Pot Regime the next month, the *Review* quoted the same intelligence sources to the effect that in some areas the local Kampuchean population had risen up in "spontaneous and scattered uprisings" against Pol Pot, and were assisting the Vietnamese and Heng Samrin troops in their attempts to mop up the defeated forces and unearth arms caches.[26] Other sources confirm this, specifying one particular uprising of this kind at Cheom Khsanh in Preah Vihear province.

Many refugees who have fled to various parts of Thailand because of the war in Kampuchea also report that the population welcomed the Vietnamese troops and those of the UFNS army. These troops established good relations with the villagers, they say.

Several peasants from northern Kampuchea were interviewed by international observers in the Surin refugee camp in February. An Hian, 22, said that, in her village, "the Vietnamese stayed four days. They did not demand food but distributed cooking instruments so villagers could eat individually if they wanted to.... I do not want to return to Kampuchea because Pol Pot might come back to power," she added.

Suon Sophoat, 25, also said that the Vietnamese "distributed food and ended communal dining." Non Loc, 76, agreed and added that "they also distributed other goods to the people." He said that Pol Pot troops had killed 140 people in his village of Kouk Mon since 1975; he did not trust them when they asked the peasants to attend a meeting after the Vietnamese troops had withdrawn. So he fled to Thailand.

Hong Var, whom Chanthou Boua and I interviewed at length in Aranyaprathet on April 2, fled to Thailand with her two daughters and 204 others on 12 March. [See "Thai Neutrality a Farce," above: she reported that the Vietnamese had reached Andaung Khlong village, re-established freedom of travel, and withdrawn. When fifty or sixty families of former Phnom Penh residents set out to return home, Pol Pot troops ambushed them twice not far from Andaung Khlong, killing nearly all, and then returned to the village.] Not long after, Var managed to join the people of the nearby village of Srae Memai, who fled to Thailand almost to the last person. In Srae Memai, seventeen men had been executed by the Pol Pot forces on their return.

William Shawcross interviewed some Kampuchean refugees in another camp in Aranyaprathet, in March 1979. He reported:

> The Vietnamese appear anxious to win the hearts and minds of the people and seem to behave well toward them. They distribute rice and cooking utensils so that families can once again eat en famille instead of en masse.

---

25. *Far Eastern Economic Review*, 22 Dec. 1978.
26. *Far Eastern Economic Review*, 26 Jan. 1979.

They also either appoint or supervise the election of new village officials. Refugees give the impression that these changes are widely welcomed, despite the fact that they are imposed by the ancient enemy of the Khmers.

But the Vietnamese are stretched too thin apparently to stay in the villages they have occupied. Invariably they move on, sometimes leaving behind a radio for emergency calls. This is ineffective. The Khmer Rouge then return, discover from spies they have left behind what has happened, kill those who collaborated (or were elected to official posts under Vietnamese guidance), take away the food and then force the people to march into the jungle.... This pattern seems to have been repeated frequently, at least in the west of Cambodia.[27]

In an analysis published in *Le Monde*[28] in May, based on interviews with other refugees, François Ponchaud concurred with this. But according to "several refugees," he added, "the Vietnamese are proceeding to empty the country of all the wealth which might still remain." This has not yet been confirmed. Finally, Ponchaud noted that "most of the refugees tell of the bad treatment of Khmer women by the Vietnamese." I asked a Bangkok Kampuchea-watcher, who works in the embassy of a country which has not exactly enjoyed close relations with the Vietnamese communists in the past twenty years, about this. He said there had been cases of rape by Vietnamese soldiers in Kampuchea, but that it was not a general phenomenon: one Vietnamese soldier was ordered shot by his superiors for raping a Khmer woman, he said. He concluded: "I don't accuse the Vietnamese of atrocities, and that includes starving the people."

Khmer and ethnic Chinese refugees from Kampuchea, interviewed in the Aranyaprathet camps by Chanthou Boua and James Pringle on May 21, provided some more recent information about the looming food problem. One of them said:

> There will certainly be famine. Everyone will die, starving to death in the next three or four months. It is the farming season now. There is rain everywhere, but no one can get into the fields to do anything. The Vietnamese told us to go and do the farming, but there is still much fighting going on, and also mines in the rice fields laid by the Pol Pot forces....

Another refugee, questioned about such mines, said: "Pol Pot laid them." The answer to the question: "Who is responsible for all that has happened in Cambodia?" was unanimous: "Pol Pot...Pol Pot...Pol Pot..." But opinions were divided as to what the new government was doing about the food problem. One refugee said that "the Vietnamese are too busy [fighting Pol Pot] to solve the food problem." Another said: "We have seen planes and trucks transporting our food away," while yet another noted: "I have not seen the Vietnamese taking rice out of Cambo-

27. *Asian Wall Street Journal*, 29 March 1979.
28. *Le Monde*, 10 May 1979.

dia." The refugees expressed general agreement with those who said: "The Khmer Rouge killed a person just like killing an ant.... Pol Pot is worse than Hitler—a fascist.... The Vietnamese did not give us any rice, but they did not hurt us." When asked whether there had been any signs that the Heng Samrin forces might kill them, they replied: "They were nice to us, but it is communism."

More than a month after the change of government, a secret meeting is reported to have taken place between representatives of the Thai Communist Party and those of the Pol Pot forces in Kampuchea. According to a detailed account in the Thai weekly *Thai Nikorn*, the meeting, among other things, "took account of the fact that about 80% of the Kampuchean people were in support of the Heng Samrin group." The meeting further noted that:

> A great number of Pol Pot soldiers have secret contacts with the Heng Samrin Government, partly because they are satisfied to an extent with the policies of the Heng Samrin government in granting certain freedoms relating to property, place of residence, etc.

> Not a few Pol Pot soldiers say that if the Heng Samrin government could push the Vietnamese soldiers out of Kampuchean territory immediately, they would support the Heng Samrin government 100% immediately. But if the Heng Samrin government could not do that, their support for it would only be limited.

Interestingly, according to *Thai Nikorn*, the meeting then went on to discuss the Khmer Serei, anti-communist Kampuchean guerrillas based in Thailand.

> Quite a number of Khmer Serei could not bring themselves to cooperate with Pol Pot in fighting against Heng Samrin according to the advice of some large countries. They are very angry about Pol Pot's massacres and confiscation of property and are satisfied to a certain extent with the democratic policies of the Heng Samrin group. Therefore they secretly and openly cooperate with the Heng Samrin government concerning the activities of the extreme rightwing groups in Thailand and of a certain number of big countries on the matter of Kampuchea, by giving detailed information speedily to the Heng Samrin government (about this)....[29]

Also in February, the Khmer Serei themselves drew up a report on the situation in Kampuchea. According to this report:

> The Heng Samrin government has given the inhabitants back their freedom. The people have been authorized to leave the cooperatives where they had been locked up by the Khmer Rouge and to return to their villages.

> The Vietnamese were accompanied by interpreters or small groups of soldiers from the new people's army.... In general they conducted themselves well and even distributed small supplies and medicine to the people. They urged the villagers to elect a new

29. *Thai Nikorn*, Bangkok (Thai-language), 14 May 1979, pp. 14-16.

village committee and often facilitated arming of self-defence units…. The villagers (now) work half a day for the state on collective tasks such as planting rice and
irrigation work. The rest of the day they can work for themselves…. In general the
people appear happy.[30]

It is significant that before this report was released, the Khmer Serei leadership had already decided to fight alongside the Pol Pot troops against Heng
Samrin's government and the Vietnamese.[31] Thai military sources, too, reported
in February that "most Kampucheans are now in favour of the new regime led
by Heng Samrin."[32]

Two non-communist journalists, Harish Chandola and Jean-Pierre Gallois,
visited several provinces of Kampuchea in late March. Both reported evidence of
the fact that the Pol Pot regime had been murderous. They also reported that the
roads in eastern Kampuchea were "filled" with people returning to their homes
after being freed from places where they had been sent to work by the Pol Pot
regime.[33] Gallois, who said he was able to talk to a number of Kampucheans
unsupervised, wrote in a report from Phnom Penh:

> The Cambodians who have returned to this broken city feel that they have been abandoned
> by the non-communist world. They cannot believe that all the Western countries are con-
> tinuing to recognise the legality and existence of the Pol Pot government. They cannot
> understand how the United Nations can disregard their views and try to destroy their only
> outside support without finding a replacement to protect them against a return of Pol
> Pot. In Chang Chamres village, at the gates of Phnom Penh, the same question came
> back dozens of times: "And what are France and United States doing?"

---

30. AFP report by Joel Henri, Bangkok, 3 March 1979. Part of this report may be found
     in *Le Matin de Paris*, 5 March 1979.
31. *Business Times*, Bangkok, 2 May 1979, carries an interview with a Khmer Serei
     officer who said the order to fight alongside the Khmer Rouge of Pol Pot "came
     through Bangkok on February 2," presumably from Paris. According to a Khmer-
     language weekly in Paris, "it is no longer a secret for anyone" that Khmer exile
     leader Son Sann met with Pol Pot representatives in Bangkok on 27-30 May 1979.
     (*Angkor*, 29/7/79.) The Thai government's role in fostering continued insecurity
     in Kampuchea was indicated by a UPI report from Bangkok by Paul Wedel on 14
     May 1979. Wedel wrote: "Khmer Serei soldiers and Khmer Rouge deserters have
     set up a camp with over 5,000 people in the Cambodian mountains supported by
     the Thai military to oppose the Vietnamese occupation army, eyewitnesses have
     said . . . A 28-year-old refugee, who asked that his name not be revealed, said he
     was among almost 1,700 refugees from a camp in Thailand who were handed over
     to the guerrillas by Thai military officers." The refugees were involuntary recruits,
     and 1,000 of the Khmer Serei soldiers were "supplied from Thailand," Wedel went
     on. According to one aid organization, a short time later: "It is reliably reported
     that already 200 of the 1,700 (civilians) are dead, through lack of food and medical
     care." *Christian Outreach*, Newsletter no. 45, p.6.
32. *Nation Review*, Bangkok, 16 Feb. 1979.
33. Ibid., 21 March 1979.

Every night the people of Chang Chamres listen to Western broadcasts in the hope of a reply. The Cambodia that survived Pol Pot is like a dismembered body coming back to life.... Meeting today the people of Phnom Penh, the visitor leaves convinced that the Cambodian people feel, at least at present, only gratitude and reassurance over the Vietnamese presence here.[34]

Chandola, for his part, reported that "there was no shortage of Kampucheans anxious to assure me they'd been saved by the Vietnamese."[35] French journalist Roger Pick received the same impression during a later visit to Phnom Penh.[36]

In May I spoke at length with an ethnic Khmer peasant from a Thai border village, who asked not to be identified. He said he had crossed into Kampuchea for five days in April, to search for relatives who used to live on the other side of the border. He visited Samron, the capital of Kampuchea's Oddar Meanchey province, as well as the village of Trabek and other places.

He said he had discovered that all but two of his relatives had died or been killed during the Pol Pot period. The surviving two had joined the UFNS army, which he said was well liked by the population and in good military control of the Province. Asked about Vietnamese troops, he said he couldn't say anything about them since he had been unable to communicate with them.

In Samrong, this peasant said, mass graves were now being unearthed; these contained the bodies of victims of Pol Pot soldiers, with their hands still bound at the wrists. Many of the dead were monks. Now, he said, the Heng Samrin government was encouraging the practice of Buddhism once again; this was a popular move, he thinks. He said people had told him they were eating better in 1979 than they had in 1978, under Pol Pot. Food was still scarce, but he said there was no starvation when he was there. He was told that because the United Nations did not recognize the new government, "the Khmer would be on their own for a while" with only limited Russian assistance. But he thought morale was quite high since people in Kampuchea were extremely happy to have done with the Pol Pot regime.

This feeling appears general but may not be unanimous. One Khmer, a former stretcher-bearer for the Pol Pot forces, arrived in the Surin camp in Thailand on May 11 from a village in Oddar Meanchey. He told international observers that the Vietnamese troops were treating the local population "pretty well"; however, he said that the Vietnamese suspected some members of the UFNS forces of aiding Pol Pot, and he saw the Vietnamese disarming some of them. The disarming of Heng Samrin troops was also reported by a refugee from Battambang, interviewed by Chanthou Boua and James Pringle on May 21. From late February 1979, when according to refugees arriving

---

34. *Agence France-Presse*, 25 March 1979.
35. *Asiaweek*, 13 April 1979.
36. Interview with *Bulletin de l'Association France-Cambodge*. July 1979.

in Aranyaprathet the Pol Pot forces regained possession of a number of villages and massacred large numbers of their inhabitants,[37] Vietnamese troops distributed arms to civilians for their self-protection. The recall of many of these weapons may signify a rationalization of the UFNS army, or, possibly, political difficulties within it.

While Kampuchean refugees continued to flee to Thailand from the fighting in their country (many of them marched along by armed Pol Pot soldiers under whose guard they remained while in Thailand),[38] some voluntarily went back the other way. These refugees, who fled Kampuchea before the change of government, headed for peaceful areas of the country where Pol Pot forces are no longer active. By early May 1979, according to the UN High Commission for Refugees, between 800 and 1,000 Khmers had returned home from the Surin camp. Later reports indicate that by the end of May another one thousand had gone back voluntarily to UFNS areas of Kampuchea from the Aranyaprathet camp.[39] Yet another thousand left for home in April from a camp 30 km. south of Pakse in Laos.

The general popularity of the new government in Kampuchea is to a large extent a reflection of the extreme unpopularity of its predecessor. But it has also had to overcome deep-rooted traditional ethnic prejudices between Kampucheans and Vietnamese. Reports about the good behavior of the Vietnamese troops towards civilians, carried by nearly all Karnpucheans who came into contact with them and are now in Thailand, are not characteristic of reports

37. See above. For further evidence, a missionary who speaks fluent Khmer and works closely with the Kampuchean refugees told me on 3 April 1979 that in several villages of Battambang province, returning Pol Pot troops had executed every single adult male in the village. He added, on the other hand, that "the Vietnamese seem OK, so far." According to U.S. Assistant Secretary of State for Asia, Richard Holbrooke, Pol Pot forces in early 1979 "massacred a large number of villagers." He told a congressional hearing that "the Pol Pot forces killed the villagers because they had accepted pots and pans from the Vietnamese." This is confirmed by many other sources. See my articles in *Nation Review* (Melbourne), 5 April, 24 May 1979.
38. Thailand has not prevented Pol Pot troops from killing, on Thai soil, a large number of Kampuchean refugees and a number of Thai citizens as well. See *Nation Review* (Melbourne) 24 May 1979, and AP dispatch from Khaw Sa-Thon, Thailand, by Visetsak Sanguangpong; W 105, R33, May 1979. The latter quotes a refugee, Tee Suphat, 25, "who admitted he had acted as a guard for the Pol Pot side," as saying that Pol Pot soldiers trekking "with the civilian columns along the border were given "permission" from higher echelons to execute suspected traitors.... He claimed to have seen the bodies of about 40 Cambodian civilians including children, stabbed to death by Pol Pot soldiers just inside Cambodia across from the Thai province of Chanthaburi. The Pol Pot soldiers he talked to said the dead were "traitors."
39. These people are quite distinct from those, said to be over 40,000, forcibly sent back to Kampuchea against their will, either into the hands of Pol Pot forces, or Khmer Serei forces, or into jungled sections of the frontier sown with minefields. For a horrifying report of these people's fate and the callous role of the Thai Special Forces, see *Liberation* (Paris) 9 July 1979, based on an eyewitness account.

about invading armies, nor of the way many Kampucheans used to talk about Vietnamese.

However, 10,000 ethnic Chinese residents of Kampuchea who crossed into Thailand in early May might have received different treatment. In a letter which they subsequently wrote to the Chinese embassy in Bangkok, these refugees made two points. Firstly, they claimed that in the years 1975-78 over half a million ethnic Chinese had died or were killed in Kampuchea. (One refugee also complained that the Chinese embassy had done "nothing" to protect the ethnic Chinese in Kampuchea during this period.) With the change of government in January, the letter went on to point out, the ethnic Chinese were at first allowed freedom to travel and earn their living at will.[40] But, in May "pressure against them" mounted and the Vietnamese "inspired disunity between the Kampucheans and the overseas Chinese," the letter said.

On being questioned about this, one of these refugees told journalists that "there was little direct abuse by the Vietnamese troops in Kampuchea." But in the letter the ethnic Chinese said they had been blamed for Beijing's support of the Pol Pot government; this "caused simple-minded people to be more hateful to overseas Chinese. They beat and seized belongings of the overseas Chinese after the Vietnamese occupation," the letter said.[41]

Not long after, Vietnamese officers in Battambang province of Kampuchea reportedly announced that those ethnic Chinese who wanted to leave Kampuchea could do so. Thousands were taken in trucks to the Thai border. Thirty-year-old Ang Hua, one of a group of 4,500, told Associated Press "that his group never would go back to Kampuchea because they would be killed by Pol Pot troops. He said the Pol Pot side had branded all who joined the new government and the Vietnamese as "traitors" and had executed many of them."[42]

According to press accounts, the Chinese were transported to Thailand by the Vietnamese in return for payment in gold.[43] During the May 21 interviews with Chanthou Boua and James Pringle, however, one ethnic Chinese at Aranyaprathet denied this, saying: "In the Chinese newspaper they said we had to pay money to leave Kampuchea, but that was not true. We were robbed when we crossed the border." Another of these refugees, asked about the difference between the regimes of Pol Pot and Heng Samrin, replied: "There is not much difference but under the Vietnamese we have our own pots and pans.... And also Heng Samrin's followers don't kill people." When asked, So why do you think that Heng Samrin is not better than Pol Pot?, the reply was: "Because they are very tough on the Chinese...but not on the Khmer."

Tae Hui Lang, an ethnic Chinese refugee who left Kampuchea in late May 1979, was interviewed at length by Chanthou Boua and myself in

---

40. *Bangkok Post*, 11 May 1979.
41. *Business Times*, Bangkok, 16 May 1979.
42. *Bangkok Post*, 23 May 1979.
43. See for instance, *Business Times*, 17 May 1979.

Paris on August 10, 1979. Her account is worth giving in detail. Lang lived nearly four years under the Khmer Rouge, an ordeal which ended with a month-long forced march through the forest of Pursat and Battambang provinces. During the battles that accompanied the march "the rural population would gather together and then run behind the Vietnamese lines,' she said. Finally her Khmer Rouge escorts were driven off, and Lang and a group of other Khmer civilians were free to do the same. After being sent by the Vietnamese to a place where they could obtain food and water, they set out for the town of Battambang.

One woman in the group gave birth to a baby along the way. Some Vietnamese soldiers felt sorry for her, and arranged for a truck to take her the rest of the way. When she arrived in Battambang the Vietnamese brought milk and medicine to her and found a place for her to live. They carried her things for her and arranged for people to look after her, much to the woman's pleasure. Lang herself, who had a two-year old baby, was assisted in carrying her things by Vietnamese soldiers along the way. Although they couldn't speak any Khmer they still made a good impression on Lang's group. "I don't know what their politics was about, but from what I saw they did good things," Lang said. While marching through the forest, the Khmer Rouge had told her that the Vietnamese would kill civilians and molest women, but it didn't turn out to be true, she said.

There were both northern and southern Vietnamese troops. In their encounters with the Khmer population, the northerners behaved much better than the southerners, according to Lang. While walking to Battambang, Lang said she depended on the Vietnamese soldiers a lot, and always made sure that there were some on the road ahead to protect her. During this trip the northern troops warned her that the southerners might be a little undisciplined, and they were, although they never did any harm to Lang or anyone with her. "Their leaders were nice," Lang said.

Lang and her family arrived in Battambang city just before the Khmer New Year in April 1979. She found Vietnamese troops quartered in the city itself; Khmer civilians coming from the countryside were told to build houses for themselves outside the town center. There were many Khmers there, mostly former city dwellers or ethnic Chinese, or farmers who had been slightly better off than others in the pre-1975 period. There were many more women than men since "all the men had been killed off by the Khmer Rouge," Lang said.

There were 100 Vietnamese soldiers for every ten Khmer troops of the new Heng Samrin government. Khmer officials were given the highest-ranking posts, such as province chief, but were flanked by Vietnamese officials from whom "they had to ask permission to get things done," according to Lang. She thinks this might have been because the Vietnamese "wanted to take over our land but at the same time give the false impression that the Khmer have power." Or alternatively it might have been because there were hardly any qualified Khmer officials, intellectuals or skilled personnel to be found. In fact, she said, there were "very few of them left, they had all been killed except for the ones who had managed to hide their backgrounds from the Khmer Rouge. Out of 100, only 2 or 3 were left."

Still, Lang says things were "like before" and that life was "normal," although the population were still scared of Khmer Rouge raids. The Khmer Rouge were by now reduced to small groups who sometimes made murderous sorties from the forest, but were no significant threat either to the population or to the Vietnamese army.

There was a Khmer New Year celebration in Battambang, organized as in pre-1975 years. The Vietnamese and the Heng Samrin troops didn't join in the dancing and festivities, but the latter appointed a committee (*kanak kammakar*) of people chosen from among the lower classes to organize the occasion. Songs were sung, and people visited newly-reopened pagodas. Although the Vietnamese army didn't provide much food for the population, Lang says the people were grateful to them for "letting us have freedom to do what we wanted.... The people like the Vietnamese much more than the Khmer Rouge. The Vietnamese have more heart than the Khmer Rouge."

This also applied to the Vietnamese treatment of their prisoners Lang said. The Vietnamese had captured "many, many Khmer Rouge...they put them in trucks, sent them to jail, and even fed them full." The people were very angry and wanted to kill these Khmer Rouge but the Vietnamese tried to prevent them, advising them to let bygones by bygones and saying that they would try to re-educate the Khmer Rouge. But in a few cases, despite the efforts of the Vietnamese to stop them, the people could not hold back their anger and a number of Khmer Rouge prisoners were killed.

An important reason for her decision to leave was that, in her opinion, "the Khmer people now hate the Chinese minority" in Kampuchea. This was despite the fact that the local Chinese community had suffered under the Khmer Rouge as much as the ethnic Khmers had: "We weren't allowed even to speak Chinese; we were accused of being capitalists by the Khmer Rouge, we were killed off." During the Khmer Rouge period, her father at one stage asked some Chinese advisors, sent to Kampuchea by Beijing, for help in relieving the hardships of life, but they refused. But the population of Battambang in mid-1979 held China responsible for their own sufferings in the previous four years, and associated local Chinese with the Beijing government. Khmer civilians were in fact preparing to hold an anti-Chinese demonstration (*patekam*) in Battambang, "to smash the Chinese in Kampuchea," they said. The Vietnamese did not allow this, and warned people not to talk in terms of the Chinese, Khmer, and Vietnamese races. A Vietnamese leader addressed the crowd, saying that the ethnic Chinese had suffered under the Khmer Rouge, too, and asked people to calm down. He also asked those who wanted to fight the Chinese to put up their hands. A few hands were raised, and he told these people to pack up their things and get ready to go to fight against the Chinese aggressors who had attacked Vietnam. He pointed out that the Chinese residents of Kampuchea were not responsible for all that had happened: many of them had died, he said. After that the crowd calmed down and there was no demonstration, but anti-Chinese feeling among the Khmers subsisted. Many ethnic Chinese felt insecure, and didn't want to stay in Kampuchea any longer. Some of them went to see the Vietnamese leaders in Battambang, who recognized the situation and gave the Chinese a free choice of whether to go or stay. Lang was not required to make any payment to the Vietnamese in order to leave.

In five months of power the People's Republic of Kampuchea managed to make an impressive political start. Paris-based representatives of Khmer exiles recognize that "the present authorities in Phnom Penh" are not mere puppets of Vietnam but in fact "could become an important national political force after the Vietnamese troops withdraw from Kampuchea."[44] Whether the UFNS can maintain its evident popularity while it attempts to deal decisively with Pol Pot's army and Pol Pot's own foreign backers, and haul the country out of economic ruin under the threat of a very severe famine, remains to be seen.

---

44. *Angkor* (Paris), 29 July 1979.

11

War and Peace in Post-Genocide Cambodia

New Light on the Origins of the Vietnam-Cambodia Conflict
Bulletin of Concerned Asian Scholars, **12:4, 1980, 61-65**

> *"Don't make pretexts about Kampuchea Krom in
> order to hide your jaw of traitor." Security regula-
> tion no. 8 for inmates at the Pol Pot regime's Tuol
> Sleng prison (S-21), Phnom Penh, 1977-8.*

On January 7, 1979, Vietnamese-backed forces captured Phnom Penh and overthrew the regime of Pol Pot, Ieng Sary and Khieu Samphan. The population of Cambodia generally welcomed the change. But many Khmers still harboured the suspicion best described by Martin Woollacott, who quoted one as saying: "Yes, the Vietnamese have saved us, but what have they saved us *for*?"[1]

The motives of the Vietnamese communists, and of the Pol Pot government, in pursuing the two-year (1977-78) border fighting that led up to Vietnam's final push have been described in a number of ways. It has been interpreted as a somehow irresolvable "frontier dispute," long-held Vietnamese plans to dominate all of Indochina, Chinese attempts to weaken Vietnam by encouraging Pol Pot raids across its borders, or Pol Pot's need to bolster his flagging internal position by creating an external conflict. However, a 1976 Pol Pot internal communist party magazine gives another angle on the problem, describing it as "the continuous non-stop struggle between revolution and counter-revolution."[2] The June 1976 issue of *Tung Padevat* (Revolutionary Flags), continues:

> We must have the standpoint that the enemy will continue to exist for 10, 20 or 30 years. The national struggle is the same as the class struggle; in a word, the struggle between revolution and counter-revolution will be continuous…. When we are strong they are weak, when they are weak we are strong...(p. 21)

---

1. *Guardian*, London, 3 April 1980.
2. This Khmer-language document may be found at Cornell University's Olin Library. I am grateful to Timothy Carney for passing it on to me. I will also deposit a copy at Monash University Library in Australia. The translation is by Chanthou Boua.

Vietnam, to which this document undoubtedly refers, was thus seen as a long-term enemy whose interests were directly opposed to those of Kampuchea. It was June 1976. What was the background to this policy conviction of the Pol Pot regime?

After the twin victories of the Vietnamese and Kampuchean communists over U.S.-backed regimes in April 1975, they immediately began fighting one another on land and sea. It is difficult to pinpoint what it was that sparked off these serious battles, but they ended with Vietnam capturing Kampuchea's Wai islands and then, in August 1975, handing them back. Further sporadic clashes took place later in the year, but these were not serious, and the year 1976 was a much more peaceful one.

The Central Committees of the Communist Parties of Vietnam and Kampuchea agreed in April 1976 to sign a border treaty in June. From May 4-18, preparatory talks were held in Phnom Penh between the two sides. It was agreed to coordinate border liaison committees, but there was little agreement on the maritime frontier, and Kampuchea postponed the June summit indefinitely. Significantly, though, "Following the meeting" of May 4-18, according to Vietnam, "border incidents decreased in number." Neither side, including Vietnam in its detailed history of border clashes, publicly mentions *any* fighting between the two countries during the rest of 1976. Vietnam's Deputy Minister and Vietnamese reporters visited Kampuchea, reporting favorably on economic reconstruction. Women's delegations from the two countries exchanged visits, and agreement was reached over air links. Interestingly, the Pol Pot regime's detailed official history of Vietnamese "aggression" against Kampuchea neglects to mention these important May 1976 talks or their aftermath.

But *Tung Padevat*, the internal magazine of Pol Pot's party, did make some interesting observations about the border situation in its June 1976 issue.

Within the general framework of the country, the enemy carried out several activities along the land and sea border from the months of November and December (1975) to January and February (1976). From March onwards, the situation has softened considerably.

Along with this we have destroyed the enemies within our country and scattered many of them. They have no strong forces...(p. 20)

Interestingly, there is again no mention of the May negotiations. The magazine goes on:

We want to build socialism quickly, we want to transform our country quickly, we want our people to be glorious quickly. But especially this is to prevent the enemy from harming us. Even now the enemy cannot persist in trying to have his way with us. (p. 42, my emphasis)...The enemy is hesitant towards us (p, 44)...We believe that we could quickly build up the country, It is impossible for the enemy to attack us...(pp. 51-51).

1976 was clearly not a year in which Kampucheans saw any serious indication of Vietnamese ambition on their country, even though Pol Pot's regime
had broken off negotiations.

Internally, however, Kampuchea in 1976 was deeply riven by political strife,
from which the Pol Pot group emerged supreme only at the end of the year.
Beginning around early 1977, a vast series of purges was launched. Leading
communists such as the Cabinet Ministers Hu Nim and Touch Phocun, and
other equally senior figures such as Non Suon, Phouk Chhay and Tiv 01, were
executed. But even more frequently, throughout three-quarters of the country
and fight down to the village level, the revolutionary cadres in place were dismissed, and in most cases executed, sometimes along with their families. Their
replacements were newly arrived cadres from the Southwest Zone, which had
become the stronghold of the Pol Pot group since victory in 1975.

According to *Tung Padevat* of April 1977:

> ...our enemies no longer possess a fifth column in the bosom of our party and people
> to use as a nucleus from which to foment counter-revolutionary activities with the aim
> of overthrowing our regime, destroying our revolution, dismantling the Communist
> Party in Kampuchea, enslaving our people, throwing our army into confusion and
> annihilating our democracy. From another point of view, they are no longer able to
> attack us militarily from the outside.

Who, then, was doing the fighting that had definitely broken out not long
before? The magazine continues:

> Faced with this encouraging situation, what position could we adopt? Should we attack
> our enemies more fiercely, or should we be content with the results obtained:

> ...We should attack them without respite on every terrain by taking our own initia-
> tives and by scrupulously following the directions of our party, both in the internal
> political field and in the field of foreign relations....We must fight the enemy coming
> from the outside in all theatres of operations and in every form.[3]

Interviews

What follows are accounts by Cambodian refugees whom I interviewed in
France during 1979-80.

Mrs. Lang Sim, a Khmer refugee now in France, was in Snuor district of
Battambang province in mid-1977 when new cadres arrived from the Southwest Zone. At a meeting in her village of Lopeak at the end of that year, these
cadres told a gathering of about thirty people at which she was present that
"Kampuchea aimed to fight to recover Kampuchea Krom [the Mekong Delta]

---

3.   I am grateful to Gareth Porter for passing on to me a partial translation of this issue
      of *Tung Padevat*.

from Vietnam, as well as Surin and other provinces from Thailand." Bopha, a Phnom Penh woman who lived in Saang district of Kandal province after the 1975 evacuation, said that the Khmer Rouge there were "all right" until April 1977 (we know from other sources that the province party secretary had been arrested on March 15). Brutality against the population then became a hallmark of government control of Saang, she said. In 1978, Bopha went on, the Khmer Rouge cadres told villagers including herself that the government of Kampuchea "aimed to fight to get back Kampuchea Krom."

Nguon Son, a worker in a large Phnom Penh "mineral factory" under the Pol Pot regime, recalls that around November 1978, Ta Khon, the director of the factory, said in a meeting that "we aim to liberate the people of Kampuchea Krom and have already liberated 10,000-20,000 of them."

A former Khmer interpreter for North Korean advisers in the Pol Pot period, who had an opportunity to travel widely in Kampuchea, said that the policy to reconquer Kamuchea Krom from Vietnam was "not official," in the sense that it was not mentioned in official statements and publications. Nevertheless, he went on, "right through 1978, from the beginning of the year until the end, everybody I met in the army was talking in those terms."

Although changes in village leadership and many aspects of policy began in various parts of Kampuchea in early 1977, as cadres selected by the Pol Pot group from the Southwest Zone started to arrive in the villages, in the case of Saut Nikom district of Siemreap province cadres from Kampot arrived in March 1978. Sovannareth, 19, was at that time working in a bean-growing production unit in the district. He recalls:

> They arrested the previous local leaders, and made us suffer more than those cadres had. They said they were "real, strong socialists" and that their predecessors were "traitors."

> At a meeting of 1,000 people in the village where I worked the Southwestern cadres put up banners denouncing the "Vietnamese aggressors of our land who are trying to form an Indochina Federation." Another banner asked the Vietnamese a question: "You want us to join a Federation: do you know how to manufacture guns?" Another said: "I am a Kampuchean, and I resolve to fight the Vietnamese," and others "Long live the great and strong Kampuchean revolution." There were many other banners as well.

> We sat on the ground during the meeting, which lasted from 6 P.M. to 10 P.M. The village chief talked about how the people resolved to work hard so that guns and ammunition could be bought to defend the country. Fifteen village chiefs from the district also talked for about ten minutes each, telling us to "destroy all bad habits and oppressive acts."

> Then, the big leader spoke. His name was Ta Meng; he was about fifty years old, and killed people like anything, right in front of others. He talked about how the country had developed, showing photographs, and about the war between the Revolutionary

Army and the Vietnamese. He said they had killed 30,000 Vietnamese in Svay Rieng province, destroyed fifty tanks and shot down four Russian-made planes. In order not to waste anything, he said, the bodies of the tanks had been used to make plates for the people to eat on...

Their plan was to take back Kampuchea Krom. He said that the Vietnamese were swallowers of Khmer land and that "the Khmer people resolve to liberate again the Khmer land in Kampuchea Krom." He talked all about "Moat Chrouk" (Chaudoc province of Vietnam) and "Prey Nokor" (Ho Chi Minh City) and so on. He called for the recruitment of ten youths from each village to join the army...

He also said that Thai planes had attacked Kampuchea's Oddar Meanchey province, and that "we are preparing to attack the Thai in order to take back the Khmer land in Thailand." Later he said: "We will have to fight Thailand in 1979, and we will certainly win. The Thais do not know how to fight because they have never fought before. For example, we went into their villages and killed them and burned their houses, and there was nothing they could do." He said they aimed to get back the provinces of Surin and Sisaket and so on from Thailand. This was in June 1978, in Koh Kong village.

Prince Sihanouk

In 1979, Prince Sihanouk described some of the background to all this in his book, *Chroniques de guerre....et d' espoir*[4]:

In September 1975, I was indeed surprised to hear Khieu Samphan, Son Sen and company say, smiling and very pleased with themselves, that their soldiers were "displeased" with "the Party," because the latter did not give them the green light to go and take back Kampuchea Krom as well as the border districts of Thailand which belonged to Kampuchea in the past (Aranya, Surin, etc.)

Later Sihanouk provided more detail about this conversation: "In the past, they said, our leaders sold out Kampuchea Krom, sold out South Vietnam to the Vietnamese. Our armies can't accept the status quo. We must make war against Vietnam to get back Kampuchea Krom. As the first step, if there are [sugar] palm trees, the soil is Khmer. In Chaudoc and Ha Tien, there are still palm trees. We must occupy."[5]

Sihanouk's book continues that after the 1975 Khmer Rouge victory, they

tried to conquer a part of Kampuchea Krom and committed horrible atrocities on a large number of Vietnamese male and female civilians (including old people, women and children).

The Pol Pot government rejected all the proposals for a peaceful solution presented on several occasions (in particular 5 February 1978) by the Hanoi government...

---

4.   Paris, Hachette-Stock, 1979.
5.   Speech to the Asia Society, New York, 22 February 1980.

In 1978 Khieu Samphan confided to me, concerning the Kampuchea-Vietnam war, that his soldiers (Khmer Rouge) were "unstoppable": whenever they saw sugar palms in the territory of Kampuchea Krom, these patriotic soldiers could not prevent themselves from crossing the frontier and advancing "until they came to the last Khmer sugarpalm"...According to Son Sen, Deputy Prime Minister in charge of National Defence, his glorious "revolutionary army of Kampuchea" considered itself capable of dealing very easily with Giap's (Vietnamese) army, and with the much more puny one of Kukrit Pramoj and Kriangsak Chamanond (Thailand)!

Although Sihanouk's account is possibly sensationalized, it is not unlikely that the Pol Pot group outlined such a policy to the Prince as early as 1975. But apart from the clashes in May-June of that year, serious attacks into Vietnamese territory did not begin until 1977. Serious incidents along the border between northeast Thailand and Kampuchea started around the same time. (This was just when Pol Pot's group was successfully consolidating its power over the internal party opposition.) These attacks by Pol Pot's Khmer Rouge or by joint Khmer Rouge-Thai communist forces were characterized by a brutal militarism quite unlike what is known of the operating methods of the communists in other parts of Thailand at that time, where the tendency was to use political persuasion rather than coercion to win the support of the population.

Around December 1977, according to the leftwing Bangkok journal *Thai Nikorn* (14/5/79), a secret agreement was reached between representatives of the Communist Party of Thailand (CPT), Northeastern Commmittee, and the Kampuchean party secretary of Oddar Meanchey province (adjacent to Surin), representing Pol Pot's Communist Party of Kampuchea (CPK). The meeting agreed

To set up a mixed force of CPT and CPK in order to act in the southern part of Northeast Thailand...

It was agreed that the Kampucheans would send one unit of forces to join the CPT movement, in order that the mixed force should use Pol Pot's lessons on how to seize power, that is, wherever the conditions are ripe for striking against the stable underpinnings of Thai civil servants, an effort should be made to strike, and every day and every night in order to terrorize Thai officials. Wherever conditions are not ripe, a report should be made to the central unit of the Kampuchean side. If it should be thought appropriate, the Kampuchean base unit will enter Thailand and strike against the base without the mixed force having to become involved.

The Thai communist guerrillas in this southern part of northeast Thailand (mostly Surin, Buriram and Sisaket provinces) were nearly all ethnic Khmers of local origin. Their movement, which enjoyed the use of about a dozen base camps inside northern Kampuchea (formalized in the December 1977 agreement), was internally known as Angkar Siem, or "the Thai Angkar," in Khmer: *angkar*, the Khmer term meaning "the Organization," was the word used by the Communist Party of Kampuchea to describe itself. It seems to me extremely curious that a Thai group would explicitly describe itself as virtually the Thai branch, as appendage of the word "Siem" implies, of a characteristically named Kampuchean movement. Unless, of course, certain "Thai military strategists" are correct in thinking that "Phnom Penh increased its support for the Thai communist insurgency along the northern Cambodian border to back irredentist claims on a wide swathe of Thai provinces settled by a mixed Khmer-descended population."[6] A similar evaluation of Pol Pot's designs by the CPT leadership, as well as a realization of the political disaster created by the use of coercion against the Thai border population, and Chinese pressure on Pol Pot to stabilize the Thai front in order to concentrate his forces against Vietnam, may have been the reason for the CPT's cracking down on the activities of Angkar Siem around mid-1978.

In this connection one may legitimately ask what purpose could have been served by the construction of a long road through the forest of northern Kampuchea parallel with the Thai frontier. Work began on this in early 1977, according to one participant in a number of work-teams of teenage Khmer peasant boys.

At almost the same time, Kampuchea began to clash with her third neighbor, Laos. After a December 1978 visit to southern Laos, Nayan Chanda wrote in the *Far Eastern Economic Review* (12/12/78): "It is now clear that the situation on the [Lao-Kampuchean] border has been deteriorating since the end of 1976."

The CPK and Vietnam

But it was against Vietnam that Kampuchean border attacks were the fiercest and most systematic. It is widely accepted that the fighting that broke out in early 1977 and continued throughout the year was initiated by the Kampuchean side, and consisted mostly of raids on villages or shelling of towns. Vietnamese civilian casualties were extremely high. Summarizing numerous reports in the press, *Keesing's Contemporary Archives* gave the following account of the conflict during 1977:

> The situation gravely deteriorated from March 1977 onwards. According to an official Vietnamese document published on 6th January 1978 the Cambodian forces made raids into the Vietnamese provinces of Kien Giang and An Giang on March 15-18 and 25-28, 1977, along a sector nearly 100 kilometres long from Ha Tien (Kien Giang) to Tinh Bien (An Giang). Strong Cambodian forces launched concerted attacks on Vietnamese army posts and on border villages in An Giang between April 30 and May 19, killing 222 civilians, and shelled Chau Doc, the provincial capital, on May 17. These reports were corroborated by Vietnamese refugees reaching other Asian countries, who stated that the civilian population had been evacuated from Ha Tien on May 16 and from Chau Doc on the following day after the two towns had been shelled...According to the Vietnamese document, fighting continued at intervals

---

6.   *Far Eastern Economic Review*, 5/8/77.

throughout mid-1977....The scale of the fighting greatly increased in the second half of September — this development coinciding with Mr. Pol Pot's resumption of the premiership and his visits to China and North Korea. The Vietnamese document of 6 January 1978, which was supported by reports from US intelligence sources, stated that from September 24 onwards Cambodian forces totalling about four divisions had launched continuous attacks along the entire border of Tay Ninh province, and that over 1,000 civilians had been killed or wounded in this area between September 24 and late November...[7]

Of course, some supporters of the Pol Pot regime dispute that Democratic Kampuchea continually instigated clashes with Vietnam during 1977. But so far they have provided little or no evidence to sustain their case. The Pol Pot regime itself accuses Vietnam of beginning its attacks that year only in June (and even for this there is no corroborating evidence), whereas we know from many independent sources that the fighting began in March. The *Black Book*, Pol Pot's detailed official history of the border conflict, in its discussion of Vietnamese "aggression" in the year 1977, mentions only the real Vietnamese cross-border offensive of December.

Two Cambodian refugees in France provide eyewitness accounts of the border fighting in 1977. Veasna fled his country for Vietnam in December 1975. He says he was allowed to live normally as a Vietnamese citizen, taking various jobs. He lived very close to the border, in the village of Ap Sase (Minit, Ha Tien, Kien Giang) and "could see the Khmer Rouge working every day." He says there was no fighting between Cambodia and Vietnam during 1976.

In mid-1977, "the Khmer Rouge started the fighting," Veasna says. "I saw this in actual fact with my own eyes, since my house was 500 metres from the border. When the Khmer Rouge crossed the border everybody ran and grabbed their children and all ran into their houses. But the Khmer Rouge came into our village and bum down houses and burnt goods, and killed about twenty people who were not able to run away..." Before that, in nearby Prey Tameang village, the Khmer Rouge had killed two hundred civilians, including ethnic Khmers as well as Vietnamese, he adds: "The population asked the Vietnamese military to fight back against the Khmer Rouge, but they replied that they didn't have orders from above to do so. In 1977 the Vietnamese did not go into Kampuchean territory" (interview in France, 7 October 1979).

Heng escaped to Vietnam from Svay Rieng province of Kampuchea in October 1975. He too was given permission to live and work as he chose, and he settled down in the mixed Khmer-Vietnamese village of Ke Mea, in Tay Ninh province. He found that the Vietnamese authorities referred to the Khmer Rouge as "brothers," and that all through 1976 there was no fighting along the border.

7.   27 October 1978, 29269. My emphasis. Quoted in Anthony Bamett's draft reply to Laura Summers' article in the *Bulletin of Concerned Asian Scholars*, 11: 4 (1979).

The local Vietnamese community, he said, were not racist in their attitudes towards the Khmers; in Vietnam "they didn't teach the children to hate (the Khmers) as in Kampuchea." Further, "Vietnamese girls liked Khmer boys."

Then, in May or June 1977, the Khmer Rouge shelled Ke Mea, killing "hundreds of people." Many of them were ethnic Khmers as well as Vietnamese, Heng says. The Vietnamese authorities still insisted that the Khmer Rouge were their "friends." Only in early 1978, according to Heng, did they mount loudspeakers in the villages "telling their people what the Khmer had done." (Interview in France, 8 October 1979.)

The Vietnamese counter-offensive of December 1977-January 1978 was followed by a Vietnamese withdrawal from inside Kampuchean territory (or a defeat), and the offer of negotiations, a mutual pullback five kilometers either side of the border, and international supervision of the border to prevent aggression across it. The traditional Vietnamese communist view of themselves, as patrons of the other Indochinese revolutions, had been overcome by a more urgent priority, the desire for a peaceful frontier. If Pol Pot had accepted this offer, made by Hanoi on 5 February 1978, his regime would most likely have survived. But this would also have meant the abandonment of policies towards Vietnam that had become clear enough over the previous year. But with Chinese backing, a desire to reconquer the Mekong Delta from Vietnam, and internal instability within Kampuchea's ruling communist party, the Pol Pot group was not prepared to abandon those policies. They refused the proposal, and their conflict with Vietnam became locked into "the continuous non-stop struggle."

A Proposal for Peace
Inside Asia, **February-March 1985**

I wish to start with a description – with which I think few would disagree – of what most of Kampuchea's population would most wish to see happen inside their country. Their objective is two-fold: the withdrawal of Vietnamese troops from the country and the removal of any threat of Pol Pot's forces returning to power. In my view Kampucheans would want these two things to occur simultaneously; they would not wish Vietnamese troops to remain after the removal of the threat of Pol Pot's forces returning, nor would they want them to leave before that occurs. I say that this is what they would want to happen to them, but the two prime objectives cannot as yet be met because of attitudes and policies outside Kampuchea and outside its control.

Not only does such an arrangement seem a "fair exchange," involving as it does concessions on both sides in the international confrontation, but is also seems, to me at least, the only practical possibility for a negotiated settlement. This is not to say that it is simply the proposal of the lowest common denominator. On the contrary, it would entail important advantages for the Khmer people in terms of peace, stability and independence, and a reduction in outside influence over Kampuchean affairs by all contending international parties. It would involve give and take on all sides.

The Vietnamese View

Vietnam has said that it wants the Chinese threat to its security removed. Following a settlement along the lines described China might well choose to remain hostile to Vietnam. However, I doubt that China would oppose any settlement reached by ASEAN. Anyway Vietnam has convincingly shown that it can handle a direct Chinese invasion from the north, while simultaneously dealing with a Chinese-backed army to its west. Removal of the threat from the west would only facilitate Vietnam's resistance against Chinese pressure. So I am not persuaded by Vietnam's claim that it requires removal of the threat of another Chinese "lesson" on its northern border before it can withdraw from Kampuchea -- at least not so long as that withdrawal ensures a removal of the Pol Pot threat to the west.

The Vietnamese position could be either a bargaining counter that it is prepared to drop when serious negotiations have begun, or else it could hide a Vietnamese desire to remain indefinitely in Kampuchea using as justification the (real but unrelated) continuing hostility of China. The only means to discover which is the case is for serious negotiations to begin, and this has yet to occur.

China's Position

China says that it wants a Vietnamese withdrawal from Kampuchea. But is also has other desires, which are at present parallel ones, but which may eventually conflict with one another. These are: a return of the Pol Pot group ("I do not understand why some want to remove Pol Pot," said Deng Xiaoping recently), or of at least another pro-Chinese government in Phnom Penh; and secondly, good relations with the ASEAN governments. Now, should ASEAN agree to remove the Pol Pot threat, China would be unlikely to oppose them, especially if a Vietnamese withdrawal went hand-in-hand with such an agreement.

Two other Chinese wishes could also conflict in the future. These are the desire to prevent Vietnam hosting increasingly sophisticated Soviet facilities to China's south, and the desire to "bleed Vietnam" economically. I am not sure which of these aims looms largest among China's priorities, but I suspect the latter because of recent statement by a Chinese diplomat that "one should not talk of compromise" over Kampuchea, and because of Deng Xiaoping's statement in December 1979 to the effect that "it is wise for China to force the Vietnamese to stay in Kampuchea because that way they will suffer more and more." These statements indicate that Deng's regime is more worried by the prospect of a healthy Vietnam than of one with Soviet bases. In any case, it was only after the 1979 Chinese invasion of Vietnam that Soviet vessels appeared in Cam Ranh Bay.

However, China alone can not indefinitely "force the Vietnamese to stay in Kampuchea." The future of that arrangement, in my view, depends on Vietnam itself and on ASEAN. Yet in the event of ASEAN agreeing to deny sanctuary and arms to Pol Pot's forces, or even to disarm them, in return for a Vietnamese withdrawal, China would not lose out --- and would certainly not lose face, given its repeated public calls for a Vietnamese withdrawal. Vietnam's influence in the region would be significantly reduced, and so would the scope of Soviet military activity. In return, though, China would have to abandon hopes of reversing the situation in Kampuchea to the one existing before 1979, and might be called on to provide a "Sinkiang dacha" for Pol Pot and his cohorts.

ASEAN'S Position

I will take, as the leading factor within ASEAN, the position of Thailand, given that it is the frontline state and the one to which the other ASEAN governments defer, even when—as is frequently the case with Indonesia—they do not agree with Bangkok's views.

Thailand naturally wants a withdrawal of the Vietnamese forces that are lined along its border, occupying its neighbor. But it also wants a new Kampuchean government, either through "national reconciliation" of all four factions in the two rival Kampuchean parties, or else through internationally supervised elections. Unlike China, Thailand does not necessarily want Pol Pot's forces to return to power, but is currently demanding that they share in power and keep their weapons. Thailand has not publicly or privately offered to deny sanctuary to the Khmer Rouge or to assist in disarming them. But disarming Pol Pot was an option put forward by ASEAN at the 1981 International Conference on Kampuchea and was rejected by China and the U.S. Furthermore, ASEAN again recently agreed on the desirability of Pol Pot's removal, but was once more blocked by China.

Now Thailand's aims of a Vietnamese withdrawal and a new Kampuchean government including Pol Pot's faction may also become contradictory ones. Thailand may be forced to choose which of the two it regards as the higher priority, just as Vietnam may have to decide whether it wants to remain in Kampuchea or have the threat posed by Pol Pot forces removed.

Recent Developments

So what developments have there been over the last year that might promise the eventual possibility of a Vietnamese withdrawal from Kampuchea in return for Thai co-operation in disarming Pol Pot's Khmer Rouge? The answer is, not many, though there have been some glimmers of hope which are worth reviewing.

The most promising of these were the visits to Australia by the Vietnamese and Thai foreign ministers in March 1984. Hanoi's Nguyen Co Thach arrived in Canberra first. After discussions with Australian foreign minister Bill Hayden, Thach thanked Australia for easing conflict in Asia, and then announced that Vietnam was prepared to discuss six issues:

1. The withdrawal of Vietnamese troops from Kampuchea;
2. The removal of Pol Pot and his associates as a political force; (Note that these were the two he mentioned first).
3. The creation of a safety zone on both sides of the Thai-Kampuchean border;
4. Security of borders, including China's border with Vietnam and Laos and the Thai-Lao border;
5. Self-determination for Kampuchea through free elections, but with Pol Pot and his associates excluded; and
6. International supervision and guarantees of all these conditions

What was most interesting here was the absence of any explicit reference by Thach to "removing the Chinese threat" to Vietnam. With some qualifications Vietnam seemed to have dropped one of its two major demands. Thailand's foreign minister Siddhi Savetsila followed Thach to Australia soon afterwards; in Canberra he released a statement welcoming the "new elements" in Hanoi's position. And the Indonesian foreign minister Mochtar Kusumaatmadja described Vietnam's new proposals as a "significant step forward."

Proposal Rejected

But back in South East Asia, meanwhile, things seemed to have gone wrong. Bangkok officials described Thach's statements as "insulting and threatening." On his way home through Indonesia, Thach was presented by President Suharto with a plan for a phased withdrawal of Vietnamese troops in return for Kampuchean "national reconciliation," that is, including Pol Pot as well as Heng Samrin, a proposal which Thach rejected. Finally, in Bangkok, Thach declined to talk with his Thai counterpart Siddhi, feigning a sore throat. But there was obviously also something which worried Thai officials. As Rodney Tasker put it (*Far Eastern Economic Review*, 5 April 1984): "Thach's announcement in Canberra that the Khmer Rouge, rather than the alleged Chinese threat to Vietnam, was Hanoi's main worry was not something the Thais wanted to discuss."

In Tasker's words, the Khmer Rouge were "ASEAN's main bargaining chip," a phrase that can only be described as regrettable in the extreme for reasons that should be evident from recent Kampuchean history. Also regrettable, however was Thach's failure to state explicitly that he had softened Vietnam's position and dropped the "threat from China" demand (though statements of this kind are rarely made in international diplomacy). Thach merely said it was not a high priority, adding "If we can eliminate Pol Pot, we can talk later" (about the Chinese threat to Vietnam). But this statement was still seen in Bangkok as clearly separating the two issues.

Despite all this, Siddhi's encouraging statement a week later after meeting Hayden, in which he welcomed the "new elements" in Thach's proposals, could have been the basis for real progress, and at the same time suggested that Hayden was playing an important role in the affair.

Hayden Rebuffed

The next diplomatic development suggested a similar thing, but in a negative way. Having just secured the acquiescence of the Australian Labor Party over the Indonesian takeover of East Timor and the denial of aid to Vietnam (both policy reversals by Canberra), Hayden left for the ASEAN meeting in Bangkok on 9-10 July 1984. There he proposed a Six (ASEAN) plus Two (Vietnam and Laos) meeting in Canberra to discuss the Kampuchean issue, a suggestion the ASEAN foreign ministers quickly rejected, apparently no longer feeling it necessary to take Hayden too seriously, since the moment Vietnam had shown some flexibility Australia had hardened its attitude towards Vietnam. In the event, the ASEAN ministers released the "strongest, hardest and most strident [statement] to have come out of any ASEAN meeting," according to a senior ASEAN official.

The next development occurred in mid-October 1984, when Thach predicted negotiations on Kampuchea between Indochinese and ASEAN countries within several months. He claimed already to have begun discussions with ASEAN foreign ministers on the date, venue and agenda. As an apparent part of this process Vietnam and Heng Samrin government each agreed to meet secretly with Norodom Sihanouk in Paris. Sihanouk, though, was unable to proceed with the meetings because of opposition from his allies, the Khmer Rouge and China. This according to Nayan Chanda (*Far Eastern Economic Review*, 1 November 1984), showed up the "fundamental difference between ASEAN and China," for ASEAN had agreed on the principle of the "elimination of Pol Pot," which China resolutely rejected. In Vietnam's words, on the other hand, the Heng Samrin government was "ready now for talks with Sihanouk and Son Sann if these [two were to leave] the ranks of Pol Pot," and Hanoi was prepared to accept international control of Kampuchea after agreement was reached.

Obstacle to Progress

It should now be clear that the "Democratic Kampuchea" coalition – Pol Pot's Khmer Rouge, Sihanouk and Son Sann – is a weighty obstacle to progress on the issue. ("Pol Pot is still in firm control of the Khmer Rouge," according to a high-ranking official of Son Sann's anti-communist KPNLF, reported the *Jakarta Post* on 10 March 1984.) It should also be clear that Sihanouk, even though nominally president of the "Coalition Government of Democratic Kampuchea," is unable to take initiatives without the support of the Khmer Rouge. Whatever his own inclinations, he remains a front person for the Pol Pot forces and, behind them, for China. And finally, it should be apparent that Vietnam and ASEAN have more in common with each other than they do with China.

One further point should be clarified. It seems that there is now a real possibility of achieving a solution on the basis I have outlined --- namely, the withdrawal of the Vietnamese troops in return for ASEAN cooperation in disarming the Pol Pot forces: Vietnam's public willingness to talk with Sihanouk and Son Sann highlights this. It is still a remote chance, perhaps, yet it is a unique opportunity, and Australia in particular (because of its regional importance) should help ensure that the chance does not pass by for lack of resolve within the South East Asian region. But for a successful outcome to occur, though, this initial step must lead on to the disarming of the Pot Pot army; exile to China of a few of its leading members, or even free elections in Kampuchea, would not of themselves remove the threat posed by some 30 – 40,000 Pol Pot guerillas.

Two points arise. Firstly, although Sihanouk and Son Sann have lent their international respectability to the Pol Pot forces, they have gained less than the latter from the coalition in terms of strength on the ground. The strategy of building up the non-communists to outnumber the Khmer Rouge in the coalition would seem to be failing badly. And secondly, the so called "Coalition Government of Democratic Kampuchea" must be recognized for what it is --- neither a coalition, nor a government, nor democratic. Not only have the Khmer Rouge been attacking and ambushing their coalition partners near the Thai border, but the non-communists are now reportedly less active against the Vietnamese than in the past, having recently suffered considerable losses. And this despite covert CIA aid to them of well over $4 million in the past two years (*Far Eastern Economic Review*, 25 October 1984).

The Heng Samrin army is now playing an important part in the fighting, something which can only be expected to increase in the future. "About 2,000 Khmers are currently estimated to be undergoing specialized training in Vietnam, the Soviet Union, and other Eastern Bloc states.... The prospect of a gradual stiffening of the government forces is already causing some concern among the non-communist resistance groups, which, unlike their stronger Khmer Rouge coalition partner, still have most of their bases on the Thai border" (*Washington Post*, 27 July 1984). Khmer fears of a return of Pol Pot will ensure this at least as long as Sihanouk claims he has the "dignity of Democratic Kampuchea" to defend (*The Age*, 22 June 1984). Inside the country, people still associate the words, "Democratic Kampuchea" with the death of up to two million Khmers. The stability of Kampuchea and perhaps even South East Asia depend on an achievement of a solution that is acceptable to the people inside Kampuchea, and not simply one that might appear good on paper from the outside.

Double Standards on Cambodia and East Timor
Sydney Morning Herald, August 13, 1985

It is now more than ten years since Saigon became Ho Chi Minh City, Cambodia became Kampuchea, and Phnom Penh lost its Australian Embassy. For more than a decade there has been no embassy or other Australian representation in the capital city of Kampuchea, a country of seven million people.

Instead of moves towards reconciliation and mutual recognition with the People's Republic of Kampuchea led by Heng Samrin, it is now reported that squatters are doing the moving – into the former Cambodian embassy in Canberra.

Perhaps next the National Trust will classify the building, after it has been "rediscovered" – like Angkor Wat – in Forrest (the leafy Canberra suburb where the embassy is located). Can there really be nothing more than a historical monument to our relations with the people of Kampuchea, or can Australians deal with them and their country as real people?

Opponents of the straightforward approach claim that time should be allowed for diplomacy to work its slovenly way. We must convince our allies first. And it should be stressed that to some extent diplomacy is working: with Australian prodding, the Vietnamese have now offered to withdraw their forces from Kampuchea if those commanded by the murderous Pol Pot are disarmed. (The stumbling block to a settlement along these lines is that our ally Thailand refuses even to stop supplying shipments of Chinese weaponry to Pol Pot forces, let alone to disarm them).

And it should be also be stressed that Australia at least (unlike ASEAN) does not recognize, as the "legitimate" government of Kampuchea, the so-called Coalition Government of Democratic Kampuchea, which in fact is neither a coalition, nor a government, nor democratic, nor does it even have any bases in Kampuchea.

Even its titular president, Norodom Sihanouk, has recently stated that he has worked out a "new arrangement" whereby he serves as President of the CGDK for six months of the year, and spends the other six working on his memoirs. The "Government" recognized by the UN as the functioning, legitimate administration of Cambodia is therefore headed by a part-time, semi-retired former prince. The facade of respectability of Pol Pot's Khmer Rouge could not be thinner, and the scandal of the Western world's abandonment of the Cambodian people could not be more damning.

At least Australia has not damned itself by recognizing the CGDK fiction as fact. But after ten years we still recognize neither side as the government of Cambodia. While this position may seem admirably even-handed, the real victims of this two-eyed blindness are the Cambodian people (and their relations with Australia), and even Australian influence in the region.

For without creditability we can have little influence, and without consistency in policy our creditability is damaged. And there are some glaring inconsistencies in our approach to South East Asia when it comes to invasions of territories.

For instance Indonesia wishes us to recognize East Timor as part of Indonesia. We do so. Vietnam wishes us to recognize the People's Republic of Kampuchea as an independent state. We refuse to do so.

Indonesia's incorporation of East Timor was not provoked by any Timorese attacks on Indonesia. Yet we recognize that incorporation. The Vietnamese invasion of Cambodia was provoked by repeated and savage Cambodian attacks. Yet we condemn it as aggression.

The Indonesian invasion of Timor led to the deaths of a fifth of the local population. Yet we recognize it. The Vietnamese invasion of Cambodia put an end to the murder by Pol Pot's regime of a fifth of the local population. Yet we condemn it. What kind of policy is this? What kind of principles are we acting upon? None at all, it seems.

Well, if principles do not apply, then perhaps some old fashioned pragmatism on this issue might have an attraction for our leaders.

Once upon a time there was an Australian Prime Minister called Sir Robert Menzies. And once upon a time, in 1940 in fact, Thailand invaded Cambodia. And not only did it invade, but it also annexed one-third of it (plus large areas of Laos), which became a new Thai province named after the Bangkok dictator of the time.

Thailand did this with the backing of an aggressive power seeking domination of Asia and threatening Australia—namely Japan. Japan had also occupied Indochina, and its objectives were even thought to include "bases like Camranh Bay." The scenario is of course very familiar to Australian inhabitants of the 1980s – if we substitute Vietnam for Thailand, and the USSR for Japan. Or at least, the Australian (and ASEAN) rhetoric of the 1980s is similar enough to the facts of the 1940s, to make such substitutions worthwhile for the purposes of argument.

Well, what did the Australian prime minister do, when confronted with this once-upon-a-time ASEAN problem? To begin with, Menzies took note of the feelings of our great and powerful friend. He reported that "the Americans had lectured the Thais on aggression and had adopted a high moral tone." As a result of Washington taking such a firm stand against Thailand (for 1985, read Vietnam), Menzies went on to say that "we might not be in a position to nail our colours to the mast without knowing the United States' attitude." (For Menzies, read Hawke.)

But Menzies' private view of the situation was quite different. For one thing, he claimed "from his own observation that there was a solid core of friendly feeling in Thailand towards Great Britain (for 1985, read Australia) which we ought not to neglect…. We should make an effort to get the Thais on our side and to stimulate resistance by Thailand to Japanese demands." Should this be our policy towards Vietnam and Soviet demands?

And as for Thailand's aggression against Kampuchea: "Mr. Menzies said that it was his practice to recognize facts. He thought it a pity that the term 'recognition' had ever been invented."

Over forty years later, Australia apparently cannot make up its mind about which Kampuchean government to recognize as the effective government of Kampuchea—the one governing the country, or the one writing its memoirs.

If ASEAN (or the United States) wish to recognize, as the legitimate government of Kampuchea, a part-time fiction-in-exile that is ASEAN's right. There is no need for Australia to criticize ASEAN over this. But if we choose to recognize, as the Government of Cambodia, the one that is governing it, let ASEAN not criticize Australia. For it is our right to recognize facts in our region.

Fictionalisation of the Cambodian drama has gone on long enough. The real tragedy is too long-running—fifteen years, its plot too horrifying—as we know from *The Killing Fields*, and the possibility of a return season is too serious.

If Thailand had the "facts" on its side in 1941, it certainly does not in 1985. ASEAN as well as Australia will eventually have to recognize the People's Republic of Kampuchea (as we did that of China after an absurd quarter-century of pretending not to see it). Therefore the sooner the better, especially if Thailand continues to block a diplomatic settlement with its demand that Pol Pot's Khmer Rouge forces keep their weapons and be returned to positions of power in Cambodia.

Son Sen: Blood on His Hands
Sun-Herald, **Sydney, 22 September 1985**

With apparent relief, Thailand's Foreign Minister Siddhi described the new Khmer Rouge commander as "a very good man." His appointment, Siddhi claimed, represents "a sort of concession" to Vietnamese demands (that Pol Pot and his immediate circle be excluded from a role in Cambodia's future after a Vietnamese withdrawal).

This was the first reaction to the news that Son Sen had allegedly replaced Pol Pot as military chief in the anti-Vietnamese Democratic Kampuchea (DK) exiled coalition. The Malaysian Government echoed the Thai view that the ball was now in Vietnam's court.

In fact, though, Son Sen is unlikely to attract much interest in Hanoi. If anything he is more pro-Chinese than Pol Pot, and his record is almost as gruesome. Son Sen served as as defense minister and deputy prime minister throughout the four years of Pol Pot's DK regime (1975 – 79), and was responsible for some of the most barbaric attacks on civilians in their villages.

On September 24, 1977, for instance, Sen's troops killed nearly 300 Vietnamese peasants in a single cross-border raid. Eleven days later, Son Sen wrote a letter to the notorious DK Security Chief, whom he addressed as "Beloved Comrade Deuch," giving him instructions on how to extract confessions from Khmer political prisoners' criticisms of the Pol Pot group. In 1978, Son Sen was closely implicated in the greatest massacre of all during the Pol Pot period, when 100,000 or more people of Kampuchea's eastern zone were murdered by DK troops. Despite being defense minister during the 1979 military rout of the DK army at the hands of the Vietnamese, Son Sen does not appear to have been punished for it. By 1980 he had been promoted to membership of Pol Pot's five-person Politburo-exile.

Return to War Leadership

A glance at the latest leadership reshuffle, announced by DK radio in early September, suggests that it has done no more than return the movement to the publicly proclaimed leadership of the 1970–75 war. At that time, Son Sen was chief of the Joint Chiefs of Staff, and Pol Pot was described only as "chief of the military conduct of the army." (Now he is said to be president of the "Higher Institute for National Defense.")

Then, as now, it was publicly denied that the Khmer Rouge, later (DK) were a communist party, and then, as now, Prince Sihanouk and Khieu Samphan served as titular heads of the movement.

But Pol Pot, secretary of the Communist Party of Kampuchea, became DK prime minister after victory, in early 1976. There seems little to prevent him repeating the exercise should his 30,000-strong army of Stalin's bumiputras win power a second time.

(A real possibility if Vietnamese forces withdraw from Kampuchea).

It is worth remembering that Pol Pot has in fact "stepped down" once before, in September 1976 (allegedly for health reasons). If this departure ever occurred, it was only temporary, and he never bothered to officially announce to the public that he had resumed his post. He went on to preside over the deaths of more than a million people in 1977-78. We should beware such Khmer Rouge leaders who pretend to be inactive.

The DK radio now claims that Pol Pot has "retired" because he has reached the age of sixty. There have also been rumours that Pol Pot was suffering variously from malignant malaria, high blood pressure, or diabetes. But there is no reason to believe that the expert treatment he has received at Bangkok hospitals in recent years has failed to ensure his recovery.

Prince Sihanouk has put his own view of the "retirement" quite frankly: "The Khmer Rouge) are my allies, so in my official capacity I must believe them. But if you ask me for my personal opinion, I would say that it is better not to believe what they say."

What recent events do show is that the DK coalition is feeling the heat of the Vietnamese and Heng Samrin government military and diplomatic offensives.

But removing Pol Pot's group from the future of Kampuchea would require the co-operation of Thailand, which supplies them with sanctuary and Chinese weapons.

At the movement all Thailand seems willing to do is help remove Pol Pot from the public eye. However, judging from the drawn-out skepticism with which much of the Western media have treated his claimed resignation, the move may have backfired. Once again, Pol Pot is back in the news.

A Bad Dream is Fading
Sydney Morning Herald, 27 August 1986

The waters of the Mekong and Sap rivers are low. But at their junction, the city of Phnom Penh is awash with bicycles. The streets are overflowing with wheels and pedals, spilling over onto the sidewalks. Eddies of bicycles form at intersections, swirling around jeeps, carrying off mobile food stalls and pedestrians alike. It is the seventh anniversary of the liberation of the country from Pol Pot's brutal Democratic Kampuchea regime, which fell to Vietnamese forces on January 7, 1979.

Over the parklands in front of the former Royal Palace and the National Museum, nearly 20,000 people have gathered. One crowd watches a traditional Khmer *yiké* comedy performance, emitting loud laughs every few seconds. Another mass of sweethearts, babies and bicycles is listening to a Western-style Khmer rock band. Couples stroll along the riverfront while eager photographers gesticulate in the din and freshening breeze.

The Central Market has finally re-opened, ten years after Pol Pot closed it and the town. Practically empty for four years, Phnom Penh now has a population of 600,000 and the whole city is decked with flags of the People's Republic of Kampuchea (PRK).

The whole city is also tightly organized by the pro-Vietnamese PRK. Heng Samrin's government apparatus has grown with the economy in recent years. The ruling People's Revolutionary Party of Kampuchea (PRPK) first emerged into the open in 1981 with less than 600 members. It now has nearly 10, 000 with another 50,000 enrolled in party recruitment cells. The composition of its leadership has also changed. In 1981, former rebels and defectors from the Khmer Rouge (Eastern Zone) administration had constituted 37 percent of the full members of the PRPK Central Committee. By 1986, they were less than 30 percent.

More dramatic was the decline of the Hanoi-trained Khmer communist veterans who had comprised eleven of the nineteen full members of the 1981 PRPK Central Committee. By 1986, they numbered only five out of thirty-one. Meanwhile, people of non-revolutionary backgrounds increased their representation on the central committee, from none out of nineteen full members to twelve out of thirty-one.

Further, revolutionaries who neither spent long years in Vietnam, nor were associated with any faction of the Pol Pot regime, increased their representation from one out of nineteen to at least five out of thirty-one full members of the committee. They, and to a greater extent the middle-class "new people," are the real beneficiaries of the party's expansion, and they are now essential allies of a dominant political faction in Kampuchea.

In the countryside this expansion is evident. In 1981 even some entire provinces had no party members at all. In 1986, many have hundreds and one small village I visited had five, with thirty-six in recruitment cells.

The Cambodian Army has grown, too. In one province, 17,000 villagers are members of armed militia. To this figure must be added the district, provincial and national armed forces stationed there.

But there are about 140,000 Vietnamese troops occupying the country as well. So long as they remain to support it, there is little chance of the PRK Government being overthrown, or even seriously threatened.

Still, the 30,000 Khmer Rouge remnants of the Pol Pot regime are making a sustained effort, with massive Chinese support. Since they lost all their bases on the Thai border eighteen months ago, the Khmer Rouge have split into small groups and spread over the much of the country.

They are capable of terrorist raids and continue to slaughter peasants and travelers in many areas, whether or not the victims played any role in the Vietnamese occupation. The Khmer Rouge are thus more active than they were in 1981, and they are the only effective military opposition to the PRK and Vietnam. Yet they are hated by Cambodians as much as ever. One million deaths in 1975-79 will never be forgiven the Khmer Rouge leaders who were responsible.

In fact, the increased activity has backfired politically. My overall impression after a month in urban and rural Kampuchea in January is that people are now resigned to Heng Samrin's PRK regime, despite some past mistrust.

The choice is generally seen as limited: either the PRK or the Khmer Rouge, and the latter would not be tolerated in any form of "coalition" unless they were to lay down arms. The international community will eventually have to recognize this --- and the PRK.

Meanwhile, people have been getting on with reconstructing their lives. Buddhist wats are being repaired and rebuilt in almost every district. The PRK Government first revived Buddhism in 1979 by sponsoring official ordination ceremonies for monks and public donations to religious causes have grown considerably as the economy has picked up.

In one rural sub-district I had visited several times in 1980-81, much new construction was evident on my return in 1986. A large rice mill and warehouse had gone up in 1982 and two more were under construction. Two new brick works and a 10-room school had been built in 1984 and 1985.

In another province, a former education department official in the 1960s, back in his old job in 1986, said there were now more children in local schools than in pre-war days. He also confirmed that the Vietnamese language was not being taught in the schools, nor the Vietnamese culture imposed on the people. The number of Vietnamese residents was no more than in the 1960s, he added.

My investigation in other border provinces and that of Michael Vickery elsewhere suggest that there may well be as few as 150,000 ethnic Vietnamese residents in Cambodia today (compared to 450,000 in 1970). The PRK is in fact building up Khmer communities along the country's eastern border, rather than encouraging settlement. Most of the "Vietnamization" charges leveled at the occupying forces in Cambodia, by critics outside the country, are as baseless as the U.S. allegation of chemical warfare recently proved false by United Kingdom and Canadian government inquiries.

But the fact is that the longer the occupation continues, the more the political structure of Kampuchea will resemble that of Vietnam. That would prevent a Khmer Rouge return to power (no matter how long China and Thailand persist in their efforts). But a much superior outcome is one now being considered in ASEAN circles: a removal of the Khmer Rouge threat to Kampuchea in return for a withdrawal of Vietnamese troops. This would address the twin issues at the heart of the international confrontation.

The security situation has been deteriorating in Cambodia since 1980, as the Khmer Rouge have been revived by the international misappropriation of aid destined for refugees and by Chinese weapons supplied through Thailand. The Vietnamese are not seriously threatened, nor are they suffering very high casualties, but they are tied down and therefore less likely to withdraw. And, predictably, the PRK has stepped up security measures to defeat the "undeclared war" against it.

Hopefully Australia will continue its effort to break the deadlock. Foreign Minister Bill Hayden's recent proposal for an international tribunal to judge the crimes of the Pol Pot leadership would certainly go some way towards removing the group that poses the major obstacle to peace.

Cambodia under the Vietnamese
The Nation (Bangkok), May 7, 1989

Last March a crowded Cambodian bus carrying passengers from the seaport to Phnom Penh was ambushed by Khmer Rouge, a few miles out of the town of Kompong Speu. Its fuel tank was hit by a B-47, and exploded. Forty-five civilians were killed, and only three survived.

Several days later, there was a total eclipse of the moon. Astrology soothsayers seemed to come out of the shadows to predict very inauspicious results. That night, as soon as the moon started to disappear, firecrackers and rockets exploded all over town. The townspeople produced an infernal din of metal on metal, to frighten off the "moon eating monster." Even the police and the army joined in firing off their guns. The night sky was besieged for several hours before the monster departed, and the full moon shone again.

It was exactly twenty years since the sky had unleashed the first American B-52 bombardment over Cambodia, helping propel the Khmer Rouge to power.

After ten years of occupation, Vietnam is now withdrawing the remainder of its military forces from Cambodia. The reason for their invasion in December 1978 was a spate of characteristically brutal attacks on Vietnamese territory by Pol Pot's Democratic Kampuchea (DK) regime. From early 1977, Khmer Rouge forces had staged fierce raids into Vietnamese territory, massacring thousands of Vietnamese civilians and causing hundreds of thousands to flee from their homes. Hanoi's complaints to this effect were corroborated at the time by both U.S. intelligence reports and the testimony of Vietnamese refugees fleeing abroad from the war zone, and they have since been extensively documented from both sides of the border.

Despite what China and Western governments have said, Hanoi's December 1978 invasion was not "aggression" (unprovoked attack). Vietnam's immediate reason for intervention in Cambodia was self-defense.

So long as the Khmer Rouge maintain an effective military capacity in Cambodia and an alliance with China, Vietnam will continue to regard them as a security threat. Nevertheless, since 1979 Hanoi has been reducing its forces in Cambodia, and in 1985 it pledged to withdraw all its troops by 1990. So far, it is ahead of schedule.

However, part of Hanoi's policy and practice in Cambodia has been to patronize the Khmer people. The government established after the Vietnamese invasion, the People's Republic of Kampuchea (PRK), has often been treated not as an equal, but as a subordinate. This lop-sided, patron-client relationship has made Cambodia vulnerable to Vietnamese political domination; best illustrated by the confinement since 1981, in Hanoi as well as in Phnom Penh, of the PRK's first prime minister, Pen Sovan.

Vietnamese advisers in Cambodian ministerial offices and local administration have varied in quality, from corrupt and arrogant to responsible and appreciated. (The Vietnamese troops have generally conducted themselves well). However, since 1980 the advisers have gradually been withdrawn as Cambodian cadres have become more experienced. The last advisers left in 1988.

Hanoi has painted its intervention in Cambodia as an exercise in international solidarity. In the outside world it would have been wiser to adhere to its case of self-defense under international law. But inside Cambodia it has preferred its stress that the three countries of Indochina will "either die together, or live together." PRK President Heng Samrin has himself asserted that "separation from Laos and Vietnam means death, while unity with Vietnam and Laos means victory." This is partly a reflection on Vietnamese dominance and partly gratitude for real Vietnamese assistance to Cambodia.

Vietnam sheltered over 300,000 refugees from the Pol Pot regime. During the threatened famine of 1979-80, Vietnam provided Cambodians with tens of thousands of tons of rice, and 50,000 tons thereafter. Other unpaid non-military assistance has been in the fields of agriculture, health, transport and communications, technical training, administration, and education. Vietnamese assistance has helped re-establish a Cambodian state from the wreckage left behind by the Pol Pot regime.

In its last years at least, the DK regime was on a genocidal track, and most Cambodians were glad to see it overthrown. Many were grateful to the Vietnamese, whom they saw risking their lives against the Khmer Rouge. In 1979 Cambodians I interviewed in France, who had quickly decided to make their way abroad, expressed the view that the Vietnamese invasion had been a genuine liberation.

Ang Ngeck Teang, an ethnic Chinese girl from Phnom Penh, was fourteen years old when the Vietnamese invaded. All ten of her family members had perished of starvation and disease under Khmer Rouge rule in 1977-78. Safe with relatives in France soon afterwards, she recalled: "When the Vietnamese came, the Khmer Rouge ran away…. The Vietnamese were good…very honest…. If we asked them for food, they gave it. If we were sick, they gave us medicine. My hand was infected, they cured it. I asked them for a life to Phnom Penh, where my elder brother found me…. My house had been destroyed by the Khmer Rouge…"

A controversial issue since 1979 has been so-called "Vietnamization" of Cambodia such as the teaching of the Vietnamese language in schools. In fact the Vietnamese language has been slow to appear in the PRK school curriculum. By 1988 it was taught only in the three final years of high school, for two hours per week. Students at this level took either Vietnamese or Russian.

In the PRK, it is the Khmer language which has occupied a more central place in the Cambodian school curriculum than ever before. In March 1988, Phnom Penh University re-opened after thirteen years, with over 2,000 students. The medium of instruction is Khmer.

Why the Khmer Rouge are Still Dangerous
The Nation (Bangkok), May 14, 1989

There was little Khmer Rouge activity in Prey Veng province, on the east bank of the Mekong River, from 1979 to 1985. The province governor was wounded when his car hit a mine in July 1986. Khmer Rouge snipers assassinated a sub-district official in Sithor Kandal district in the north of Prey Veng near Kompong Cham and then made their escape. Later, on the night of January 20, 1989, 90-100 Khmer Rouge massed and attacked the district town of Sithor Kandal. The province governor and other officials were conducting a meeting there. The governor escaped but four Vietnamese troops, nine civilians and two Khmer soldiers were killed. The district chief escaped only in his underpants. The Khmer Rouge burnt down "everything," including the district office. They beheaded their dead comrades and took the severed heads with them as they retreated, so that they could not be recognized.

These Khmer Rouge were led by Khan Soeun, commander of DK's 920th Brigade. Soeun's parents, who were natives of the area, were taken in for questioning by PRK officials. They said he had joined the Khmer Rouge in 1970, and disappeared until 1975, when he came home for three days after the war ended. His parent claimed that they had never seen him again until 1986. He is variously said to have been a regimental commander in the district from 1975 to 1979, or even vice minister of defense under Pol Pot's deputy prime minister, Son Sen. Soeun had obviously retreated to the west with the DK forces in the face of the Vietnamese onslaught of 1979.

Khan Soeun returned to visit his parents early in 1986. Locals quickly reported his unit's arrival to the PRK authorities; but troops sent out to capture them were unable to locate them, and the Vietnamese forces in the area were disinclined to believe the story. It appears that the Khmer Rouge were mostly locals who had returned from the Thai border and were able to count on their relatives to supply them with food. The district chief turned out to be Khan Soeun's cousin. After his bare escape, he was demoted to a member of the district committee.

On January 8, 1987, Khan Soeun's forces returned to the fray in Prey Veng and attacked a district/provincial armed forces base at Khum Kompong Prang in Peareang district. They were well armed. (A section of ten Khmer Rouge is reported to have seven AK-47s and three B-40 rocket launchers). It is not known whether they inflicted any casualties in this attack, but that night I overheard a PRK officer say that if there were any, it would be kept quiet "The situation is not good, "he said. "Wow, they even dared to attack an army position," a militia guard said after the officer had left.

In August 1987, the last Vietnamese advisers withdrew from Sithor Kandal district, and they were followed by the remaining Vietnamese troops. But in December 1987-January 1988, Soeun's band came back to his village there on five occasions, looking for food. The local authorities did not discover this until the group had again crossed the Mekong and returned to Kompong Thom province, where they hide out during the rainy season. But before then they struck again. On January 4, 1988, 20 of Soeun's guerillas disguised themselves as civilians to attend a video screening in a village near Chihe in neighbouring Kompong Cham province. After the screening was over, the infiltrators opened fire from the crowd, killing the sub-district police chief and one militia member, and wounding two others.

Three days later, while the country celebrated the defeat of the Pol Pot regime, a force of ninety of Soeun's troops was seen on the road between Prek Pou and Koh Sautin. Soon afterwards they returned to Kompong Thom, and there were no more incidents in the area in 1988. But fighting broke out again in Sithor Kandal in January 1989, following the usual pattern of the previous three years.

These incidents in Prey Veng may be a good illustration of the war in Cambodia. The Khmer Rouge are able to strike in many parts of the country, even those far from the Thai border. They are well armed and they benefit from local limited local support; but they also have many enemies who will report their movements to the PRK, and their ability to damage the PRK is limited even in province like Prey Veng where there are few if any Vietnamese troops. The PRK has had to pour out much of its budget on defense, but six incidents in three years have not disturbed its control of the province. The PRK militia in Prey Veng consists of 17,000 armed villagers, and there are least ten battalions of PRK district forces, plus a provincial regiment. These face about 100 Khmer Rouge, but have been unable to destroy them so far.

The PRK army is now much stronger than most outsiders suspect, but it would be unwise to write off the Khmer Rouge after the Vietnamese withdrawal is completed this year. And as long as Prince Sihanouk, supported by China and the USA, continues to demand that his Khmer that his Khmer Rouge allies be included in a new Cambodian government, they can be hopeful of an easier route to power.

Talk of an "International peacekeeping force" is also misleading. The Khmer Rouge still have the support of the United Nations and most major powers. The only way to ward off the Khmer Rouge is stop their supply of bullets before they are fired. This means cutting their supply lines in Thailand, denying them sanctuary there and international recognition as the "legitimate" government of the country, and recognizing the People's Republic of Kampuchea (now the State of Cambodia) – which has now governed the country for over ten years.

For the international community to avoid these necessary steps, yet hope to defend the country from the Khmer Rouge monster, would be like shooting at the moon.

The Balance of Forces in Cambodia, 1989
The Nation, Bangkok, 13 October 1989

A tripartite coalition, which excludes the Khmer Rouge, is the best option for Cambodia.

This year has been a key year in the Cambodian conflict. The pro-Vietnamese Cambodian government has been in power for ten years. The last Vietnamese troops have been withdrawn. Hanoi's advisers have already left. Pol Pot's Khmer Rouge insurgency appears to have peaked, and security has markedly improved in the past two years.

The Cambodian army of Prime Minister Hun Sen is now much stronger than most outsiders suspect. It probably has 150,000 troops under arms, plus 200,000 militia. Estimates of Khmer Rouge strength range from 15,000-40,000. They are well-supplied and still a threat, but Hun Sen seems confident his government can hold on after its Vietnamese allies departed late last month.

That is because in both the military and diplomatic arenas, the balance of forces has gradually been shifting in favor of Hanoi and Phnom Penh.

The Guerrilla War

Four years ago, a Cambodian village thirty miles north of Phnom Penh was attacked by Khmer Rouge forces. The terrified villagers were unarmed and unable to prevent the attackers from burning down a government office and destroying a rice mill. Losses totaled 40,000 riels, or about $400.

A year later, 800 Khmer Rouge marched through the village in broad daylight, according to a village woman who witnessed the show of force. Each carried two B-40 rocket launchers. They didn't harm anyone this time, but most feared and distrusted them because of their murderous record, the woman said.

By 1987, she said, Vietnamese and Cambodian government forces were in a much stronger position. The Khmer Rouge mounted no further attacks. "There is no problem now," she claimed. By 1989, the same woman expressed much greater confidence, saying the Cambodian 33rd Regiment "protects the area" from the Khmer Rouge, still active but now confined to a distant forest.

In Prey Veng province in eastern Cambodia, much the same is true. Since 1986, a band of 100 Khmer Rouge have staged six attacks on government outposts. The attacks occurred only each January, were limited to one of the ten districts, and have decreased in seriousness from year to year. Vietnamese advisers and troops have long withdrawn from the area leaving Prey Veng to the Cambodian forces of at least ten battalions and militia of over 17,000 armed peasants.

The Diplomatic Arena

There are three levels to the conflict: the Cambodian, the regional Southeast Asian, and the big power levels. Developments since 1979 have favored a settlement at the regional level. The Cambodian factions disagree on a role for the Khmer Rouge, and the diminishing role of the great powers has created dilemmas, for China especially.

The conflict started in 1977 with Khmer Rouge regime attacks into Vietnam. After Pol Pot refused to negotiate, Vietnamese forces overthrew his regime in early 1979. Pol Pot's Chinese ally Deng Xiaoping retaliated by launching his own invasion of Vietnam.

Vietnamese troops remained in Cambodia, demanding two concessions: exclusion of Pol Pot's forces from the country, and an end to the Chinese threat to Vietnam. China, Asean and the West, on the other hand, demanded unconditional Vietnamese withdrawal, recognized the ousted Pol Pot regime as the "legitimate" representative of the Cambodian people, and re-armed and supplied its forces via Thailand.

From 1982, Hanoi began partial withdrawals of its troops, as its Cambodian ally consolidated its position. In early 1985, Vietnamese forces captured all twenty opposition camps along the Thai-Cambodian border. China's protection of its clients proved unreliable. Hanoi then dropped its demand for an end to the Chinese threat before a full withdrawal from Cambodia.

In Hanoi in March 1985, Australia's then Foreign Minister Bill Hayden heard new Vietnamese proposals which he claimed were "a considerable advance." Hayden also met Hun Sen, the first regional leader to do so.

Hun Sen told him: "We are ready to make concessions to Prince Sihanouk and other people if they agree to join with us to eliminate Pol Pot." Hun Sen later announced that the Vietnamese troops would all leave Cambodia by 1990, or earlier if there was a settlement.

Vietnam insisted only that the Khmer Rouge be prevented from returning to power. This meant that the two major prongs of the Cambodian problem could now be resolved within Southeast Asia, principally by Thailand cutting off sanctuary and supplies to the Khmer Rouge, and by Vietnam withdrawing its troops. China's cooperation was no longer necessary.

Against this background, the policy of the frontline state shifted. This year Bangkok has hosted three visits by Hun Sen. Sensing advantage, the new Thai government wants to turn Indochina "from a battlefield into a trading ground." Indonesia also welcomes this. In Southeast Asia, the Cambodian issue is the major one dividing the region, and the momentum exists for a settlement.

But to the great powers, small countries like Cambodia can be ignored for years. One British diplomat remarked, "We're only talking about six million people." The USA also appears unenthusiastic about a settlement arrived at independently in Southeast Asia. China has nothing to gain from the isolation of its Khmer Rouge client, and it resists moves toward regional concord, preferring a Balkanized Southeast Asia with many roads to Beijing." But an agreement between Asean-backed Thailand and Vietnam to isolate the Khmer Rouge, would be hard for Beijing to ignore.

Any settlement between the Cambodian parties, too, would likely exclude at least the Khmer Rouge military. Hun Sen may welcome Sihanouk and the other small faction leader, Son Sann, back to Phnom Penh, but not Pol Pot's army.

Whether Sihanouk and Son Sann would ever accept this is unclear. As heads of the two smallest factions, they depend most on their great figurehead president of the exiled Coalition Government of Democratic Kampuchea, dominated by Pol Pot's Khmer Rouge and supported by China and the USA.

Since 1987, Prince Sihanouk has had several meetings with Hun Sen, and a few fairly successful rounds of talks in Indonesia. The consensus there has usually favored a settlement that would exclude both Vietnamese troops and the Khmer Rouge – potential common ground common ground with Hanoi. But now Sihanouk has rejected the Southeast Asian consensus, for great power interests.

That is why the Paris peace talks broke down last August. The greatest danger to the Cambodian people is not continuing Khmer Rouge insurgency after the Vietnamese withdrawal. It is the possibility of Pol Pot's Khmer Rouge being included in a new government, with the Khmer Rouge guerrillas brought into the country and included in a new Cambodian army. Given the genocidal record of Pol Pot's Khmer Rouge, this is a recipe for breakdown, and for a new civil war far more destabilizing than the military status quo.

A quadripartite government that included the Khmer Rouge military would not function anyway. Popular support does not exist to offer the Khmer Rouge hope of power by peaceful means. They privately target the other three parties as "enemies," and they would merely hide their time before attempting to a coup. Their army would be there when needed.

Talk of a UN Peacekeeping Force to ward the Khmer Rouge off is misleading, because they occupy the UN seat. The only way to ward off the Khmer Rouge is to stop their supply of bullets before they are fired. This means cutting their supply lines in Thailand, denying them sanctuary and recognition as the "legitimate" government. Further, Western nations should offer to resettle many of the refugees currently held captive by the Khmer Rouge and their allies in camps in Thailand, and Bangkok should be encouraged to allow this.

No all-party Cambodian agreement would admit the Khmer Rouge army into a new government. There is more chances of a three-party coalition between Hun Sen, Sihanouk and Son Sann, excluding the Khmer Rouge armed forces. Agreement along these lines would most likely be backed by Southeast Asian countries.

Bibliography

Ainsztein, Reuben. *The Warsaw Ghetto Revolt* (New York: Holocaust Library, 1979).

Arad, Yitzhak. *The Partisans: From the Valley of Death to Mount Zion* (Washington, DC: United States Holocaust Memorial Museum, 1990).

Arad, Yitzhak. "The Armed Jewish Resistance in Eastern Europe: Its Unique Conditions and its Relations with the Jewish Councils (Judenrate) in the Ghettoes," in *The Holocaust and History: The Known, the Unknown, the Disputed, and the Re-examined*, ed. Michael Berenbaum and Abraham J. Peck (Bloomington: Indiana University Press, 1998), 591-600.

Ball, Patrick D., Paul Kobrak, and Herbert F. Spirer. "Populations in Resistance," ch. 20 of *State Violence in Guatemala, 1960-1996: A Quantitative Reflection* (Washington, DC: American Association for the Advancement of Science, 1999): http://shr.aaas.org/guatemala/ciidh/qr/english/chap20.html

Bastholm Jensen, Mette. *Solidarity in Action: A Comparative Study of Rescue Efforts in Nazi-occupied Denmark and the Netherlands*. Ph.D. dissertation, Sociology Department, Yale University, 2007.

Budiardjo, Carmel, and Liem Soei Liong. *The War Against East Timor* (London: Zed, 1984).

Burr, William, and Michael L. Evans, eds. *East Timor Revisited: Ford, Kissinger and the Indonesian Invasion, 1975-76*, National Security Archive Electronic Briefing Book No. 62, Washington, D.C., 2001: www.gwu.edu/~nsarchiv/NSAEBB/NSAEBB62.

Carey, Peter. Historical introduction to *Generations of Resistance: East Timor*, with photographs by Steve Cox (London: Cassell, 1995).

Carey, Peter. "Third-World Colonialism, the *Geração Foun*, and the Birth of a New Nation: Indonesia through East Timorese Eyes, 1975-99," *Indonesia* 76 (Oct. 2003), 23-67.

Carey, Peter. "East Timor under Indonesian Occupation, 1975-99," in *Handbook on Terrorism and Insurgency*, ed. Andrew Tan (Malvern, 2006).

Chamberlain, Ernest. *The Struggle in Iliomar: Resistance in Rural East Timor*, Point Lonsdale, Vic., Australia, 2003.

Comisión para le Esclarecimiento Histórico (CEH). "Agudización de la Violencia y Militarización del Estado (1979-1985)" and "Afrontando la Violencia," in *Guatemala: Memoria del Silencio*, Guatemala, UNOPS, 1999, capitulo 1: 359-461, 3: 609-98: http://shr.aaas.org/guatemala/ceh/mds/spanish/toc.html

Commission for Reception, Truth and Reconciliation in Timor-Leste (CAVR). *Chega ! The Report of the Commission for Reception, Truth and Reconciliation in Timor-Leste*, October 2005: www.cavr-timorleste.org

Cook, Susan E., ed. *Genocide in Cambodia and Rwanda: New Perspectives* (New Brunswick, NJ: Transaction Publishers, 2005).

Corfield, Justin J. *A History of the Cambodian non-Communist Resistance, 1975-1983*, (Clayton, Vic.: Monash University Centre of Southeast Asian Studies, 1991).

Dunn, James. *Timor: A People Betrayed* (Milton, Qld.: Jacaranda, 1983).

Gunn, Geoffrey C. *Complicity in Genocide: Report to the East Timor "Truth Commission" on International Actors* (Macao: Tipgrafia Macau Hung Heng, 2006).

Gusmão, Xanana (Sarah Niner, ed.). *To Resist is to Win! The Autobiography of Xanana Gusmão* (Melbourne, Vic.: Aurora Books, 2000).

Hamerow, Theodore S. *On the Road to the Wolf's Lair: German Resistance to Hitler* (Cambridge, MA: Harvard University Press, 1997).

Hill, Helen M. *Stirrings of Nationalism in East Timor: Fretilin 1974-1978* (Sydney: Otford, 2002).

Horowitz, Irving Louis. *Taking Lives: Genocide and State Power* (New Brunswick, NJ: Transaction Publishers, 1997).

Jolliffe, Jill. *East Timor: Nationalism and Colonialism* (St. Lucia: University of Queensland Press, 1978).

Kiernan, Ben. *How Pol Pot Came to Power: Colonialism, Nationalism and Communism in Cambodia, 1930-1975* (London: Verso, 1985); 2nd ed. (New Haven, CT, Yale University Press, 2004).

Kiernan, Ben. *Cambodia: Eastern Zone Massacres* (New York: Columbia University Center for the Study of Human Rights, Documentation Series no. 1, 1986).

Kiernan, Ben. "Ke Pauk," *Guardian* (London), February 21, 2002: www.guardian.co.uk/Archive/Article/0,4273,4360122,00.html

Kiernan, Ben. *The Pol Pot Regime: Race, Power and Genocide in Cambodia under the Khmer Rouge, 1975-1979* (New Haven, CT: Yale University Press, 1996); 2nd ed., 2002.

Kiernan, Ben. *Blood and Soil: Genocide and Extermination in World History from Carthage to Darfur* (New Haven, CT: Yale University Press, 2007).

Levene, Mark. *Genocide in the Age of the Nation State*, 4 vols. (London: I.B. Tauris, 2005).

MacDonald, Callum. *The Killing of SS Obergruppenführer Reinhard Heydrich* (New York, Free Press, 1989).

Michalczyk, John J., ed. *Confront!: Resistance in Nazi Germany* (New York: P. Lang, 2004).

Pribbenow, Merle L., II. "A Tale of Five Generals: Vietnam's Invasion of Cambodia," *Journal of Military History* 70 (January 2006), 459-86.

Reynolds, Henry. *The Other Side of the Frontier: Aboriginal Resistance to the European Invasion of Australia* (Ringwood, Vic., Penguin, 1982).

Rungswasdisab, Puangthong. "Thailand's Response to the Cambodian Genocide," in Susan E. Cook, ed., *Genocide in Cambodia and Rwanda: New Perspectives* (New Brunswick, NJ: Transaction Publishers, 2005), 79-126.

Scott, James C. *Domination and the Arts of Resistance: Hidden Transcripts* (New Haven, CT: Yale University Press, 1990).

Scholl, Inge. *Students against Tyranny: the Resistance of the White Rose, Munich, 1942-1943*. Translated from the German by Arthur R. Schultz (Middletown, CT: Wesleyan University Press, 1970).

Selden, Mark, and Alvin Y. So, eds. *War and State Terrorism: the United States, Japan, and the Asia-Pacific in the Long Twentieth Century* (Lanham, MD: Rowman and Littlefield, 2004).

Semelin, Jacques. *Unarmed against Hitler: Civilian Resistance in Europe, 1939-1943* (Westport, CT: Praeger, 1993).

Slocomb, Margaret. "Chikreng Rebellion: Coup and Its Aftermath in Democratic Kampuchea," *Journal of the Royal Asiatic Society*, Series 3, 16:1 (2006), 59-72.

Stanton, Gregory H. "Blue Scarves and Yellow Stars: Classification and Symbolization in the Cambodian Genocide," *Occasional Paper*, Montreal Institute for Genocide Studies, April 1989: www.genocidewatch.org/bluescarves. htm

Stanton, Gregory H. "The Cambodian Genocide and International Law," in Ben Kiernan, ed., *Genocide and Democracy in Cambodia: The Khmer Rouge, the United Nations, and the International Community* (New Haven, CT: Yale Council on Southeast Asia Studies, 1993).

Stroop, Jürgen. *The Stroop Report: The Jewish Quarter of Warsaw is No More!*, translated from the German by Sybil Milton, introduction by Andrzej Wirth (New York: Pantheon, 1979).

Suhl, Yuri. *They Fought Back: The Story of the Jewish Resistance in Nazi Europe* (New York: Crown, 1967).

Tanter, Richard. "The Military Situation in East Timor," *Pacific Research,* VIII, 1977, 2:1-6.

Tanter, Richard, Mark Selden and Stephen R. Shalom, eds. *Bitter Flowers, Sweet Flowers: East Timor, Indonesia and the World Community* (Lanham, MD, Rowman & Littlefield, 2001), 254-56.

Taylor, John. *East Timor: The Price of Freedom* (London: Zed, 1999).

Waugh, Colin M. *Paul Kagame and Rwanda: Power, Genocide, and the Rwandan Patriotic Front* (Jefferson, NC: McFarland, 2004).

Index

Sin Song, 42, 45, 75-76
Smith, Beverley, 242
Smith, Nancy deWolf, 233
Soares, Abilio, 255
Soares, Aquiles, 124
Soares, Guido, 144-146
Soares, Osorio, 112-113
Sos Man, 33
Stanton, Gregory H., 204, 226
Sudrajad, Yahyat, 255
Suharto, 1, 105-106, 110, 111, 248, 253-254
Suratman, Tono, 256

Tasker, Rodney, 316-317
Thach, Bunroeun, 224, 237
Thach, Nguyen Co, 316
Thailand, 287-292, 315-323
Timorese Social Democratic Association, 112
Truth Commission,
  report on East Timor resistance, 137-192

UDT (Timorese Democratic Union), 111-114, 137-138, 154, 180, 244

UN Genocide Convention of 1948, 107-108
United Nations, 2
  report on East Timor resistance, 137-192

Vickery, Michael, 227-228
Vietnam, 24-25, 70, 74, 251, 305-306
  Khmer Rouge, 2, 107
  view on Kampuchea, 314
Vietnam Workers' Party, 30
Vietnam War, 1, 105, 107

Wall Street Journal, 230, 232, 237
Walsh, Patrick, 244
Wheeldon, John, 253
Wheeler, John Parsons III, 235-236
Wiesel, Elie, 216
Windshuttle, Keith, 263-266
Woolcott, Richard, 249
Woollacott, Martin, 305
Wold, James W., 234
World Genocide Convention, 215
World War II, 243, 251

Yin Sophi, 35, 41, 87-88